P~~~~
West Coast
Australia

**Broome &
the Kimberley**
p204

**Coral Coast &
the Pilbara**
p183

**Monkey Mia &
the Central West**
p165

**Around
Perth**
p89

**Perth &
Fremantle**◉
p46

South Coast
p143

**Margaret River & the
Southwest Coast**
p118

THIS EDITION WRITTEN AND RESEARCHED BY

Brett Atkinson
Steve Waters

PLAN YOUR TRIP

ON THE ROAD

FEARGUS COONEY/GETTY IMAGES ©

QUOKKA P94

KATY CLEMMANS/GETTY IMAGES ©

MITCHELL FALLS P223

Contents

SPECIAL FEATURES

Welcome to Perth & West Coast Australia

If you subscribe to the 'life's a beach' school of thought, you'll fall in love with Western Australia (WA) and its 12,500km of spectacular coastline.

An Immense, Sparsely Populated Land

If the huge expanses of WA were a separate nation, it would be the planet's 10th-largest country. Most of the state's population clings to the coast, yet you can wander along a beach for hours without seeing another footprint, or be one of a handful of campers stargazing in a national park.

The south is a playground of white-sand beaches, expanses of springtime wildflowers and lush green forests teeming with life. Up north in the Kimberley, you'll encounter wide open spaces that conceal striking gorges, waterfalls and ancient rock formations.

Action Stations

WA has plenty for the active traveller. Traverse the 963km Bibbulmun Track (or focus on a few spectacular day walks), or mountain bike the 1000km Munda Biddi Trail. Shorter but equally interesting walks include wandering amid the wildflowers of the Stirling Range National Park and negotiating Porongurup's granite formations. Dive and snorkel in stunning marine parks and around fascinating shipwrecks, or surf around Margaret River and kiteboard and windsurf off Lancelin's expansive beaches.

All Creatures Great & Small

WA's fauna includes kangaroos, emus and colourful parrots, and there is also the chance to get acquainted with lesser-known local critters like quokkas, bilbies and potoroos. The WA coast's lengthy dalliance with the Indian and Southern Oceans means opportunities to spot marine wildlife also abound. Each year about 30,000 whales cruise the coast-hugging 'Humpback Hwy'. At Ningaloo Marine Park you can dive with the world's largest fish, the whale shark, and at Rockingham, Bunbury and Monkey Mia you can interact with wild dolphins.

The Finer Things in Life

Perth and neighbouring Fremantle are cosmopolitan cities, yet both retain a laid-back feel courtesy of their fantastic beaches and parks. The mining boom continues to add a glitzy sheen to everything in the shadow of its skyscrapers, and earlier boom times have left grand architectural legacies in Fremantle, Albany, Guildford and York.

Around Margaret River and the southwest, vignerons and brewers craft world-class wines and beers, complemented by the inventive menus of the region's restaurants. Truffles are grown down south, and WA's seafood is consistently sublime.

Why I Love Perth & West Coast Australia

By Brett Atkinson, Author

Despite being very familiar with Australia's eastern states, I always find the country's far west a compellingly different destination. Perth's pride at being the world's most remote capital is reflected in the verve and independence of the locals, and I love exploring the state's emerging culinary scene, which combines great wine and local produce. Fremantle's historic townscape – and excellent pubs serving great craft beer – is worth multiple leisurely explorations, and the state's combination of the outback's elemental red-dirt expanses and cliff-studded coastline is truly like nowhere else I've been.

For more about our authors, see page 280

Above: Greens Pool, William Bay National Park (p147)

Perth & West Coast Australia

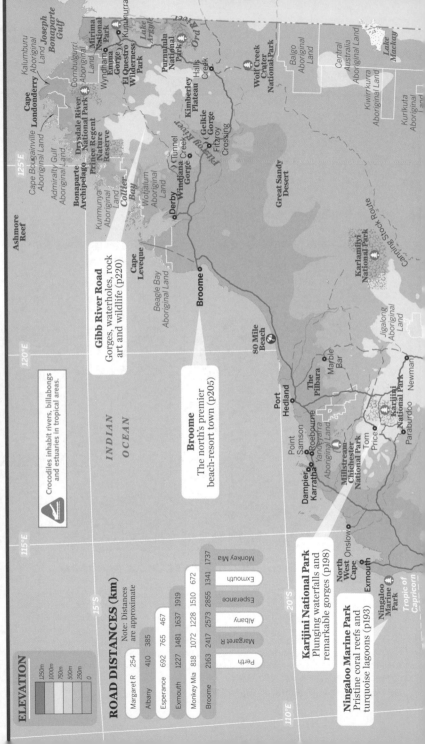

ELEVATION

- 1250m
- 1000m
- 750m
- 500m
- 250m
- 0

ROAD DISTANCES (km)

Note: Distances are approximate

	Perth	Margaret R	Albany	Esperance	Exmouth
Margaret R	254				
Albany	410	385			
Esperance	692	765	467		
Exmouth	1227	1481	1637	1919	
Monkey Mia	818	1072	1228	1510	672
Broome	2163	2417	2573	2855	1341	1737

Crocodiles inhabit rivers, billabongs and estuaries in tropical areas.

Gibb River Road
Gorges, waterholes, rock art and wildlife (p220)

Broome
The north's premier beach-resort town (p205)

Karijini National Park
Plunging waterfalls and remarkable gorges (p198)

Ningaloo Marine Park
Pristine coral reefs and turquoise lagoons (p193)

INDIAN OCEAN

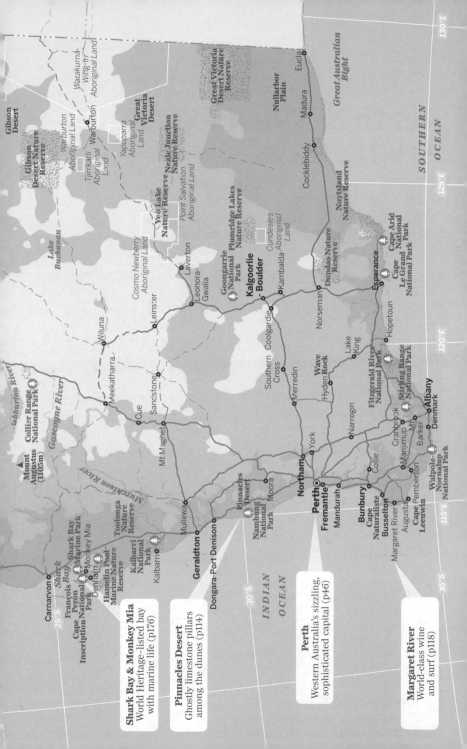

Gibson Desert

Ashburton River

Collier Range National Park

Gascoyne River

Mount Augustus (1105m)

Carnarvon

Shark Bay

François Peron Marine Park

Cape Peron

Shark Bay Inscription National Park

Hamelin Pool Marine Nature Reserve

Denham

Monkey Mia

Murchison River

Kalbarri National Park

Kalbarri

Toolonga Nature Reserve

Meekatharra

Wiluna

Lake Buchanan

Sandstone

Cue

Mt Magnet

Leinster

Leonora

Gwalia

Laverton

Warburton

Gibson Desert Nature Reserve

Warburton Aboriginal Land

Wanarri-Wilngu Aboriginal Land

Waakurna Aboriginal Land

Cosmo Newberry Aboriginal Land

Tjirrkarli Aboriginal Land

Yeo Lake Nature Reserve

Point Salvation Aboriginal Land

Yapuparra Aboriginal Land

Neale Junction Nature Reserve

Great Victoria Desert

Great Victoria Desert Nature Reserve

Great Victoria Desert Nature Reserve

Goongarrie National Park

Plumridge Lakes Nature Reserve

Kalgoorlie-Boulder

Kambalda

Cundeelee Aboriginal Land

Nullarbor Plain

Madura

Eucla

Great Australian Bight

Mullewa

Geraldton

Dongara-Port Denison

Pinnacles Desert

Nambung National Park

Moora

Northam

Perth

Fremantle

Mandurah

Bunbury

Cape Naturaliste

Busselton

Margaret River

Augusta

Cape Leeuwin

Collie

York

Merredin

Southern Cross

Coolgardie

Wave Rock

Hyden

Lake King

Narrogin

Cranbrook

Manjimup

Mt Barker

Pemberton

Walpole-Nornalup National Park

Fitzgerald River National Park

Stirling Range National Park

Denmark

Albany

Hopetoun

Dundas Nature Reserve

Norseman

Kambalda Aboriginal Land

Cocklebiddy

Nuytsland Nature Reserve

Esperance

Cape Le Grand National Park

Cape Arid National Park

SOUTHERN OCEAN

INDIAN OCEAN

25°S

30°S

35°S

115°E

120°E

125°E

130°E

Shark Bay & Monkey Mia
World Heritage–listed bay with marine life (p176)

Pinnacles Desert
Ghostly limestone pillars among the dunes (p114)

Perth
Western Australia's sizzling, sophisticated capital (p46)

Margaret River
World-class wine and surf (p118)

8

Perth & West Coast
Australia's
Top 12

Ningaloo Marine Park

1 Swim alongside 'gentle giant' whale sharks, snorkel among pristine coral, surf off seldom-visited reefs and dive at one of the world's premier locations at this World Heritage–listed marine park (p193), which sits off the North West Cape on the Coral Coast. Rivalling the Great Barrier Reef for beauty, Ningaloo has more easily accessible wonders: shallow, turquoise lagoons are entered straight from the beach for excellent snorkelling. Development is very low-key, so be prepared to camp, or take day trips from the access towns of Exmouth and Coral Bay.

Margaret River Wine Region

2 The joy of drifting from winery to winery along country roads shaded by tall gum trees is just one of the delights of Australia's most beautiful wine region (p127). Right on its doorstep are the white sands of Geographe Bay, and even closer to the vines are the world-famous surf breaks of Yallingup and Margaret River Mouth. And then there are the caves – magical subterranean palaces of limestone, scattered along the main wine-tasting route. Sup, swim, surf, descend – the only difficulty is picking the order.

AUSCAPE / UIG/GETTY IMAGES ©

JON ARNOLD IMAGES LTD/ALAMY ©

Shark Bay & Monkey Mia

3 The aquamarine waters of World Heritage–listed Shark Bay (p176) teem with an incredible diversity of marine life, from Monkey Mia's world-famous dolphins to Hamelin Pool's ancient stromatolites. Enjoy simple coastal camping; excellent indigenous cultural tours explain how to care for and understand the country. Explore remote Edel Land, with its towering limestone cliffs, cross over to historically rich Dirk Hartog Island or relax, lie back and sail after the elusive, sea-grass-munching dugong.

Dolphins, Monkey Mia

Pinnacles Desert

4 It could be mistaken for the surface of Mars: scattered among Nambung National Park's dunes, thousands of ghostly limestone pillars rise like a vast, petrified alien army. One of the West's most bizarre landscapes, the Pinnacles (p114) attract thousands of visitors each year. It's easily enjoyed as a day trip from Perth, but staying overnight in nearby Cervantes allows for multiple visits to experience the full spectrum of colour changes at dawn, sunset and full moon, when most tourists are back in their hotels.

PHOTO BY MARTIN COHEN WILD ABOUT AUSTRALIA/GETTY IMAGES ©

CHERYL FORBES/GETTY IMAGES ©

Perth & Fremantle

5 Perth (p46) may be isolated, but it's far from being a backwater. Scattered across the city are sophisticated restaurants showcasing modern Australian cuisine, while chic cocktail bars bubble away in unlikely laneways and restored heritage buildings. In contrast to the flashy face that Perth presents to the river, charmingly grungy inner suburbs echo with the hum of guitars and turntables, and the sizzle of woks. Just downstream, the lively port of Fremantle has a pub on just about every corner, most pouring craft brews from around Western Australia and the world.

City skyline, Perth

Karijini National Park

6 Hidden deep in the heart of the Pilbara, the shady pools and plunging waterfalls of Karijini (p198) offer cool respite from the oppressive heat of the surrounding ironstone country. While most are content to explore the open gorges, booking an adventure trip will take you beyond the public areas as you abseil, swim, dive, climb and paddle through deep waterworn passages. Up top, witness the amazing spring transformation as wildflowers carpet the plains, and get some altitude on the state's highest peaks, including Mt Bruce (1235m).

Fern Pool, Dales Gorge

Broome

7 You can bitch and moan about the price of beer or how long your twice-cooked pork belly takes to arrive, but one thing is for certain: when that boiling crimson sun starts sinking slowly behind a conga-line of camels into a languid Indian Ocean at Cable Beach, you'll realise there's no other place like it in the world. Broome (p205) is a melting pot of travellers, one of the world's great crossroads, and you'll find everything you need (though perhaps not everything you want) in the back streets, bars and markets, and on the noticeboards.

Water Adventures

8 If you can't catch a wave on WA's 12,000km of coastline, mate, you're doing it wrong. In which case, head straight to one of Perth's surf schools (p55) and leave Margaret River and Gnaraloo to the pros, where breaks with nicknames like 'suicides' and 'tombstones' beckon the fearless. Diving and snorkelling are excellent in many spots, and WA is the place to swim with your favourite marine animal. Windsurfers breeze off to gusty Lancelin (p113) and Gnaraloo Bay (p182), while paddlers splash their way along the many rivers.

Bushwalking

9 Western Australia has 96 national parks, not counting dozens of other nature reserves and regional parks. These special places present oodles of opportunities to go walkabout on the many waymarked trails, and camp in isolated spots. The Bibbulmun Track (p35), the mother of them all, starts on the outskirts of Perth and heads nearly 1000km to Albany on the south coast, sheltered by the cooling giant eucalypts of the southern forests. At the Valley of the Giants (p145) you can walk through the canopy on the 40m-high Tree Top Walk.

Valley of the Giants

Gibb River Road

10 Launch yourself into Australia's last frontier on a wild drive down this old cattle road (p220) into the heart of the Kimberley. This is not for the faint-hearted; you'll need a serious 4WD, good planning and plenty of fuel, spares, food and water. Bring big doses of self-reliance, flexibility and humour. The rewards are fantastic gorges, hidden waterholes, incredible rock art and amazing wildlife, and you'll gain a first-hand insight into life in the outback. Did we mention there are also flies, dust and relentless heat?

Wildlife

11 Welcome to an idiosyncratic menagerie of species: endangered numbats, woylies, bilbies and boodies in the Dryandra Woodland (p102), quokkas on Rottnest Island (p94), freshwater crocodiles in Windjana Gorge National Park (p222), migratory shorebirds at Parry Lagoons Nature Reserve (p226), beautiful red-tailed tropicbirds of the southwest coast, migrating humpback whales, dolphins at Monkey Mia (p179) and whale sharks in Ningaloo Reef (p193).

Numbat

Indigenous Art

12 From urban galleries featuring contemporary art to centuries-old rock carvings, the culture and spirit of indigenous WA infuses this land. In Perth and Fremantle, visit excellent Indigenart (p75) and Japingka (p87) galleries; in the Kimberley, visit Short Street Gallery (p209), before looking back across the eons at Wandjina and Gwion Gwion rock-art sites (p250). Near spectacular Wave Rock (p102) to the south, visit the 450 stencils and hand prints of the nearby Mulkas Cave.

Wandjina figures, Mitchell Plateau

Need to Know

For more information see Survival Guide (p253)

Currency
Australian dollar ($)

Language
English

Money
ATMs widely available. Credit cards accepted in most hotels and restaurants.

Visas
All visitors require a visa, although New Zealanders receive one on arrival. Residents of Canada, the US, and many European and some Asian countries can apply online.

Mobile Phones
Australia's network is compatible with most European phones, but generally not with the US or Japanese systems. The main service providers offer prepaid SIMs.

Time
Western Standard Time (GMT/UTC plus eight hours). Daylight saving does not operate in WA.

When to Go

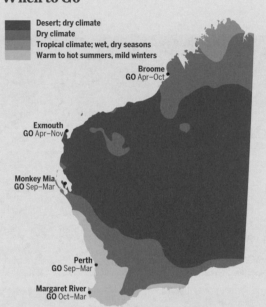

Desert; dry climate
Dry climate
Tropical climate; wet, dry seasons
Warm to hot summers, mild winters

Broome
GO Apr–Oct

Exmouth
GO Apr–Nov

Monkey Mia
GO Sep–Mar

Perth
GO Sep–Mar

Margaret River
GO Oct–Mar

High Season (Dec–Mar)

➡ In the south the weather is at its hottest and driest.

➡ The season peaks from Christmas to the end of the school holidays in January.

➡ In the north, this is the wet (low) season.

Shoulder (Apr, May & Sep–Nov)

➡ Wildflowers are in bloom from September.

➡ Also the months to visit the north.

➡ Humpback whales from September to November, whale sharks from April to June. Monkey Mia's dolphins are seen throughout the year.

Low Season (Jun–Aug)

➡ Wettest and coolest time in Perth and the south.

➡ Lows in the south are usually over 10°C.

➡ High season for the Coral Coast, the Pilbara, Broome and the Kimberley; dry and usually above 30°C.

Websites

Lonely Planet (www.lonely planet.com/australia) Destination information, traveller forum and more.

Tourism Western Australia (www.westernaustralia.com) Official tourist site.

Tourism Australia (www.aus tralia.com) Transport, event and destination information.

West Australian (www.thewest .com.au) Online version of the newspaper.

Department of Environment and Conservation (www.dec .wa.gov.au) Details on national parks. Some camp sites can be prebooked.

Important Numbers

Drop the zero from the area code if calling from outside Australia (61-8). If calling a WA number while in WA, drop the 08 prefix.

International access code	0011
Australia's country code	61
WA area code	08
Emergency (police, fire, ambulance)	000
Directory assistance	12455

Exchange Rates

Canada	C$1	$0.97
Euro	€1	$1.23
Japan	¥100	$1.20
New Zealand	NZ$1	$0.79
UK	£1	$1.54
USA	US$1	$0.96

For current exchange rates see www.xe.com.

Your Daily Costs

Budget: Up to $150

➡ Campsite (two people): $14–45

➡ Dorm bed: $24–48

➡ Private room in hostel: $80–120

➡ Mainly self-catering but having an occasional budget meal out: $25

Midrange: $150–275

➡ Double room in a midrange hotel: $120–220

➡ Lunch and dinner in cafes and pubs: $60

➡ Car hire: $40–50 per day

Top End: Over $275

➡ Mains in top restaurants: over $35

➡ Double room in a top hotel: from $250

Opening Hours

Note that, outside Perth, shops may not be open on weekends. Vineyard restaurants are usually only open for lunch, and many cafes also open later for dinner. Sunday shopping was introduced to the Perth CBD in August 2012, and most central-city stores now open seven days a week.

Banks 9.30am to 4pm Monday to Friday

Restaurants noon to midnight

Cafes 7am to 4pm

Pubs 11am to midnight

Shops 9am to 5pm Monday to Saturday, 11am to 5pm Sunday

Arriving in Perth & West Coast Australia

Perth Airport (p265) The Connect Shuttle runs every 50 minutes to Perth ($18), less frequently to Fremantle ($33). A taxi is about $40 to central Perth and $60 to Fremantle. Buses run every 10 to 30 minutes to the city, hourly after 7pm; journey time is 44 minutes.

Getting Around

Rental Car The most flexible way to get around, especially in attraction-packed areas like Margaret River. Distances are huge in other parts of the state, though, so investigate combining a one-way hire and a flight back to your starting point. See p268 for more information.

Airlines A good option to cover WA's huge distances quickly. Consider flying from Perth to Esperance, Exmouth or Broome, and then renting a car locally if your focus is only around those areas.

Train A good option for day trips south of Perth to Mandurah and Rockingham. Regular trains make Fremantle a worthwhile base for exploring Perth.

Bus Extensive coverage and relatively good frequency throughout the state. Good links from Perth to Margaret River and the southwest, and north to Geraldton and Exmouth.

Public Transport Both Perth and Fremantle have excellent urban bus and train networks. Be sure to use the free CAT bus services.

For much more on transport, **see p265**

What's New

Brookfield Place

A precinct of heritage buildings along St Georges Terrace in central Perth has been lovingly restored to house the city's coolest new opportunities for eating and drinking. (p65)

The Terrace Hotel

Another careful heritage makeover in central Perth, this time transforming an expansive 19th-century terrace house into the city's newest and most luxurious boutique hotel. (p58)

The Rise (& Rise) of Craft Beer

Western Australia has always been a craft-beer hot spot, but new microbreweries in the Swan Valley and Margaret River now make it an essential destination for travelling beer buffs. (p33)

Jewel Cave & Moondyne Cave

Experience the stunning new Jewel Cave Preservation Centre before donning a hard hat and overalls to explore the adjacent and recently opened Moonydne Cave. (p136)

Margaret River Gourmet Escape

Some of the planet's truly great chefs celebrate a four-day food-and-wine adventure amid Margaret River's verdant vineyards. (p127)

Cooking Schools

Harness WA's fine natural produce by cooking up a storm at Wildwood Valley near Yallingup and Foragers Field Kitchen in Pemberton. (p128) & (p142)

Castle Rock Granite Skywalk

Negotiate this newly opened walkway for spectacular views of the idiosyncratic rocky landscapes and karri forests of the Porongurup National Park. (p156)

Broome's Short Street Gallery

Broome's oldest gallery throws open its stock room, containing incredible canvases from indigenous artists scattered across the Kimberley and beyond. (p209)

Yarliyil Gallery

A new initiative from Halls Creek Shire provides local indigenous artists with a commercial outlet. (p218)

Duncan Road

Hauntingly beautiful and remote, this historic Kimberley route sees little tourist traffic yet is no more technical than its more famous cousin the Gibb River Road. (p222)

For more recommendations and reviews, see **lonelyplanet.com/ australia/western-australia**

If You Like...

Beaches

You're in luck. Western Australia (WA) has some of Australia's finest, which makes them among the best in the world. And you'll have many of them completely to yourself.

Cottesloe Perth's most iconic beach, with cafes and bars close at hand. (p54)

Bunker Bay Brilliant white sand edged by bushland; you'll have to look hard to spot the few houses scattered about. (p126)

Hellfire Bay Sand like talcum powder in the middle of Cape Le Grand National Park (p164), which is precisely in the middle of nowhere.

Shark Bay 1500km of remote beaches and towering limestone cliffs. (p176)

Turquoise Bay A beautiful bay in Ningaloo Marine Park, with wonderful snorkelling. (p194)

Eighty Mile Beach You're guaranteed at least 79 miles of solitude on this remote, white-sand beach. (p205)

William Bay National Park Sheltered swimming around the granite boulders of Greens Pool and Elephant Rocks. (p147)

Cable Beach Surely the most famous, camel-strewn, sunset-photographed beach in WA. (p205)

Diving & Snorkelling

Reefs and wrecks are plentiful around WA and the marine life is lush, providing a smorgasbord of options for geared-up diving pros or gung-ho first-time snorkellers.

Mettams Pool Excellent snorkelling within Perth's city limits. (p54)

Rottnest Island Over a dozen wrecks and two underwater snorkelling trails make this an excellent option. (p91)

Busselton Lots to see around the southern hemisphere's longest timber jetty, plus the wreck of a decommissioned Navy destroyer not far away. (p123)

Albany Look for sea dragons among the coral reefs and the wreck of the HMAS *Perth*. (p149)

Ningaloo Marine Park Australia's largest fringing reef, where you can snorkel and dive with the world's largest fish, the whale shark, along with turtles, dolphins and dugongs. (p193)

Houtman Abrolhos Islands Dive, snorkel, bushwalk or fish around these historic islands that rarely see tourists. (p172)

Surfing & Windsurfing

Wax the board and fire up the Kombi van: WA's surfing is legendary.

Trigg Beach Perth's surfers come here straight from work to catch a few waves. (p54)

Lancelin A mecca for windsurfers and kiteboarders, a great spot to learn to surf. (p113)

Yallingup/Margaret River 'Yals' and 'Margs' are the hub of the WA surf scene – with a major pro competition held there every year. (p127) (p131)

Ocean Beach, Denmark You might find yourself sharing this beautiful bay with whales. (p146)

Geraldton The surrounding beaches are thrilling for both wind- and wave-powered surfers. (p168)

Gnaraloo Surfers flock here in winter to try their luck at the

---

IF YOU LIKE... FINE FOOD

Foodies shouldn't resist a visit to the Wine & Truffle Co (p139) in Manjimup, where you can take part in a truffle hunt.

famous Tombstones break; in summer the windsurfers take their place. (p182)

North West Cape Big swells hit the west of the cape from July to October. (p195)

Forests & Bushwalking

You might be forgiven for thinking that WA was all about white sand and red dirt. There is an awful lot of both, but the state's arboreal delights are also worthy of exploration.

Lesueur National Park A huge diversity of flora with many rare and endemic trees. (p115)

Karri Forest Explorer This shady circuit passes through three national parks surrounding Pemberton. (p140)

Valley of the Giants Tree Top Walk A wobbly walkway arches through the lofty canopy of the tingle forest. (p145)

Bibbulmun Track The big one – stretching nearly 1000km from the edge of Perth through the southern forests to Albany. (p35)

Cape to Cape Track Enjoy Indian Ocean views on this 135km trail from Cape Naturaliste to Cape Leeuwin. (p127)

Walyunga National Park Explore the trails in this beautiful park, where the Avon River cuts through the Darling Range. (p104)

Derby With its bloated trunk and often bare, scrawny branches, the alien-looking boab tree is emblematic of this Kimberley town. (p217)

Stirling Range National Park This rugged range is known for its flora and chameleon-like ability to change colour. (p157)

Top: Little Creatures brewery (p85), Fremantle
Bottom: Kayaking near Mornington Wilderness Camp (p221)

Marine Mammals

It's extraordinarily easy to come close to the great creatures of the deep along WA's coast.

Perth & Fremantle Thirty thousand whales cruise past between mid-September and early December, and boat trips will take you out to cheer them on. (p55)

Rottnest Island The sharp-of-eye may spot New Zealand fur seals, dolphins and whales. (p94)

Rockingham Wild Encounters Cruise out to swim with dolphins and spot seals. (p96)

Sea Lion Charters, Green Head Splash with sea lions in the shallows. (p117)

Dolphin Discovery Centre, Bunbury Wade next to the wild dolphins that regularly drop by, or take a boat trip to swim with them. (p122)

Albany Between July and mid-October the bay turns into a whale nursery, with mothers and calves easily spotted from the beach, and cruises to take you a little closer. (p151)

Monkey Mia Watch dolphins feeding in the shallows and take a dugong-spotting cruise. (p179)

Beer, Wine & Food

WA's wine industry is now being complemented by innovative craft breweries, and vineyard restaurants and provedores also abound.

Swan Valley Within Perth's eastern reaches, this semirural area's cosy wineries and bustling microbreweries are packed with city folk at the weekend. (p104)

Fremantle The traditional home of WA craft beer, from mighty Little Creatures to the marvellous Sail & Anchor (43 taps and counting). (p86)

Margaret River Known for its Bordeaux-style varietals, chardonnay and sauvignon blanc, and a growing number of craft breweries. (p127)

Pemberton Another esteemed wine area, producing extremely good pinot noir, chardonnay and sauvignon blanc. (p139)

Denmark Notable wineries and craft breweries dot this picturesque area of the cool-climate Great Southern region. (p146)

Mt Barker & Porongurup Considered the most significant part of the Great Southern, with cool climes suiting riesling, pinot noir and cabernet sauvignon. (p156)

Aboriginal Art & Culture

Around 59,000 Aboriginal people still call WA home, comprising many different Indigenous groups, speaking distinct languages.

Art Gallery of Western Australia A treasure trove of indigenous art. (p50)

Yanchep National Park Didgeridoo and dance performances, and history and cultural tours with Noongar guides. (p113)

Wardan Aboriginal Centre Learn about Wardandi beliefs and way of life; try your hand at stone-tool making, and boomerang and spear throwing. (p127)

Kepa Kurl Eco Cultural Discovery Tours Day tours to visit rock art and waterholes, sample bush food and hear ancient stories. (p162)

Wula Guda Nyinda Aboriginal Cultural Tours Offers bushwalks and kayak tours, where you'll learn some of the local Malgana language, and how to identify bush tucker. (p179)

Dampier Peninsula Interact with remote communities and learn how to spear fish and catch mud crabs. (p216)

The Kimberley View artists' cooperatives, visit ancient rock art, and get to know 'country' on a cultural tour. (p218)

Getting Off the Beaten Path

In a destination so varied and expansive, there are plenty of spectacular opportunities to craft your own journey of discovery.

Mornington Wilderness Camp The 95km stretch from the Gibb River Road to this riverside oasis is some of WA's most exquisite and loneliest country. (p221)

Dryandra Woodland Less than two hours from Perth, but a world away, with endangered populations of endemic wildlife. (p102)

Gnaraloo Station Come for a night and stay for a month as your skills are put to work on this sustainable marvel. (p182)

Middle Lagoon Life doesn't get much more laid-back than at this Dampier Peninsula beachside campground far from anywhere. (p216)

Mt Augustus Uluru is a mere pup compared to this art-adorned monolith five hours from the closest asphalt. (p197)

Duncan Road A real outback adventure without the masses, Duncan Rd is both a destination itself and a 'long-cut' to the Northern Territory. (p222)

Marble Bar Burnt into the Australian psyche by the sun's rays, the Iron Clad Hotel is surrounded by incredibly scenic and empty landscapes. (p203)

Month by Month

January

The peak of the summer school holidays sees families head to the beach en masse. Days are hot and dry, except in the far north, where the wet season is in full force.

☆ Busselton's Big Music Festival

The Southbound Festival starts off the new year with three days of alternative music and camping in Busselton. Featuring big-name international artists, it's Western Australia's Glastonbury, but with less mud. (p124)

🏄 Lancelin's Windsurfing Challenge

In early January, tiny Lancelin's renowned blustery conditions attract thousands for its world-famous windsurfing event, the Lancelin Ocean Classic. Held over four days, the event starts with wave sailing on the Thursday and Friday, followed by the marathon on Saturday and the Sunday slalom. (p113)

February

The kids head back to school, freeing up some room at the beach and taking some of the pressure off coastal accommodation. It's still hot and dry (and soggy in the north).

☆ Alternative Music Festival, Perth

The Big Day Out is Australia's biggest touring music festival, attracting leading alternative artists and lots of local up-and-comers. It comes to Claremont Showground in early February. (p57)

🎭 Perth International Arts Festival

Held over 25 days from mid-February, Perth's festival attracts an international line-up, spanning theatre, classical music, jazz, visual arts, dance, film, literature – the whole gamut. It's worth scheduling your trip around. (p57)

☆ Leeuwin Concert Series

Leeuwin Estate winery in Margaret River hosts world-class performers of popular music, opera and the stage (Roxy Music, kd lang, Sting) during its annual event in mid-February; other concerts run from January to April. (p135)

🎭 Boyup Brook Country Music Festival

Good ol' boys and gals descend on a tiny southern forest town for five days of country music, bush poetry, markets and the annual 'Ute & Truck Muster'. Recent acts have included Kasey Chambers. (p138)

March

It's still beach weather, but it's not quite as swelteringly hot in the south. It's hot and steamy in the north, however, with rain still bucketing down. Prices shoot up at Easter.

🏃 Margaret River Surfing Pro

Officially called the Drug Aware Pro, this World Qualifying Series (WQS) event, held over six days in mid-March, sees the world's best up-and-coming surfers battle it out in the epic surf at Margaret River. (p127)

April

Another pleasant month in Perth, with the temperatures dropping to the mid-20s and a little more rainfall. Up north, it's finally starting to dry out and a great time for a Kimberley flyover.

🍴 Margaret River Wine Festival

This five-day festival titillates the taste buds with the best of the southwest's wine, food, art, music and outdoor adventures. It includes carnivals, master classes, the Slow Food Long Table Feast and a cricket match at Cowaramup Oval. (p127)

☆ Blues 'n' Roots Festival

Held in Fremantle Park, this festival interprets its remit widely: the 2012 line-up featured Crosby, Stills and Nash, My Morning Jacket and The Specials. Its 10th anniversary was held in 2013. (p83)

May

Temperatures creep down and Broome and Exmouth both finally drop below the 30s, making them particularly appealing – especially now the box jellyfish have retreated. Autumn showers are more common in the south.

🏃 Ord Valley Muster

For two weeks Kununurra hits overdrive during this annual collection of sporting, charity and cultural events, leading up to a large outdoor concert under a full moon on the banks of the Ord River. (p225)

June

Winter hits Perth, with plenty of rain and possibly some snow on the Stirling Range further south. The warm, dry north, however, heads into peak season. Whale watching commences in Augusta.

🍴 Avon Valley Food & Wine

Gourmet food from around the world, tasty goodies from more local producers, and the best of the expanding Avon Valley wine scene are all showcased at this welcome winter festival in Northam. (p108)

🎊 Derby Boab Festival

Derby strings out its party season from late May to early July with concerts, mud footy, horse and mud-crab races, film festivals, poetry readings, art exhibitions, street parades and a dinner out on the mudflats.

☆ Denmark Festival of Voice

Rousing choruses blow away the cobwebs from the south-coast town of Denmark during the Festival of Voice held over the June long weekend. The town is flooded with soloists, duos, choristers and their admirers. It's accompanied by a workshop program. (p147)

July

It's still wet and cold in the south and beautiful in the north – sparking a winter-break exodus from Perth. Whales congregate in the bays around Albany.

🎊 Indigenous Cultural Celebrations

Indigenous art exhibitions and performances take place throughout WA during National Aboriginal & Islander Day Observance Committee week, which celebrates the history, culture and achievements of indigenous people. (p210)

August

Much the same as July climate-wise, although temperatures start to edge up. Manjimup truffles come into season, to the delight of Perth's chefs and their customers; whales continue to hang out on the south coast.

🎊 Avon River Festivities

Northam and Toodyay both turn on festivals the day before the Avon Descent, a gruelling 133km whitewater rafting event for powerboats, kayaks and canoes between the two towns. Northam hosts the Avon River Festival, while Toodyay has a Festival of Food. (p108)

Broome Race Round

Local fillies and stallions frock up and get slaughtered as the Broome Race Round heads towards a frenzied climax with the Kimberley Cup, Ladies Day and the Broome Cup, all in early August. There's also some horse racing. (p210)

☆ Opera Under the Stars, Broome

World-class opera performers sing under clear Kimberley night skies at the Cable Beach Amphitheatre, their vocal pyrotechnics accompanied by a fireworks display. The event (www.operaunderthestars.com.au) is now preceded by the Oper-Arte fundraising art auction.

September

Spring brings a flurry of excitement, with wildflowers blooming and whales heading up the west coast. Broome pops back into the 30s and the tourists start to head south again.

☆ Red Earth Arts Festival, Pilbara

Spread across the Pilbara's coastal mining towns during most of September, the Red Earth Arts Festival is an eclectic mix of live music (all genres), theatre, comedy, visual arts (including film, photography and sculpture) and storytelling. (p196)

Festival of the Pearl

Starting either in late August or early September, Broome's Shinju Matsuri celebrates its pearl industry and multicultural heritage with a carnival of nations, a film festival, art exhibitions, food, concerts, fireworks and dragon-boat races. (p210)

Perth's Wildflower Festival

In September and early October, Kings Park and the Botanic Garden are filled with colourful wildflower displays for the annual Kings Park Festival, which celebrates WA's unique, spectacular flora. Includes guided walks, talks and live music every Sunday. (p57)

October

The last of the whales depart the south coast and hit the west-coast leg of the Humpback Hwy. The weather's warmer and drier, and the wildflowers are still wonderful.

Geraldton Greenough Sunshine Festival

It started in 1959 as a tomato festival, but now Geraldton's solar celebrations (www.sunshinefestival.com.au) include dragon-boat races, parades, sand sculptures and parties, held over nine days in early October. Sunshine guaranteed.

November

A great time to be in Fremantle, with temperatures in the mid-20s, very little rain and a convoy of whales passing by. In the far north, box-jellyfish season begins.

Margaret River Gourmet Escape

The culinary world's heavy hitters – David Chang and AA Gill attended the inaugural event in 2012 – descend on Margaret River for four days of culinary inspiration (www.gourmetescape.com.au). Australia's growing crew of celebrity chefs usually attend as well.

Fremantle Festival

Ten days of parades, performances, music, dance, comedy, visual arts, street theatre and workshops. Founded in 1905, it's Australia's longest-running festival (www.fremantle.wa.gov.au). Highlights: the Kite Extravaganza on South Beach and the Wardarnji Indigenous Festival.

Broome Mango Festival

Broome celebrates its mango harvest with four days of mango-themed everything (www.broome.wa.au/events/broome-mango-festival). So how exactly do you celebrate mangos? With a quiz night, a fashion parade and a Great Chefs of Broome Cook-Off, apparently. If you don't end up with sweet, sticky fingers, you're doing it wrong.

Itineraries

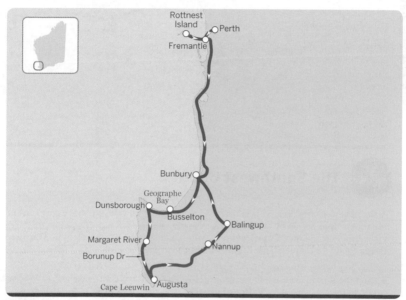

Rottnest
Island
Perth
Fremantle

Bunbury

Geographe
Bay
Dunsborough
Busselton
Balingup

Margaret River
Nannup

Borunup Dr

Cape Leeuwin Augusta

1 WEEK A Southwest Short Circuit

If you've got limited time, this itinerary offers a taste of the best of the state – city life, colonial history, beaches, wildlife, wine, forests and rural roads. Base yourself in either **Perth** (p47) or **Fremantle** (p77) and spend three days exploring the conjoined cities and one day on **Rottnest Island** (p91). Hire a car and head south, stopping first at **Bunbury** (p120) for lunch and a visit to the Dolphin Discovery Centre. Continue on to **Geographe Bay** (p120), basing yourself in either **Busselton** (p123) or **Dunsborough** (p125), and use the rest of the day to explore the beaches. Pick up a wine-region map and spend day six checking out the wineries, surf beaches and caves, all of which are close by. Base yourself in the **Margaret River** (p132) township that night and head to Settlers Tavern, the local pub. The next morning, head to **Augusta** via Caves Rd and take the scenic detour through the karri forest along unsealed **Borunup Drive** (p134). Visit **Cape Leeuwin** (p136), where the Indian and Southern Oceans meet, before heading back to Bunbury on a picturesque rural drive through **Nannup** (p137) and **Balingup** (p137). From here it's a two-hour drive back to Perth.

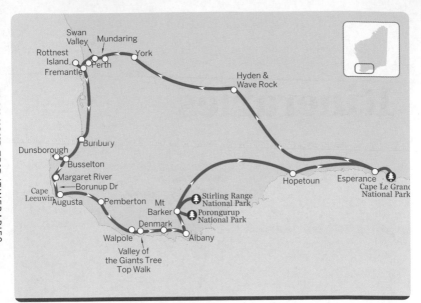

 The Southwest Uncut
3 WEEKS

Australia's southwest is a magical part of the continent and this itinerary covers its main highlights. Bump it up by another week to really relax into it. Start by following the previous itinerary as far as **Cape Leeuwin** (p136), but spend a second night in **Margaret River** (p132) for more winery, brewery and beach action.

Continue to **Pemberton** (p139), amid three forested national parks, for more wineries and the Karri Forest Explorer scenic drive. The next day, continue through **Walpole** (p145) to the extraordinary **Valley of the Giants Tree Top Walk** (p145), then press on to **Denmark** (p1460). Check out the beaches, wineries and breweries before making the short hop to **Albany** (p149) the next day. Spend two days here swimming (in summer), whale watching (in winter) and exploring the nearby coastal national parks.

Head north for more wineries at **Mt Barker** (p156) before scuttling east to spend the night at **Porongurup National Park** (p156). Spend the next day (or two) tackling the mountainous tracks here or at **Stirling Range National Park** (p157) further north.

From here the driving distances get longer. Continue through Ongerup and Jerramungup to the South Coast Hwy and at Ravensthorpe hop down to **Hopetoun** (p1600) to spend the night. This will take about three hours from the Stirling Range, so you can spend the afternoon at the beach. The following day, head back to the South Coast Hwy and continue east to **Esperance** (p161), a drive of around 2½ hours. Stay there for at least two days, spending one exploring gorgeous **Cape Le Grand National Park** (p164).

Head back on the South Coast Hwy and turn north just past Ravensthorpe for the road to **Hyden** (p102) and extraordinary **Wave Rock** (p102); allow four hours' driving. The following day, head west on Hwy 40 to Brookton and then turn north on the Great Southern Hwy and follow the Avon Valley to quaintly colonial **York** (p107); allow 3½ hours. For your last day, take a leisurely drive back to Perth via **Mundaring** (p103), stopping at the **Swan Valley** (p104) wineries en route.

To make this itinerary shorter, head straight to Hyden from the Stirling Range, or take the Albany Hwy directly to Perth from Mt Barker.

Above: Mitchell Falls (p223)

Right: Swan River, Perth

FRANCES ANDRIJICH/GETTY IMAGES ©

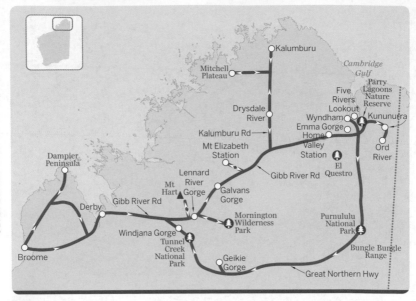

The Gibb River Road & Kimberley Outback

The biggest adventure in the west leaves **Broome** (p205) during the Dry and traverses the heart of the rugged Kimberley by 4WD. First stop is the **Dampier Peninsula** (p216), with its Aboriginal communities, beautiful beaches and mud crabs, and your last salt-water swim. Take the back road to **Derby** (p217), with its boabs, then on to the **Gibb River Road** (p220), where **Lennard River** (p221) is the first of many inviting gorges. Explore wildlife and gorges at **Mt Hart** (p221) and remote **Mornington Wilderness Camp** (p221) and look for Wandjina at **Galvans Gorge** (p221) and **Mt Elizabeth Station** (p222). Turn off onto the **Kalumburu Road** (p221), check the road conditions at **Drysdale River** (p223) and drive on to the **Mitchell Plateau** (p223), with its forests of Livistona and mind-blowing falls. Marvel at the area's rock art before hitting the northern coast and excellent fishing at **Honeymoon Bay** (p221), just beyond the mission community of **Kalumburu** (p221).

It's all downhill from here as you retrace your route back to the Gibb, then turn left for wonderful **Home Valley Station** (p222), where someone else can do the cooking and the soft beds make a pleasant change from camping. Nearby **El Questro** (p222) has gorges aplenty, none more beautiful than **Emma Gorge** (p222). Soon you're back on asphalt, but not for long as you take in the amazing bird life of **Parry Lagoons Nature Reserve** (p226). Let Wyndham's **Five Rivers Lookout** (p225) blow your mind with its view of Cambridge Gulf, before heading for the civility of **Kununurra** (p225), with its excellent food and supplies. Look for fruit-picking work, ride a canoe down the mighty Ord River, or jump back behind the wheel for the wonders of **Purnululu National Park** (p224), home to the orange-domed **Bungle Bungle Range** (p224). Darwin and the Northern Territory are beckoning, or you can follow the Great Northern Hwy back to Broome, stopping in at beautiful **Geikie Gorge** (p223) for a relaxing boat cruise where you might spot freshwater crocs. If you don't see any, don't worry, as nearby **Windjana Gorge** (p222) has loads sunning on the river banks. Grab your torch and head for a cold wade through the icy waters of **Tunnel Creek** (p223), with its bats and rock art, before planting the pedal back to Broome, where you won't care how much that beer costs any more.

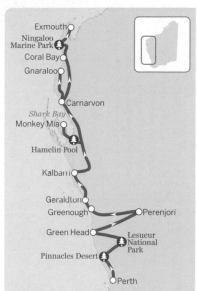

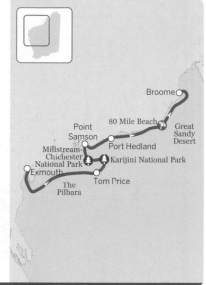

Indian Ocean Dreaming

2 WEEKS

Beautiful beaches, spectacular sunsets and diverse wildlife are constants on this coastal cruise. Take Indian Ocean Dr north from **Perth** (p47) to Cervantes for sunset on the otherwordly **Pinnacles Desert** (p114). Cruise the wildflower-laden Kwongan back roads and marvel at **Lesueur National Park's** (p115) flora before snorkelling with sea lions at **Green Head** (p117). Follow the flowers out to **Perenjori** (p112), then hit the cafes and museums of **Geraldton** (p168). Have a surf on a kiteboard, then move on to the wonderful **Kalbarri** (p172) coastline. Enjoy a canoe in the gorges before sampling the outback on the long drive to World Heritage–listed **Shark Bay** (p176). Watch dolphins at **Monkey Mia** (p179), go sailing with dugongs, and learn about country on an indigenous cultural tour. Check out the stromatolites of **Hamelin Pool** (p176), before putting in more road time on the stretch to **Carnarvon** (p180). Drop into **Gnaraloo** (p182) for world-class waves before arriving at tiny **Coral Bay** (p186) and **Exmouth** (p188), where whale sharks, manta rays and turtles inhabit the exquisite **Ningaloo Marine Park** (p193). You can fly out of Exmouth, drive back to Perth in two days, overnighting in historic **Greenough** (p170), or push on to the gorges of **Karijini** (p198).

Pilbara Jewels

1 WEEK

You'll camp most of the way on this link between Ningaloo and Broome, with long empty beaches, shady pools and surprisingly good food. From **Exmouth** (p188), take Burkett Rd back to the highway, and head north, turning off at Nanutarra for the long, scenic haul up to **Tom Price** (p198). After stocking up, spend the next few days camped in **Karijini National Park** (p198), exploring the sublime gorges and indulging in a spot of peak bagging among the state's highest mountains. Don't miss a swim at Hamersley Gorge en route to restful, shady Crossing Pool in **Millstream-Chichester National Park** (p198). Admire the mesas and breakaways of the Chichester Range before dropping down to the coast and some snorkelling at lovely **Point Samson** (p197). Take the North West Coastal Hwy directly to **Port Hedland** (p201), and scoff some wonderful coffee and cake in the Silver Star railcar, before camping at remote **80 Mile Beach** (p205), where you might spot nesting turtles. Your last leg is a long stretch of nothing as you skirt the Great Sandy Desert to arrive in tropical **Broome** (p205). You can bail out here or tool up for the Kimberley. Alternatively, skip the country on a direct Bali flight from Port Hedland.

Off the Beaten Track

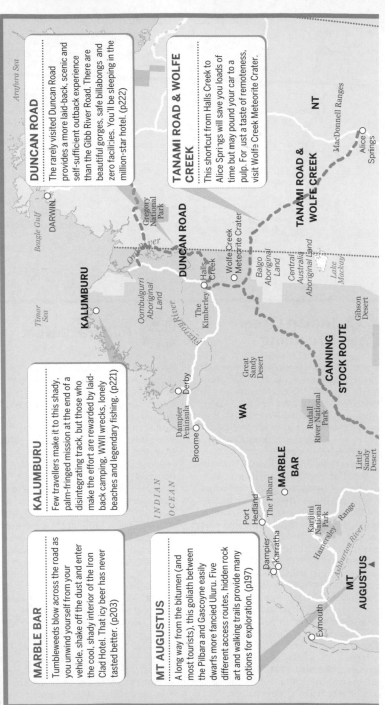

MARBLE BAR

Tumbleweeds blow across the road as you unwind yourself from your vehicle, shake off the dust and enter the cool, shady interior of the Iron Clad Hotel. That icy beer has never tasted better. (p203)

KALUMBURU

Few travellers make it to this shady, palm-fringed mission at the end of a disintegrating track, but those who make the effort are rewarded by laid-back camping, WWII wrecks, lonely beaches and legendary fishing. (p221)

DUNCAN ROAD

The rarely visited Duncan Road provides a more laid-back, scenic and self-sufficient outback experience than the Gibb River Road. There are beautiful gorges, safe billabongs and zero facilities. You'll be sleeping in the million-star hotel. (p222)

TANAMI ROAD & WOLFE CREEK

This shortcut from Halls Creek to Alice Springs will save you loads of time but may pound your car to a pulp. For ust a taste of remoteness, visit Wolf Creek Meteorite Crater.

MT AUGUSTUS

A long way from the bitumen (and most tourists), this goliath between the Pilbara and Gascoyne easily dwarfs more fancied Uluru. Five different access routes, hidden rock art and walking trails provide many options for exploration. (p197)

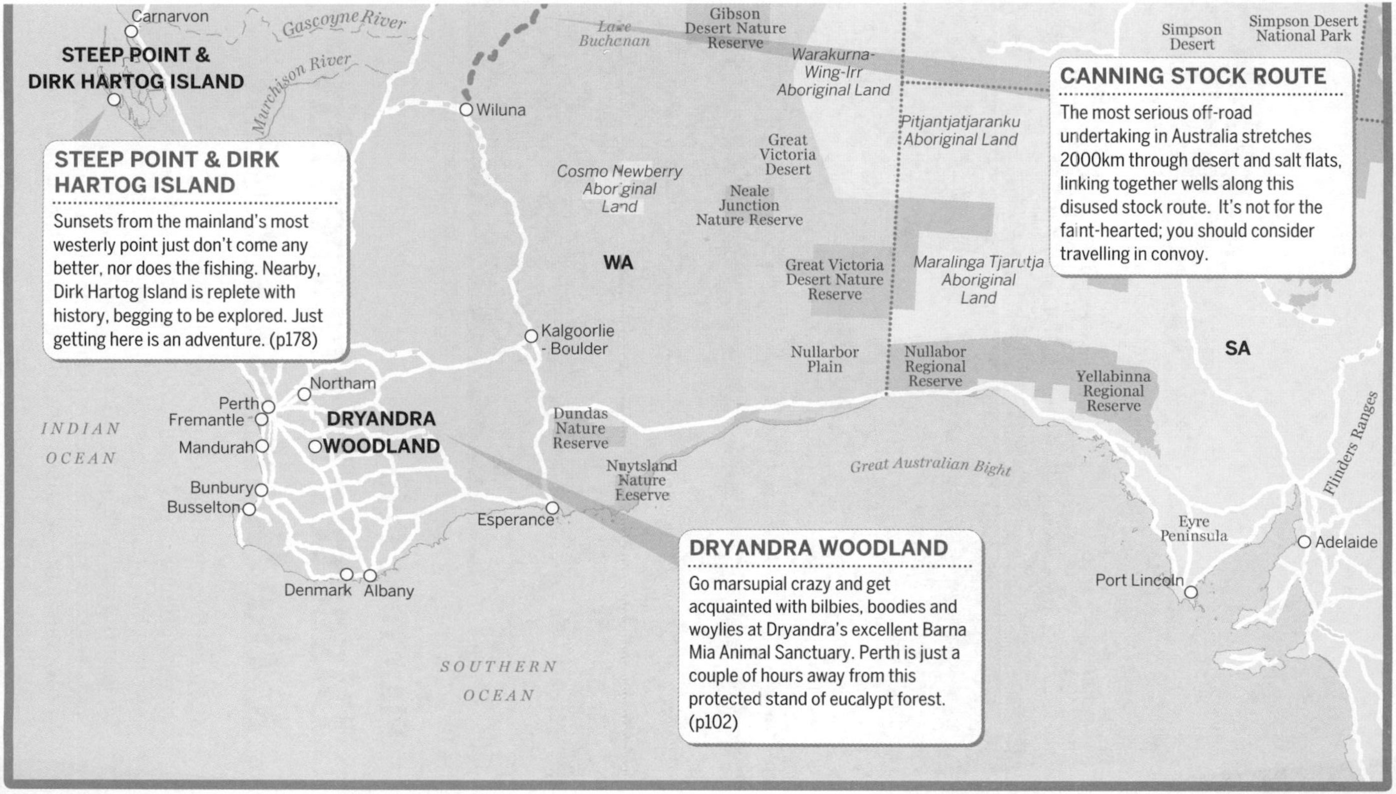

CANNING STOCK ROUTE

The most serious off-road undertaking in Australia stretches 2000km through desert and salt flats, linking together wells along this disused stock route. It's not for the faint-hearted; you should consider travelling in convoy.

DRYANDRA WOODLAND

Go marsupial crazy and get acquainted with bilbies, boodies and woylies at Dryandra's excellent Barna Mia Animal Sanctuary. Perth is just a couple of hours away from this protected stand of eucalypt forest. (p102)

STEEP POINT & DIRK HARTOG ISLAND

Sunsets from the mainland's most westerly point just don't come any better, nor does the fishing. Nearby, Dirk Hartog Island is replete with history, begging to be explored. Just getting here is an adventure. (p178)

Simpson Desert National Park

Simpson Desert

Adelaide

Flinders Ranges

SA

Eyre Peninsula

Port Lincoln

Yellabinna Regional Reserve

Maralinga Tjarutja Aboriginal Land

Pitjantjatjarraku Aboriginal Land

Nullarbor Regional Reserve

Great Australian Bight

Nullarbor Plain

Great Victoria Desert Nature Reserve

Warakurna Wing-Irr Aboriginal Land

Gibson Desert Nature Reserve

Great Victoria Desert

Neale Junction Nature Reserve

WA

Cosmo Newberry Aboriginal Land

Lake Buchanan

Kalgoorlie -Boulder

Dundas Nature Reserve

Nuytsland Nature Reserve

Esperance

SOUTHERN OCEAN

Wiluna

Gascoyne River

Murchison River

Carnarvon

STEEP POINT & DIRK HARTOG ISLAND

Northam

Perth

Fremantle

Mandurah

Bunbury

Busselton

DRYANDRA WOODLAND

Denmark Albany

INDIAN OCEAN

Contos Beach, Leeuwin-Naturaliste National Park (p127)

Plan Your Trip

Discover Margaret River & the Southwest Coast

Margaret River features family-friendly beaches, brilliant surfing, labyrinthine caves studded with limestone formations, and a world-class gourmet scene – all in a relatively compact area. Vineyards producing excellent chardonnays and Bordeaux-style reds segue to rural backroads punctuated with craft breweries, providores, cheese shops, chocolate shops, and art galleries.

Best of the Region

Best Wineries

Vasse Felix (☑08-9756 5000; www
.vassefelix.com.au; cnr Caves & Harmans
Rds) Regional pioneer leading the way with
its Heytesbury Cabernet blend and Heytesbury Chardonnay.

Cullen Wines (p131) Another Margaret River
pioneer, with the 2009 Diana Madeline cabernet sauvignon merlot awarded Wine of the
Year in the *Australian Wine Annual 2012*.

Leeuwin Estate (p135) Wonderful wines,
especially its Art Series chardonnay and
sauvignon blanc.

Watershed Premium Wines (p135) One of
WA's best vineyard restaurants and renowned
for its Awakening cabernet sauvignon.

Ashbrook (p131) Great quality, good value;
try the cabernet merlot.

Four Things
You Wouldn't Expect

Artworks by Arthur Boyd and Sidney Nolan in
the **Bunbury Regional Art Gallery** (p120).

A highly rated French-Australian film festival,
CinéfestOZ (p124), is held annually in
beachy Busselton.

A colony of **red-tailed tropicbirds** roosts off
Cape Naturaliste.

Most of the best restaurants aren't open in
the evenings.

Plan Your Attack
What's the Layout?

The sheltered white sands of Geographe
Bay arch from south of Bunbury to Cape
Naturaliste, with Busselton and Dunsborough its main towns. At Cape Naturaliste
the coastline pirouettes and runs nearly
due south to Cape Leeuwin. The wine
region runs parallel to this coast with
Margaret River cutting roughly east to
west through the centre, passing through
its namesake town. Wineries are scattered
around, but most are north of the river.

Where to Stay

➜ **For a beach holiday** Busselton or
Dunsborough

➜ **For surfing** Yallingup, Prevelly or Margaret
River

➜ **For wineries** Yallingup, Margaret River or
anywhere in between

➜ **For caves** Anywhere between Yallingup and
Augusta

➜ **For peace and quiet** Augusta

When to Go

➜ **For a beach holiday** December to March

➜ **For surfing** Anytime, but the big surf pro is
in March

➜ **For wineries, breweries and caves** All year

➜ **For whale watching** June to September
from Augusta, September to December from
Dunsborough

➜ **For French films** August

When to Avoid

➜ January in Busselton, unless you're going to
the Southbound music festival or have booked
well in advance

➜ November in Dunsborough, when the place is
overrun by end-of-school revellers

➜ Weekends in Margaret River, accommodation
prices are higher and there are loads of people –
but at least everything will be open

What to Do
Surfing the Wineries

The two main north–south routes are the
Bussell Hwy (passing through Cowaramup,
Margaret River and Augusta) and leafy
Caves Rd (running south from Dunsborough). Numerous bucolic back roads link
the two. Pick up one of the excellent free
maps, squabble over who's going to be the
nondrinking driver, and dive right in. The
other alternative is to take a tour – public
transport is not a workable option.

Most of the wineries offer tastings between 10am and 5pm daily. At busy times
(this includes every weekend), consider
booking ahead for lunch before you set out.

Tasting the Waves

Known to surfers as 'Yals' (around Yallingup) and 'Margs' (around the mouth of

OLAVER CARROLL/GETTY IMAGES ©

Above: Lake Cave (p134)

Left: Leeuwin Estate (p135), Margaret River

the Margaret River), the beaches between Capes Naturaliste and Leeuwin offer powerful reef breaks, mainly left-handers (the direction you take after catching a wave). The surf at Margs has been described by surfing supremo Nat Young as 'epic', and by world surfing champ Mark Richards as 'one of the world's finest'.

As is the way with such hot spots, surfers can be quite territorial, so respect the etiquette and defer to locals if you're unsure. If you're planning on spending a lot of time on the breaks, call into the surf shops and get to know some locals.

Around Dunsborough, the better locations include Rocky Point (short left-hander) and the Farm and Bone Yards (right-handers), which are between Eagle and Bunker Bays. Near Yallingup there are the Three Bears (Papa, Mama and Baby, of course), Rabbits (a beach break towards the north of Yallingup Beach), Yallingup (reef with breaks left and right), and Injidup Car Park and Injidup Point (right-hand tube on a heavy swell; left-hander). You'll need a 4WD to access Guillotine/Gallows (right-hander), north of Gracetown. Also around Gracetown are Huzza's (an easy break within the beach), South Point (popular break) and Lefthanders (the name says it all). The annual surfer pro is held around Margaret River Mouth and Southside ('Suicides') in March.

Pick up a surfing map from one of the visitor centres.

Surfing is never without its risks. Two people have been killed by sharks in the vicinity of Gracetown in the last six years.

Going Underground

The main cave complexes are spread, perhaps unsurprisingly, along Caves Rd. Ngilgi Cave sits by itself near Yallingup, but the other main complexes are between Margaret River township and Augusta, and are split between those run by the Department of Environment and Conservation (Calgardup Cave and Giants Caves) and the more commercialised CaveWorks caves (Lake Cave, Jewel Cave and Mammoth Cave). Caveworks offers a combined ticket for its

> ### BEST FAMILY ACTIVITIES
> ....
> ➡ Dolphin Discovery Centre (p122), Bunbury
>
> ➡ Bunbury Wildlife Park (p120)
>
> ➡ Busselton Drive-in Outdoor Cinema (p125)
>
> ➡ Busselton Jetty (p123)
>
> ➡ Margaret River Chocolate Company (p131)

three caves. If you're feeling adventurous, don overalls and a hard hat and explore the recently reopened Moondyne Cave on a guided tour.

Getting Crafty

The hoppy wave of craft beer that's sweeping many countries has also washed up on WA shores, and an innovative generation of brewers is proving there's more to beer than innocuous Euro lagers. Look forward to a global array of beer styles including India Pale Ales, Belgian Ales and Chocolate Porters, and decide on a designated driver or join a tour. See p130 for our picks of the best of Margaret River's craft brewing scene. Most are open for drinks and food from around 11am to 5pm.

Other Attractions

➡ **Beaches** – and lots of them; they're particularly beautiful between Dunsborough and Cape Naturaliste.

➡ **Walking** – there are excellent tracks around Cape Naturaliste and between the capes.

➡ **Diving** – trips leave from Busselton and Dunsborough to explore local wrecks and reefs.

➡ **Whale watching** – cruises leave from Augusta (starting in June) and Dunsborough (starting in September).

➡ **Lighthouses** – both capes have them and both can be visited. From Cape Leeuwin you can watch the Indian and Southern Oceans collide.

➡ **Adventure sports** – from mountain biking to climbing and kayaking. See p34.

Quokka (p94), Rottnest Island (Wadjemup)

Plan Your Trip

West Coast Australia Outdoors

With incredible landscapes and seascapes, intriguing wildlife, and all that brilliant sunshine, Western Australia (WA) is the perfect playground for outdoor enthusiasts, with numerous tracks to follow, waves to surf and reefs to explore.

Best Outdoors

Best for Daredevils

Karijini National Park Scramble, abseil, slide and dive through the gorges

Horizontal waterfalls, Derby Ride the surge in a speedboat

Best Wildlife Encounters

Whales Whale-watching boats leave from Perth, Fremantle, Dunsborough, Augusta, Albany, Coral Bay, Exmouth, Kalbarri, Broome and the Dampier Peninsula

Whale sharks and manta rays Ningaloo Marine Park

Dolphins Rockingham, Bunbury, Monkey Mia

Sea lions Rockingham, Green Head

Seals Rottnest Island

Dugongs Monkey Mia

Little marsupials Rottnest Island, Dryandra Woodland

Huge lizards Anywhere in the Kimberley

Kangaroos and parrots Everywhere

Bushwalking

WA's excellent bushwalking terrain includes the southwest's cool forests, the expansive Bibbulmun Track and the north's rugged national parks.

See www.bushwalkingwa.org.au for details of local bushwalking clubs, and to contact potential walking buddies, or buy and sell gear, see the forums on www.bushwalk.com.

For responsible-bushwalking tips, see the camping and bushwalking guidelines online at www.dec.wa.gov.au.

THE BIBBULMUN TRACK

Taking around eight weeks to walk, the 963km **Bibbulmun Track** (www.bibbulmuntrack.org.au) goes from Kalamunda, 20km east of Perth, through mainly natural environment to Walpole and Albany.

Terrain includes jarrah and marri forests, wildflowers, granite outcrops, coastal heath country and spectacular coastlines.

Comfortable camp sites are spaced regularly, and the best time to do it is from August to October.

Perth & Surrounds

With hiking and camping facilities, John Forrest National Park has an easy 15km walk to waterfalls, and the rugged Walyunga National Park features a medium-to-hard 18km walk that fords the Avon River and has excellent wildlife viewing. The Yanchep National Park has short strolls and challenging full-day walks. The Yaberoo Budjara trail follows an Aboriginal walking trail.

Down South

Serious walkers gravitate to the ruggedly beautiful Stirling Range National Park. Popular are the Bluff Knoll climb (6km, three to four hours), and the park's 1500 species of wildflower. Visit from September to November for the park's flowering glory, and be prepared for wind chill and rain (and sometimes snow) in winter.

North of Albany is the smaller Porongurup National Park, with spectacular granite rocks and dense karri forest. Trails include the 10-minute Tree in the Rock stroll, the medium-grade Hayward and Nancy Peaks (three hours) and the challenging three-hour Marmabup Rock hike. Wildflowers and bird activity make springtime the peak season for Porongurup, but it can be visited year-round.

Spectacular coastal highlights are walks through Walpole, Fitzgerald River and Cape Le Grand National Parks. The Cape to Cape Track (p127) follows the coastline 135km from Cape Naturaliste to Cape Leeuwin, taking five to seven days, and featuring wild camp sites en route.

BEST WILDFLOWER SPOTS

➡ Kings Park, Perth, especially the Botanic Garden

➡ Fitzgerald River National Park, between Albany and Esperance

➡ Porongorup National Park, north of Albany

➡ Stirling Range National Park, also north of Albany

➡ Mulleaw, in the central midlands, especially at August's annual flower show

➡ Kalbarri National Park, on the Batavia Coast

➡ Wongan Hills and Morawa in the central midlands

Bungle Bungle Range, Purnululu National Park (p224)

Up North

Summer's no picnic in the sweltering, remote national parks of the north, and high season for many bushwalkers is from April to October. The arid terrain can be treacherous, so research carefully, be prepared with water and supplies, and check in with rangers before setting out.

Kalbarri National Park showcases scenic gorges, thick bushland and rugged coastal cliffs. The popular six-hour loop features dramatic seascapes, including spectacular Nature's Window.

Rugged, sometimes hazardous treks can be taken into the dramatic gorges of Karijini National Park. The walk to the Mt Bruce summit (9km, five hours) is popular with experienced bushwalkers.

Visitors to the Kimberley's Purnululu National Park come to see the striped beehive-shaped domes of the World Heritage–listed Bungle Bungles. Walks include the easy Cathedral Gorge walk, and the more difficult overnight trek to Piccaninny Gorge. The park is only open from April to December.

Camping

It's very easy to 'get away from it all' in WA, and in the state's national parks, sleeping in a swag under the stars is almost obligatory. The weather is a factor, though: it can be uncomfortable in the north during summer due to heat and flash flooding, and cold down south during winter. School holidays can be very busy.

Surfing & Windsurfing

Beginners, intermediates, wannabe pros and adventure surfers will all find excellent conditions to suit their skill levels. WA gets huge swells (often over 3m), so it's critical to align the surf and the location with your ability. Look out for strong currents, sharks and territorial local surfers.

WA's traditional surfing home is the southwest, particularly from Yallingup to Margaret River. This stretch has many different breaks to explore.

Around Perth the surf is smaller, but there are often good conditions at bodyboard-infested Trigg and Scarborough. If the waves are small, head to Rottnest Island for (usually) bigger and better waves. Check out Strickland Bay.

Heading north, there are countless reef breaks waiting to be discovered (hint: take a 4WD). Best known are the left-hand

Salmon Holes, Torndirrup National Park (p154)

point breaks of Jakes Point near Kalbarri; Gnaraloo Station, 150km north of Carnarvon, and Surfers Beach at Exmouth. Buy the locals a beer and they might share a few more secret world-class locations.

Windsurfers and kitesurfers have plenty of choices with excellent flat-water and wave sailing. Kitesurfers appreciate the long, empty beaches and offshore reefs.

After Perth's city beaches, head to Lancelin, home to a large summertime population of surfers. Flat-water and wave sailing are excellent here. Further north, Geraldton has the renowned Coronation Beach. The Shark Bay area has excellent flat-water sailing and Gnaraloo Station is also a world-renowned wave-sailing spot.

Wildlife Watching

Whales

Because so many southern right and humpback whales (upwards of 30,000) cruise along the WA coast, it has become known as the Humpback Hwy. From June onwards their annual pilgrimage begins

from Antarctica to the warm tropical waters of the northwest coast, and mothers with calves seek out the shallower bays and coves of King George Sound in Albany from July to October. In whale-watching season, whales can be spotted from coastal clifftops, and often from the beach as well.

NATIONAL PARK PASSES

Thirty of WA's 96 national parks charge vehicle entry fees (per car/motorcycle $11/5), which are valid for any park visited that day. If you're camping within the park, the entry fee is only payable on the first day (camping fees are additional). If you plan to visit more than three WA parks with entry fees – which is quite likely if you're travelling outside Perth – get the four-week Holiday Pass ($40). All DEC offices sell them, and if you've already paid a day-entry fee in the last week (and have the voucher to prove it), you can subtract it from the cost of the pass.

Longreach Bay (p93), Rottnest Island (Wadjemup)

Dolphins

Dolphins can be seen up close at the Dolphin Discovery Centre in Bunbury, around Rockingham, and at Monkey Mia. Monkey Mia also has 10% of the world's dugong population.

Birds

The Broome Bird Observatory attracts a staggering 800,000 birds each year, and the Yalgorup National Park near Mandurah is another important waterbird habitat. The Lesueur National Park is home to the endangered Carnaby's cockatoo, and migratory shorebirds flock to Parry Lagoons Nature Reserve in the Kimberley.

Cycling

WA's southwest is good for cycle touring, and while there are thousands of kilometres of flat, virtually traffic-free roads elsewhere in the state, the distances between towns makes it difficult to plan.

Perth is a relatively bike-friendly city, with good recreational bike paths, including routes that run along the Swan River to Fremantle, and paths overlooking the city through Kings Park.

Cyclists rule on virtually car-free Rottnest Island, with long stretches of empty roads circumnavigating the island and its beaches. Geraldton also has great cycle paths.

The most exciting route for mountain bikers is the **Munda Biddi Trail** (www.mundabiddi.org.au), meaning 'path through the forest' in the Noongar Aboriginal language. The 1000km mountain-biking equivalent of the Bibbulmun Track, all the way from Mundaring on Perth's outskirts to Albany on the south coast, was projected to be completed around April 2013. Camp sites are situated a day's easy ride apart, and maps are available online and at visitor centres.

Diving & Snorkelling

WA's fascinating diving and snorkelling locations include stunning marine parks and shipwrecks.

Close to Perth, divers can explore wrecks and marine life off the beaches of Rottnest Island, or explore the submerged reefs and historic shipwrecks of the West Coast Dive Park within Shoalwater Islands Marine Park, near Rockingham. You can take a dive course in Geographe Bay with companies based in Dunsborough or Busselton; the bay offers excellent dives under the Busselton jetty, on Four Mile Reef (a 40km limestone ledge about 6.5km off the coast) and the scuttled HMAS *Swan*.

Other wrecks include the HMAS *Perth* (at 36m), deliberately sunk in 2001 in King George Sound near Albany; and the *Sanko Harvest,* near Esperance. Both teem with marine life on the wrecks' artificial reefs.

Divers seeking warmer water should head north. Staggering marine life can be found just 100m offshore within the Ningaloo Marine Park, fantastic for both diving and snorkelling. In Turquoise Bay, underwater action is equally accessible, and one of the planet's most amazing underwater experiences is diving or snorkelling alongside the incredible whale shark, the world's largest fish. Tours leave from Exmouth and Coral Bay.

Above: Snorkelling off Busselton (p123)

Right: Corellas, Yalgorup National Park (p99)

AUSCAPE / UIG/GETTY IMAGES ©

REDUCING THE RISK OF SHARK ATTACK

This list of shark safety guidelines is from WA's Department of Fisheries. After a spate of fatal shark attacks in 2012, the WA government also announced a $20-million safety program including a system to track, catch and potentially kill any sharks posing an imminent threat. See www.fish.wa.gov.au.

➡ Swim between the flags at patrolled beaches.

➡ Swim close to shore.

➡ Swim, dive or surf with other people.

➡ Avoid areas close to bird rookeries or where there are large schools of fish, dolphins, seals or sea lions.

➡ Avoid areas where animal, human or fish waste enter the water.

➡ Avoid deep channels or areas with deep drop-offs nearby.

➡ Do not remain in the water with bleeding wounds.

➡ Look carefully before jumping into the water from a boat or jetty.

➡ If spearing fish, don't carry dead or bleeding fish attached to you and remove all speared fish from the water as quickly as possible.

➡ If schooling fish or other wildlife start to behave erratically or congregate in large numbers, leave the water.

➡ If you see a shark, leave the water as quickly and calmly as possible – avoid excessive splashing or noise.

There's also excellent diving and snorkelling around the Houtman Abrolhos Islands.

Fishing

From sailfish in the north to trout in the south, all types of fishing are on offer along WA's immense coastline. Fishing is the state's largest recreational activity, with many locals catching dinner nearly every time.

Close to Perth, Rottnest Island has plentiful schools of wrasse and Western Australian dhufish (previously called jewfish).

South of Perth, popular fishing hot spots include Mandurah, with options for deep-sea fishing, catching tailor from the beach or nabbing Mandurah's famed blue manna crabs and king prawns in the estuaries. In Augusta you can chase salmon in the Blackwood River or whiting in the bay, or drop a line from the Busselton Jetty.

Sunny Geraldton's popular spots include Sunset Beach and Drummond Cove, and fishing charters go to the nearby Houtman Abrolhos Islands. There's great fishing all along the coast, and lots of charters in the hotter, steamier northwest. There's a good chance to hook a monster fish at Exmouth, the Dampier Archipelago and the game-fishing nirvana of Broome. The northern Kimberley is good for barramundi.

Buy a recreational fishing licence (RFL; $40) if you intend to catch marron (freshwater crayfish) or rock lobsters, use a fishing net or go freshwater angling in the southwest. If you're fishing from a motorised boat, someone on the boat will need to have a Recreational Fishing from Boat Licence (RFBL; $30). Licences can be obtained online (www.fish.wa.gov.au) or from Australia Post offices. Note that there are strict licence, bag and size limits – see the Fisheries website for specific details.

Plan Your Trip
Travel with Children

With lots of sunshine, beaches and big open spaces, Western Australia (WA) is a wonderful destination for children of all ages. Australians are famously laid-back and their generally tolerant, 'no worries' attitude extends to children having a good time and perhaps being a little raucous.

West Coast Australia for Kids

Interacting with Australia's native fauna, in either the wild or wildlife parks, will create lifetime memories for your kids. The wildlife can be dangerous, but in reality you're unlikely to strike any problems if you take sensible precautions.

The sun's harshness is more of a concern. Don't underestimate how quickly you and your kids can get sunburnt, even on overcast days. A standard routine for most Australian parents is to lather their kids in high-protection sunscreen (SPF 30-plus) before heading outside for the day. It's a habit worth adopting. Avoid going to the beach in the middle of the day. Head out in the morning or mid-afternoon instead.

On hot days, dehydration is a problem, especially for small children. Always carry fluids, especially on long car journeys.

Babies & Toddlers

Perth and most major towns have public rooms where parents can nurse their baby or change nappies; check with the local visitor centre. While many Australians are relaxed about public breastfeeding or nappy changing, some aren't.

Best Regions for Kids

Perth & Fremantle
See p56 and p79.

Margaret River & the Southwest
Geographe Bay features family-friendly beaches, Yallingup has a surf school, and Bunbury has the Dolphin Discovery Centre and Bunbury Wildlife Park. The region also features whale watching.

Monkey Mia & the Central West
Beaches, and lots of marine wildlife, especially Monkey Mia's dolphins and dugongs, Kalbarri's pelicans, and Denham's Ocean Park aquarium.

Coral Coast & the Pilbara
Coral Bay has plenty of safe-water options and like-minded families.

Broome & the Kimberley
While there's plenty of wildlife interaction such as camel rides and crocodile-park tours, it's the camping experiences, gorge swimming and Indigenous culture the Kimberley offers that kids will find most memorable, particularly in the Dampier Peninsula and along the Gibb River Road.

Many motels and larger caravan parks have playgrounds and swimming pools, and can supply cots and baby baths. Motels in touristy areas may have in-house children's videos and child-minding services. Top-end and midrange hotels usually welcome families with children, but some B&Bs market themselves as child-free havens.

Many eateries lack a specialised children's menu, but others do have kids' meals or will provide smaller servings. Some supply high chairs.

Medical services and facilities are of a high standard, and baby food, formula and disposable nappies are widely available. Major car-hire companies will supply and fit booster seats for a fee.

School-Age Kids

The biggest challenge is a sudden attack of the 'are-we-there-yets?'. Adults – let alone kids – find the long drives tedious. Bring along books, computer games, iPads and child-friendly CDs. Consider hiring a car with a backseat screen for playing DVDs.

Snacks are essential for journeys where shops might be 200km or further apart, and toilet paper is also a blessing.

Have a word to the kids about insects, snakes and spiders, stressing the need for them to keep their distance, particularly for kids who like to prod things with sticks. While bushwalking, make sure they wear socks with shoes or boots.

Children's Highlights

Beaches

Beaches are a big part of the WA experience. Ensure the kids swim between the flags, and ask the locals about the safer beaches.

Wildlife Parks & Zoos

There are wildlife parks throughout WA, especially in tourist areas. Many have walk-in aviaries, so prepare for a freak-out when an over-friendly parrot lands on little Jimmy's shoulder. Watch out for emus: those beady eyes and pointy beaks are even more intimidating when they're attached to something that's double your height.

Whale Watching

If you're in the right part of the coast at the right time of year, you'll definitely see whales from the shore. Organised whale-watching boat trips depart from Perth, Fremantle, Dunsborough, Augusta, Albany, Coral Bay, Broome, Kalbarri, Exmouth and the Dampier Peninsula.

Other Marine Mammals

➡ **Rockingham Wild Encounters** (p56) Swimming with wild dolphins for over-fives.
➡ **Dolphin Discovery Centre** (p122) Wade into the shallows alongside the dolphins in Bunbury.
➡ **Monkey Mia** (p179) Watch dolphins being fed in the bay or head out on a cruise to spot dolphins and dugongs.
➡ **Sea Lion Charters** (p117) Splash about with sea lions in the shallows.

Surf Schools

➡ **Surfschool, Perth and Lancelin** Lessons for kids aged 11 and over.
➡ **Yallingup Surf School** (p128) 'Microgrom' lessons for the under 10s.

Amusement Parks & Rides

➡ Adventure World (p56) Perth's amusement park.
➡ Perth Royal Show (p57) Annual event.

Planning

When booking accommodation and rental cars, specify whether you need cots, high chairs and car booster seats. If travelling with an infant, bring a mosquito net to drape over the cot. Bring rash tops for the beach and warm clothes if travelling south in winter. Anything you forget can be easily purchased when you arrive.

Discounts

Child concessions (or family rates) often apply for tours, admission fees (babies and infants are often free) and public transport. Note: a 'child' can vary from under 12 to under 18 years. Accommodation concessions usually apply to children under 12 years. On major airlines, infants travel free if they don't occupy a seat.

Regions at a Glance

Perth & Fremantle

Beaches
Museums & Galleries
Historic Buildings

Beaches
They may not offer the solitude and pristine natural surroundings of elsewhere in WA, but Perth and Fremantle's long beaches are popular playgrounds for city dwellers. Surfers, snorkellers and swimmers can all find a stretch of sand to suit.

Museums & Galleries
Perth's public institutions include the Art Gallery of Western Australia, housing traditional and contemporary art. Nearby is the edgy Perth Institute of Contemporary Art and the Western Australian Museum. Fremantle showcases the superb maritime museum and Shipwreck Galleries.

Historic Buildings
Relics of the colonial era and gold rushes abound. Fremantle has a frozen-in-time streetscape with a wonderful historic ambience. The drawcard is the old convict-built prison, its murky stories brought to life through fascinating guided tours.

p46

Around Perth

Beaches
Wildlife
Heritage Towns

Beaches
Rottnest Island is ringed by gorgeous beaches that are often deserted midweek. Mandurah, Rockingham and Yanchep are built-up beach 'burbs bustling with cafes and marinas. Guilderton sits on a picturesque lagoon, while Lancelin is windsurfing heaven.

Wildlife
Whales, dolphins, sea lions, seals, penguins, kangaroos, possums, quokkas, bilbies, boodies, woylies – it's quite amazing how much wildlife lives in such close proximity to the city.

Heritage Towns
The quaint townships in the forests, hills and river valleys surrounding Perth make perfect day trips. York has contiguous rows of historic buildings, preserving a gold-rush atmosphere.

p89

Margaret River & the Southwest Coast

Beaches
Wineries
Forests

Beaches
The sandy beaches of Geographe Bay are perfect for a bucket-and-spade family holiday. The most beautiful spots are near Cape Naturaliste, and the state's primo surf breaks also roll ashore to the south.

Wineries
Australia's most beautiful wine region also produces some of the country's best wine. The cool-climate vineyards around Pemberton are worth exploring too.

Forests
Studded with tuart and karri, WA's forests of tall trees are an impressive sight. Some of the larger specimens are rigged with spikes, allowing the fit and fearless to climb up to 68m into the canopy.

p118

South Coast

Beaches
Wineries
National Parks

Beaches

Glorious, isolated bays of powdery white sand are spread all along this long stretch of coast. On many you'll be more likely to spot a whale than another person.

Wineries

The wineries of the Great Southern region are constantly growing in stature. Sup your way from Denmark to Mt Barker and on to Porongurup.

National Parks

This region's parks encompass the dramatic Tree Top Walk in Walpole-Nornalup and end with the silky sands of Cape Arid. Also, don't miss the rugged Porongurup and Stirling Range National Parks, or the vast wild heath of Fitzgerald River.

p143

Monkey Mia & the Central West

Beaches
Adventure
History

Beaches

The white shell beaches of Shark Bay – with famous visitors, the Monkey Mia dolphins – are just part of a turquoise coastline stretching from family-friendly Port Denison to the wilds of Gnaraloo Station.

Adventure

Surfers and windsurfers flock to Geraldton and Gnaraloo for winter swells and summer winds; fisherfolk and explorers head west to Edel Land. Bushwalkers prefer Kalbarri in winter.

History

Historic artefacts, shipwrecks and 19th-century buildings stud this rugged coastline, including Greenough's pioneer settlement and the 1629 *Batavia* wreck off the Houtman Abrolhos Islands.

p165

Coral Coast & the Pilbara

Beaches
Adventure
Wildlife

Beaches

Superb isolated beaches lead down to shallow lagoons hemmed by World Heritage–listed Ningaloo Marine Park. World-class snorkelling and diving are only a short wade from shore, and camping is right behind the dunes.

Adventure

Karijini National Park is the Pilbara's adventure playground, with deep, narrow gorges inviting exploration, and the state's highest peaks begging to be climbed.

Wildlife

Whale sharks, manta rays, turtles and migrating whales all visit Ningaloo, while inland birds flock to the oasis pools of Millstream-Chichester National Park, and pythons and rock wallabies hide in the shadows of Karijini.

p183

Broome & the Kimberley

Beaches
Indigenous Culture
Adventure

Beaches

Don't miss the sunset camel trains of iconic Cable Beach. Equally spectacular are the seldom-visited beaches of the Dampier Peninsula and Coloumb Nature Reserve.

Indigenous Culture

Learn traditional practices from the Aboriginal communities of the Dampier Peninsula. Follow Broome's Lurujarri Dreaming Trail, before exploring the Kimberley's amazing Wandjina and Gwion Gwion images.

Adventure

Drive the bone-shaking Gibb River Rd, detouring to Mitchell Falls and remote Kalumburu. Zip on a speedboat to the horizontal waterfalls, or negotiate a canoe down the mighty Ord River.

p204

On the Road

Perth & Fremantle

Best Places to Eat

➡ Duende (p68)
➡ Namh Thai (p67)
➡ Print Hall (p65)
➡ Il Lido (p69)
➡ Cantina 663 (p67)

Best Places to Stay

➡ Eight Nicholson (p60)
➡ Wickham Retreat (p60)
➡ Durack House (p60)
➡ Above Bored (p60)
➡ Norfolk Hotel (p84)

Why Go?

Planted by a river and beneath an almost permanent canopy of blue sky, the city of Perth is a modern-day boom town, stoking Australia's economy from its glitzy central business district. Yet it remains as relaxed as the sleepy Swan River – black swans bobbing atop – which winds past the skyscrapers and out to the Indian Ocean.

Even in its boardrooms, Perth's heart is down at the beach, tossing around in clear ocean surf and stretching out on the sand. The city's beaches trace the western edge of Australia for some 40km, and you can have one to yourself on any given day – for a city this size, Perth is sparsely populated.

Perth has sprawled to enfold Fremantle within its suburbs, yet the port city maintains its own distinct personality – proud of its nautical ties, working-class roots, bohemian reputation and, especially, its football team.

When to Go
Perth

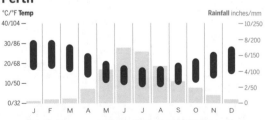

Feb Perth's Arts Festival is on and school starts, so the beaches are less crowded.

Mar Warm and dry, so great weather for the beach, and not as sweltering hot.

Sep Kings Park wildflowers, the Perth Royal Show and the Parklife festival.

PERTH

POP 1.75 MILLION

Laid-back, liveable Perth has wonderful weather, beautiful beaches and an easygoing character. About as close to Bali as to some of Australia's eastern state capitals, Perth's combination of big-city attractions with relaxed and informal surrounds offers an appealing lifestyle for locals and lots to do for visitors. It's a sophisticated, cosmopolitan city with myriad bars, restaurants and cultural activities all vying for attention. When you want to chill out, it's easy to do so. Perth's pristine parkland, nearby bush, and river and ocean beaches – along with a good public transport system – allow its inhabitants to spread out and enjoy what's on offer.

Relaxed doesn't mean static, though. The mining boom of Western Australia (WA) continues to see Perth blossom like the state's wildflowers in spring. Those on the gravy train are out eating, socialising, spending money and flexing their muscles in the sun.

The city of Perth lies along a wide sweep of the Swan River. The river borders the city centre to the south and east, and links Perth to its neighbouring port city, Fremantle. Follow the river north from the city and you'll reach prosperous nooks such as Claisebrook Cove, lined with ostentatious houses, cafes and public sculpture.

Train tracks divide the city centre from the Northbridge entertainment enclave, immediately to the north. Here's where you'll find Perth's cultural institutions, most of its hostels and the lively Little Asia restaurant strip.

Continue northeast along Beaufort St and you'll reach the sophisticated suburbs of Highgate and Mt Lawley. Heading west there's Mt Hawthorn and hip Leederville. To the west of the central city rises Kings Park, with well-heeled Subiaco beyond it. Go further west and you'll hit the beaches.

History

The discovery of stone implements near the Swan River suggests that Mooro, the site on which the city of Perth now stands, has been occupied for around 40,000 years. The indigenous Wadjuk people, a subgroup of the Noongar, believed that the Swan River (Derbal Yaragan) and the landforms surrounding it were shaped by two Wargal (giant serpentlike creatures), which lived under present-day Kings Park.

In December 1696 three ships in the Dutch fleet commanded by Willem de Vlamingh anchored off Rottnest Island. On 5 January 1697 a well-armed party landed near present-day Cottesloe Beach and then marched eastward to a river near Freshwater Bay. They tried to make contact with the local people to enquire about survivors of the *Ridderschap van Hollant,* lost in 1694, but were unsuccessful, so they sailed north. It was de Vlamingh who bestowed the name Swan on the river.

Modern Perth was founded in 1829 when a hopeful Captain James Stirling established the Swan River Colony, and named the main settlement after the Scottish hometown of the British Secretary of State for the Colonies. The original settlers paid for their own passage and that of their servants, and in return they received 200 acres for every labourer they brought with them.

At the time Mooro belonged to a Wadjuk leader called Yellagonga and his people, whose main camp was at Boorloo, near where the colony was founded. Relations were friendly at first, the Noongar believing the British to be the returned spirits of their dead, but competition for resources led to conflict. Yellagonga moved his camp first to Lake Monger and, by the time of his death in 1843, his people had been dispossessed of all of their lands around Perth's city centre and were forced to camp around the swamps and lakes to the city's north.

Midgegooroo, an elder from south of the Swan River, along with his son Yagan, led resistance to the British settlement. In 1833 Midgegooroo was caught and executed by firing squad, while Yagan was shot a few months later by teenage settlers whom he had befriended. Yagan's head was removed, smoked and sent to London where it was publicly displayed as an anthropological curiosity.

Life for the settlers was much harder than they had expected it to be. The early settlement grew very slowly until 1850, when convicts alleviated the labour shortage and boosted the population. Convict labour was also responsible for constructing the city's substantial buildings such as Government House and the Town Hall. Even then, Perth's development lagged behind that of the cities in the eastern colonies. That is, until the discovery of gold inland in the 1890s increased Perth's population fourfold in a decade and initiated a building bonanza.

Perth & Fremantle Highlights

1 Stretching out on the lawn in **Kings Park** (p51) with the glittering river and city spread out below you

2 Doing time with the ghosts of convicts past in World Heritage–listed **Fremantle Prison** (p78)

3 Experiencing Perth's emerging restaurant scene in the bustling eateries of **Mt Lawley** (p67), **Northbridge** (p66) and the **city centre** (p64)

4 Exploring a wealth of local art, indigenous and otherwise, at the **Art Gallery of Western Australia** (p50)

5 Soaking up the decaying gold-rush grandeur of **Fremantle's historic streetscape** (p82)

6 Enjoying the sunset with a sundowner in hand after a hard day's beaching at **Cottesloe** (p54)

7 Hitting **Fremantle's pubs** (p86) and letting the bands of Bon Scott's hometown shake you all night long

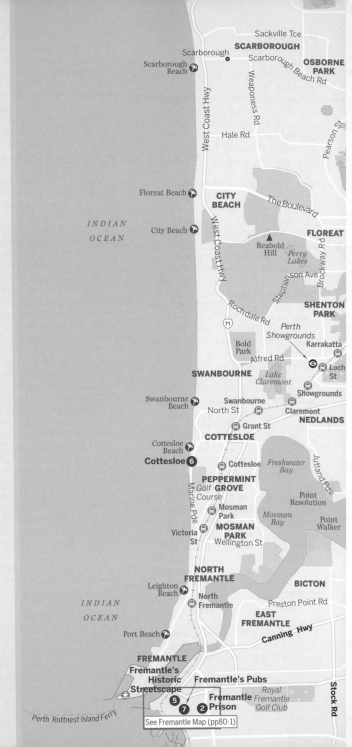

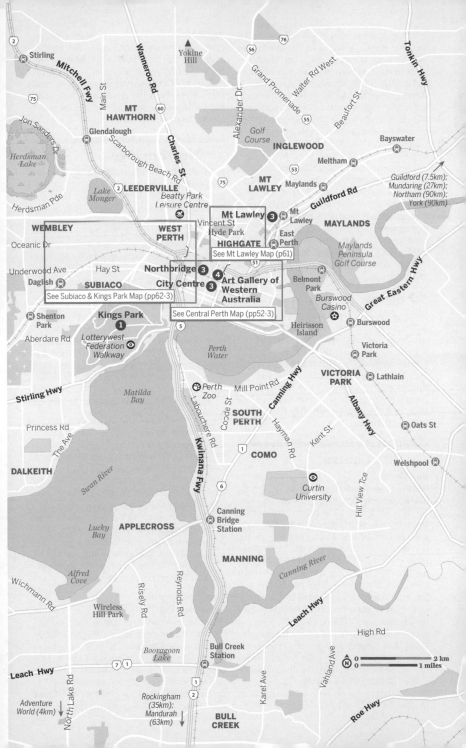

The mineral wealth of WA has continued to drive Perth's growth. In the 1980s and '90s, though, the city's clean-cut, nouveau-riche image was tainted by a series of financial and political scandals. Today Perth is thriving once again, thanks to another mining boom throughout the state. Rumours of a slowdown by the Chinese and Indian economies continue to bubble away, but obviously no-one's told more than a few of the fiscally confident locals.

Largely excluded from this race to riches are the Noongar people. In 2006, the Perth Federal Court recognised native title over the city of Perth and its surrounds, but this was appealed by the WA and Commonwealth governments. In December 2009 an agreement was signed in WA's parliament, setting out a two-year time frame for negotiating settlement of native-title claims across the southwest.

◉ Sights

Many of Perth's main attractions are within walking distance of the inner city, several in the Perth Cultural Centre precinct past the railway station in Northbridge. Most of the farther-flung sights, including the beaches, can be reached by public transport, although you'll find it easier to hop between them with a car. There are several easy day trips, including the Swan Valley, that can be reached from the city.

◉ City Centre

Bell Tower
LANDMARK
(Map p52; www.thebelltower.com.au; adult/child $14/9; ☺10am-4pm, ringing noon-1pm Mon, Tue, Thu, Sat & Sun) This pointy glass spire fronted by copper sails contains the royal bells of London's St Martin's-in-the-Fields, the oldest of which dates to 1550. They were given to WA by the British government in 1988, and are the only set known to have left England. Clamber to the top for 360-degree views of Perth by the river.

The tower sits on land that was reclaimed in the 1920s and 1930s, and now forms a green strip between the river and the city. Long, thin Langley Park is still occasionally used as an airstrip for light aircraft demonstrations. Stirling Gardens and Supreme Court Gardens have lawns and formal gardens which fill up with city workers at lunchtime.

Perth Mint
HISTORIC BUILDING
(Map p52; www.perthmint.com.au; 310 Hay St; adult/child $15/5; ☺9am-5pm) Dating from 1899, the oddly compelling mint displays a collection of coins, nuggets and gold bars. You can fondle a bar worth over $200,000, mint your own coins and watch gold pours (on the hour, starting 10am).

◉ Northbridge

Art Gallery of Western Australia
GALLERY
(Map p52; www.artgallery.wa.gov.au; Perth Cultural Centre; ☺10am-5pm Wed-Mon) **FREE** Founded in 1895, this excellent gallery houses the state's pre-eminent art collection. It contains important post-WWII works by Australian luminaries such as Arthur Boyd, Albert Tucker, Grace Cossington Smith, Russell Drysdale, Arthur Streeton and Sidney Nolan, but it's the Indigenous galleries that provide the highlight.

Work ranges from canvases to bark paintings and sculpture, and artists include Rover Thomas, Angilya Mitchell, Christopher Pease and Phyllis Thomas. The annual WA Indigenous Art Awards entries are displayed here from August to December. Free tours take place at 11am and 1pm on Sunday, Monday, Wednesday and Thursday, at 12.30pm and 2pm on Friday, and at 1pm on Saturday.

Perth Institute of Contemporary Arts
GALLERY
(PICA; Map p52; www.pica.org.au; Perth Cultural Centre; ☺11am-6pm Tue-Sun) **FREE** Commonly referred to by its acronym, PICA (pee-kah) may have a traditional wrapping (it's housed in an elegant 1896 red-brick former school), but inside it's anything but, being one of Australia's principal platforms for cutting-edge contemporary art – installations, performance, sculpture, video works and the like. It actively promotes new and experimental art, and exhibits graduate works annually.

Western Australian Museum – Perth
MUSEUM
(Map p52; www.museum.wa.gov.au; Perth Cultural Centre; ☺9.30am-5pm) **FREE** The state's museum is a six-headed beast, with branches also in Fremantle, Albany, Geraldton and Kalgoorlie. This one includes dinosaur, mammal, butterfly and bird galleries, a **children's discovery centre**, and an excellent **WA Land and People** display covering indigenous and colonial history.

In the courtyard, set in its own preservative bath, is Megamouth, a curious-looking species of shark with a soft, rounded head. Only about five of these benign creatures have ever been found; this one beached itself near Mandurah, south of Perth.

The museum complex includes Perth's original gaol, built in 1856 and used until 1888 – the site of many hangings.

Hyde Park   PARK
(Map p61; William St) One of Perth's most beautiful parks, suburban Hyde Park is a top spot for a picnic or lazy book-reading session on the lawn. A path traces the small lake, and mature palms, firs and Moreton Bay figs provide plenty of shade. It's within walking distance of Northbridge; continue northeast along William St.

⊚ Subiaco & Kings Park

★ **Kings Park & Botanic Garden**   PARK
(Map p62; www.bgpa.wa.gov.au; ⊘ Lotterywest Federation Walkway 9am-5pm, guided walks 10am, noon & 2pm) Rising above the Swan River on the western flank of the city, the 400-hectare bush-filled expanse of Kings Park is Perth's pride and joy. When the sun's shining (which isn't exactly a rare occurrence) it's a good spot for a picnic under the trees or to let the kids off the leash in one of the playgrounds. Its numerous tracks are popular with walkers and joggers all year round, with an ascent of

the steep stairs from the river rewarded with wonderful views from the top.

The Noongar people knew this area as Kaarta Gar-up and used it for thousands of years for hunting, food gathering, ceremonies, teaching and tool-making. A freshwater spring at the base of the escarpment, now known as Kennedy Fountain but before that as Goonininup, was a home of the Wargal, mystical snake-like creatures that created the Swan River and other waterways.

At the park's heart is the 17-hectare Botanic Garden, containing over 2000 plant species indigenous to WA. In spring there's an impressive display of the state's famed wildflowers. A highlight is the **Lotterywest Federation Walkway**, a 620m path through the gardens that includes a beautifully designed, 222m-long, glass-and-steel bridge that passes through the canopy of a stand of eucalypts.

The main road leading into the park, Fraser Ave, is lined with towering lemon-scented gums that are dramatically lit at night. At its culmination are the State War Memorial, a cafe, a gift shop, Frasers restaurant and the Kings Park Visitor Centre. Free guided walks leave from here.

To get here take bus 37 (39 on weekends), heading west along St Georges Tce (S-stand), to the visitor centre. You can also walk up (steep) Mount St from the city or climb Jacob's Ladder from Mounts Bay Rd, near the Adelphi Hotel

PERTH & FREMANTLE PERTH

A CITY IN TRANSITION

With Perth's population increasing faster than that of any other Australian state capital, it's also a city rapidly transitioning from a relatively sleepy centre into an international hub with its commercial gaze resting as much on China, India and Indonesia as it does on Sydney and Melbourne.

Major civic works under consideration include an audacious light-rail plan and a new football stadium, and visitors to Perth can already witness ongoing work on two major reboots of the central city's urban landscape.

Historically, Northbridge's entertainment and cultural precinct has been awkwardly separated from the CBD by the labyrinth of train tracks around Perth railway station. The Perth City Link project is scheduled to take until 2016 to complete, and will transform the area between Northbridge and the CBD by installing train tracks and the Wellington St bus station underneath pedestrian malls. See www.pta.wa.gov.au/perthcitylink.

At the opposite end of the CBD, the Elizabeth Quay development will revamp around 10 hectares of riverfront land between Barrack and William Sts, and link the central city back to the Swan River. Public parks and retail and hospitality precincts are planned, and the development is also scheduled to be completed by 2016. See www.mra.wa.gov.au.

Come back in a few years, and there's a good chance you won't recognise the city.

Central Perth

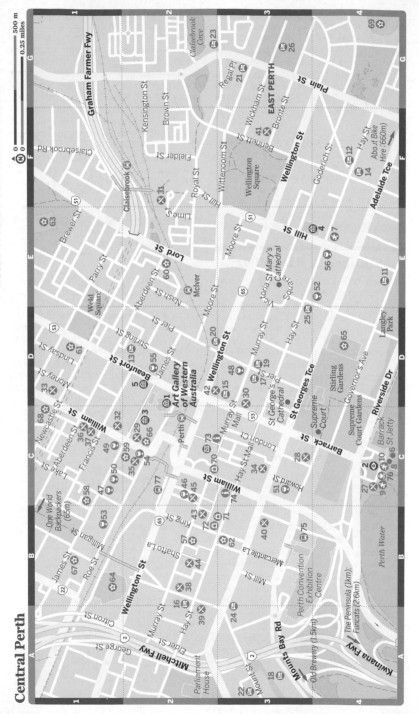

Central Perth

◎ Top Sights
1 Art Gallery of Western Australia........... D2

◎ Sights
2 Bell Tower C4
3 Perth Institute of Contemporary
   Arts C2
4 Perth Mint E4
5 Western Australian Museum –
   Perth D2

⊕ Activities, Courses & Tours
6 Captain Cook Cruises........................... C4
  Captain Cook Cruises................... (see 10)
7 Cycle Centre E4
8 Golden Sun Cruises.............................. C4
9 Oceanic Cruises.................................... C4
10 Swan Jet... C4

⊟ Sleeping
11 City Waters E4
12 Comfort Hotel Perth City....................... F4
13 Emperor's Crown D2
14 Mantra on Hay....................................... F4
15 Medina Executive Barrack Plaza D3
16 Melbourne... B2
17 Miss Maud... D3
18 Mounts Bay Waters............................... A3
19 Pensione Hotel D3
20 Perth City YHA D2
21 Regal Apartments................................. G3
22 Riverview on Mount Street A3
23 The Sebel Residence............................ G2
24 The Terrace Hotel................................. A3
25 Travelodge Perth D3
26 Wickham Retreat G3

✕ Eating
27 Annalakshmi.. C4
28 Balthazar.. C3
29 Bivouac Canteen & Bar......................... C2
30 Cabin Fever D3
31 City Farm Organic Growers
   Market F2
32 Flipside.. C1
33 Good Fortune Roast Duck
   House D1
34 Greenhouse C3
35 Kakulas Bros... C2
36 La Cholita.. C1
37 Little Willy's... C1
38 Mama Tran B2
39 Matsuri A2
40 Print Hall B3
41 Restaurant Amusé................................. F3
   Secret Garden .... (see 43)
   Taka .... (see 42)
42 Taka D2

The Trustee................................... (see 40)
43 Tiger, Tiger.. B2
44 Tom's Kitchen.. B2
45 Venn Cafe & Bar C2
   Viet Hoa .... (see 68)

☕ Drinking & Nightlife
46 1907..C2
47 Air C1
48 Ambar.. D3
49 Brass Monkey C1
   Cheeky Sparrow............................ (see 43)
   Ezra Pound.................................... (see 35)
50 Geisha C1
   Greenhouse................................... (see 34)
51 Helvetica... C3
52 Hula Bula Bar E4
   Mechanics Institute....................... (see 32)
53 Metro City... B1
54 The Bird.. C2
55 The Court.. D2
56 The Grosvenor...................................... E4
   Wolfe Lane.................................... (see 43)

✪ Entertainment
57 Amplifier B2
58 Cinema Paradiso C1
59 Connections.. C2
60 Devilles Pad.. E2
61 Ellington Jazz Club............................... D1
62 His Majesty's Theatre........................... B3
63 NIB Stadium.. E1
64 Perth Arena B1
65 Perth Concert Hall................................ D4
66 State Theatre Centre............................ C2
67 The Bakery B1
68 The Moon.. C1
   Universal....................................... (see 49)
69 WACA.. G4

⊞ Shopping
70 78 Records C2
71 Elizabeth's Bookshop B3
   Perth Map Centre......................... (see 70)
   Pigeonhole.................................... (see 30)
   Pigeonhole.................................... (see 44)
72 Wheels & Doll Baby.............................. B2

ⓘ Information
73 i-City Information Kiosk......................... C2
74 WA Visitor Centre................................. C3

ⓘ Transport
75 Esplanade Busport................................ B3
76 Ferries to South Perth &
   Fremantle.. C4
77 Integrity Coach Lines............................ C2

◎ Beaches

When the mercury rises the only sensible decision is to head west to cool down on one of Perth's many clean, sandy beaches. Most of them are comparatively undeveloped, which is just how the locals like it. The most famous of them, Cottesloe, gets by quite well with a beachside pavilion, a couple of giant pubs and a scattering of other businesses delineating the edge of suburbia.

Run by the Surf Life Saving Club of WA, the website www.mybeach.com.au has a profile of all the city beaches, including weather forecasts and information about buses, amenities and beach patrolling. Note that many can be rough, with strong undertows and rips – swim between the flags.

The following are the main beaches, listed from south to north.

Port & Leighton Beaches BEACH
Popular for surfing; the Port (south) end is slightly better for swimming, and has some eateries. Leighton Beach is a short walk from North Fremantle station.

Hamersley Pool, North, Watermans & Sorrento Beaches BEACH
Excellent swimming, picnic areas, BBQs, bike path through scrub.

Cottesloe Beach BEACH
The safest swimming with cafes, pubs, pine trees and fantastic sunsets. From Cottesloe station (on the Fremantle line) it's 1km to the beach. Bus 102 (William St) goes there.

Swanbourne Beach BEACH
Safe swimming, and an unofficial nudist and gay beach. From Grant St station it's a 1.5km walk to the beach (2km from Swanbourne station). Catch bus 102 from William St.

City Beach BEACH
Swimming, surfing, lawn and amenities. Take bus 84 (85 on weekends) from Wellington St (40 minutes, hourly).

Floreat Beach BEACH
Less crowded but sometimes windy, with swimming, surfing, cafes and playground. Bus to City Beach and walk north 800m.

Scarborough Beach BEACH
Popular young surfers' spot. Swim between flags as it can be dangerous. Has lots of shops and eateries. Bus 400 from Wellington St.

Trigg Beach BEACH
Better surf and a more hardcore group of locals who come out when the surf's up; dangerous when rough and prone to rips – always swim between the flags.

Mettams Pool BEACH
This beach is like a turquoise paddle pool – good for snorkelling.

Aquarium of Western Australia AQUARIUM
(AQWA; ☑08-9447 7500; www.aqwa.com.au; Hillarys Boat Harbour; adult/child $28/16; ⊙10am-5pm) Dividing WA's vast coastline into five distinct zones (Far North, Coral Coast, Shipwreck Coast, Perth and Great Southern), AQWA offers the chance to enjoy its underwater treasures without getting wet. Or eaten, stung or otherwise poisoned (the displays of WA's most poisonous fish, octopi, shells and sea snakes is particularly interesting).

Wander through a 98m underwater tunnel as gargantuan stingrays, turtles, fish and sharks stealthily glide over the top of you. Moon jellyfish billow iridescently through a giant cylinder lit up like a school disco, while sea horses and sea dragons drift on delicate underwater currents.

The daring can snorkel or dive with the sharks in the giant aquarium with the help of the in-house dive master; book in advance ($159 with your own gear; hire snorkel/dive gear $20/40; 1pm and 3pm). Another interactive option is donning a wetsuit and breathing tube and negotiating an underwater seascape as a Reefwalker ($20). You can also simply dip your hands into the touch pool and get to know harmless guys like the Port Jackson shark, sea stars, sea cucumbers and the Western stingaree.

To get here on weekdays, take the Joondalup train to Warwick station and then transfer to bus 423. By car, take the Mitchell Fwy north and exit at Hepburn Ave, or take the coastal road north from Scarborough Beach. AQWA is by the water at Hillarys Boat Harbour, behind Hillarys shopping centre.

◎ Other Areas

Perth Zoo ZOO
(www.perthzoo.wa.gov.au; 20 Labouchere Rd; adult/child $28/14; ⊙9am-5pm) Part of the fun of a day at the zoo is getting there – taking the ferry across the Swan River from Barrack Street Jetty to Mends Street Jetty (every half-hour) and walking up the hill. Zoo zones include Reptile Encounter, African Savan-

nah (rhinos, cheetahs, zebras, giraffes and lions), Asian Rainforest (elephants, tigers, sun bears, orangutans) and, of course, Australian Bushwalk (kangaroos, emus, koalas, dingos).

If you don't fancy the ferry ride, catch bus 30 or 31 from the Esplanade Busport.

Lake Monger   PARK
(Lake Monger Dr) In spring, black swans and their cygnets plod about the grounds – something of a meeting place for the local bird life – nonplussed by the joggers circling the lake on the flat 3.5km path. There's plenty of grass for cricket, football and picnics. It's walking distance from Leederville train station; exit on the side opposite the shops, turn right onto Southport St and veer left onto Lake Monger Dr.

🏃 Activities

Whale Watching
The whale-watching season runs from mid-September to early December, when 30,000 of them take the 'Humpback Highway' up the coast. Tour operators offer either a refund or a repeat trip in the unlikely event that whales aren't spotted. Tour boats are also fitted with underwater hydrophones, so you can listen to the whales singing.

Mills Charters   WHALE WATCHING
(☑08-9246 5334; www.millscharters.com.au; adult/child $80/65) Informative three- to four-hour trips departing from Hillarys Boat Harbour at 9am on Wednesday.

Oceanic Cruises   WHALE WATCHING
(Map p52; ☑08-9325 1191; www.whalewatching.com.au; adult/child $77/34) Departs Barrack Street Jetty at 8.30am, returning at 5.45pm after spending the afternoon in Fremantle. Daily departures during the school holidays, otherwise Wednesday and Friday to Sunday only.

Cycling
Cycling is an excellent way to explore Perth. Kings Park has some good bike tracks and there are cycling routes along the Swan River, running all the way to Fremantle, and along the coast. Bikes can be taken free of charge on ferries at any time and on trains outside of weekday peak hours (7am to 9am and 4pm to 6.30pm) – with a bit of planning you can pedal as far as you like in one direction and return via public transport. Bikes can't be taken on buses at any time, except some regional coaches (for a small charge).

For route maps, see www.transport.wa.gov.au/cycling/ or call into a bike shop.

About Bike Hire   BICYCLE RENTAL
(☑08-9221 2665; www.aboutbikehire.com.au; 1-7 Riverside Dr, Causeway Carpark; per day/week from $36/80; ⊙9am-5pm) Also hires kayaks (per hour/day $16/65).

Cycle Centre   BICYCLE RENTAL
(Map p52; ☑08-9325 1176; www.cyclecentre.com.au; 313 Hay St; per day/week $25/65; ⊙9am-5.30pm Mon-Fri, 9am-3pm Sat, 1-4pm Sun) See the website for recommended rides.

Gecko Bike Hire   BICYCLE RENTAL
(☑0439 989 610; www.geckobikhire.com.au) Excellent company with four locations around the city. See the website for route maps.

Other Activities

Surf Sail Australia   WINDSURFING, KITESURFING
(Map p62; ☑1800 686 089; www.surfsailaustralia.com.au; 260 Railway Pde; ⊙10am-5pm Mon-Sat) When the afternoon sea breeze blusters in, windsurfers take to the Swan River, Leighton and beaches north of Perth. Here's where you can hire or buy your gear.

Australasian Diving Academy   DIVING
(☑08-9389 5018; www.ausdiving.com.au; 142 Stirling Hwy) Hires diving gear (full set per day/week $75/200) and offers diving courses (four-day open-water $495). There are a variety of sites in the vicinity, including several around Rottnest Island and four wrecks.

Funcats   SAILING
(☑0408 926 003; www.funcats.com.au; Coode Street Jetty; per hr $40; ⊙Oct-Apr) These easy-to-sail catamarans are for hire on the South Perth foreshore. Each boat holds up to three people.

Surfschool   SURFING
(☑08-9447 5637; www.surfschool.com; Scarborough Beach; adult/child $55/50) Two-hour lessons at Scarborough Beach (at the end of Manning St), including boards and wetsuits.

Beatty Park Leisure Centre   SWIMMING
(Map p62; ☑08-9273 6080; www.beattypark.com.au; 220 Vincent St; swimming adult/child $5.70/4.30; ⊙5.30am-8.30pm Mon-Fri & 8am-4pm Sat & Sun) Originally built for the 1962 Commonwealth Games, this recently expanded complex has indoor and outdoor pools, water slides and a gym. Turn left at the top of William St and continue on Vincent St to just past Charles St.

PERTH FOR CHILDREN

With a usually clement climate and plenty of open spaces and beaches to run around in, Perth is a great place to bring children. Of the beaches, Cottesloe is the safest and a family favourite. With older kids, arrange two-wheeled family expeditions along Perth's riverside and coastal bike paths. Kings Park has playgrounds and walking tracks.

The Perth Royal Show (p57), held late September, is an ever-popular family outing – all sideshow rides, showbags and proudly displayed poultry. Many of Perth's big attractions cater well for young audiences, especially the Aquarium of Western Australia (p54), Perth Zoo (p54), the Western Australian Museum – Perth (p50) and the Art Gallery of Western Australia (p50).

Scitech (Map p62; www.scitech.org.au; Sutherland St, City West Centre; adult/child $14/9; ☺10am-4pm) is another rainy-day option, with over 160 hands-on, large-scale science and technology exhibits.

Adventure World (www.adventureworld.net.au) has exciting rides such as 'Bounty's Revenge', a giant swinging pirate boat, as well as pools, water slides and a castle. From Perth, come off the Kwinana Fwy at Farrington Rd, turn right and follow the signs.

Look for the **LetsGoKids** (www.letsgokids.com.au) booklet at the WA Visitor Centre (p76) for loads more kid-friendly information.

WA Skydiving Academy   SKYDIVING
(Map p61; ☎1300 137 855; www.waskydiving.com.au; 458 William St; ☺Mon-Thu) Tandem jumps from 8000/10,000/12,000ft from $300/340/380.

☞ Tours

Indigenous Tours WA   INDIGENOUS CULTURE
(www.indigenouswa.com) See Perth through the eyes of the local Wadjuk people. Options include the **Indigenous Heritage Tour** (☎08-9483 1106; adult/child $25/15; ☺1.30pm) – a 90-minute guided walk around Kings Park – and an indigenous-themed stroll (p83) around Fremantle.

City Sightseeing Perth Tour   BUS TOUR
(☎08-9203 8882; www.citysightseeingperth.com; adult/child $28/10) Hop-on, hop-off double-decker bus tour, with loop routes taking in the central city, Kings Park and the Burswood Entertainment Complex. Tickets are valid for two days. The Kings Park section can be purchased separately (adult/child $6/3).

Two Feet & A Heartbeat   WALKING TOUR
(☎1800 459 388; www.twofeet.com.au; per person $40-50) Daytime walking tours of Perth, and a popular after-dark Small Bar Tour. Tight Arse Tuesdays are just $20 for the Perth tour.

**Rockingham
Wild Encounters**   WILDLIFE INTERACTION
(☎08-9591 1333; www.rockinghamwildencounters.com.au; cnr Arcadia Dr & Penguin Rd) 🖋 Long-standing and laden with ecotourism awards, these guys are the only operator licensed to take people to Penguin Island, and they also run a variety of low-impact tours. The most popular is the **dolphin swim tour** (departs Val Street Jetty; tours $205-225; ☺8am Sep-May), which lets you interact with some of the 200 wild bottlenose dolphins in the marine park. If you don't fancy getting wet, there are two-hour **dolphin-watch tours** (departs Mersey Street Jetty, Shoalwater; adult/child $85/50; ☺10.45am Sep-May). Pickups can also be arranged from Perth hotels.

There's also a 45-minute **penguin and sea lion cruise** (departs Penguin Island; adult/child $36.50/27.50; ☺10.15am, 11.15am & 1.15pm Sep-May), which heads around the islands in a glass-bottomed boat.

Swan Jet   BOAT TOUR
(Map p52; ☎1300 554 026; www.swanjet.com.au; Barrack Street Jetty; adult/child $55/25) Exciting jetboat blasts on the Swan River.

Captain Cook Cruises   CRUISE
(Map p52; ☎08-9325 3341; www.captaincookcruises.com.au) Cruises to the Swan Valley or Fremantle, with an array of add-ons such as meals, wine tastings and tram rides.

Golden Sun Cruises   CRUISE
(Map p52; ☎08-9325 9916; www.goldensuncruises.com.au) Cheaper and with fewer frills than Captain Cook Cruises.

Beer Nuts   BREWERY
(☎08-9295 0605; www.beernuts.com.au) Visits five Swan Valley microbreweries and a rum distillery.

Out & About WINE TASTING
(☑ 08-9377 3376; www.outandabouttours.com.
au) Wine-focused tours of the Swan Valley
and historic Guildford. Some include river
cruises, cheese and chocolate stops, or the
opportunity to make your own wine blend.

Swan Valley Tours FOOD, WINE TASTING
(☑ 03-9274 1199; www.svtours.com.au) Food- and
wine-driven tours that cruise up to and/or
drive through the Swan Valley.

Rottnest Air Taxi SCENIC FLIGHTS
(☑ 08-9292 5027; www.rottnest.de) Thirty-
minute joy flights over the city, Kings Park
and Fremantle ($88 to $115), leaving from
Jandakot airport.

🌟 Festivals & Events

Perth Cup HORSE RACING
(www.perthracing.org.au) New Year's Day sees
Perth's biggest day at the races, with the
party people heading to 'Tentland' for DJs
and daiquiris.

Summadayze MUSIC
(www.summadayze.com) Electronic beeps and
beats get booties shaking at Paterson's Stadium in Subiaco in early January.

Australia Day Skyworks NATIONAL
(www.perth.wa.gov.au/skyworks; ⊘ 26 Jan)
Around 250,000 people come down to the
riverside for a whole day of family entertainment, culminating in a 30-minute fireworks
display at 8pm.

Big Day Out MUSIC
(www.bigdayout.com; Claremont Showgrounds;
⊘ early Feb) Australia's biggest music festival,
attracting big-name alternative bands and
lots of local up-and-comers.

Laneways MUSIC
(http://perth.lanewayfestival.com.au; ⊘ early Feb)
Perth's skinny-jean and floppy-fringe hip-
sters party to the planet's up-and-coming
indie acts. The über-cool festival takes place
in early February around the Perth Cultural
Centre in Northbridge.

Perth International Arts Festival ARTS
(www.perthfestival.com.au; ⊘ mid-Feb) Artists
like Laurie Anderson, Dead Can Dance and
Philip Glass perform alongside top local tal-
ent. Held over 25 days, it spans theatre, classical music, jazz, visual arts, dance, film and
literature. Worth scheduling a trip around,
especially for nocturnal types.

Kings Park Festival WILDFLOWERS
(www.kingsparkfestival.com.au; ⊘ Sep) Festival
held throughout September to coincide with
the wildflower displays, it includes live music every Sunday, guided walks and talks.

Perth Royal Show AGRICULTURE FESTIVAL
(www.perthroyalshow.com.au; Claremont Showground; ⊘ late Sep-early Oct) A week of fun-fair
rides, spun sugar and showbags full of plastic junk. Oh, and farm animals.

Parklife MUSIC
(www.parklife.com.au; Wellington Sq; ⊘ late Sep) A
one-day festival of international indie bands
of a more danceable bent.

**Awesome International
Festival for Bright Young Things** CHILDREN
(www.awesomearts.com; ⊘ school holidays Oct)
This 13-day contemporary-arts festival celebrates young creativity with exhibitions,
film, theatre, dance and wacky instruments.
It strikes a balance between international
performers and participation.

🛏 Sleeping

Perth is very spread out, so choose your location carefully. Northbridge is backpacker/
boozer central, and can be noisy. The CBD
and Northbridge are close to public transport, making hopping out to inner-city
suburbs such as Leederville and Mt Lawley
straightforward.

If you care most for the beach, consider
staying there, as public transport to this part
of town can be time-consuming.

Fuelled by the ongoing mining boom,
Perth is an expensive town for accommodation. Book as early as you can, and see our
other tips to maximise your Perth travel
budget (see boxed text, p59).

🛏 City Centre

Perth City YHA HOSTEL $
(Map p52; ☑ 08-9287 3333; www.yha.com.au; 300
Wellington St; dm $39, r with/without bathroom
$120/95; ❋ @ 🛜 🖳) Occupying an impres-
sive 1940s art-deco building by the train
tracks, the centrally located YHA has a slight
boarding-school feel in the corridors, but the
rooms are clean and there are good facilities
including a gym. Like many Perth hostels,
it's popular with FIFO ('fly-in, fly-out') mine
workers, so the traditional YHA's travellers'
vibe has been diminished.

Riverview on Mount Street APARTMENT $$
(Map p52; ✆08-9321 8963; www.riverviewperth.
com.au; 42 Mount St; apt from $140; ❄@🛜) There's a lot of brash new money up here on Mount St, but character-filled Riverview stands out as the best personality on the block. Its refurbished 1960s bachelor pads sit neatly atop a modern foyer and a relaxed cafe. Rooms are sunny and simple; the front ones have river views, while the back ones are quieter.

**Medina Executive
Barrack Plaza** APARTMENT $$
(Map p52; ✆08-9267 0000; www.medina.com.au; 138 Barrack St; apt from $229; ❄❄) The meticulously decorated apartment-sized hotel rooms of the Medina are minimalist yet welcoming. All one-bedrooms have balconies, and rooms on Barrack St tend to have more natural light (not always easy to obtain in central Perth).

Pensione Hotel BOUTIQUE HOTEL $$
(Map p52; ✆08-9325 2133; www.pensione.com.
au; 70 Pier St; d from $155; ❄🛜) Formerly the budget-oriented Aarons, this central-city 98-room property has recently had a shiny boutique sheen applied to become the Pensione Hotel. The standard rooms definitely veer to cosy and (very) compact, but classy decor and a good location are two definite pluses in an expensive city.

Miss Maud HOTEL $$
(Map p52; ✆08-9325 3900; www.missmaud.com.
au; 97 Murray St; s/d $189/239; ❄@🛜) Anyone with a love of Scandinavia, kitsch or *The Sound of Music* will find a few of their favourite things in the alpine murals and dainty rooms. The Scandinavian rooms are best, as they're bigger and well maintained. The smorgasbords (lunch/dinner $34/45) are enough to feed a goat herd.

City Waters MOTEL $$
(Map p52; ✆08-9325 1566; www.citywaters.com.
au; 118 Terrace Rd; s/d $130/150; ❄) Apricot-hued City Waters is one of a dying breed of old-fashioned Perth waterfront motels. Rooms are small and simple and face onto the car park, but they're clean and airy, and the waterfront location is top-notch. Top-floor rooms are best; river views exist but are difficult to secure.

Melbourne HOTEL $$
(Map p52; ✆08-9320 3333; www.melbourneho
tel.com.au; cnr Hay & Milligan Sts; r $190-330;

❄🛜) Classic country charm wafts through this heritage-listed hotel. Built in the gold-rush era, its facade – particularly the deep corrugated-iron balcony that wraps around the building – recalls a mining-town pub perched on the edges of the red-dust desert. Rooms are unpretentious and comfortable, though 1st-floor rooms facing Milligan St can be noisy.

Travelodge Perth HOTEL $$
(Map p52; ✆08-9238 1888; www.travelodge.com.
au; 417 Hay St; r from $189; ❄🛜) No surprises here, just unassuming well-kept rooms, some with views. Occasional online deals are good value in an expensive city.

Mantra on Hay APARTMENT $$$
(Map p52; ✆1300 987 604; www.mantra.com.au; 201 Hay St; apt from $239; ❄@🛜❄) Low-key but classy, Mantra's roomy apartments have laundries, dishwashers, good-sized benches and all the utensils you'll need.

Comfort Hotel Perth City HOTEL $$
(Map p52; ✆9220 7000; www.comforthotelperth
city.com.au; 200 Hay St; r from $170; ❄@🛜) Generic and outmoded, but rooms are large, the staff friendly and the breakfast spread excellent.

Mounts Bay Waters APARTMENT $$$
(Map p52; ✆08-9213 5333; www.mounts-bay.com.
au; 112 Mounts Bay Rd; apt from $290; ❄❄) Giant apartment complex, where 165 out of 440 units are available for short-term lease.

The Terrace Hotel BOUTIQUE HOTEL $$$
(Map p52; ✆08-9214 4444; www.terracehotel
perth.com.au; 237 St Georges Tce; d from $432; ❄🛜) Opened in late 2012, the Terrace Hotel fills a heritage-listed terrace house in Perth's historic West End. There are just 15 deluxe rooms and suites, all with a clubby and luxurious ambience. Modern accoutrements include huge flat-screen TVs, Apple TV and iPads, and king-size four-poster beds with Egyptian-cotton linen.

🛏 Northbridge

Most of Perth's hostels are in Northbridge, and it's possible to walk around and inspect rooms before putting your money down. We've only listed the better ones, and note that many hostels have long-term residents working in Perth, and this can alter the ambience for short-term visitors and travellers.

Emperor's Crown
HOSTEL $

(Map p52; ☑ 08-9227 1400; www.emperorscrown. com.au; 85 Stirling St; dm $36, r with/without bathroom from $130/110; ✳ @ 🛜) One of Perth's best hostels has a great position (close to the Northbridge scene without being in the thick of it), friendly staff and high housekeeping standards. Granted, it's a bit pricier than most, but it's worth it.

Witch's Hat
HOSTEL $

(Map p61; ☑ 08-9228 4228; www.witchs-hat.com; 148 Palmerston St; dm/tw/d $34/88/99; ✳ @ 🛜) Witch's Hat is like something out of a fairy tale. The 1897 building itself could be mistaken for a gingerbread house, and the witch's hat (an Edwardian turret) stands proudly out the front, beckoning the curious to step inside. Dorms are light and uncommonly spacious, and there's a red-brick BBQ area out the back.

One World Backpackers
HOSTEL $

(☑ 08-9228 8206; www.oneworldbackpackers. com.au; 162 Aberdeen St; dm $28-30, d $80; @) 🍃 Polished floorboards beam brightly in all the rooms of this nicely restored old house, and the dorms are big and sunny, if a little messy sometimes. The kitchen is large and functional, with everything provided, and the hostel tends to be quieter on weeknights. Like most Perth hostels, though, it can get noisy.

Coolibah Lodge
HOSTEL $

(Map p61; ☑ 08-9328 9958; www.coolibahlodge. com.au; 194 Brisbane St; dm $32, r $80; ✳ @ 🛜) Built from two big old houses, Coolibah Lodge is comfortable and homely but nothing fancy. Dorms are tidy if a bit poky, and doubles are of a good standard. Expect a mix of travellers and longer-term guests. Breakfast is included. Brisbane St runs off William St, north of Northbridge.

Pension of Perth
B&B $$

(Map p61; ☑ 08-9228 9049; www.pensionperth. com.au; 3 Throssell St; s/d from $150/165; ✳ @ 🛜) Pension of Perth's French belle époque style lays luxury on thick: chaise lounges, rich floral rugs, heavy brocade curtains, open fireplaces and gold-framed mirrors. Two doubles with bay windows (and small bathrooms) look out onto the park, and there are two rooms with spa baths. Location wise, it's just across the road from gorgeous Hyde Park.

Hotel Northbridge
HOTEL $$

(Map p61; ☑ 08-9328 5254; www.hotelnorthbridge. com.au; 210 Lake St; r from $160; ✳ @) Hotel Northbridge isn't the hippest kid in town, but there's a spa bath in every room, and it's a quieter part of a sometimes noisy neighbourhood.. The classic pub rooms in the budget wing ($65) face onto a broad verandah but share shabby toilets.

ⓘ HOW TO MAXIMISE YOUR PERTH TRAVEL BUDGET

Everything you've heard is true. Compared to other Australian state capitals, Perth is expensive. Central city hotels especially are in high demand, and prices can be significantly higher than in east-coast Australia. Follow these tips to make the most of your dollars when visiting the city.

➡ Book accommodation as far ahead as possible.

➡ Accommodation can be significantly cheaper from Friday to Sunday.

➡ Consider a self-contained apartment with full cooking facilities.

➡ Perth B&Bs are usually good value.

➡ Consider Fremantle, especially for B&B accommodation, as a base while visiting Perth.

➡ Use Perth and Fremantle's free-of-charge Central Area Transit (CAT) bus services.

➡ Look out for good-value lunch deals at central city pubs and cafes.

➡ Cheaper ethnic restaurants dot the streets around Northbridge.

➡ Visit markets and other specialist stores for self-catering supplies (see boxed text, p64).

➡ Free Perth attractions include the Art Gallery of Western Australia, the Perth Institute of Contemporary Arts and the Western Australian Museum.

East Perth

★Wickham Retreat HOSTEL $
(Map p52; ☑08-9325 6398; www.facebook.com/WickhamRetreatBackpackers; 25-27 Wickham St; dm $35-40, d $70-100; @🗟) Located in a residential neighbourhood east of the city centre, Wickham Retreat has a quieter vibe compared to other hostels around town. Most of the guests are international travellers, drawn by the colourful rooms and dorms, and a funky AstroTurf garden. Free food (including rice, fresh bread and vegies) stretches travel budgets eroded by Perth's high prices.

Regal Apartments APARTMENT $$
(Map p52; ☑08-9221 8614; www.regalapartments.com.au; 11 Regal Pl; apt from $230; ❉@) Tucked in behind good-value Asian restaurants east of the city centre, these recently redecorated one- and two-bedroom apartments are spacious and modern. Fully-equipped kitchens and private laundry facilities make them ideal for families watching their dollars. Pretty Claisebrook Cove is just a short walk away.

The Sebel Residence APARTMENT $$$
(Map p52; ☑08-9223 2500; www.mirvachotels.com/perth; 60 Royal St; apt from $315; ❉🗟) Modern and chic apartments with self-contained kitchenettes and a classy hotel vibe. Adjacent Claisebrook Cove Promenade has a few nights' worth of restaurants, cafes and bars.

Highgate & Mt Lawley

★Durack House B&B $$
(☑08-9370 4305; www.durackhouse.com.au; 7 Almondbury Rd; s $160, d $175-190; 🗟) It's hard to avoid words like 'delightful', when describing this cottage, set on a peaceful suburban street behind a rose-adorned white picket fence. The three rooms have plenty of old-world charm, paired with thoroughly modern bathrooms. It's only 250m from Mt Lawley station; turn left onto Railway Pde and then first right onto Almondbury Rd.

Billabong Backpackers Resort HOSTEL $
(Map p61; ☑08-9328 7720; www.billabongresort.com.au; 381 Beaufort St; dm $29-31, r $82; ❉@🗟) This large hostel (about 150 beds) has a busy poolside area. It's popular with longstay guests and can be noisy, but it's close to Mt Lawley's bars and cafes.

Above Bored B&B $$
(☑08-9444 5455; www.abovebored.com.au; 14 Norham St; d $190-200; ❉🗟) In a quiet residential neighbourhood, this 1927 Federation house is owned by a friendly TV scriptwriter. The two themed rooms in the main house have eclectic decor, and in the garden there's a cosy self-contained cottage with a kitchenette. In an expensive town for accommodation, Above Board is great value. Northbridge and Mt Lawley are a short drive away.

Subiaco & Kings Park

★Eight Nicholson BOUTIQUE HOTEL $$$
(☑08-9382 1881; www.8nicholson.com.au; 8 Nicholson Rd; r from $369; ❉🗟) Concealed behind the whitewashed walls of this stylishly renovated heritage house is accommodation that's one-part luxury boutique hotel and one-part welcoming B&B. Hip but elegant decor and interesting artworks are evidence of the well-travelled owners' eclectic tastes, and it's just a short walk to Kings Park or Subiaco's cafes and restaurants.

Richardson HOTEL $$$
(Map p62; ☑08-9217 8888; www.therichardson.com.au; 32 Richardson St; r from $520; ❉🗟❊) Ship-shaped and shipshape, the Richardson offers luxurious, thoughtfully designed rooms – some with sliding doors to divide them into larger suites. The whole complex has a breezy, summery feel, with pale marble tiles, creamy walls and interesting art. There's an in-house spa centre if you require additional pampering.

The Outram HOTEL $$$
(Map p62; ☑08-9322 4888; www.wyndhamvrap.com.au; 32 Outram St; r $380-410; ❉🗟) Discreet and understated, the Outram (aka the unwieldly Wyndham Vacation Resorts Asia Pacific Perth) is stylish, with compact openplan rooms, a bathroom with a walk-through shower, king-size beds and flat-screen TVs.

Beaches

Ocean Beach Backpackers HOSTEL $
(☑08-9384 5111; www.oceanbeachbackpackers.com; 1 Eric St; dm/s/d $26/70/80; @🗟) Offering (some) ocean views, this big, bright hostel in the heart of Cottesloe is just a short skip from the sand. Rooms are basic, but all have private bathrooms, and you'll probably just be here to sleep given the

Mt Lawley

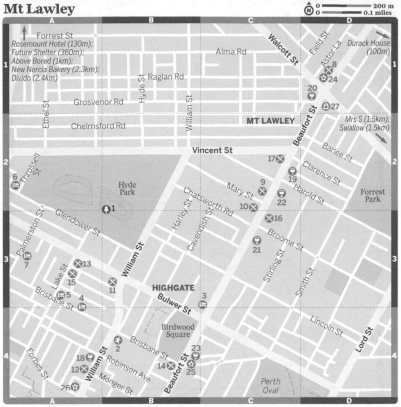

Mt Lawley

Subiaco & Kings Park

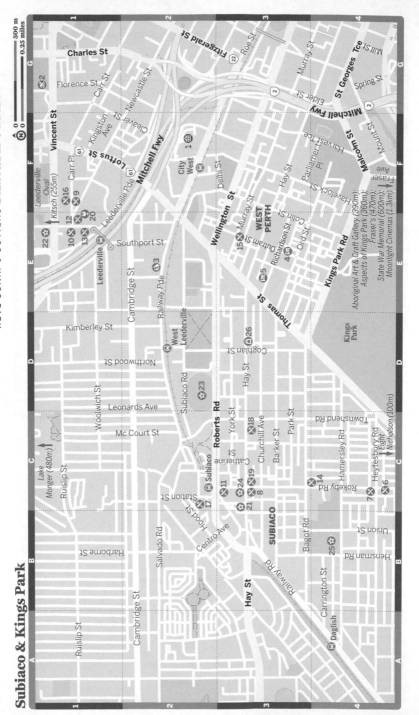

500 m
0.25 miles

Charles St

Florence St

Vincent St

Carr St

Newcastle St

Kingston Ave

Cleaver St

Loftus St

Mitchell Fwy

Leederville Oval

Kitsch (255m)

Carr Pl

Leederville Pde

Southport St

Leederville

Cambridge St

Railway Pde

Kimberley St

West Leederville

Northwood St

Woolwich St

Leonards Ave

Mc Court St

Ruislip St

Harborne St

Lake Monger (480m)

Salvado Rd

Cambridge St

Ruislip St

Hood St

Station St

Centro Ave

Subiaco Rd

Catherine St

York St

Roberts Rd

Churchill Ave

Barker St

Park St

Hay St

Coghlan St

Hay St

SUBIACO

Bagot Rd

Carrington St

Hensman Rd

Union St

Townshend Rd

Hamersley Rd

Rokeby Rd

Heytesbury Rd

Nicholson (100m)
Eight

Daglish

Railway Rd

Fitzgerald St

Roe St

Murray St

St Georges Tce

Mill St

Spring St

Mitchell Fwy

Elder St

Harvest Tce

Parliament Pl

WEST PERTH

Havelock St

Hay St

Colin St

Old St

Richardson St

Kings Park Rd

Murray St

Outram St

Wellington St

Thomas St

Delhi St

City West

Malcolm St

Mount St

Fraser Ave

Kings Park

Aboriginal Art & Craft Gallery (390m);
Aspects of Kings Park (360m);
Fraser's (470m);
State War Memorial (500m);
Moonlight Cinemas (1.3km)

Subiaco & Kings Park

great location. Hire a bike to get around locally, or take advantage of the hostel's free bodyboards and surfboards.

Western Beach Lodge HOSTEL **$**
(☑08-9245 1624; www.westernbeach.com; 6 Westborough St; dm $30-34, d with shared bathroom $75; @🛇) A real surfer hang-out, this sociable, homely hostel has surfboards and boogie boards available, and a good, no-frills feel.

Trigg Retreat B&B **$$**
(☑08-9447 6726; www.triggretreat.com; 59 Kitchener St; r $190; ❄@🛇) Quietly classy, this three-room B&B offers attractive and supremely comfortable queen bedrooms in a modern house a short drive from Trigg Beach. Each has fridge, TV, DVD player and tea- and coffee-making facilities. A full cooked breakfast is included in the rates. When we last dropped by, the beautiful jarrah floors were getting a makeover.

Sunmoon Boutique Resort HOTEL **$$**
(☑08-9245 8000; www.sunmoon.com.au; 200 West Coast Hwy; r from $175; ❄🛇≋) Separated from Scarborough Beach by a busy road and a petrol station, this Balinese-themed complex has wooden pathways leading to shady palm gardens and fishponds. Batik furnishings adorn large rooms with terracotta-tiled floors, and all rooms have been recently refurbished. Check online for good discounts.

Ocean Beach Hotel HOTEL **$$**
(☑08-9384 2555; www.obh.com.au; cnr Marine Pde & Eric St; r $170-250; ❄🛇) A good midrange option facing Cottesloe Beach, this accommodation is slightly removed from the raucously popular pub of the same name. Rooms are large and pretty good value, either in an older art-deco area, or in a towering new block. It's a good alternative to the pricey hotels of central Perth *and* the Indian Ocean is just across the road.

Other Areas

Discovery Holiday Parks – Perth CAMPGROUND **$**
(☑08-9453 6877; www.discoveryholidayparks.com. au; 186 Hale Rd; powered sites for 2 people $38-45, units $125-187; ❄@🛇≋) This well-kept holiday park, 15km out of the city, has a wide range of cabins and smart-looking units, many with deck, TV and DVD player.

The Peninsula APARTMENT **$$**
(☑08-9368 6688; www.thepeninsula.net; 53 South Perth Esplanade; apt from $205; ❄@🛇) While only the front few apartments have full-on views, the Peninsula's waterfront location lends itself to lazy ferry rides and sunset strolls along the river. It's a sprawling, older-style complex, but it's kept in good nick. The apartments all have kitchenettes and there's a communal laundry room.

SELF-CATERING

These are the pick of the crop.

Boatshed Market (www.boatshedmarket.com.au; 40 Jarrad St, Cottesloe; ⊙ 6.30am-8pm) Upmarket shed stacked with fresh produce, meat, fish, delicatessen goods, pastries and bread.

Chez Jean-Claude Patisserie (Map p62; www.chezjeanclaudepatisserie.com.au; 333 Rokeby Rd, Subiaco; ⊙ 6am-6.30pm Mon-Fri) Line up with the locals for brioche and baguettes.

City Farm Organic Growers Market (Map p52; www.perthcityfarm.org.au; 1 City Farm Pl, Fast Perth; ⊙ 8am-noon Sat) Local organic producers sell eggs, fruit, vegetables and bread.

Kailis Bros (Map p62; www.kailisbrosleederville.com.au; 101 Oxford St, Leederville; ⊙ 8am-6pm) Big, fresh seafood supplier with cafe attached.

Kakulas Bros (Map p52; www.kakulasbros.com.au; 183 William St, Northbridge;) Provisions store overflowing with sacks and vats of legumes, nuts and olives, plus a deli counter, well stocked with cheese. There's another branch, Kakulas Sister (p85), down in Fremantle.

Station St Markets (Map p62; www.subiacomarkets.com; Station St, Subiaco; ⊙ 7.30am-5.30pm Fri-Mon) Covered market selling fresh produce.

🍴 Eating

Where many of Australia's other state capitals might have a handful of top restaurants charging over $40 a main, in Perth those prices are fast becoming the norm for any establishment that considers itself above average. Unfortunately, the experience doesn't always match the outlay, and inferior and lax service is more prevalent than it should be.

It's still possible to eat cheaply, especially in the Little Asia section of William St, Northbridge. Many restaurants are BYO, meaning you can bring your own wine; check first. The better cafes are good places to go for a midrange meal, and good coffee and free wi-fi are becoming more prevalent. Some establishments listed under Drinking blur the line between bar, cafe and restaurant, and offer good dining as well.

The happening neighbourhoods for new cafes and restaurants are Northbridge, Mt Lawley and more recently Maylands, and the city centre has also seen many new options open around the Brookfield Pl precinct (www.brookfieldplace.com.au) on St George's Terrace.

🍴 City Centre

Mama Tran   VIETNAMESE $
(Map p52; www.mamatran.com.au; 36-40 Milligan St; snacks & mains $8-12; ⊙ 7am-4pm) Now you don't have to truck across to Northbridge for a hearty bowl of *pho* (Vietnamese noo-dle soup). The hip Mama Tran also does excellent coffee, fresh rice-paper rolls, and Asian salads. Grab a spot on one of the big shared tables and order up a storm including plump *banh mi ga* (Vietnamese chicken baguettes).

Tiger, Tiger   CAFE $
(Map p52; ☑ 08-9322 8055; www.tigertigercoffee bar.com; Murray Mews; mains $8-20; ⊙ 7am-5pm Mon & Sat, to 8pm Tue-Thu, to midnight Fri; 🛜) In a laneway off Murray St, Tiger, Tiger has a shabby-chic interior that isn't as popular as its outdoor setting. The free wi-fi's a draw-card, but the food is also excellent – all the regular breakfast favourites, along with pasta, curry, tarts, soups and baguettes on the lunch menu. Table service kicks in at lunchtime; before that you'll need to order at the counter.

Cabin Fever   CAFE $
(Map p52; 88 Barrack St, Bon Marche Arcade; snacks $5-10; ⊙ 7am-5pm Mon-Fri, 10am-5pm Sat; 🛜) Hidden away in a central Perth shopping arcade, Cabin Fever features quirky retro decor last seen at your aunt's place circa 1973. It's like bees to a heritage honeypot for Perth's cool kids, drawn also by free wi-fi, homestyle baking and excellent coffee. And just when you thought this part of town wasn't very interesting.

Annalakshmi   INDIAN $
(Map p52; ☑ 08-9221 3003; www.annalakshmi.com. au; 1st fl, Western Pavilion; pay by donation; ⊙ noon-

2.30pm & 6.30-9pm Tue-Sun) While the 360-degree views of the Swan River are worth a million dollars, the food's literally priceless. Run by volunteers (formidable baby-boomers, in the main), this place asks for payment by donation. An eclectic mix of hippies, Hindus and the just plain hungry line up for spicy vegetarian curries and fragrant dhal. Chilled coconut-milk and cardamom desserts cleanse the palate.

Secret Garden   CAFE $
(Map p52; www.secretgardencafe.com.au; Murray Mews; mains $10-19; ⊙7am-3pm Mon-Fri; 🛜) Tucked away down a boho laneway off Murray St, Secret Garden has good coffee, enticing counter food and all-day breakfasts for hangovers. Free wi-fi is the perfect partner for a robust espresso.

Taka   JAPANESE $
(www.takaskitchen.iinet.net.au; mains $7-10; ⊙11am-9pm Mon-Sat) This straightforward Japanese eatery whips out standards like teriyaki, udon and sushi. Great for a quick bite if you're out drinking. It has branches at **Barrack St** (Map p8; 150-152 Barrack St)and **Shafto Lane** (Map p8; shops 5 & 6 Shafto Lane).

Greenhouse   TAPAS $$
(Map p52; ☑08-9481 8333; www.greenhouseperth.com; 100 St Georges Tce; tapas $10-19; ⊙7am-midnight Mon-Sat) 🍴 Groundbreaking design – straw bales, plywood, corrugated iron and living exterior walls covered with 5000 individual pot plants – combines with excellent food at this hip tapas-style eatery. Asian and Middle Eastern influences inform a sustainably sourced menu including spiced lamb with yoghurt and quinoa, or lamb with pistachio and pomegranate.

Venn Cafe & Bar   CAFE $$
(Map p52; www.venn.net; 16 Queen St; mains $13-28, pizza $15; ⊙7am-5pm Mon-Tue, 7am-midnight Wed-Fri, 9am-midnight Sat) Equal parts design store, gallery, bar and cafe, and more proof that Perth is a foodie city on the rise. Breakfast and lunch team with good coffee – try the quinoa and banana pancakes or carpaccio of Margaret River Wagyu beef – and later at night pizza and charcuterie combine with a surprising wine list and craft beers from around Australia.

Tom's Kitchen   CAFE $$
(Map p52; ☑08-9321 0345; www.tomskitchenwa.com.au; Shafto Lane; lunch 2/3 courses $21.50/28.50, dinner mains $30-35; ⊙6.30am-9pm Mon-Fri, from 6pm Sat) Cafe by day, dining room by night, Tom's Kitchen is a standout amid the ethnic eateries and rambunctious pubs of Shafto Lane. Good-value multi-course lunches feature classy comfort food, and are a great way to battle the impact of Perth's expensive menus. Evenings showcase warming dishes like slow-cooked pork belly and crispy-skin salmon.

Matsuri   JAPANESE $$
(Map p52; www.matsuri.com.au; 250 St Georges Tce; mains $18-23; ⊙noon-2.30pm Mon-Fri, 6-10pm Mon-Sat) You'll feel a bit like a carp in a fish tank here – floor-to-ceiling glass runs the perimeter of this large, long-standing Japanese restaurant. Excellent teriyaki, tempura and sashimi combine with slightly formal but friendly service.

Print Hall   ASIAN, MODERN AUSTRALIAN $$$
(Map p52; www.printhall.com.au; 125 St Georges Tce; snacks $10-18, mains $25-45; ⊙noon-midnight Mon-Fri, 4pm-midnight Sat) Formerly the base of the *West Australian* newspaper, this sprawling complex in the Brookfield Place precinct includes the Apple Daily, featuring Southeast Asian–style street food, and the expansive Print Hall Dining Room, with an oyster bar and grilled WA meat and seafood. Don't miss having a drink and Spanish tapas in the rooftop Bob's Bar, named after Australia's larrikin former prime minister, Bob Hawke.

Restaurant Amusé   MODERN AUSTRALIAN $$$
(Map p52; ☑08-9325 4900; www.restaurantamuse.com.au; 64 Bronte St; degustation $125; ⊙6.30pm-late Tue-Sat) The critics have certainly been amused by this degustation-only establishment, regularly rated as WA's finest. The latest gong was for Perth's Restaurant of the Year in the 2013 *Good Food Guide*. Book well ahead and come prepared for a culinary adventure.

The Trustee   BISTRO $$$
(Map p52; www.thetrustee.com.au; 133 St Georges Tce; bar snacks $13-25, mains $33-39; ⊙11.45am-midnight Mon-Fri, from 5pm Sat) Just one of the new eateries and bars filling the heritage buildings around central Perth's Brookfield Place precinct, The Trustee channels a European bistro vibe with dishes like chicken black bean cassoulet and confit duck leg. A spectacular wine list draws Perth's movers and shakers, and the flash bar snacks are pricey but delicious.

Balthazar   MODERN AUSTRALIAN **$$$**
(Map p52; ☑ 08-9421 1206; 6 The Esplanade; mains $30-45; ☺ noon-late Mon-Fri, 6pm-late Sat) Low lit, discreet and sophisticated, with a hipster soundtrack and charming staff, Balthazar's informal cool vibe is matched by exquisite food and a famously excellent wine list. The menu here is refreshingly original, combining European and Asian flavours with not-at-all-reckless abandon.

✖ Northbridge

Little Willy's   CAFE **$**
(Map p52; 267 William St; mains $5-14; ☺ 6am-6pm Mon-Fri, 8am-4pm Sat & Sun) It's tiny and it's on William St, and it's a go-to spot to grab a sidewalk table and tuck into robust treats like the city's best breakfast burrito and bircher museli. It's also a preferred coffee haunt for the hip Northbridge indie set. BYO skinny jeans.

Viet Hoa   VIETNAMESE **$**
(Map p52; 349 William St; mains $10-23; ☺ 10am-10pm) Don't be fooled by the bare-bones ambience of this corner Vietnamese restaurant – or you'll miss out on the fresh rice-paper rolls and top-notch *pho*. Greenery creeping up the beams gives the place an offbeat feel.

Source Foods   CAFE **$**
(Map p61; www.sourcefoods.com.au; 289 Beaufort St; mains $10-19; ☺ 7.30am-3pm; 🔊) 🍴 Unassuming cafe committed to sustainable practices; free wi-fi also. Pop along for 'Burger Night' on a Friday – try the harissa steak burger ($16).

Flipside   BURGERS **$**
(Map p52; www.flipsideburgerbar.com.au; 222 William St; burgers $10.50-14.50; ☺ 11.30am-10pm Tue-Sat, to 9pm Sun) Gourmet burgers with the option of takeout upstairs at Mechanics Institute bar (p70).

★ Namh Thai   THAI **$$**
(Map p17; ☑ 08-9328 7500; 223 Bulwer St; mains $22-40; ☺ 6-10pm Mon-Sat) Not your average Thai restaurant, Namh experiments with interesting taste combinations – duck with lychees is the speciality, but we love the soft-shell crab with watermelon – and serves them in an elegant candlelit dining room. Friday and Saturday are given over to banquet-style dining. Bulwer St intersects William St, north of Northbridge.

Bivouac Canteen & Bar   CAFE **$$**
(Map p52; www.bivouac.com.au; 198 William St; mains $16-36, pizzas $21-24; ☺ noon-late Tue-Fri, 10am-late Sat) Bivouac is another of the cool recent openings on William St resurrecting the area as a hip destination. Mediterranean-style cuisine partners with a good wine list, and gourmet pizzas go well with boutique beers and artisan ciders. The coffee is excellent, and Bivouac's utilitarian decor is softened with a rotating roster of work from local artists.

Tarts   CAFE **$$**
(Map p61; www.tartscafe.com.au; 212 Lake St; mains $14-33; ☺ 7am-10pm Tue-Fri, to 5pm Sat-Mon) Massive tarts piled with berries, apples or lime curd; rich scrambled eggs tumbling off thickly sliced sourdough; mini custard tarts stacked with glazed strawberries. Packed like a picnic hamper on weekends, and a worthy bistro-style dinner option during the week.

Good Fortune Roast Duck House   CHINESE **$$**
(Map p52; www.goodfortuneduckhouse.com.au; 344 William St; mains $10-24; ☺ 10am-10pm Wed-Mon) This is the real thing – just like being in China. Locals charge in for family-sized feeds of barbecue pork, roast duck and noodles – the front window is crammed with options. A half-serve of boneless duck is $21, and seafood options include crispy soft-shell crab.

La Cholita   MEXICAN **$$**
(Map p52; cnr Aberdeen & William Sts; snacks $6-12, mains $26-28; ☺ 5pm-late Wed-Sun) *Sí*, the Mexican culinary wave has also washed up on Western Australian shores, and La Cholita's energetic combo of Mexican street food, ice-cold *cerveza* and gutsy tequilas is *muchas* fun. Don't come expecting a quiet romantic evening – you may have to share tables – and there are no reservations, so arrive early.

Sayers Sister   CAFE **$$**
(Map p61; www.sayersfood.com.au; 236 Lake St; mains $10-27; ☺ 7am-5pm Tue-Sun) Top-notch breakfasts and lunches (including scrambled eggs with feta, truffle and smoked salmon) and a convenient Northbridge location.

Red Teapot   CHINESE **$$**
(Map p61; www.redteapotrestaurant.com.au; 413 William St; mains $11-22; ☺ 11.30am-3pm & 5.30-10pm Mon-Sat) An intimate restaurant, always busy with diners enjoying stylishly executed Chinese favourites like fragrant prosperous chicken and chilli salt squid.

Highgate & Mt Lawley

Veggie Mama   VEGETARIAN $
(Map p61; www.veggiemma.com.au; cnr Beaufort
& Vincent Sts; mains $10-20; ☺7am-5pm Mon-Fri,
from 8am Sat & Sun; ☜) ✎ Loads of vegan and
gluten-free options shine at this cute corner
cafe where flavour is definitely not compro-
mised. The menu includes delicious salads,
smoothies, vegie curries and burgers – try
the polenta and butternut burger with mango salsa – and weekend breakfasts are very
popular. There's free wi-fi, and it's all really
well priced.

Cantina 663   MEDITERRANEAN $$
(Map p61; ☑08-9370 4883; www.cantina663.com;
663 Beaufort St; lunch $12-28, dinner $26-34;
☺8am-late Mon-Sat, to 3pm Sun) It's a mini cu-
linary World Cup, featuring Spain, Portugal
and Italy, at this cool but casual cantina with
tables spilling into the arcade. Service can
be a bit too cool for school, but it's worth
waiting for dishes like Ortiz anchovies with
lemon and charred bread, or braised baby
goat with pearl barley and yoghurt.

The Beaufort St Merchant   CAFE $$
(Map p61; ☑08-9328 6299; www.beaufortmer
chant.com; 488 Beaufort St; breakfast $13-22,
lunch & dinner $24-37; ☺7am-10pm) Our favour-
ite cafe in Mt Lawley, and one of our favourites in Perth – especially for a leisurely
breakfast over the papers and a couple of
coffees. Go for the chorizo and manchego-
cheese tortilla, and work out what you'd
order if you came back for dinner. Maybe
the lime-baked ocean trout or crab linguini,
we reckon.

El Público   MEXICAN $$
(Map p61; ☑0418 187 708; www.elpublico.com.
au; snacks $9-16, mains $22-28; ☺5pm-midnight
Wed-Fri, from noon Sat & Sun) El Público in Mt
Lawley is one of Perth's hippest new eater-
ies. Look forward to interesting and authen-
tic spins on Mexican street food, all served
as small plates that are perfect for sharing.
Menu standouts include fish soft-shell tacos,
and tequila-infused marshmallows for des-
sert. Bring along a few friends, and groove
to the occasional DJs.

Jackson's   MODERN AUSTRALIAN $$$
(Map p61; ☑08-9328 1177; www.jacksonsrestau
rant.com.au; 483 Beaufort St; mains $41-49, de-
gustation $125; ☺6pm-late Mon-Sat) The finest
of fine dining is offered in this upmarket
dining room, where the wait staff don white

gloves to present you with wonderfully creative treats from the kitchen of Neal Jackson,
one of Perth's most established chefs.

Must Winebar   FRENCH $$$
(Map p61; ☑08-9328 8255; www.must.com.au; 519
Beaufort St; mains $39-46; ☺noon-midnight) Not
content with being Perth's best wine bar,
Must is one of its best restaurants as well.
The Gallic vibe is hip, slick and a little bit
cheeky, and the menu marries classic French
bistro flavours with the best local produce.

Mt Hawthorn

New Norcia Bakery   BAKERY, CAFE $
(www.newnorciabaker.com.au; 163 Scarborough
Beach Rd; mains $11-17; ☺7am-6pm) Perth's best
bread, delicious pastries and a bright cafe
as well. It gets crammed on the weekends.
There's another more central branch **Subi-
aco** (Map p62; Bagot Rd, The Cloisters; ☺7.30am-
6pm Mon-Sat, to 4pm Sun) for takeaway baked
goodies.

Divido   ITALIAN $$
(☑08-9443 7373; www.divido.com.au; 170 Scarbor-
ough Beach Rd; mains $33-39, 6-course degustation
$95; ☺6pm-late Mon-Sat) Italian but not rig-
idly so (the chef is of Croatian extraction, so
delicious Dalmatian-style doughnuts make
it onto the dessert menu), this romantic
restaurant serves handmade pasta dishes
and delicately flavoured mains. Good-value
'Champagne Mondays' feature three courses
and a glass of bubbles for $65.

Leederville

Snags & Sons   FAST FOOD $
(Map p62; www.snagsandsons.com.au; 749 New-
castle St; sausages $5-10; ☺11am-10pm Tue-Sat,
to 9pm Sun & Mon) ✎ It's sausage heaven at
Snags & Sons. Tasty spins on the humble
snarler – often made from free range and
organic produce – include smoked cheese
kransky, Thai red curry or North African
lamb. Sauces include tamarind chutney,
harissa yoghurt and horseradish cream, and
healthy single-serve salads are also on offer.

Green's & Co   CAFE $
(Map p62; 123 Oxford St; cakes $5-8; ☺8am-
midnight) Dive into great coffee and a 'how-
do-I-choose?' selection of cakes, and see if
your favourite band is featured on the post-
ers adorning the walls.

WORTH A TRIP

MAYLANDS: THE NEXT BIG THING?

If the recent expansion of new bars, cafes and restaurants in Mt Lawley makes the suburb the 'new Subiaco', we reckon Maylands just to the east could be the 'new Mt Lawley'. It's early days, with just a few eating and drinking spots huddled on Whatley Cres, but there's a definite foodie buzz around the neighbourhood. It's also very easy to reach by train, just a short Zone 1 hop ($2.70) to the Maylands station on the Midland line.

Mrs S (178 Whatley Cres; mains $10-17; ⊙7am-5pm Tue-Fri, 8am-4pm Sat & Sun) Mrs S has a quirky retro ambience, the perfect backdrop for excellent homestyle baking or a lazy brunch. Menus – presented in Little Golden children's books – feature loads of innovative variations on traditional dishes. Try the breakfast tortilla with poached eggs, spicy beans and a lime sour cream. Weekends are *wildly* popular, so try to visit on a weekday.

Swallow (198 Whatley Cres; snacks $10-24; ⊙4pm-late Mon-Sat. from noon Sun) Channeling an art deco ambience with funky lampshades and vintage French advertising, Swallow is the kind of place you'd love as your local. Wine and cocktails are exemplary, and the drinks list includes Spanish wheat beers and French ciders. DJs often play on Sunday afternoons in the courtyard, and bar snacks also come with a Euro accent.

Jus Burgers   BURGERS $
(www.jusburgers.com.au;burgers$11-14; ⊙11.30am-10pm) 🍴 Carbon-neutral gourmet burgers; branches in **Leederville** (Map p62; 743 Newcastle St) and **Subiaco** (Map p62; 1 Rokeby Rd).

★Duende   TAPAS $$
(Map p62; ☑08-9228 0123; www.duende.com.au; 662 Newcastle St; tapas & mains $14-29; ⊙7.30am-late) Sleek Duende occupies a corner site amid the comings and goings of Leederville. Stellar modern-accented tapas are served: make a meal of it or call in for a late-night glass of dessert wine and *churros* (doughnuts served with hot chocolate sauce). We're also very partial to starting the day with an espresso and Duende's crab-and-chorizo omelette.

Kitsch   ASIAN $$
(www.kitschbar.com.au; 229 Oxford St; small plates $5-19; ⊙5pm-midnight Tue-Sat) Southeast Asian–style street food, Thai beers and an eclectic, slighty overgrown garden make Kitsch a great spot for a few laid-back hours of tasty grazing. Standout dishes include the son-in-law eggs with tamarind and pork crackling, or the five-spice pork with plums and ginger chilli caramel. Expect to stay (and eat) longer than you planned.

Sayers   CAFE $$
(Map p62; www.sayersfood.com.au; 224 Carr Pl; mains $10-27; ⊙7am-3pm) This classy cafe's counter groans under the weight of its alluring cakes. The breakfast menu includes eggy treats such as beetroot-cured salmon omelette, and lunch highlights include a zingy calamari, watermelon and fresh mint salad.

🍴 Subiaco & Kings Park

Stimulatte   CAFE $
(Map p62; 361 Hay St; brunch $7.50-12.50; ⊙7am-3pm) It's worth taking the short stroll from central Subiaco to this cool neighbourhood cafe. Big-format photos of New York adorn the walls, providing a cosmopolitan backdrop for interesting brunches and serious coffee. The brekky wrap or the homemade baked beans with ciabatta toast are recommended.

Boucla   CAFE $
(Map p62; www.boucla.com; 349 Rokeby Rd; mains $11-22; ⊙7am-5pm Mon-Fri, to 3.30pm Sat) A locals' secret, this Greek- and Levantine-infused haven is pleasingly isolated from the thick of the Rokeby Rd action. Baklava and cakes tempt you from the corner, and huge tarts filled with blue-vein cheese and roast vegetables spill off plates. The salads are great too.

Subiaco Hotel   GASTROPUB $$
(Map p62; ☑08-9381 3069; www.subiacohotel. com.au; 465 Hay St; mains $19-34; ⊙7am-late) A legendary boozer with a makeover, the Subi's buzzy dining room is the suburb's main place to see and be seen. The menu ranges from lighter fare like Caesar salads and Asian-inspired pork belly to perfectly cooked steaks and excellent fish dishes. Around the corner, the main bar (p71) is still relatively old school.

Old Brewery STEAKHOUSE $$
(📝 08-9211 8910; www.theoldbrewery.com.au; 173 Mounts Bay Rd; mains $29-48; ☺ breakfast Sun, lunch & dinner daily) Even Perth's steakhouses are glamorous, evidenced by this designer joint in the historic Swan Brewery building (1838). There are river views across to the city, but hardcore carnivores will be more interested in the beef aging gracefully in glass display cabinets. Splash out on a 300g Wagyu scotch fillet ($79). Craft-beer fans won't go thirsty either.

Chutney Mary's INDIAN $$
(Map p62; www.chutneymarys.com.au; 67 Rokeby Rd; mains $15-28; ☺ noon-2.30pm Mon-Sat, 5.30pm-late daily) The feisty, authentic Indian food here is much loved and a sizeable chunk of the large menu is devoted to vegetarian favourites.

Perugino ITALIAN $$
(Map p62; 📝 08-9321 5420; www.perugino.com.au; 77 Outram St; mains $27-41; ☺ noon-3pm Tue-Fri, 7pm-late Tue-Sat) Traditional, formal Italian restaurant with a three-course lunch for $52.

Fraser's MODERN AUSTRALIAN $$$
(📝 08-9481 7100; www.frasersrestaurant.com. au; Fraser Ave; mains $36-44; ☺ noon-late) Atop Kings Park, overlooking the city and the glittering Swan River, Fraser's is in a wonderful location. Thankfully, the food is also excellent, making it a popular spot for business lunches and romantic dinners on the terrace on balmy summer nights. Pair the turmeric, snapper and king prawn curry with a Leeuwin Estate riesling from Margaret River.

🏖 Beaches

Dancing Goat CAFE $
(14 Railway St; mains $10-15; ☺ 6am-4pm Mon-Fri, 7.30am-12.30pm Sat) The hip and bohemian Dancing Goat is the best place in the beach suburbs for a coffee. It's near the Swanbourne train station.

John St Cafe CAFE $
(37 John St; mains $10-25; ☺ 7am-4pm) Tucked up a residential street, five minutes from the beach, John St is another fine Cottesloe breakfast spot.

Il Lido ITALIAN $$
(www.illido.com.au; 88 Marine Pde; mains $20-35; ☺ 7.30am-late) Il Lido's al fresco area is popular with Cotteslocals and their dogs, but we prefer the sunny interior of this self-styled 'Italian canteen'. Breakfast and coffee attract the early-bird swimmers, and throughout the day antipasto plates, pasta and risottos, and a good beer and wine list continue the culinary buzz. Maybe linger for cocktails and an Indian Ocean sunset.

Naked Fig CAFE $$
(www.thefig.com.au; 278 Marine Pde; breakfast & lunch $16-33, dinner $27-36; ☺ 7am-late, closed dinner Mon; 🖥) 🍴 It's all about the location here, especially the sublime ocean-gazing deck near Swanbourne beach. Modern Australia and Mediterranean flavours make perfect sense given the stunning view, and the sustainable menu tends to free-range this and organic that.

🍷 Drinking & Nightlife

Once upon a time, licences to sell alcohol in WA were tightly restricted and massively expensive. Venues therefore had to be built on a grand scale in order to recoup the investment, and big booze barns became part of the culture.

A law change a few years back has given birth to a new breed of quirky little bars that are distinctly Melbourne-ish in their hipness and difficulty to locate. They're sprouting up all over the place, including in the formerly deserted-after-dark central city. Northbridge is also a happy-hunting ground for more idiosyncratic drinking establishements.

One of the by-products of the mining boom has been the rise of the Cashed-Up Bogan (CUB) – young men with plenty of cash to splash on muscle cars, beer and drugs. A spate of fights and glassings in bars has caused many venues, particularly around Northbridge, to step up security. Most pubs now have lockouts, so you'll need to be in before midnight in order to gain entry. You may need to present photo ID to obtain entry and it would pay to keep your wits about you in pubs and on the streets after dark.

🍸 City Centre

Greenhouse COCKTAIL BAR
(Map p52; www.greenhouseperth.com; 100 St Georges Tce; ☺ 7am-midnight Mon-Sat) In a city so in love with the great outdoors, it's surprising that nobody's opened a rooftop bar in the central city before now. Hip, eco-conscious Greenhouse is leading the way, mixing up a

storm amid the greenery with great cocktails and an interesting beer and wine list.

Helvetica   BAR
(Map p52; www.helveticabar.com.au; rear 101 St Georges Tce; ☺3pm-midnight Tue-Thu, noon-midnight Fri, 6pm-midnight Sat) Clever artsy types tap their toes to delicious alternative pop in this bar named after a typeface and specialising in whisky and cocktails. The concealed entry is off Howard St: look for the chandelier in the lane behind Andaluz tapas bar.

Cheeky Sparrow   BAR, CAFE
(Map p52; www.cheekysparrow.com.au; 1/317 Murray St; ☺11.30am-late Tue-Fri, from 4pm Sat) Cheeky Sparrow's multi-level labyrinth of leather banquettes and bentwood chairs is great for everything from brunch and coffee through to pizza and cheese and charcuterie plates. If you're feeling peckish later at night, pop in for robust bar snacks including chorizo croquettes and chickpea fritters. Cocktail fans certainly won't be disappointed. Access is via Wolfe Lane.

Hula Bula Bar   COCKTAIL BAR
(Map p52; www.hulabulabar.com; 12 Victoria Ave; ☺4pm-midnight Wed-Fri, 6pm-1am Sat) You'll feel like you're on *Gilligan's Island* in this tiny Polynesian-themed bar, decked out in bamboo, palm leaves and tikis. A cool but relaxed crowd jams in here on weekends to sip ostentatious cocktails out of ceramic monkey's heads.

Wolfe Lane   COCKTAIL BAR
(Map p52; www.wolflane.com.au; Wolfe Lane; ☺4pm-midnight Tue-Sat) Exposed bricks, classic retro furniture and high ceilings create a pretty decent WA approximation of a New York loft. A serious approach to cocktails and wine combines with an eclectic beer selection, and bar snacks include share plates of cheese and chorizo. Here's where to come for the last drink(s) of the night.

The Grosvenor   PUB
(Map p52; www.thegrosvenorperth.com.au; cnr Hay & Hill Sts; ☺11am-midnight) The perfect spot for a lazy afternoon drink. This classic corner pub – complete with wrought-iron balconies and one of Perth's best garden bars – draws a crowd of loyal locals, nearby desk jockeys and thirsty students.

1907   COCKTAIL BAR
(Map p52; www.1907.com.au; 26 Queen St; ☺4pm-midnight Wed-Sat) Hidden away down a lane, behind a gate and down the side of a building, this modern-day speakeasy has a backlit bar and Rat Pack photos on the walls. Blue Note Thursdays feature $10 cocktails.

Metro City   CLUB
(Map p52; www.metroconcertclub.com; 146 Roe St) Thumping super-club (capacity 2000), which doubles as a concert venue.

Ambar   CLUB
(Map p52; www.boomtick.com.au/ambar; 104 Murray St) Perth's premier club for breakbeat, drum'n'bass and visiting international DJs.

🍺 Northbridge
Northbridge is the rough-edged hub of Perth's nightlife, with dozens of pubs and clubs clustered around William and James Sts. It's so popular, it even has its own website (www.onwilliam.com.au). A few recent openings have lifted the tone of the area.

Mechanics Institute   BAR
(Map p52; www.mechanicsinstitutebar.com.au; 222 William St; ☺noon-midnight Tue-Sun) Negotiate the laneway entrance around the corner on James St to discover one of Perth's most down-to-earth small bars. Share one of the big tables on the deck or nab a stool by the bar. Craft beers from Two Birds Brewing are on tap, and you can even order in a gourmet burger from Flipside (p66) downstairs.

Ezra Pound   BAR
(Map p52; www.epbar.com.au; 189 William St; ☺1pm-midnight Thu-Tue) Down a much-graffitied lane leading off William St, Ezra Pound is favoured by Northbridge's bohemian set. It's the kind of place where you can settle into a red velvet chair and sup a Tom Collins out of a jam jar. Earnest conversations about Kerouac and Kafka are strictly optional.

399   BAR
(Map p61; www.399bar.com; 399 William St; ☺10am-midnight Mon-Sat, to 10pm Sun; 🖥) This friendly neighbourhood bar has booths along one side and a long bar down the other, making it easy to interact with the engaging bar staff. Cocktails are artfully crafted, and there's a serious approach to beer and wine. Good-value tapas are three for $19, and 399 is also a good espresso and wi-fi stop during the day.

The Brisbane   PUB
(Map p61; www.thebrisbanehotel.com.au; 292 Beaufort St; ☺11.30am-late) It was a very

clever architect indeed who converted this classic corner pub (1898) into a thoroughly modern venue, where each space seamlessly blends into the next. Best of all is the large courtyard where the phoenix palms and ponds provide a balmy holiday feel. Dining, shooting pool or lazing on a lounge are all options.

Brass Monkey
PUB

(Map p52; www.thebrassmonkey.com.au; cnr James & William Sts; ⊗ 11am-1am Wed-Sat, to 10pm Sun) A massive 1897 pub with several different component parts, each with its own vibe: sit up on a stool at the bar, lean back in the relaxed beer garden, or hunker down on a chesterfield by the fire (and sports screen). Semidetached GrapeSkin is the Monkey's (slightly) more upmarket wine and tapas bar.

The Bird
BAR

(Map p52; http://williamstreetbird.com; 181 William St; ⊗ 1pm-midnight) Grungy indie bar that's always worth a look for local bands and DJs. Upstairs there's a bricklined deck with city views.

Air
CLUB

(Map p52; www.airclub.com.au; 139 James St; ⊗ from 9pm Fri & Sat) Serious clubbers head here for nonstop house, techno and trance.

Geisha
CLUB

(Map p52; www.geishabar.com.au; 135a James St; ⊗ 11pm-6am Fri & Sat) A small-and-pumping DJ-driven, gay-friendly club; the vibe's usually music-focused and chilled out.

Highgate & Mt Lawley

Five Bar
CRAFT BEER, CAFE

(Map p61; www.fivebar.com.au; 560 Beaufort St; ⊗ 11am-midnight) More than 50 international and Australian craft beers – and a few interesting ciders – make Mt Lawley's Five Bar worth seeking out by the discerning drinker. Wine lovers are also well catered for, and the menu leans towards classy comfort food.

Must Winebar
WINE BAR

(Map p61; www.must.com.au; 519 Beaufort St; ⊗ noon-midnight) With cool French house music pulsing through the air and the perfect glass of wine in your hand (40 offerings by the glass, 500 on the list), Must is hard to beat. Upstairs is an exclusive, bookings-only Champagne bar.

Luxe
COCKTAIL BAR

(Map p61; www.luxebar.com; 446 Beaufort St; ⊗ 8pm-late Wed-Sun) With retro wood panelling, big, sexy lounge chairs and velvet curtains, Luxe is knowingly hip. It's also armed with turntables, and the gregarious bar staff are good for a chat while they shake their stuff.

Queens
PUB

(Map p61; www.thequeens.com.au; 520 Beaufort St; ⊗ 10am-midnight Mon-Sat, to 10pm Sun) Big, nicely renovated Federation-style pub, popular on Sunday. A cold beer in the dappled courtyard is the standard routine.

Flying Scotsman
PUB

(Map p61; www.theflyingscotsman.com.au; 639 Beaufort St; ⊗ 11am-midnight) Old-style pub that attracts the Beaufort St indie crowd. A good spot before a gig up the road at the Astor.

Velvet Lounge
PUB

(Map p61; www.theflyingscotsman.com.au; 639 Beaufort St) Out the back of the Flying Scotsman is this small, red-velvet-clad lounge with ska, punk and indie beats. Upstairs, the Defectors bar channels cocktails and chilled dub and dance beats.

Leederville

Leederville Hotel
PUB

(Map p62; www.leedervillehotel.com; 742 Newcastle St; ⊗ 11am-late) The good old Leederville has been turning out beers and Jägerbombs for many years. The something-for-everyone philosophy is etched out in the sports screens, dance floors and pool tables. Wednesday is big with the younger folk, and Retro Friday is the go for any lapsed 1980s New Romantics. Next door is the Garden, the Leederville's decent stab at a 21st-century gastropub.

Subiaco & Kings Park

Subiaco Hotel
PUB

(Map p62; www.subiacohotel.com.au; 465 Hay St; ⊗ 11am-late) The Subi's the locals' institution of choice for a morning coffee with the papers or a pre-footy beer. Middie-clutching men perch themselves for hours in the side bar, friends banter in lounges by the central bar and the Sunday sundowner crowd settle into the sun-speckled courtyard to squeeze the last drops out of the weekend.

Old Brewery
MICROBREWERY

(www.theoldbrewery.com.au; 173 Mounts Bay Rd; ⊙noon-late) Cowhide stools gather around the bar, gazing towards the shiny copper vats making the magic (ales and wheat beers, actually), carrying on the tradition of the Swan Brewery, which opened on this site in 1879. It's the perfect place for a riverside sundowner. Check the website for regular seasonal brews.

 Beaches

Elba
BAR

(www.elbacottesloe.com.au; 29 Napoleon St; ⊙3pm-late Mon-Thu, noon-late Fri-Sun) In the swanky residential part of Cottesloe, not the chilled-out beach strip, Elba has taken its street name as inspiration and produced a slick Napoleonic bar complete with a gilt-framed portrait of the little man. Come dressed for cocktails, although perhaps in flat shoes out of deference. Small plates (obviously) complete the picture for a worthwhile evening assignation.

Cottesloe Beach Hotel
PUB

(www.cottesloebeachhotel.com.au; 104 Marine Pde; ⊙11am-midnight Mon-Sat, to 10pm Sun) Grab a spot on the lawn in the massive beer garden, or watch the sun set from the balcony. Sunday is big. A recent trendy makeover has installed a specialist craft-beer bar downstairs.

Ocean Beach Hotel
PUB

(www.obh.com.au; cnr Marine Pde & Eric St; ⊙11am-midnight Mon-Sat, to 10pm Sun) Backpackers and locals drink up the beer and soak up the sun at this rambling beachside pub, especially on Sunday.

☆ **Entertainment**

Live Music

Ellington Jazz Club
LIVE MUSIC

(Map p52; www.ellingtonjazz.com.au; 191 Beaufort St; ⊙7pm-1am Mon-Thu, to 3am Fri & Sat, 5pm-midnight Sun) There's live jazz nightly in this handsome, intimate venue. Standing-only admission is $10, or you can book a table (per person $15) for tapas and pizza.

Perth Arena
LIVE MUSIC

(Map p52; www.pertharena.com.au; 700 Wellington St) Opened in November 2012, and used for big concerts by major international acts like Elton John and Russell Brand. It's also used by the Perth Wildcats NBL basketball franchise.

The Bakery
LIVE MUSIC

(Map p52; www.nowbaking.com.au; 233 James St; ⊙7pm-late) Run by Artrage, Perth's contemporary arts festival body, the Bakery draws an arty crowd. Popular indie gigs are held almost every weekend.

Amplifier
LIVE MUSIC

(Map p52; www.amplifiercapitol.com.au; rear 383 Murray St) The good old Amplifier is one of the best places for live (mainly indie) bands. Part of the same complex is Capitol, used mainly for DJ gigs.

The Moon
LIVE MUSIC

(Map p52; www.themoon.com.au; 323 William St; ⊙6pm-late Mon-Tue, 11am-late Wed-Sun) Low-key, late-night cafe with singer-songwriters on Wednesday, jazz on Thursday, poetry slams on Saturday afternoon and '10 Minute Tuesday', when it's guaranteed that 10 minutes of oddness will occur.

Universal
LIVE MUSIC

(Map p52; www.universalbar.com.au; 221 William St; ⊙7am-late) The unpretentious Universal is one of Perth's oldest bars and much-loved by jazz and blues enthusiasts.

Rosemount Hotel
LIVE MUSIC

(www.rosemounthotel.com.au; cnr Angove & Fitzgerald Sts, North Perth; ⊙noon-late) Local and international bands play regularly in this spacious art-deco pub with a laid-back beer garden.

Charles Hotel
LIVE MUSIC

(www.charleshotel.com.au; 509 Charles St, North Perth) Hosts lots of live music, including the Legendary Perth Blues Club on Tuesday.

Astor
CONCERT VENUE

(Map p61; www.liveattheastor.com.au; 659 Beaufort St) The beautiful art-deco Astor still screens the odd film but is mainly used for concerts these days.

Cabaret & Comedy

Devilles Pad
CABARET

(Map p52; www.devillespad.com; 3 Aberdeen St; ⊙6pm-midnight Thu, to 2am Fri & Sat) The devil goes to Vegas disguised as a 1950s lounge lizard in this extremely kooky venue. Punters are encouraged to dress to match the camp interiors (complete with erupting volcano). Burlesque dancers, live bands and assorted sideshow freaks provide the entertainment, and good food is available. Thursday is rock 'n' roll karaoke night, so bring along your Elvis A-game.

Lazy Susan's Comedy Den COMEDY
(Map p61; www.lazysusans.com.au; 292 Beaufort St; ⊘8.30pm Tue, Fri & Sat) Shapiro Tuesday offers a mix of first-timers, seasoned amateurs and pros trying out new shtick (for a very reasonable $5). Friday is for more grown-up stand-ups, including some interstaters. Saturday is the Big Hoohaa – a team-based comedy wrassle. The Den is at the Brisbane Hotel.

Theatre & Classical Music

Check the *West Australian* for what's on. Book through www.ticketek.com.au.

His Majesty's Theatre THEATRE
(Map p52; www.hismajestystheatre.com.au; 825 Hay St) The majestic home to the **West Australian Ballet** (www.waballet.com.au) and **West Australian Opera** (www.waopera.asn. au), as well as lots of theatre, comedy and cabaret.

Perth Concert Hall CONCERT HALL
(Map p52; www.perthconcerthall.com.au; 5 St Georges Tce) Home to the **Western Australian Symphony Orchestra** (WASO; www.waso. com.au).

State Theatre Centre THEATRE
(Map p52; www.statetheatrecentrewa.com.au; 174 William St) Opened in 2011, this flash new complex includes the 575-seat Heath Ledger Theatre and the 234-seat Studio Underground. It's home to the Black Swan State Theatre Company and Perth Theatre Company.

Subiaco Arts Centre THEATRE
(Map p62; www.subiacoartscentre.com.au; 180 Hamersley Rd) Indoor and outdoor theatres used for drama and concerts; home to Barking Gecko young people's theatre (www. barkinggecko.com.au).

Regal Theatre THEATRE
(Map p62; www.regaltheatre.com.au; 474 Hay St) Popular musicals and stage shows.

Cinema

Somerville Auditorium CINEMA
(www.perthfestival.com.au; 35 Stirling Hwy; ⊘Dec-Mar) A quintessential Perth experience, the Perth Festival's film program is held here on the University of WA's beautiful grounds surrounded by pines. Picnicking before the film is a must.

Luna CINEMA
(Map p62; www.lunapalace.com.au; 155 Oxford St) Art-house cinema with Monday double features and a bar. Screens outdoor movies in summer.

Cinema Paradiso CINEMA
(Map p52; www.lunapalace.com.au; 164 James St) Art-house cinema in the Galleria complex.

PERTH & FREMANTLE PERTH

GAY & LESBIAN PERTH

Perth is home to all of WA's gay and lesbian venues. Before you get excited, let's clarify matters: it has precisely two bars, one club and one men's sauna. Many other bars, especially around Highgate and Mt Lawley, are somewhat gay-friendly, but it's hardly what you'd call a bustling scene.

For a head's up on what's on, pick up the free monthly newspaper **Out In Perth** (www.outinperth.com). **Perth Pride** (www.pridewa.asn.au) runs a three-week festival in October, starting with a fair day and culminating in the Pride Parade.

The Court (Map p52; www.thecourt.com.au; 50 Beaufort St, Northbridge; ⊘noon-midnight Sun-Thu, to 2am Fri & Sat) A large, rambling complex consisting of an old corner pub and a big, partly covered courtyard with a clubby atmosphere. Wednesday is drag night, with kings and queens holding court in front of a young crowd.

Connections (Map p52; www.connectionsnightclub.com; 81 James St, Northbridge; ⊘10pm-late Wed, Fri & Sat) Reputedly the oldest surviving gay-and-lesbian venue in Australia, Connections keeps on keeping on, with DJs, drag shows and the occasional bit of lesbian mud wrestling.

Honey Lounge (Map p62; 663 Newcastle St, Leederville; ⊘Tue-Sun) Ladies only on Queen Bee nights, the first Thursday of every month.

Perth Steam Works (Map p61; www.perthsteamworks.com.au; 369 William St, Northbridge; admission $21; ⊘noon-1am Sun-Thu, to 3am Fri & Sat) Gay men's sauna. Entry on Forbes St.

Ace Subiaco CINEMA
(Map p62; www.moviemasters.com.au; 500 Hay St)
Four-screen multiplex screening Hollywood
fare.

Moonlight Cinema CINEMA
(www.moonlight.com.au; Synergy Parklands, Kings
Park) Bring a picnic and blanket and enjoy a
romantic moonlit movie; summer only.

Camelot Outdoor Cinema CINEMA
(www.lunapalace.com.au; 16 Lochee St, Memorial
Hall; ⊗ Dec-Easter) Seated open-air cinema in
Mosman Park.

Sport
In WA 'football' means Aussie Rules and
during the Australian Football League (AFL)
season it's hard to get locals to talk about
anything but the two local teams – the **West
Coast Eagles** (www.westcoasteagles.com.
au) and the **Fremantle Dockers** (www.fre
mantlefc.com.au) – and the joy of beating 'the
Vics' (any Victorian team is considered an
arch-enemy). Rugby League (considered an
east-coast game) doesn't get a look in, even
during the finals season.

Patersons Stadium FOOTBALL
(Subiaco Oval; Map p62; ☑ 08-9381 2187; www.pater
sonsstadium.com.au; 250 Roberts Rd) The home
of Aussie Rules and huge concerts; you're
guaranteed a great atmosphere.

WACA CRICKET
(Western Australian Cricket Association; Map p52;
☑ 9265 7222; www.waca.com.au; Nelson Cres) In
summer, cricket fans while away lazy afternoons here watching a test or state match.

NIB Stadium SOCCER, RUGBY
(Perth Oval; Map p52; www.nibstadium.com.au; Lord
St) Both the **Perth Glory** (www.perthglory.com.
au) soccer (football) team and the **Western
Force** (www.westernforce.com.au) Super 15 rugby union team play here, and it's the home
of WA rugby league.

Challenge Stadium NETBALL
(www.venueswest.wa.gov.au; Stephenson Ave, Mt
Claremont) Home to the **West Coast Fever**
(www.westcoastfever.com.au) netball team.

🛍 Shopping

🛍 City Centre
Murray St and Hay St Malls are the city's
shopping heartland, while King St is the

place for swanky boutiques. London Court
arcade has opals and souvenirs.

Wheels & Doll Baby CLOTHING
(Map p52; www.wheelsanddollbaby.com; 26 King
St; ⊗ 10am-6pm Mon-Sat, 11am-5pm Sun) Punky
rock-chick chic with a bit of baby doll mixed
in. Perhaps Perth fashion's coolest export,
and worn by Courtney Love, Katy Perry and
Debbie Harry.

Pigeonhole CLOTHING, ACCESSORIES
(Map p52; www.pigeonhole.com.au; Shop 16, Bon
Marche Arcade, 80 Barrack St; ⊗ 10am-5.30pm
Mon-Sun) Hip clothing, and stylish retro ac-
cessories and gifts. There are five stores
around the city – the main store is adjacent
to the associated Cabin Fever (p64) cafe
in Bon Marche Arcade – and Pigeonhole's
Shop 9 (Shop 9; Map p52; 9 Shafto Lane; ⊗ 10am-
6pm Mon-Sun, to 9pm Fri) features local and international fashion.

78 Records MUSIC
(Map p52; www.78records.com.au; upstairs 255
Murray St Mall; ⊗ 9am-5pm Mon-Sat, from 11am
Sun) Independent record shop with a massive range of CDs and lots of specials. Also
good for vinyl and tickets to rock and indie
gigs.

Elizabeth's Bookshop BOOKS
(Map p52; www.elizabethsbookshop.com.au; 820
Hay St; ⊗ 9am-7pm) Fremantle institution's
city-centre branch with lots of second-hand
tomes.

Perth Map Centre BOOKS, MAPS
(Map p52; www.mapworld.com.au; 900 Hay St;
⊗ 9am-5.30pm Mon-Fri, 10am-3pm Sun) Maps
and travel guides.

🛍 Northbridge, Highgate & Mt Lawley

William Topp DESIGN
(www.williamtopp.com; 452 William St; ⊗ 11am-
6pm Tue-Fri, to 5pm Sat & 4pm Sun) Lots of cool
knick-knacks.

Planet BOOKS, MUSIC
(Map p61; www.planetvideo.com.au; 636-638 Beaufort St; ⊗ 10am-late) Stacked with books, CDs
and lots of obscure DVDs. Pop next door for
coffee and cake at its new **Daily Planet** cafe.

Future Shelter HOMEWARES
(www.futureshelter.com; 56 Angove St, North Perth;
⊗ 10am-6pm Mon-Sat) Quirky clothing, gifts

and homewares designed and manufactured locally. Surrounding Angove St is an emerging hip North Perth neighbourhood.

⌂ Leederville

Leederville's Oxford St is the place for groovy boutiques, eclectic music and bookshops.

Atlas Divine CLOTHING
(Map p62; www.atlasdivine.com; 121 Oxford St; ⊙9am-9pm) Hip women's and men's clobber: jeans, quirky tees, dresses etc.

⌂ Subiaco & Kings Park

Upmarket Rokeby Rd and Hay St boast fashion, art and classy gifts.

Indigenart INDIGENOUS ART
(Map p62; www.mossensongalleries.com.au; 115 Hay St; ⊙10am-5pm Mon-Fri, 11am-4pm Sat) Reputable Indigenart carries art from around the country but with a particular focus on WA artists. Works include weavings, paintings on canvas, bark and paper, sculpture and limited-edition prints. See p251 for guidelines on the ethical purchase of Aboriginal art.

**Aboriginal Art &
Craft Gallery** INDIGENOUS ART
(www.aboriginalgallery.com.au; Fraser Ave; ⊙10.30am-4.30pm Mon-Fri, 11am-4pm Sat-Sun) Has a mixture of work from around WA; tends to be more populist than high-end or collectable.

Aspects of Kings Park ART, SOUVENIRS
(www.aspectsofkingspark.com.au; Fraser Ave; ⊙9am-5pm) Australian art, craft and books.

⌂ Other Areas

æ'lkemi CLOTHING
(www.aelkemi.com; Times Square Centre, 337 Stirling Hwy; ⊙10am-5.30pm Mon-Sat) Top WA designer's signature store, showcasing his feminine frocks and distinctive prints.

Karrinyup MALL
(www.karrinyupcentre.com.au; 200 Karrinyup Rd) Big mall east of Trigg Beach.

Garden City MALL
(www.gardencity.com.au; 125 Riseley St) Another large shopping centre; south of the river.

ⓘ Information

EMERGENCY
Police Station (☎13 14 44; www.police.wa.gov.au; 60 Beaufort St)
Sexual Assault Resource Centre (☎08-9340 1828, freecall 1800 199 888; www.kemh.health.wa.gov.au/services/sarc; ⊙24hr)

INTERNET ACCESS
State Library of WA (www.slwa.wa.gov.au; Perth Cultural Centre; ⊙9am-8pm Mon-Thu, 10am-5.30pm Fri-Sun; @ 🛜) Free wi-fi and internet access. At the time of writing, Perth City was also trialling free wi fi access in the Murray Street Mall between William St and Barrack St.

MEDIA
Look for free listings booklets, such as *Your Guide to Perth & Fremantle,* available at hostels, hotels and tourist offices.
Drum Media (www.facebook.com/drumperth) Music, film and culture listings.
Go West (www.gowesternaustralia.com.au) Backpacker magazine with information on activities throughout WA and seasonal work opportunities.
Urban Walkabout (www.urbanwalkabout.com) Handy free pocket guides covering hip eating, drinking and shopping spots in key inner-Perth neighbourhoods and Fremantle.
West Australian (www.thewest.com.au) Local newspaper with entertainment and cinema listings.
X-Press Magazine (www.xpressmag.com.au) Long-running street press and a good source of live-music information.

MEDICAL SERVICES
Lifecare Dental (☎08-9221 2777; www.dentistinperth.com.au; 419 Wellington St; ⊙8am-8pm) In Forrest Chase.
Royal Perth Hospital (☎08-9224 2244; www.rph.wa.gov.au; Victoria Sq) In the CBD.
Travel Medicine Centre (☎08-9321 7888; www.travelmed.com.au; 5 Mill St; ⊙8am-5pm Mon-Fri) Travel-specific advice and vaccinations.

MONEY
ATMs are plentiful, and there are currency-exchange facilities at the airport and major banks in the CBD.

POST
Main Post Office (GPO; ☎13 13 18; 3 Forrest Pl; ⊙8.30am-5pm Mon-Fri, 9am-12.30pm Sat)

TOURIST INFORMATION
i-City Information Kiosk (Map p52; Murray Street Mall; ⊙9.30am-4.30pm Mon-Thu & Sat, to 8pm Fri, 11am-3.30pm Sun) Volunteers answer your questions and run walking tours.

WA Visitor Centre (Map p52; ✆08-9483 1111, 1800 812 808; www.bestofwa.com.au; 55 William St; ☺9am-5.30pm Mon-Fri, 9.30am-4.30pm Sat, 11am-4.30pm Sun) A good resource for a trip anywhere in WA.

WEBSITES

www.heatseeker.com.au Gig guide and ticketing.

www.perth.citysearch.com.au Entertainment and restaurants.

www.perthnow.com.au Perth and WA news and restaurant reviews

www.scoop.com.au Entertainment.

www.showticketing.com.au Gig guide and ticketing.

www.whatson.com.au Events and travel information.

❶ Getting There & Away

AIR

For details on flights to Perth from international, interstate and other WA destinations, see the Transport chapter (p265 and p266).

BUS

Greyhound (✆1300 473 946; www.greyhound.com.au) has services from the East Perth terminal to Broome ($277 to $431, 34 hours, thrice weekly) via Geraldton, Carnarvon, Karratha and Port Hedland.

Integrity Coach Lines (Map p52; ✆08-9574 6707; www.integritycoachlines.com.au; Wellington Street Bus Station) runs services between Perth and Port Hedland ($232, 22 hours, weekly) via Mt Magnet, Cue, Meekatharra and Newman. Also has a service from Perth to Geraldton on Indian Ocean Dr via Lancelin, Jurien Bay and Cervantes.

South West Coach Lines (✆08-9261 7600; www.veoliatransportwa.com.au) focuses on the southwestern corner of WA, running services from the Esplanade Busport (some stopping at the airport) to most towns in the region, including:

Dunsborough (four hours, daily) via Mandurah, Bunbury and Busselton.

Augusta (five hours, daily) via Bunbury, Busselton, Cowaramup and Margaret River.

Manjimup (five hours, daily except weekends) via Mandurah, Bunbury, Balingup and Bridgetown.

Transwa (✆1300 662 205; www.transwa.wa.gov.au) operates services from the bus terminal at East Perth train station to/from many destinations around the state. These include:

SW1 to Augusta ($48, six hours, 12 per week) via Mandurah, Bunbury, Busselton and Dunsborough.

SW2 to Pemberton ($51, 5½ hours, thrice weekly) via Bunbury, Balingup and Bridgetown.

GS1 to Albany ($58, six hours, daily) via Mt Barker.

GE2 to Esperance ($87, 10 hours, thrice weekly) via Mundaring, York and Hyden.

N1 to Geraldton ($61, six hours, daily) and on to Northampton and Kalbarri ($76, 8½ hours, three weekly).

TRAIN

Transwa runs the following services:

Australind (twice daily) Perth to Pinjarra ($16, 1¼ hours) and Bunbury ($30, 2½ hours).

AvonLink (thrice weekly) East Perth to Toodyay ($16, 1¼ hours) and Northam ($19, 1½ hours).

Prospector (daily) East Perth to Kalgoorlie–Boulder ($82, seven hours).

❶ Getting Around

TO/FROM THE AIRPORT

The domestic and international terminals of Perth's airport are 10km and 13km east of Perth respectively, near Guildford. Taxi fares to the city are around $40 from the domestic and international terminals, and about $60 to Fremantle.

Connect (✆1300 666 806; www.perthairportconnect.com.au) runs shuttles to and from hotels and hostels in the city centre (one way/return $18/30, every 50 minutes) and in Fremantle (one way/return $33/58, approximately every 1½ hours). Prices are slightly cheaper between Perth and the domestic terminal and substantially discounted for groups of two to four people (check the website for details). Bookings are essential for all services to the airport and are recommended for services to Fremantle. No bookings are taken for shuttles from the airport to Perth's city centre.

Transperth bus 37 travels to the domestic airport from St Georges Tce, near William St ($4, 55 minutes, every 10 to 30 minutes, hourly after 7pm).

CAR & MOTORCYCLE

Driving in the city takes a bit of practice, as some streets are one way and many aren't signed. There are plenty of car-parking buildings in the central city but no free parks. For unmetered street parking you'll need to look well away from the main commercial strips and check the signs carefully.

A fun way to gad about the city is on a moped. **Scootamoré** (✆08-9380 6580; www.scootamore.com.au; 356a Rokeby Rd, Subiaco; day/week/month $45/200/400) hires 50cc scooters with helmets (compulsory) and insurance included (for those over 21, $500 excess).

PUBLIC TRANSPORT

Transperth (☎ 13 62 13; www.transperth.
wa.gov.au) operates Perth's public buses, trains
and ferries. There are Transperth information offices at Perth station (Wellington St), Wellington
St bus station, Perth underground station (off
Murray St) and the Esplanade Busport (Mounts
Bay Rd). There's a good online journey planner.

From the central city, the following fares apply
for all public transport:

Free Transit Zone (FTZ) Covers the central
commercial area, bounded (roughly) by Fraser
Ave, Kings Park Rd, Thomas St, Newcastle St,
Parry St, Lord St and the river (including the
City West and Claisebrook train stations, to the
west and east respectively).

Zone 1 Includes the city centre and the inner
suburbs ($2.70).

Zone 2 Fremantle, Guildford and the beaches
as far north as Sorrento ($4).

Zone 3 Hillarys Boat Harbour (AQWA), the
Swan Valley and Kalamunda ($4.90).

Zone 5 Rockingham ($7.10).

Zone 7 Mandurah ($9.40).

DayRider Unlimited travel after 9am weekdays
and all day on the weekend in any zone ($11).

FamilyRider Lets two adults and up to five
children travel for a total of $11 on weekends,
after 6pm weekdays and after 9am on weekdays during school holidays.

If you're in Perth for a while, consider buying a SmartRider card, covering bus, train and
ferry travel. It's $10 to purchase, then you add
value to your card. The technology deducts the
fare as you go, as long as you tap in and tap out
(touch your card to the electronic reader) every
time you travel, including within the FTZ. The
SmartRider works out 15% cheaper than buying
single tickets and automatically caps itself at
the DayRider rate if you're avoiding the morning
rush hour.

Bus

As well as regular buses the FTZ is well covered
during the day by the three free Central Area
Transit (CAT) services. The Yellow and Red CATs
operate east–west routes, Yellow sticking mainly
to Wellington St, and Red looping roughly east
on Murray St and west on Hay St. The Blue Cat
does a figure eight through Northbridge and the
south end of the city; this is the only one to run
late – until 1am on Friday and Saturday nights
only. Pick up a copy of the free timetable (widely
available on buses and elsewhere) for the exact
routes and stops. They run every five to eight
minutes during weekdays and every 15 minutes
on weekends. Digital displays at the stops advise
when the next bus is due.

The metropolitan area is serviced by a wide
network of Transperth buses. Pick up timetables

from any of the Transperth information centres
or use the online journey planner.

Ferry

The only ferry runs every 20 to 30 minutes
between Barrack Street Jetty and Mends Street
Jetty in South Perth – use it to get to the zoo or
for a bargain from-the-river glimpse of the Perth
skyline.

Train

Transperth operates five train lines from around
5.20am to midnight weekdays, and until about
2am Saturday and Sunday. Your rail ticket can
also be used on Transperth buses and ferries
within the ticket's zone. You're free to take your
bike on the train in nonpeak times. The lines and
useful stops include:

Armadale Thornlie Line Perth, Burswood.

Fremantle Line Perth, City West, West Leederville, Subiaco, Shenton Park, Swanbourne,
Cottesloe, North Fremantle, Fremantle.

Joondalup Line Esplanade, Perth Underground, Leederville.

Mandurah Line Perth Underground, Esplanade,
Rockingham, Mandurah.

Midland Line Perth, East Perth, Mt Lawley,
Guildford, Midland.

TAXI

Perth has a decent system of metered taxis,
though the distances make frequent use costly
and on busy nights you may have trouble flag-
ging one down off the street. The two main
companies are **Swan Taxis** (☎ 13 13 30; www.
swantaxis.com.au) and **Black & White** (☎ 13 10
08; www.bwtaxi.com.au); both have wheelchair-
accessible cabs.

FREMANTLE

POP 28,100

Creative, relaxed, open-minded: Fremantle's
spirit is entirely distinct from Perth's. Perhaps it has something to do with the port
and the city's working-class roots. Or the
hippies, who first set up home here a few
decades ago and can still be seen casually
bobbling down the street on old bicycles. Or
perhaps it's just that a timely 20th-century
economic slump meant that the city re-
tained an almost complete set of formerly
grand Victorian and Edwardian buildings,
creating a heritage precinct that's unique
among Australia's cities today.

Whatever, today's clean and green Freo
makes a cosy home for performers, profes-
sionals, artists and more than a few eccen-
trics. There's a lot to enjoy here – fantastic

museums, edgy galleries, pubs thrumming with live music and a thriving coffee culture. On weekend nights the city's residents vacate the main drag, leaving it to kids from the suburbs, who move in to party hard and loud.

History

This was an important area for the Wadjuk Noongar people, as it was a hub of trading paths. Some of these routes exist to this day in the form of modern roads. Before the harbour was altered, the mouth of the river was nearly covered by a sandbar and it was only a short swim from north to south. The confluence of the river and ocean, where Fremantle now stands, was known as Manjaree (sometimes translated as 'gathering place'). The Fremantle coast was called Booyeembara, while inland was Wallyalup, 'place of the eagle'.

Manjaree was mainly occupied in summer when the Wadjuk would base themselves here to fish. In winter they would head further inland, avoiding seasonal flooding.

Fremantle's European history began when the ship HMS *Challenger* landed in 1829. The ship's captain, Charles Fremantle, took possession of the whole of the west coast 'in the name of King George IV'. Like Perth, the settlement made little progress until convict labour was used. Convicts constructed most of the town's earliest buildings; some of them, such as the Round House, Fremantle Prison and Fremantle Arts Centre, are now among the oldest in WA.

As a port, Fremantle wasn't up to much until the engineer CY O'Connor created an artificial harbour in the 1890s, destroying the Wadjuks' river crossing in the process. This caused such disruption to their traditional patterns of life that it's said that a curse was placed on O'Connor; some took his later suicide at Fremantle as evidence of its effectiveness.

The port blossomed during the gold rush and many of its distinctive buildings date from this period. Economic stagnation in the 1960s and 1970s spared the streetscape from the worst ravages of modernisation. It wasn't until 1987, when Fremantle hosted the America's Cup, that it transformed itself from a sleepy port town into today's vibrant, artsy city.

The cup was lost that year, but the legacy of a redeveloped waterfront remains. In 1995 the Fremantle Dockers played their first game, quickly developing one of the most fanatical fan bases in the AFL, boosted in 2010 and 2012 by a semifinals berth. We reckon it's only a matter of time before they go all the way.

◉ Sights

Fremantle Prison HISTORIC BUILDING
(☑08-9336 9200; www.fremantleprison.com.au; 1 The Terrace; torchlight tours $25/21; ⊘9am-5.30pm) With its foreboding 5m-high walls enclosing a nearly 6-hectare site, the old convict-era prison still dominates present-day Fremantle, with its tales of adventure and hardship living on in the city's imagination. In 2010 its cultural status was recognised, along with that of 10 other penal buildings, as part of the Australian Convict Sites entry on the Unesco World Heritage list.

The first convicts were made to build their own prison, constructing it from beautiful pale limestone dug out of the hill on which it was built. From 1855 to 1991, 350,000 people were incarcerated here, although the highest numbers held at any one time were 1200 men and 58 women. Of those, 43 men and one woman were executed on-site, the last of which was serial killer Eric Edgar Cooke in 1964.

Entry to the gatehouse, including the Prison Gallery, gift shop (where you can purchase fetching arrow-printed prisoner PJs) and Convict Cafe is free. To enter the prison proper, you'll need to take a tour. During the day there are two fascinating 1¼-hour tours on offer, timed so that you can take one after the other on a combined ticket (single tour adult/child $19/10, combined adult/child $26/17), although you can return for the second tour anytime in the next fortnight.

The Doing Time Tour (departs every 30 minutes, first 10am, last 5pm) takes in the kitchens, men's cells (the original 2.1m by 1.2m convict cells are smaller than modern toilets), the black-as-hell solitary-confinement cells (the longest anyone did here was six months on bread and water), the exercise areas, the whipping post (people could be sentenced to up to 100 lashes of the cat o' nine tails, although most would die after 30), the gallows, an interesting display on the 1988 riot, and the big, light-filled chapel (daily attendance was compulsory).

The Great Escapes Tour (departs every hour, first 11.45am, last 4.45pm) introduces you to famous inmates such as bushranger and famed escape artist Moondyne Joe and bank robber Brenden Abbott, who escaped in a prison guard's uniform. It also takes in the women's prison and the rifle range.

Bookings are required for the two more intense experiences on offer. Torchlight Tours (90 minutes, adult/child $25/21, Wednesday and Friday evenings) are designed to chill, focusing on the creepy and unpleasant aspects of the prison's history. The 2½-hour Tunnels Tour (adult/child over 12yr $60/40) takes you 20m underground to tunnels built by prisoners sentenced to hard labour. You'll be kitted out in overalls and hard hats with headlamps for the descent, which includes an underground boat ride. Children must be 12 years or older for the Tunnels Tour.

Western Australian Museum – Maritime
MUSEUM

(www.museum.wa.gov.au; Victoria Quay; museum adult/child $10/3, submarine $10/3, museum & submarine $16/5; ⊙9.30am-5pm) Housed in an intriguing sail-shaped building on the harbour, just west of the city centre, this is a fascinating exploration of WA's relationship with the ocean. It faces out to the sea, which has shaped so much of the state's, and Fremantle's, destiny.

Various boats are on display, including Australia II, the famous winged-keel yacht that won the America's Cup yachting race in 1983 (ending 132 years of American domination of the competition – an achievement which is the source of much Sandgroper pride). Other boats on show include an Aboriginal bark canoe; an Indonesian outrigger canoe, introduced to the Kimberley and used by the Indigenous people; and a pearl lugger used in Broome. Even a classic 1970s panel van (complete with fur lining) makes the cut – because of its status as the surfer's vehicle of choice.

Well-presented displays cover a wide range of topics, from Aboriginal fish traps to the sandalwood trade. If you're not claustrophobic, take an hour-long tour of the submarine HMAS *Ovens*. The vessel was part of the Australian Navy's fleet from 1969 to 1997. Tours leave every half-hour from 10am to 3.30pm.

Western Australian Museum – Shipwreck Galleries
MUSEUM

(www.museum.wa.gov.au; Cliff St; admission by donation; ⊙9.30am-5pm) **FREE** Housed in an 1852 commissariat store, the Shipwreck Galleries is considered the finest display of maritime archaeology in the southern hemisphere. The highlight of the display is the **Batavia Gallery**, where a section of the hull of Dutch merchant ship *Batavia*, wrecked in 1629, is displayed. Nearby is a large stone gate, intended as an entrance to Batavia Castle, which was being carried when it sank.

Other items of interest include the inscribed pewter plate left on Cape Inscription by Willem de Vlamingh in 1697, positioned next to a replica of the plate left by Dirk Hartog in 1616 during the first confirmed European landing in WA.

Round House
HISTORIC BUILDING

(✆08-9336 6897; www.fremantleroundhouse.com.au; admission by donation; ⊙10.30am-3.30pm) **FREE** Commenced in 1830 and 1831, shortly after the founding of the colony, this odd 12-sided stone prison is the oldest surviving building in WA. It was the site of the colony's first hangings, including that of 15-year-old John Gavin (convicted of murdering his employer's son). Later, it was used for holding Aboriginal people before they were taken to Rottnest Island.

To the Noongar people, it's a sacred site because of the number of their people killed while incarcerated here. Freedom fighter Yagan was held here briefly in 1832.

On the hilltop outside is the Signal Station, where at 1pm daily a time ball and cannon blast were used to alert seamen to the correct time. The ceremony is re-enacted daily; book ahead if you want to fire the cannon.

Beneath is an impressive 1837 Whalers' Tunnel carved through sandstone and used for accessing Bathers Beach, where whales were landed and processed.

FREMANTLE FOR CHILDREN

You can let the littlies off the leash at Esplanade Reserve, watch buskers at the market, make sand castles at Bathers Beach or have a proper splash about at South or Port Beaches. Older kids might appreciate the creepier aspects of the prison and the innards of the submarine at the Maritime Museum, where they can also poke about on actual boats. Adventure World (p56) is nearby for funfair rides. Finish up with fish and chips at Fishing Boat Harbour.

Fremantle

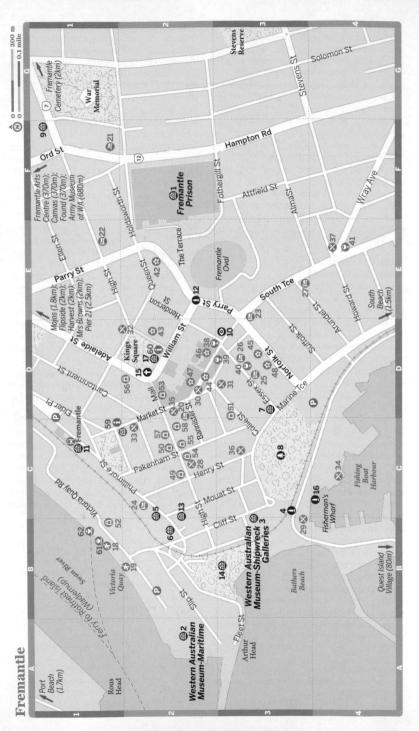

0 ———— 200 m
0 ———— 0.1 mile

Port Beach (1.7km)

Rous Head

Swan River

Ferry to Rottnest Island (Wadjemup)

Quest Island Village (80m)

Victoria Quay

Western Australian Museum–Maritime 2

Arthur Head

Bathers Beach

Fishing Boat Harbour

Fisherman's Wharf

Western Australian Museum–Shipwreck Galleries 3

Victoria Quay Rd

Phillimore St

Cliff St

Mouat St

High St

Henry St

Pakenham St

Market St

Cantonment St

Adelaide St

Parry St

Ellen St

High St

Holdsworth St

Ord St

Queen St

Henderson St

William St

Kings Square

Elder Pl

Mall

Bannister St

Essex St

Collie St

Marine Tce

Norfolk St

South Tce

Suffolk St

Arundel St

Howard St

Alma St

Attfield St

Fothergill St

Hampton Rd

Stevens St

Solomon St

Wray Ave

Stevens Reserve

Fremantle Prison 1

Fremantle Oval

War Memorial

Fremantle Cemetery (2km)

The Terrace

South Beach (1.5km)

Fremantle Arts Centre (370m); Canvas (370m); Found (370m); Army Museum of WA (680m)

Mojos (1.8km); Flipside (2km); Harvest (2km); Mrs Browns (2km); Pier 21 (2.5km)

Fremantle 11

Fremantle

◎ Top Sights
1 Fremantle Prison F2
2 Western Australian Museum
– Maritime A2
3 Western Australian Museum
– Shipwreck Galleries B3

◎ Sights
4 Bon Scott Statue C3
5 Chamber of Commerce
Building C2
6 Customs House B2
7 Esplanade Hotel.....................................D3
8 Esplanade Reserve C3
9 Fremantle Grammar School F1
10 Fremantle Markets D3
11 Fremantle Train Station.........................C1
John Curtin Statue ....(see 17)
12 Mark of the Century E2
13 Old German Consulate...........................C2
Pietro Porcelli Statue ....(see 15)
14 Round House..B3
15 St John's Anglican Church D2
16 To the Fishermen....................................C4
17 Town Hall D2

◎ Activities, Courses & Tours
Fremantle Tram Tours.................(see 17)
18 Oceanic Cruises......................................B1
19 STS Leeuwin II..B2

◎ Sleeping
20 Bannister Suites Fremantle D2
21 Fothergills of Fremantle.........................F1
22 Fremantle Colonial
Accommodation E1
23 Norfolk Hotel E3
24 Old Firestation Backpackers.................C2
25 Pirates D3
26 Port Mill B&B D3
27 Terrace Central B&B Hotel....................E3

◎ Eating
28 Cafe 55 ....C2
29 Cicerello's B3
30 Gino's..D2
31 iPho..D3

32 Juicy Beetroot...D2
33 Kakulas Sister...C2
34 Little Creatures.......................................C4
35 Maya..D2
36 Moore & Moore..C3
37 Wild Poppy E4

◎ Drinking & Nightlife
Little Creatures.............................(see 34)
Norfolk Hotel.................................(see 23)
38 Sail & Anchor D2
39 The Monk..D3
40 Whisper D3
41 Who's Your Mumma E4

◎ Entertainment
42 Fly by Night Musicians Club..................E2
43 Hoyts...D2
44 Kulcha...D2
45 Luna on SX D3
46 Metropolis Fremantle D2
47 Newport Hotel..D2
48 X-Wray Cafe D3

◎ Shopping
49 Bill Campbell Secondhand
Book Seller...C2
50 Bodkin's Bootery.....................................C2
51 Chart & Map Shop...................................D3
52 E Shed Markets..B1
53 Elizabeth's Bookshop D2
Elizabeth's Bookshop ....(see 47)
Japingka...(see 28)
54 Jarrahcorp..C2
55 Love in Tokyo...C2
56 Mills Records...D2
57 New Edition C2
58 Record Finder C2
Remedy...(see 58)

◎ Information
59 TravelLounge C1
60 Visitor Centre..D2

◎ Transport
61 Oceanic Cruises......................................B1
62 Rottnest Express.....................................B1

PERTH & FREMANTLE FREMANTLE

Fremantle Arts Centre   GALLERY
(www.fac.org.au; 1 Finnerty St; ◷10am-5pm)
FREE An impressive neo-Gothic building surrounded by lovely elm-shaded gardens, the Fremantle Arts Centre was constructed by convict labourers as a lunatic asylum in the 1860s. Saved from demolition in the 1960s, it houses interesting exhibitions and the ◐excellent Canvas (p85) cafe. During summer there are concerts, courses and workshops.

Fremantle Markets   MARKET
(www.fremantlemarkets.com.au; cnr South Tce & Henderson St; ◷8am-8pm Fri, to 6pm Sat & Sun)
FREE Originally opened in 1897, these colourful markets were reopened in 1975 and today draw slow-moving crowds, combing over souvenirs like plastic boomerangs and swan-shaped magnets. The fresh-produce section is a good place to stock up on snacks.

PERTH & FREMANTLE FREMANTLE

Gold Rush Buildings HISTORIC BUILDINGS
Fremantle boomed during the WA gold rush in the late 19th century, and many wonderful buildings remain that were constructed during, or shortly before, this period. High St, particularly around the bottom end, has some excellent examples including several old hotels.

Chamber of Commerce Building HISTORIC BUILDING
(16 Phillimore St) In its original use since 1873.

St John's Anglican Church CHURCH
(Kings Sq) Built 1882.

Fremantle Grammar School HISTORIC BUILDING
(200 High St) Built as an Anglican public school in 1885.

Town Hall HISTORIC BUILDING
(Kings Sq) Opened on Queen Victoria's jubilee in 1887.

Samson House HISTORIC BUILDING
(cnr Ellen & Ord Sts) A well-preserved 1888 colonial home, owned by the National Trust but not currently open to the public.

Esplanade Hotel HISTORIC BUILDING
(Marine Tce) Attractive colonnaded hotel, built in 1896.

Old German Consulate HISTORIC BUILDING
(5 Mouat St) Built 1903; now a B&B.

Fremantle Train Station HISTORIC BUILDING
(Phillimore St) Built from Donnybrook sandstone in 1907; we're not sure why the swans are white rather than black.

Customs House HISTORIC BUILDING
(cnr Cliff & Phillimore Sts) Built in 1908 in a Georgian style.

Public Sculptures MONUMENTS
Enlivening Fremantle's streets are numerous bronze sculptures, many by local artist Greg James (www.gregjamessculpture.com). Perhaps the most popular, certainly with black-clad pilgrims, is the statue of **Bon Scott** (1946–80) strutting on a Marshall amplifier in Fishing Boat Harbour. The AC/DC singer moved to Fremantle with his family in 1956, and his ashes are interred in **Fremantle Cemetery** (Carrington St); it's reputedly the most-visited grave in Australia, with many travellers stopping in for 'a beer with Bon'. Enter the cemetery at the entrance near the corner of High and Carrington Sts.

Bon's plaque is on the left around 15m along the path.

Also in Fishing Boat Harbour is **To The Fishermen** (Fishing Boat Harbour), a cluster of bronze figures, unloading and carrying their catch up from the wharf. There's a lively statue of former member for Fremantle and wartime Labor prime minister **John Curtin** (1885–1945) in Kings Sq, outside the Town Hall. Nearby is a Greg James sculpture of fellow sculptor **Pietro Porcelli** (1872–1943), in the act of making a bust.

Another quirky bronze is **Mark of the Century** (Parry St) outside Fremantle Oval. For those not au fait with AFL, a mark is where a player cleanly catches a kicked ball, and the mark in question was by South Fremantle's John Gerovich in 1956. Gerovich is depicted leaping boldly above his opposing player Ray French.

Beaches & Parks BEACHES
There are plenty of green spaces around Fremantle, including **Esplanade Reserve** (Marine Tce), shaded by Norfolk Island pines and dividing the city from Fishing Boat Harbour.

Although you could theoretically swim at neighbouring **Bathers Beach**, most people content themselves with wandering along the sand here and save the soaking for beaches further from the port. **South Beach** is sheltered, swimmable, only 1.5km from the city centre and on the free CAT bus route. The next major beach is **Coogee Beach**, 6km further south.

Army Museum of WA MUSEUM
(www.armymuseumwa.com.au; Burt St; adult/child $10/7; ⊙ 11am-4pm Wed-Sun) Situated within the imposing Artillery Barracks, this little museum pulls out the big guns, literally. Howitzers and tanks line up outside, while inside you'll find cabinets full of uniforms and medals.

 Activities

Fremantle Trails WALKING
(www.fremantlewa.com.au) Pick up trailcards from the visitor centre for the 11 self-guided walking tours on offer: Art & Culture, Convict, CY O'Connor (a pioneering civil engineer), Discovery (a Fremantle once-over), Fishing Boat Harbour, Hotels & Breweries, Maritime Heritage, Manjaree Heritage (Indigenous), Retail & Fashion, Waterfront and Writers.

Oceanic Cruises WHALE WATCHING
(☑ 08-9325 1191; www.oceaniccruises.com.au;
adult/child $67/29; ⊘ mid-Sep–early Dec) De-
parts B Shed, Victoria Quay, at 10.15am for
a two-hour tour. Days of operation vary by
month, so check the website.

STS Leeuwin II SAILING
(☑ 08-9430 4105; www.sailleeuwin.com; Berth
B; adult/child $95/60) Take a trip on a 55m,
three-masted tall ship; see the website for
details of breakfast, afternoon or twilight
sails. Most sailings are from Friday to Sunday and on holidays.

Tours

Fremantle Tram Tours CITY
(☑ 08-9433 6674; www.fremantletrams.com.au;
departs Town Hall) Looking like a heritage
tram, this bus departs from the Town Hall
on an all-day hop-on, hop-off circuit around
the city (adult/child $24/5). The Ghostly
Tour (adult/child $70/50) runs from 6.45pm
to 10.30pm Friday and visits the prison,
Round House and Fremantle Arts Centre
(former asylum) by torchlight. Combos include: Lunch & Tram (adult/child $79/42),
which is the tram plus lunch cruise on river;
Triple Tour (adult/child $85/40), the tram,
river cruise and Perth sightseeing bus; Tram
& Prison (adult/child $42/13), the tram and
prison tour

Captain Cook Cruises CRUISES
(Map p52; ☑ 08-9325 3341; www.captaincookcruis
es.com.au; C Shed) Cruises between Fremantle
and Perth (adult/child $25/15), departing
Fremantle at 11.15am, 12.45pm and 3.45pm
(the last is one-way only). A three-hour
lunch cruise departs at 12.45pm (adult/child
$62/41).

**Fremantle Indigenous
Heritage Tours** WALKING TOUR
(☑ 08-9431 7878; www.indigenouswa.com; adult/
child $25/15; ⊘ 10.30am daily) Highly regarded
tour covering the history of Fremantle and
the Noongar and Wadjuk people. Book
through the Fremantle visitors centre.

Two Feet & A Heartbeat WALKING TOUR
(☑ 1800 459 388; www.twofeet.com.au; per person
$20-40; ⊘ 10am daily) Operated by a younger,
energetic crew, with the focus on Fremantle's often rambunctious history. 'Tight Arse
Tuesdays' are good value.

Festivals & Events

West Coast Blues 'n' Roots Festival MUSIC
(www.westcoastbluesnroots.com.au) Held late
March to early April and interpreting its
remit widely: recent festivals have featured
Steve Earle, Grace Jones, Elvis Costello and
My Morning Jacket.

Blessing of the Fleet RELIGIOUS
(Esplanade Reserve, Fishing Boat Harbour) An October tradition since 1948, brought to Fremantle by immigrants from Molfetta, Italy.
It includes the procession of the Molfettese
Our Lady of Martyrs statue (carried by men)
and the Sicilian Madonna di Capo d'Orlando
(carried by women), from St Patrick's Basili-
ca (47 Adelaide St) to Fishing Boat Harbour,
where the blessing takes place.

Fremantle Festival CULTURE
(www.fremantle.wa.gov.au) In November, the
city's streets and concert venues come alive
with parades and performances in Australia's longest-running festival.

Sleeping

Old Firestation Backpackers HOSTEL $
(☑ 08-9430 5454; www.old-firestation.net; 18 Phillimore St; dm $27-31, d $72; @ 🛜) There's entertainment aplenty in this converted fire
station: free internet, foosball, movies and a
sunny courtyard. Dorms have natural light
and the afternoon sea breeze fluttering in,
and there's a female-only section. The hippy
vibe culminates in late-night guitar-led sing-
alongs around the campfire; bring earplugs
if you value sleep. Yoga sessions were on offer when we last dropped by.

Pirates HOSTEL $
(☑ 08-9335 6635; www.piratesbackpackers.com.
au; 11 Essex St; dm $29-31, d $65; @ 🛜) Attracting a diverse international crew, this sun-
and fun-filled hostel in the thick of the Freo
action is a top spot to socialise. Rooms are
small and reasonably basic, but the bathrooms are fresh and clean. The kitchen area
is well equipped, there's a shady courtyard,
and eye-catching marine murals remind you
that an ocean swim is minutes away.

Woodman Point Holiday Park CAMPGROUND $
(☑ 08-9434 1433; www.aspenparks.com.au; 132
Cockburn Rd; sites for 2 people $45, d $135-255;
※ @ 🛜 ≋) A particularly pleasant spot,
10km south of Fremantle. It's usually quiet,
and its location makes it feel more summer
beach holiday than outer-Freo staging post.

Coogee Beach Holiday Park CARAVAN PARK $
(☑08-9418 1810; www.aspenparks.com.au; 3 Powell Rd; sites $50, d $120-199; ✹🤶) No camp sites, only paved caravan spaces and a range of cabins, motel units and chalets. It's popular with young families, and has a tennis court and cafe. Off Cockburn Rd.

Norfolk Hotel HOTEL $$
(☑08-9335 5405; www.norfolkhotel.com.au; 47 South Tce; s/d without bathroom $100/140, d with bathroom $180; ✹🤶) While eucalypts and elms stand quietly in the sun-streaked beer garden, the old limestone Norfolk harbours a secret upstairs: its rooms. Far above your standard pub digs, they've all been tastefully decorated in muted tones and crisp white linen, and there's a communal sitting room. It can be noisy on weekends, but the bar closes at midnight.

Fothergills of Fremantle B&B $$
(☑08-9335 6784; www.fothergills.net.au; 18-22 Ord St; r $175-225; ✹🤶) Naked bronze women sprout from the front garden, while a life-size floral cow shelters on the verandah of these neighbouring mansions on the hill. Inside, the decor is in keeping with their venerable age (built 1892), aside from the contemporary art scattered about, which includes some wonderful Aboriginal pieces. Breakfast is served in the sunny conservatory.

Port Mill B&B B&B $$
(☑08-9433 3832; www.portmillbb.com.au; 3/17 Essex St; r $179-299; ✹🤶) One of the most luxurious B&Bs in town, this is clearly the love child of Paris and Freo. Crafted from local limestone (it was built in 1862 as a mill), inside it's all modern Parisian-style, with gleaming taps, contemporary French furniture and wrought-iron balconies. French doors open out to the sun-filled decks, where you can tinkle the china on your breakfast platter.

Terrace Central B&B Hotel B&B $$
(☑08-9335 6600; www.terracecentral.com.au; 79-85 South Tce; d $190-215; ✹@🤶) Terrace Central may be a character-filled B&B at heart, but its larger size gives it the feel of a boutique hotel. The main section has been created from an 1888 bakery and an adjoining row of terrace houses. There are also modern one- and two-bedroom apartments out the back. You'll find ample off-street parking.

Bannister Suites Fremantle HOTEL $$
(☑08-9435 1288; www.bannistersuitesfremantle.com.au; 22 Bannister St; r from $199; ✹) Modern and fresh, boutiquey Bannisters is a stylish highlight of central Fremantle's accommodation scene. It's worth paying extra for one of the suites with the deep balconies, where you can enjoy views over the rooftops while lounging on the upmarket outdoor furniture.

Fremantle Colonial Accommodation APARTMENT $$
(☑08-9430 6568; www.fremantlecolonialaccommodation.com.au; 215 High St; d from $165; ✹@) Rambling two-storey terrace or historic prison cottage? Whichever you choose, both embrace the colonial theme with gusto. White-painted wrought-iron bed frames, floral quilt covers and dusty-pink walls open out onto lacework balconies.

Number Six APARTMENT $$
(☑08-9299 7107; www.numbersix.com.au; studios/1-bedroom apt from $105/150; ✹) Self-contained and stylish studios, apartments and houses available for overnight to long-term stays in great locations around Freo.

Quest Harbour Village APARTMENT $$$
(☑08-9430 3888; www.questharbourvillage.com.au; Mews Rd, Challenger Harbour; apt from $292; ✹🤶) At the end of a wharf, these attractive, two-storey, sandstone and brick one- to three-bedroom apartments make the most of their nautical setting; one-bedroom units have views over the car park to the Fishing Boat Harbour, while the others directly front the marina. Downstairs, rooms are light and simple, and kitchens are fully equipped.

Pier 21 APARTMENT $$$
(☑08-9336 2555; www.pier21.com.au; 9 John St; apt from $320; ✹@🤶) Pier 21 is in a tucked-away spot on the riverside in North Freo. It's more like a motel than you'd expect for the price, but there's a tennis court, pool and spa.

✗ Eating

Although it doesn't have Perth's variety of fine-dining places (or, thankfully, its prices), eating and drinking your way around town are two of the great pleasures of Freo. The main areas to browse before you graze are around the town centre, Fishing Boat Harbour and East Freo's George St and riverbank. People-watching from outdoor tables on South Tce is a legitimate lifestyle choice. The Fremantle Markets are a good place to stock up on fruit and other picnic items.

City Centre

Moore & Moore
CAFE $

(www.mooreandmoorecafe.com; 46 Henry St; mains $8-22; ⊘8am-4pm; 🐾) An urban-chic cafe that spills into the adjoining art gallery and overflows into a flagstoned courtyard. With great coffee, good cooked breakfasts, pastries, wraps and free wi-fi, it's a great place to linger. Look forward to the company of a few Freo hipsters, and the international crew of students studying at Fremantle's University of Notre Dame.

IPho
VIETNAMESE $

(1/25 Collie St; mains $12.50-22; ⊘11.30am-9.30pm Tue-Sun) This place has a damn fine name for a Vietnamese restaurant and is excellent value for Fremantle. Settle into the mod-Asian decor and multitask your way through the menu including crispy *cha gio* (spring rolls), plump *banh xeo* (Vietnamese crepes) and hearty noodle-filled bowls of *pho*. A hip young crew delivers everything with a smile, making sure you leave very 'appy.

Juicy Beetroot
VEGETARIAN $

(mains $10-15; ⊘10am-4pm Mon-Fri) 🍃 This popular meat-free zone serves tasty vego and vegan dishes of the wholefood variety (tofu burgers, curries etc), and zingy fresh juices. Look past the bad New Age art to the posters advertising Freo's more eclectic events. It's tucked up an alley off High St with outdoor seating.

Kakulas Sister
DELI $

(29-31 Market St; ⊘9am-5pm Mon-Fri, 10am-5pm Sat & Sun) This provedore, packed with nuts, quince paste and Italian rocket seeds, is a cook's dream, and is excellent for energy-filled snacks. If you've been to Kakulas Bros in Northbridge, you'll know the deal.

Cafe 55
ASIAN $

(55 High St; mains $8-12.50; ⊘7.30am-3pm Mon-Fri, 9am-3pm Sat) Asian food with a Freo feel, this bright cafe's fragrant soups - *pho, bun bo Hue* (spicy beef noodle soup) and Malaysian laksa - are fantastic. Plus there are baguettes just like you'd get in the former French colony of Vietnam.

Canvas
CAFE $$

(www.canvasatfremantleartscentre.com; Fremantle Arts Centre; mains $10-25; ⊘8.30am-4pm) Freo's best cafe is stylishly concealed in the Fremantle Arts Centre with a diverse menu channelling Middle Eastern, Spanish and North African influences. Breakfast highlights are the baked-egg dishes - try the Israeli-style Red Shakshuka or the Spanish eggs Flamenco - and lunch presents everything from citrus-cured salmon, scallops or WA's best beef burger. Eclectic beers and wines too.

Maya
INDIAN $$

(📝08-9335 2796; www.mayarestaurant.com.au; 77 Market St; mains $18-29; ⊘6pm-late Tue-Sun, noon-3pm Fri) Maya's white tablecloths and wooden chairs signal classic style without the pomp. Its well-executed meals have made it a popular local spot for years, earning it the reputation of WA's best Indian restaurant.

Gino's
CAFE $$

(www.ginoscafe.com.au; 1 South Tce; mains $15-30; ⊘6am-late; 🐾) Old-school Gino's is Freo's most famous cafe, and while it's become a tourist attraction in its own right, the locals still treat it as their second living room, only with better coffee. For the uninitiated, you'll need to order and pay and then collect your own coffee.

Fishing Boat Harbour

Little Creatures
PUB $$

(www.littlecreatures.com.au; 40 Mews Rd; pizzas $18-34, shared plates $9-24; ⊘10am-midnight) Little Creatures is classic Freo: harbour views, fantastic brews (made on the premises) and excellent food. In a cavernous converted boatshed overlooking the harbour, it can get chaotic at times, but a signature Pale Ale with a wood-fired pizza will be worth the wait. More substantial shared plates include chickpea tagine and pork belly with fennel. No bookings.

Cicerello's
FISH & CHIPS $$

(www.cicerellos.com.au; 44 Mews Rd; fish & chips $14, mains $17-28; ⊘10am-late) Since 1903, Cicerello's has been a quintessential Freo experience. Leave the kids staring at the large aquariums (filled with living coral, bright fish, an octopus and a hemmed-in shark), choose your fish and chips, then pick a spot out on the boardwalk and soak up the sun - just watch those seagulls.

✖ East & North Fremantle

Flipside
BURGERS $
(www.flipsideburgers.com.au; 239 Queen Victoria St; $10.50-13.50; ⊙5.30-9.30pm Tue-Thu, noon-2.30pm Thu, noon-9pm Fri-Sun) Gourmet burgers with the option of dining in next door at Mrs Browns (p86).

Harvest
MODERN AUSTRALIAN $$$
(⌨08-9336 1831; www.harvestrestaurant.net.au; 1 Harvest Rd; mains $38-42; ⊙6pm-late Tue-Thu, noon-late Fri, 8am-late Sat, 8am-3pm Sun) First you'll find a green-painted cottage, complete with picket fence, next to some fields. Swing through the heavy, fuchsia-painted metal doors and into the dark-wood dining room lined with artworks and curios. Then settle down to comforting Mod Oz dishes cooked with panache. Breakfast and lunch are less expensive.

✖ South Fremantle

Wild Poppy
CAFE $$
(2 Wray Ave; breakfast $6-16, lunch $16-22; ⊙7am-4pm; 🐾) Lace doilies, kitschy furniture and a stupendous collection of retro portaits and landscapes make this hip cafe in up-and-coming South Freo worth seeking out. Soup and salad specials team with good coffee, beer and cider, and the chilli eggs are a great way to start the day. For lunch, ask if the Cape Malay fish curry is on the menu.

♟ Drinking & Entertainment

Most of Fremantle's big pubs are lined up along South Tce and there are some character-filled old taverns on High St. Freo's pubs have long been incubators for local musos, including world-famous-in-Australia acts like Eskimo Joe and John Butler. A couple of interesting smaller bars also lurk in North and South Fremantle.

Little Creatures
MICROBREWERY
(www.littlecreatures.com.au; 40 Mews Rd, Fishing Boat Harbour; ⊙10am-midnight) Try the Pale Ale and Pilsner, and other beers and ciders under the White Rabbit and Pipsqueak labels. Pop in at 4pm on Thursday for its regular 'Firkin Experiment' where limited one-off brews are given a whirl. Creatures Loft is an adjacent lounge bar with regular live entertainment and DJs. Live jazz kicks off at 4pm on Sunday.

Who's Your Mumma
BAR
(cnr Wray Ave & South Tce; ⊙4pm-late Mon-Thu, 8am-late Fri-Sun) Industrial-chic lightbulbs and polished-concrete floors are softened by recycled timber at the laidback Who's Your Mumma. An eclectic crew of South Freo locals crowd in for great-value combo specials (around $15) including 'Taco Tuesdays' and 'Schnitzel Mondays'. Other moreish bar snacks include fluffy pork buns, and it opens for a leisurely brekky at the weekend.

Sail & Anchor
PUB
(www.sailandanchor.com.au; 64 South Tce; ⊙11am-midnight Mon-Sat, to 10pm Sun) Built in 1854, this Fremantle landmark has been impressively restored to recall much of its former glory. Downstairs is big and beer focused, with 43 taps delivering a stunning range of local and international beers. Welcome to the best destination for the travelling beer geek in Western Australia. Occasional live music completes the picture.

Mrs Browns
BAR
(www.mrsbrownbar.com.au; 241 Queen Victoria St; ⊙4.30pm-late Tue-Thu, 1pm-late Fri-Sun) Exposed bricks and a copper bar combine with retro and antique furniture to create North Fremantle's most atmospheric bar. The music could include all those cult bands you thought were *your* personal secret, and an eclectic menu of beer, wine and tapas targets the more discerning, slightly older bar hound. And you can order in burgers from Flipside (p86) next door.

Norfolk Hotel
PUB
(www.norfolkhotel.com.au; 47 South Tce; ⊙11am-midnight Mon-Sat, to 10pm Sun) Slow down to Freo pace and take your time over one of the many beers on tap at this 1887 pub. Lots of interesting guest brews create havoc for the indecisive drinker, and the pub food and pizzas are very good. We love the heritage limestone courtyard, especially when sunlight peeks through the elms and eucalypts.

The Monk
CRAFT BEER
(www.themonk.com.au; 33 South Tce; ⊙11.30am-late) Park yourself on the spacious front terrace or in the chic interior, partly fashioned from recycled railway sleepers, and enjoy the Monk's own brews (kolsch, mild, wheat, porter, rauch and pale ale). The bar snacks and pizzas are also good, and guest beers and

regular seasonal brews always draw a knowledgeable crowd of local craft-beer nerds.

Whisper
WINE BAR

(www.whisperwinebar.com.au; 1/15 Essex St; ⊘noon-late Wed-Sun) Yes, there is more to Freo than craft beer. In a lovely heritage building, this classy French-themed wine bar also does shared plates of charcuterie and cheese.

Fly by Night Musicians Club
LIVE MUSIC

(www.flybynight.org; Parry St) Variety is the key at Fly by Night, a not-for-profit club that's been run by musos for musos for years. All kinds perform here, and many local bands made a start here. It's opposite the car park below the old Fremantle Prison.

Kulcha
CLUB, LIVE MUSIC

(☑08-9336 4544; www.kulcha.com.au; 13 South Tce, 1st fl) World music of all sorts is the focus here. At the time we researched the line-up included Gypsy swing, Indigenous Australian reggae and rap, and melancholy Portuguese *fado*. Book ahead.

X-Wray Cafe
LIVE MUSIC

(http://xwraymusic.tumblr.com; 3-13 Essex St; ⊘10am-11pm Mon-Wed, 9am-midnight Thu-Sat, 8am-9pm Sun) There's something on every night (live jazz, rock, open piano) at this hipster hang-out, comprising a smallish indoor area and a large canvas-covered terrace. Light meals are available.

Mojo's
LIVE MUSIC

(www.mojosbar.com.au; 237 Queen Victoria St, North Fremantle; ⊘7pm-late) Good old Mojo's is one of Freo's longest running live-music venues. Local and national bands (mainly Aussie rock and indie) and DJs play at this small place, and there's a sociable beer garden out the back. First Friday of the month is reggae night; every Monday is open-mic night.

Metropolis Fremantle
LIVE MUSIC

(www.metropolisfremantle.com.au; 58 South Tce) A great space to watch a gig, and is also a proper nightclub on the weekends. International and popular Australian bands and DJs perform here.

Newport Hotel
LIVE MUSIC

(www.thenewport.com; 2 South Tce; ⊘noon-midnight Mon-Sat, to 10pm Sun) Local bands play Saturday and Sunday, with DJs other nights. The recently opened Tiki Bar is worth a kitsch cocktail or two.

Luna on SX
CINEMA

(www.lunapalace.com.au; Essex St) Art-house films; set back in a lane between Essex and Norfolk Sts.

Hoyts
CINEMA

(www.hoyts.com.au) Blockbusters at **Millennium** (Collie St) and **Queensgate** (William St).

🔒 Shopping

The bottom end of High St is the place for interesting and quirky shopping. Fashion stores run along Market St, towards the train station. Queen Victoria St in North Fremantle is the place to go for antiques. Don't forget Fremantle Markets for clothes, souvenirs and knick-knacks.

Japingka
INDIGENOUS ART

(www.japingka.com.au; 47 High St; ⊘10am-5.30pm Mon-Fri, noon-5pm Sat & Sun) Specialising in Aboriginal fine art, from WA and beyond. Purchases come complete with extensive notes about the works and the artists that painted them.

New Edition
BOOKS

(www.newedition.com.au; 82 High St; ⊘7.30am-6pm Mon-Sat, 9am-6pm Sun) A bookworm's dream with comfy armchairs for browsing and a funky cafe attached. See you in a leisurely three hours.

Jarrahcorp
FURNITURE

(www.jarrahcorp.com.au; cnr High & Pakenham Sts; ⊘11am-4pm Mon-Sat, noon-4pm Sun) Traditional and contemporary furniture and gifts crafted from jarrah and marri timber salvaged from old buildings or ancient logs. At the time of writing, the owner was also planning on opening a wine bar called Epicure adjacent to the shop.

Found
ARTS & CRAFTS

(www.fac.org.au; 1 Finnerty St; ⊘10am-5pm) The Fremantle Arts Centre shop stocks an inspiring range of WA art and craft.

Love in Tokyo
CLOTHING

(www.loveintokyo.com.au; 61-63 High St; ⊘10am-5pm Mon-Sat, 1-5pm Sun) Local designer turning out gorgeously fashioned fabrics for women.

Elizabeth's Bookshop
BOOKS

(www.elizabethsbookshop.com.au) One of Australia's biggest second-hand booksellers, with a staggering range. Elizabeth's is a Fremantle institution with branches in **Fremantle** (High Street Mall; ⊘9am-6pm) and

South Terrace (8 South Tce; ⊘9am-10.30pm Sun-Thu).

Record Finder   MUSIC
(87 High St; ⊘10am-5pm) A treasure trove of old vinyl, including rarities and collectables.

Bodkin's Bootery   SHOES
(www.bodkinsbootery.com; 72 High St; ⊘9am-5pm Mon-Sat, noon-5pm Sun) Men's and women's boots and hats.

Chart & Map Shop   MAPS
(www.chartandmapshop.com.au; 14 Collie St; ⊘10am-5pm) Maps and travel guides.

Bill Campbell
Secondhand Book Seller   BOOKS
(48 High St; ⊘10am-5pm Mon-Fri, noon-5pm Sat & Sun) For those out-of-print Penguin classics you always meant to read.

Remedy   GIFTS
(www.remedyonline.net.au; 95 High St; ⊘9am-5pm) An eclectic collection of goodies, including kids' clothes, adults' tees, gifts and the Aesop range of toiletries.

Mills Records   MUSIC
(www.mills.com.au; 22 Adelaide St; ⊘9am-5pm Mon-Sat, noon-5pm Sun) Music, including some rarities, and tickets. Check out the 'Local's Board' for recordings by Freo and WA acts.

E Shed Markets   MARKET
(www.eshedmarkets.com.au; ⊘market 9am-5pm Fri-Sun, food court to 8pm; 🔊) An old wharf shed with market stalls, a food court, cafes and bars.

❶ Information

For free wi-fi, try Moore & Moore (p85), or the FREbytes hot spot in the vicinity of the Town Hall and library.

Fremantle City Library (🖉08-9432 9766; www.frelibrary.wordpress.com; Kings Sq, Town Hall; ⊘9.30am-5.30pm Mon, Fri & Sat, to 8pm Tue-Thu; @ 🔊) Free wi-fi and internet terminals.

Fremantle Hospital (🖉08-9431 3333; www.fhhs.health.wa.gov.au; Alma St)

Post Office (🖉13 13 18; 1/13 Market St; ⊘9am-5pm Mon-Fri)

TravelLounge (🖉08-9335 8776; www.thetravellounge.com.au; 16 Market St; internet per hr $5; @) Private agency offering information, bookings and internet terminals.

Visitor Centre (🖉08-9431 7878; www.fremantlewa.com.au; Kings Sq, Town Hall; ⊘9am-5pm Mon-Fri, 10am-3pm Sat, 11.30am-2.30pm Sun) Free maps and brochures, and bookings for accommodation, tours and hire cars. Check the website for what's on.

❶ Getting There & Around

Fremantle sits within Zone 2 of the Perth public-transport system (Transperth) and is only 30 minutes away by train. There are numerous buses between Perth's city centre and Fremantle, including routes 103, 106, 107, 111 and 158.

Another very pleasant way to get here from Perth is by the 1¼-hour river cruise run by Captain Cook Cruises (p83).

There are numerous one-way streets and parking meters in Freo. It's easy enough to travel by foot or on the free CAT bus service, which takes in all the major sights on a continuous loop every 10 minutes from 7.30am to 6.30pm on weekdays, until 9pm on Friday and 10am to 6.30pm on the weekend.

Bicycles (Kings Sq, Fremantle Visitors Centre; ⊘9.30am-4.30pm Mon-Fri, to 3.30pm Sat, 10.30am-3.30pm Sun) can be rented for free at the visitor centre, an ideal way to get around Freo's storied streets. A refundable bond of $200 applies.

Around Perth

Best Places to Eat

➡ RiverBank Estate (p106)

➡ Dear Friends (p106)

➡ M on the Point (p98)

➡ Cervantes Country Club (p116)

➡ Rustico (p97)

Best Places to Stay

➡ Faversham House (p108)

➡ Amble Inn (p116)

➡ Mundaring Weir Hotel (p103)

➡ Rottnest Island Authority Cottages (p94)

➡ Lancelin Lodge YHA (p114)

Why Go?

Although Western Australia (WA) is huge, you don't have to travel too far from the capital to treat yourself to a tantalising taste of what the state has to offer. A day trip could see you frolicking with wild dolphins, snorkelling with sea lions, scooping up brilliant-blue crabs or spotting bilbies in the bush. Active types can find themselves canoeing, rafting, surfing, windsurfing, sandboarding, diving, skydiving and ballooning. Those who prefer pursuits less likely to ruffle one's hair can linger at vineyards or craft breweries, settle down for a culinary feast, or explore historic towns classified by the National Trust.

We've designed this chapter so that the main headings can be tackled as day trips, or better still, overnighters. If you're embarking on a longer trip, whether north, south or east, you'll find your first stop within these pages.

When to Go
Mandurah

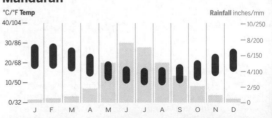

Mar Good beach weather and a fine time to spot thrombolites in Lake Clifton.

Jun Food and wine excellence at the Avon Valley Gourmet Food & Wine Festival in Northam.

Aug Wildflowers bloom, and brave paddlers take on the Avon River Descent in Northam.

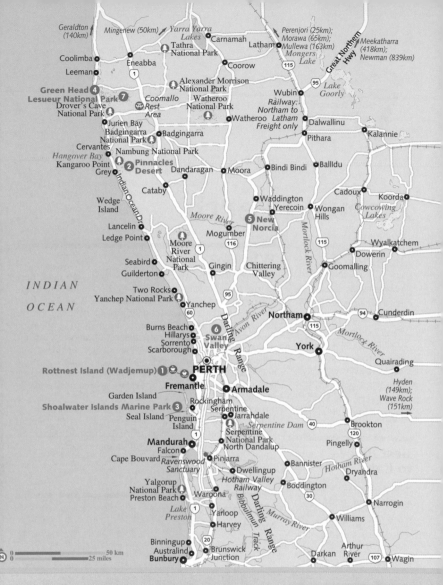

Geraldton (140km)
Mingenew (50km)
Yarra Yarra Lakes
Carnamah
Perenjori (25km); Morawa (65km); Mullewa (163km)
Meekatharra (418km); Newman (839km)

Coolimba
Tathra National Park
Latham
Mongers Lake

Leeman
Eneabba
Coorow
115

Green Head 4
Lesueur National Park 7
Alexander Morrison National Park
Wubin
Railway: Northam to Latham Freight only
Lake Goorly
95

Drover's Cave National Park
Coomallo Rest Area
Watheroo National Park
Watheroo
Dalwallinu

Jurien Bay
Badgingarra
Badgingarra National Park
Badgingarra
Pithara
Kalannie

Cervantes
Nambung National Park
Ballidu

Kangaroo Point 2 Pinnacles Desert
Dandaragan
Moora
Bindi Bindi
Cadoux
Koorda

Grey
Cataby
Waddington
Yerecoin
Wongan Hills
Cowcowing Lakes

Wedge Island
Moore River
5 New Norcia
Wyalkatchem

Lancelin
Mogumber
116
Mortlock River
115
Dowerin

Ledge Point
Moore River National Park
Gingin
Chittering Valley
Goomalling

Seabird
Guilderton
95
Avon River

INDIAN
Two Rocks
Yanchep National Park
Yanchep
60
Northam
94
Cunderlin

OCEAN
Burns Beach
Hillarys
Sorrento
Scarborough
Darling Range
115
Mortlock River

Swan Valley
York
Quairading

Rottnest Island (Wadjemup) 1
PERTH
Hyden (149km); Wave Rock (151km)

Fremantle
Armadale

Garden Island
Shoalwater Islands Marine Park 3
Rockingham
Serpentine
Jarrahdale
Serpentine Dam
40
Brookton

Seal Island
Penguin Island
Serpentine National Park
North Dandalup
Pingelly
120

Mandurah
Falcon
Pinjarra
Bannister
Hotham River
Dryandra

Cape Bouvard
Ravenswood Sanctuary
Dwellingup
Boddington

Yalgorup National Park
Preston Beach
Waroona
Hotham Valley Railway
30
Narrogin

Lake Preston
Yarloop
Harvey
Darling Range
Murray River
Williams

Binningup
Australind
Bunbury
20
Brunswick Junction
Darkan
Arthur River
107
Wagin

0 ——— 50 km
0 ——— 25 miles

Around Perth Highlights

1 Cycling your way to a private slice of coastal paradise on **Rottnest Island** (Wadjemup; p91), then spending the afternoon swimming, sunning and snorkelling

2 Enjoying a sublime sunset over the other-worldly **Pinnacles Desert** (p114)

3 Getting chipper with Flipper while palling about with scores of wild dolphins in **Shoalwater Islands Marine Park** (p96) off Rockingham

4 Splashing about with sea lions at **Green Head** (p117)

5 Exploring the intriguing monastery town of **New Norcia** (p110)

6 Getting your foodie fix at the vineyards, breweries and artisan producers of the **Swan Valley** (p104)

7 Immersing yourself in the wonderful wildflowers of the **Lesueur National Park** (p115)

ROTTNEST ISLAND (WADJEMUP)

POP 475

'Rotto' has long been the family holiday playground of choice for Perth locals. Although it's only about 19km offshore from Fremantle, this car-free, off-the-grid slice of paradise, ringed by secluded beaches and bays, feels a million miles from the metropolis.

Cycling around the 11km-long, 4.5km-wide island is a real pleasure; just ride around and pick your own bit of beach to spend the day on. You're bound to spot quokkas on your journey. These are the island's only native land mammals, but you might also spot New Zealand fur seals splashing around off magical **West End**; dolphins; and, in season, whales. King skinks are common, sunning themselves on the roads until you draw near – and then they're just as likely to scuttle into the path of your bike as they are to scuttle in the opposite direction.

Snorkelling, fishing, surfing and diving are also all excellent on the island. In fact, there's not a lot to do here that's not outdoors, so you're better off postponing your day trip if the weather is bad. It can be unpleasant when the wind really kicks up.

Rotto is also the site of annual schoolleavers' and end-of-uni-exams parties, a time when the island is overrun by kids 'getting blotto on Rotto'. Depending on your age, it's either going to be the best time you've ever had or the worst – check the calendar before proceeding.

In early September, the annual **Rottofest** (http://rottofest.com.au) immerses the island in two days of music, film and comedy.

History

The island was originally called Wadjemup (place across the water), but Wadjuk oral history recalls that it was joined to the mainland before being cut off by rising waters. Modern scientists date that occurrence to before 6500 years ago, making these memories some of the world's oldest. Archaeological finds suggest that the island was inhabited 30,000 years ago, but not after it was separated from the mainland.

Dutch explorer Willem de Vlamingh claimed discovery of the island in 1696 and named it Rotte-nest ('rat's nest', in Dutch) because of the king-sized 'rats' (which were actually quokkas) he saw there.

From 1838 it was used as a prison for Aboriginal men and boys from all around the state. At least 3670 people were incarcerated here, in harsh conditions, with around 370 dying (at least five were hanged). Although there were no new prisoners after 1903 (by which time holiday-makers from the mainland had already discovered the island), some existing prisoners served their sentences until 1931. Even before the prison was built, Wadjemup was considered a 'place of the spirits', and it's been rendered even more sacred to indigenous people because of the hundreds of their people, including prominent resistance leaders, who died there. Many avoid it to this day.

During WWI, approximately a thousand men of German or Austrian extraction were incarcerated here, their wives and children left to fend for themselves on the mainland. Ironically most of the 'Austrians' were actually Croats who objected to Austro-Hungarian rule of their homeland. Internment resumed during WWII, although at that time it was mainly WA's Italian population who were imprisoned.

There's an ongoing push to return the island to its original name. One suggested compromise is to adopt a dual name, Wadjemup/Rottnest.

⦿ Sights

Most of Rottnest's historic buildings, built mainly by Aboriginal prisoners, are grouped around Thomson Bay, where the ferry lands.

Quod & Aboriginal Burial Ground   HISTORIC SITE

(Kitson St) Built in 1864, this octagonal building with a central courtyard was once the Aboriginal prison block but is now part of the Rottnest Lodge hotel. During its time as a prison, several men would sleep in each 3m by 1.7m cell, with no sanitation (most of the deaths were due to disease). Unless you're staying here, the only part of the complex that can be visited is a small whitewashed chapel to the left of the main entrance. A weekly Sunday service is held at 9.30am. The cells have been redeveloped into hotel rooms, but an undeniable darkness and melancholia lingers around this area.

Immediately adjacent to the Quod is a wooded area where hundreds of Aboriginal prisoners are buried in unmarked graves. Until relatively recently, this area was used as a camping ground, but it's now fenced off with signs asking visitors to show respect to

Rottnest Island (Wadjemup)

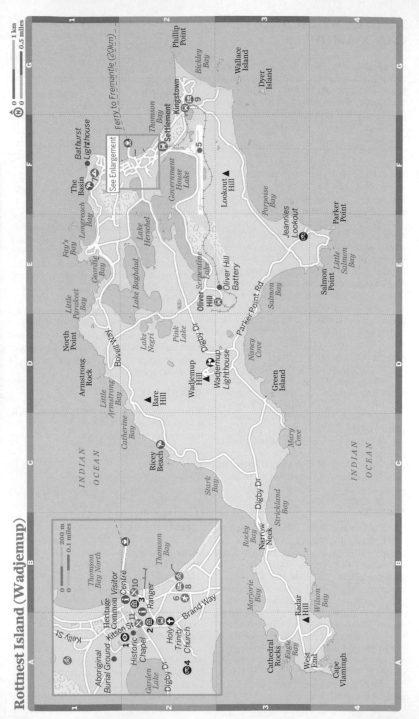

Rottnest Island (Wadjemup)

what is considered a sacred site. Plans are under way to convert the area into a memorial, in consultation with Aboriginal elders.

Rottnest Museum   MUSEUM
(Kitson St; admission by gold coin donation; ⊙11am-3.30pm) Housed in the old hay-store building, this little museum tells the island's natural and human history, warts and all, including dark tales of shipwrecks and incarceration.

Salt Store   HISTORIC BUILDING
(Colebatch Ave) **FREE** A photographic exhibition in this 19th-century building looks at a different chapter of local history: when the island's salt lakes provided all of WA's salt (between 1838 and 1950). It's also the meeting point for walking tours.

Vlamingh's Lookout   LOOKOUT
Not far away from Thomson Bay (go up past the old European cemetery), this unsigned vantage point offers panoramic views of the island, including its salt lakes. It's on View Hill, off Digby Dr.

🏃 Activities

Beaches   SWIMMING
Most visitors come for Rottnest's beaches and aquatic activities. **The Basin** is the most popular beach for family-friendly swimming as it's protected by a ring of reefs. Other popular spots are **Longreach Bay** and **Geordie Bay**, though there are many smaller secluded beaches such as **Little Parakeet Bay**.

Reefs & Wrecks   SNORKELLING, DIVING
Excellent visibility in the temperate waters, coral reefs and shipwrecks makes Rottnest a top spot for scuba diving and snorkelling. There are snorkel trails with underwater plaques at **Little Salmon Bay** and **Parker Point. The Basin, Little Parakeet Bay, Longreach Bay** and **Geordie Bay**

are also good. **Rottnest Island Bike Hire** (☎9292 5105; www.rottnestisland.com; cnr Bedford Ave & Welch Way; per hr $16, 1/2/3/4/5 days $28/45/56/67/79; ⊙8.30am-4pm, to 5.30pm in summer) has masks, snorkels and fins available, as well as kayaks.

Over a dozen boats have come a cropper on Rottnest's reefs, the earliest significant one being the schooner *Transit* in 1842. Marker plaques around the island tell the sad tales of how and when the ships sank. The only wreck that is accessible to snorkellers without a boat is at **Thomson Bay**. The Australasian Diving Academy (p55) takes diving trips to some of the wrecks.

Surfing   SURFING
The best surf breaks are at **Strickland, Salmon** and **Stark Bays,** towards the western end of the island. Boards can be hired at Rottnest Island Bike Hire.

Birds   BIRDWATCHING
Rottnest is ideal for twitchers because of the varied habitats: coast, lakes, swamps, heath, woodlands and settlements. Coastal birds include pelicans, gannets, cormorants, bar-tailed godwits, whimbrels, oystercatchers, majestic ospreys and fairy, bridled and crested terns. For more, grab a copy of *A Bird's Eye View of Rottnest Island* from the visitor centre.

👉 Tours

Check the times online or at the Salt Store, or call the visitor centre.

Rottnest Voluntary Guides   WALKING
(☎08-9372 9757; www.rvga.asn.au) **FREE** Free, themed walks leave from the central Salt Store daily: History; Reefs, Wrecks & Daring Sailors; Vlamingh Lookout & Salt Lakes; and the Quokka Walk. They also run tours of Wadjemup Lighthouse (adult/child $7/3)

QUOKKAS

These cute little docile bundles of fur have suffered a number of indignities over the years. First Willem de Vlamingh's crew mistook them for rats as big as cats. Then the British settlers misheard and mangled their name (the Noongar word was probably *quak-a* or *gwaga*). But worst of all, a cruel trend of 'quokka soccer' by sadistic louts in the 1990s saw many kicked to death before a $10,000 fine was imposed; occasional cases are still reported.

These marsupials of the macropod family (relatives of kangaroos and wallabies) were once found throughout the southwest but are now confined to forest on the mainland and a population of 8000 to 10,000 on Rottnest Island. You will see plenty of them during your visit. Don't be surprised if one comes up to you looking for a titbit (don't oblige them, as human food isn't good for them) – many are almost tame, or, at least, fearless.

and Oliver Hill Gun & Tunnels (adult/child $8/3.50); you'll need to make your own way there for the last two.

Oliver Hill Train & Tour　　　TRAIN RIDES
(www.rottnestisland.com; adult/child $28/16) The Oliver Hill gun battery was built in the 1930s and played a major role in the defence of the WA coastline and Fremantle harbour. This trip takes you by train to Oliver Hill (departing from the train station twice daily) and includes the Gun & Tunnels tour run by Rottnest Voluntary Guides.

Discovery Coach Tour　　　BUS TOUR
(www.rottnestisland.com; adult/child $35/17; ☉ departs 11.20am, 1.40pm & 1.50pm) Leaves from Thomson Bay three times daily (book at the visitor centre) and includes a commentary and a stop at West End.

Rottnest Adventure Tour　　　CRUISE
(www.rottnestexpress.com.au; adult/child $50/25; ☉ late Sep–early Jun) Ninety-minute cruises around the coast with a special emphasis on spotting wildlife, including whales in season from October to November. Packages are also available from Perth (adult/child $130/67) and Fremantle ($115/57).

Charter 1　　　SAILING
(☎ 0428 604 794; www.charter1.com.au; ☉ mid-Sep–Apr) Excursions on the *Capella*, a state-of-the-art catamaran, include whale-watching eco-cruises (adult/child $58/29), guided snorkelling trips (adult/child $68/34), and twilight sails (adult/child $48/29) for taking in a Rottnest sunset.

Rottnest Air Taxi　　　SCENIC FLIGHTS
(☎ 1800 500 006, 0411 264 547; www.rottnest.de) Ten-minute flights over the island ($38).

🛏 Sleeping

Rotto is wildly popular in summer and school holidays, when accommodation is booked out months in advance. Prices can rise steeply at these times – low-season rates are given here. Check websites for off-peak deals combining transport to the island, especially incorporating a weekday visit.

Kingston Barracks Youth Hostel　　　HOSTEL $
(☎ 08-9432 9111; www.rottnestisland.com; dm/f $50/106) This hostel is located in old army barracks that still have a rather institutional feel, and few facilities. Check in at the visitor centre before you make the 1.8km walk, bike or bus trip to Kingston.

Allison Tentland　　　CAMPGROUND $
(☎ 08-9432 9111; www.rottnestisland.com; Thomson Bay; sites per person $13) Camping on the island is restricted to this leafy camping ground with barbecues. Be vigilant about your belongings, especially your food – cheeky quokkas have been known to help themselves.

**Rottnest Island
Authority Cottages**　　　RENTAL HOUSE $
(☎ 08-9432 9111; www.rottnestisland.com; cottages $100-228) There are more than 250 villas and cottages for rent around the island. Some have magnificent beachfront positions and are palatial; others are more like beach shacks. Prices rise by around $60 for Friday and Saturday nights, and they shoot up by up to $120 in peak season (late September to April). Check online for the labyrinthine pricing schedule.

Rottnest Lodge　　　HOTEL $$
(☎ 08-9292 5161; www.rottnestlodge.com.au; Kitson St; r $190-300; mains $27-34; ☣) It's claimed there are ghosts in this comfortable complex, which is based around the former Quod and boys' reformatory school. If that worries you, ask for a room in the new section, looking

onto a salt lake. The lodge's Riva restaurant channels Italian flavours amid the island's vaguely Mediterranean ambience, especially when the sun is shining.

Hotel Rottnest   PUB $$$
(☑08-9292 5011; www.hotelrottnest.com.au; 1 Bedford Ave; r $270-320; ✸) Based around the former summer-holiday pad for the state's governors (built in 1864) the former Quokka Arms has been completely transformed by a stylish renovation. The whiter-than-white rooms are smart and modern, if a tad pricey. Some have beautiful sea views.

✖ Eating & Drinking

Most visitors to Rotto self-cater. The general store is like a small supermarket (and also stocks liquor), but if you're staying a while, you're better to bring supplies with you. Another option is to pre-order food from the general store, and they'll equip your accommodation with food and drinks before your arrival. Fir details, see the general store's website: www.rottnestgeneralstore.com.au.

All of the following are in Thomson Bay, but service, quality of food, and value for money can be mediocre during weekends and holiday periods.

Rottnest Bakery   BAKERY $
(Malley St; mains $5-12) Traditional Aussie bakery, with pies, burgers, soup and ice cream.

Hotel Rottnest   PUB $$
(www.hotelrottnest.com.au; 1 Bedford Ave; mains $19-38; ⊘11am-late) It's hard to imagine a more inviting place for a sunset pint of Little Creatures than the AstroTurf 'lawn' of this chic waterfront hotel. A big glass pavilion creates an open and inviting space, and bistro-style food and pizza is reasonably priced given the location and ambience. Bands and DJs regularly boost the laid-back island mood during summer.

Riva   SEAFOOD $$
(Kitson St, Rottnest Lodge; mains $27-34; ⊘noon-late) Classy Italian restaurant with a strong focus on local seafood. Prawns, squid, mussels and oysters all receive an elegant touch of the Med, and there are also wood-fired pizzas and interesting spins on duck, chicken and lamb.

Aristos   SEAFOOD $$
(www.aristosrottnest.com.au; Colebatch Ave; breakfast $10-17, lunch & dinner mains $27-42; ⊘8am-late) An upmarket, but pricey, option for

seafood, steaks and salads, fish and chips, burgers, ice cream or excellent coffee, right on the waterfront near the main jetty. Grab a table on the deck for absolute sea views, and push the boat (way) out with a seafood platter for two people ($125).

❶ Information

At the Thomson Bay settlement, behind the main jetty, there's a shopping area with an ATM.

Ranger (☑08-9372 9788) For fishing and boating information.

Visitor Centre (www.rottnestisland.com) Thomson Bay (☑9372 9732; www.rottnestisland.com; ⊘7.30am-5pm Sat-Thu, 7.30am-7pm Fri, extended in summer) Fremantle (☑9432 9300; www.rottnestisland.com; E Shed, Victoria Quay) The Thomson Bay office, at the end of the main jetty, handles check-ins for all the island authority's accommodation. There's a bookings counter at the Fremantle office, near where the ferry departs.

❶ Getting There & Away

AIR

Rottnest Air-Taxi (☑0411 264 547; www.rottnest.de) flies from Jandakot airport in four-seater (one-way/same-day return/extended return $230/330/430) or six-seater planes (one-way/extended return $350/550). Prices include up to three passengers in the four-seater and five passengers in the six-seater.

BOAT

Rottnest Express (☑1300 467 688; www.rottnestexpress.com.au) Fremantle (B Shed, Victoria Quay; adult/child $72.50/40) Northport (1 Emma Pl, Rous Head; adult/child $72.50/40) Perth (Pier 2, Barrack St Jetty; adult/child $92.50/50) The prices listed are for return day trips and include the island admission fee; add $10 for an extended return. Ferry schedules are seasonal, though those listed here are roughly the minimum: Perth (1¾ hours, twice daily), Fremantle (30 minutes, five times daily) and North Fremantle (30 minutes, three times daily). Secure parking is available at Northport; the Perth and Fremantle departure points are handy to train stations. Various packages are available, which can add bike hire, snorkelling equipment, meals and tours.

Rottnest Fast Ferries (☑08-9246 1039; www.rottnestfastferries.com.au; adult/child $83/45) Departs from Hillarys Boat Harbour (40 minutes; three times daily). Packages also available. Hillarys Boat Harbour is around 40 minutes' drive north of Perth. See www.hillarysboatharbour.com.au for public transport details.

ℹ Getting Around

BIKE

Bicycles are the time-honoured way of getting around the island. Rottnest is just big enough (and with enough hills) to make a day's ride good exercise.

Bikes can be booked in advance online or on arrival through **Rottnest Island Bike Hire** (☑ 08-9292 5105; www.rottnestisland.com; cnr Bedford Ave & Welch Way; ⊘ 8.30am-4pm, to 5.30pm summer). A $25 bond is required if you don't have photo ID. It's the only operator to have a pick-up service if you're unable to return to the office due to injury or damage to the bike.

The ferry companies also hire out bikes. Rottnest Express has them waiting as you get off the boat ($28/41/56 per one/two/three days). They don't provide locks but neither do they check them off when you return them. Bikes aren't usually stolen (it would be too hard to smuggle them off the island without the ferry companies noticing), but it's not unheard of for an unlocked bike to be grabbed and used by someone else.

BUS

A free shuttle runs between Thomson Bay, the main accommodation areas and the airport, departing roughly every 35 minutes, with the last bus at 7pm. The Bayseeker (day pass adult/child $14/6) is a hop-on, hop-off service that does an hourly loop around the island with the first bus at 8.30am and the last at 3.30pm. Between Geordie Bay and Thomson Bay it's free.

ROCKINGHAM

POP 100,000

Just 46km south of Perth, Rockingham's main attractions are good beaches and the Shoalwater Islands Marine Park, where you can observe dolphins, sea lions and penguins in the wild.

Rockingham was founded in 1872 as a port, although this function was taken over by Fremantle in the 1890s. There's still a substantial industrial complex to the north, at Kwinana.

Most places of interest are stretched along Rockingham Beach.

◎ Sights & Activities

**Shoalwater Islands
Marine Park**   NATURE RESERVE
(www.marineparks.wa.gov.au) 𝄐 Just a few minutes' paddle, swim or boat ride from the mainland is tiny, fabulous and strictly protected **Penguin Island**. Home to about 600 breeding pairs of seriously cute little penguins, and several thousand pairs of ground-nesting and in-your-face silver gulls, the island also has an informal and informative feeding centre (for long-term injured or orphaned penguins), boardwalks, swimming beaches and picnic tables for day visitors. It's lovely, low-key and very ecoconscious; no food is sold on the island, toilets are composting, and the island is closed for nesting from June to mid-September.

Apart from birdwatching (pied cormorants, pelicans, crested and bridled terns, and oystercatchers), you can swim and snorkel in the crystal-clear waters. Nearby **Seal Island** is home to a colony of Australian sea lions and off-limits to the public. The naval base of Garden Island can be reached only by private boat.

The **Penguin Island ferry** (Mersey Point Jetty; ferry $12; ⊘hourly 9am-3pm mid-Sep–May) is run by Rockingham Wild Encounters (p56). Tickets combining the ferry with entry to the island's discovery centre penguin-feeding (adult/child $18/15) are available.

At low tide it's possible to wade the few hundred metres to the island across the sandbar. However, take heed of warning signs, as people have drowned here after being washed off the bar during strong winds and high tides.

West Coast Dive Park   DIVING
(www.westcoastdivepark.com.au; diving permits per day/week $25/50) Diving within the marine park became even more interesting after the sinking of the *Saxon Ranger*, a supposedly jinxed 400-tonne fishing vessel. Permits to dive at this site are available from the visitor centre. Contact the Australasian Diving Academy (p55) about expeditions to this wreck and the wrecks of three other boats, two planes and various reefs in the vicinity.

☞ Tours

Capricorn Seakayaking   KAYAKING
(☑0427 485 123; www.capricornseakayaking.com.au; ⊘mid-Sep–early Jun) Full-day sea-kayaking tours around Penguin and Seal Islands from Perth, Fremantle or Rockingham ($159) plus wildlife-watching and snorkelling.

🛏 Sleeping & Eating

Beachside Apartment Hotel   APARTMENT **$$**
(📞08-9529 3777; www.beachsideapartment.com.
au; 58 Kent St; apt $210-302; 🅿️🏠) Right on the
esplanade, these apartments are spacious,
sunny and secure. The block's not super-
modern, but there's an up-to-date feel to the
decor and discounts for stays longer than a
week.

Pengo's Cafe   CAFE **$**
(153 Arcadia Dr; snacks & mains $8-18; ☺8am-
4.30pm Sep-May, reduced hours in winter) Good
coffee, gourmet burgers and fresh salads
shine at this excellent cafe near the Rocking-
ham Wild Encounters ticket office. There's
a nice alfresco deck and lots of grass for the
kids to run around on.

Rustico   CAFE, TAPAS **$$**
(www.rusticotapas.com.au; 61 Rockingham Beach
Rd; tapas $11-19, pizzas $14-16.50; ☺noon-late
Mon-Sat, to 10pm Sun) This stylish cafe is renowned for authentic Spanish-style tapas.
Secure a seat on the expansive corner terrace with ocean views, and tuck into chicken
empanadas or scallops with chorizo. Good
pizzas and larger shared plates are also
available, and there's live acoustic music on
Sunday afternoons.

Bettyblue Bistro   SEAFOOD **$$**
(📞08-9528 4228; www.bettybluebistro.com; 3-4
The Boardwalk; mains $18-34; ☺8am-2pm Mon-Tue,
9am-late Wed-Sun) The vibe at this licensed
bistro is casual, with tables that allow you to
gaze straight out to sea. Try the pomegranate-
glazed barramundi with a salad of Israeli
couscous.

ℹ️ Information

Visitor Centre (📞08-9592 3464; www.
rockinghamvisitorcentre.com.au; 19 Kent St;
☺9am-5pm; @) Accommodation listings if you
want to overnight.

ℹ️ Getting There & Around

Rockingham sits within Zone 5 of the Perth
public transport system, **Transperth** (📞13 62
13; www.transperth.wa.gov.au). Regular trains
depart, via the Mandurah line, to Perth Under-
ground/Esplanade ($7.10, 34 minutes) and
Mandurah ($4.90, 18 minutes).

Rockingham station is around 4km southeast
of Rockingham Beach and around 6km east of
Mersey Point, from where the Penguin Island
ferries depart; catch bus 551 or 555 to the beach
or stay on the 551 to Mersey Point.

PEEL REGION

Taking in swaths of jarrah forest, historic
towns and the increasingly glitzy coastal re-
sort of Mandurah, the Peel region can easily
be tackled as a day trip from Perth or as the
first stopping point of a longer expedition
down the South Western Hwy (Rte 1).

As you enter the Peel, you'll pass out of
Wadjuk country and into that of their fellow
Noongar neighbours, the Pinjarup (or Bin-
jareb) people.

Mandurah

POP 68,300

Shrugging off its fusty retirement-haven im-
age, Mandurah has made concerted efforts
to reinvent itself as an upmarket beach re-
sort, taking advantage of its new train link
to Perth's public-transport network. And,
although its linked set of redeveloped 'pre-
cincts' and 'quarters' may sound a little pre-
tentious, the overall effect is actually pretty
cool. You can wander along the waterfront
from the Ocean Marina (boats, cafes and
the Dolphin Quay indoor market), past the
Venetian Canals (glitzy apartments linked
by Venetianish sandstone bridges), through
the Boardwalk and Cultural Precinct (more
eateries, visitor centre, cinema, arts centre)
to the Bridge Quarter (still more restau-
rants and bars). At the time of writing the
local debate was whether to continue de-
velopment of Mandurah's shiny new image,
or refocus on the city's more laidback and
authentic past. Watch this space.

The bridge spans the Mandurah Estuary,
which sits between the ocean and the large
body of water known as the Peel Inlet. It's
one of the best places in the region for fish-
ing, crabbing, prawning (March and April)
and dolphin spotting.

HEADING SOUTH

The fastest and simplest route south
from central Perth is to jump on the
Kwinana Fwy. Rather than visiting Rock-
ingham and the Peel region as separate
day trips, you could turn them into a
220km loop: Perth–Rockingham–
Mandurah–Pinjarra–Dwellingup–
Jarrahdale–Perth. A good overnight
stop is Mandurah.

◉ Sights & Activities

Beaches SWIMMING

There are plenty of beautiful beaches within walking distance of the Mandurah waterfront. **Town Beach** is just across from the marina, at the southern end of **Silver Sands** – perhaps the best of the ocean beaches. There's a designated, boat-free swimming area on the far side of the estuary, just north of Mandurah Bridge. Here dolphins have been known to swim up to unwitting kids for a frolic. Facing the ocean, west of the mouth of the estuary, is family-friendly **Doddi's Beach**.

Mandurah Ferry Cruises CRUISE

(📞 08-9535 3324; www.mandurahferrycruises.com; Boardwalk) Take a one-hour **Dolphin & Mandurah Waterways Cruise** (adult/child $28/14; ⊙ on the hour 10am-4pm), a half-day **Murray River Lunch Cruise** (adult/child $79/49; ⊙ Sep-May) and, through December, a one-hour **Christmas Lights Canal Cruise** (adult/child $30/15; ⊙ Dec–mid-Jan), that gawps at millionaires' mansions under the pretence of admiring their festive displays. Other cruise options incorporate catching and cooking Mandurah's famous blue manna crabs, and a heritage cruise highlighting the region's history.

Mandurah Boat & Bike Hire BOATING, CYCLING

(📞 08-9535 5877; www.mandurahboatandbikehire.com.au; Boardwalk; bike hire per hr/day $10/33) Chase the fish on a four-seat dinghy or six-seat pontoon (per hour/day from $50/320).

Australian Sailing Museum MUSEUM

(www.australiansailingmuseum.com.au; Ormsby Tce; adult/child $10/5; ⊙ 9am-5pm) A very cool building housing 200 model yachts and tall ships, as well as a replica of the America's Cup and a cafe.

Hall's Cottage HISTORIC BUILDING

(Leighton Pl, Halls Head; admission by gold coin donation; ⊙ 10am-3pm Sun) An 1830s cottage and one of the first dwellings in the state.

🛏 Sleeping

Mandurah Ocean Marina Chalets MOTEL $$

(📞 08-9535 8173; www.marinachalets.com.au; 6 The Lido; studios & chalets $116-165) The ambience is a bit like a British holiday camp, but the chalets and motel units are spotless and modern with fully equipped kitchens. A shared barbecue area – complete with a crab-cooking facility – make it easy to meet other travelling families, and the canals and restaurants of Ocean Marina and Dolphin Quay are a short walk away.

Seashells Resort RESORT $$

(📞 08-9550 3000; www.seashells.com.au; 16 Dolphin Dr; apt from $199; 🅿 ❄) Seashells' apartments are cool and spacious, and there's a beach on its doorstep and a lovely infinity-lipped pool just metres away. Check into one of its luxury beachfront villas and you may not want to leave.

Sebel APARTMENT $$

(📞 08-9512 8300; www.mirvachotels.com; 1 Marco Polo Dr; r/apt from $159/259; 🅿 @ 🛜 ❄) If this was actually Venice, you'd have to be staying in the Doge's Palace for a better location. This big white apartment block offers well-appointed modern apartments and studio rooms, all with views. There's plenty of free parking plus a heated pool and small gymnasium. Downstairs is the excellent M on the Point bar and restaurant.

🍴 Eating

Restaurants and cafes abound on the Boardwalk and Dolphin Quay. At the time of writing, planned new openings included an oyster bar, and Thai and Indian eateries.

Cafe Moka CAFE $

(www.cafemoka.com.au; Dolphin Quay; breakfast $10-17, lunch $13-26; ⊙ 8am-4pm) Mandurah's best brekkie option is well positioned to soak up the morning sun on the edge of the marina.

Cicerello's FISH & CHIPS $$

(www.cicerellos.com.au; 73 Mandurah Tce; mains $18-28; ⊙ 9.30am-11.30pm) A boardwalk-facing branch of the Fremantle institution.

M on the Point INTERNATIONAL $$

(www.mbarandrestaurant.com.au; 1 Marco Polo Dr; pizzas $20-25, mains $28-37; ⊙ noon-late) The three classy bars beneath the Sebel are the perfect place for a Sunday sundowner, and the attached restaurant has been recognised by the *Good Food Guide*. Either kick back with a cold one and gourmet pizza in the Long Bar, or try sophisticated food like lemongrass butter poached salmon in the restaurant.

Taste & Graze CAFE $$

(www.tasteandgraze.com.au; 16 Mandurah Tce, Shop 3/4; mains $15-30, shared-plate menus per person

$45; ⊙9am-4pm Sun-Thu, till late Fri & Sat) Back in town in 'old' Mandurah, and perfectly located to catch the afternoon sun. Outdoor seating and a versatile Modern Australian menu covering breakfast, lunch and shared smaller plates make it a cosmopolitan slice of cafe cool. It's also handily adjacent to the Brighton Hotel if you're looking to kick on.

Taku Japanese Kitchen   JAPANESE $$
(52 Mandurah Tce, Shop 2, Scott's Plaza; mains $10-18; ⊙11.30am-2.30pm & 5-9pm Tue-Sun) Away from Mandurah's tourist glitz, this friendly family-run operation across the road from the town beach turns out excellent tempura, sashimi and sushi. Grab a good-value bento box and settle in for a lazy seaside lunch.

🍸 Drinking & Entertainment

Brighton Hotel   PUB
(www.brightonmandurah.com.au; 10-12 Mandurah Tce) Watch the sun set over the estuary with a glass of wine, and return after 9pm on the weekends to move to the DJs.

Mandurah Performing Arts Centre   CONCERT VENUE
(☑08-9550 3900; www.manpac.com.au; Ormsby Tce) The main regional centre for theatre, dance and concerts.

Reading Cinema   CINEMA
(www.readingcinemas.com.au; 7 James Service Pl) Blockbusters and occasional arthouse surprises; located just off the boardwalk.

ℹ Information

Visitor Centre (☑08-9550 3999; www.visitmandurah.com; 75 Mandurah Tce; ⊙9am-5pm; @) On the estuary boardwalk.

ℹ Getting There & Away

Mandurah is 72km from central Perth; take the Kwinana Fwy and follow the signs.

It sits within the outermost zone (7) of the Perth public transport system and is the terminus of Transperth's Mandurah line. There are direct trains from Mandurah to Perth Underground/Esplanade ($9.40, 50 minutes) and Rockingham ($7.10, 18 minutes).

Transwa (☑1300 662 205; www.transwa.wa.gov.au) coach routes include:

➜ SW1 (12 per week) to East Perth ($16, 1½ hours), Bunbury ($16, two hours), Busselton ($24, 2¾ hours), Margaret River ($33, four hours) and Augusta ($35, 4¾ hours).

➜ SW2 (thrice weekly) to Balingup ($27, three hours), Bridgetown ($30, 3½ hours) and Pemberton ($41, 4½ hours).

➜ GS3 (weekly) to Denmark ($65, 7¼ hours) and Albany ($71, eight hours).

South West Coach Lines (☑08-9261 7600; www.veoliatransportwa.com.au) has services to/from Perth's Esplanade Busport ($18, 1¼ hours, twice daily), Bunbury ($18, 1¼ hours, twice daily), Busselton ($30, 2½ hours, daily), Dunsborough ($32, 3¼ hours, daily) and Bridgetown ($32, 3¼ hours, weekdays).

Yalgorup National Park

Fifty kilometres south of Mandurah is this beautiful 12,000-hectare coastal park, consisting of 10 tranquil lakes and their surrounding woodlands and sand dunes. The park is recognised as a wetland of international significance for seasonally migrating waterbirds, with 130 species identified.

Amateur scientists can visit the distinctive **thrombolites** of Lake Clifton, which are descendants of the earliest living organisms on earth (they are the only life form known to have existed over 650 million years ago). These rocklike structures are most easily seen when the water is low, particularly during March and April. There's a viewing platform on Mt John Rd off Old Coast Rd; keep an eye out for long-neck tortoises below the boardwalk. A 5km **walking track** starts from here and loops around the lake.

Lake Pollard trail (6km) begins about 8km down Preston Beach North Rd (not Preston Beach Rd, as marked on some maps). The pleasant Martins Tank Lake campground is to the right of the entrance. The trail takes in tuart, jarrah and bull banksia on its way to the lake, which is known for its black swans (October to March).

The **Heathlands trail** (4.5km) to Lake Preston starts at the information bay on Preston Beach Rd (before the turn-off to Preston Beach North Rd) and explores the tuart woodland. Further along Preston Beach Rd is **Preston Beach**.

Pinjarra
POP 3300

Stretching along the Murray River, genteel Pinjarra now seems the epitome of peace and quiet. Yet it's best known as the site of a bloody incident in 1834 that was once remembered as the Battle of Pinjarra and is now known as the Pinjarra Massacre.

PINJARRA: BATTLE OR MASSACRE?

The popular myth of Australia's Indigenous people sitting back passively while the British took their land doesn't fly in the Peel region. From the outset, after Thomas Peel was 'granted' this land, its Pinjarup owners asserted their rights – spearing stock and destroying crops. An uneasy truce was reached, with the Pinjarup given regular rations of flour, which they probably viewed as a kind of rent.

In 1834 the cutting of flour rations led Pinjarup leader Calyute to stage a raid on a flour mill. Four of his men were arrested in Mandurah and taken to Perth, where they were publically flogged. Retribution was taken on a 19-year-old British servant (fair game under Noongar law as he was considered a member of the offending party's tribe), who was killed and then ritually mutilated.

This caused an uproar among the settlers, with Peel strongly urging Governor Stirling to take action. Stirling led a party of soldiers and settlers, including Peel, to Pinjarra, where they surprised Calyute's people and opened fire on their encampment. What happened then is contested. Stirling's official report put the death toll at 15 men, while the *Perth Gazette* reported 25 to 30 dead. The Pinjarup claim that the camp consisted mainly of women and children and that the death toll was far higher. There was only one British casualty.

Stirling's threat to the survivors, that 'if any other person should be killed by them, not one (of their people) would be allowed to remain alive on this side of the mountain', seemed to have had the desired effect, and curtailed any future resistance.

Sights & Activities

Town Centre
HISTORIC BUILDINGS

The South Western Hwy passes through Pinjarra's small historic precinct, immediately after crossing the Murray. **St John's Church**, built 1861–62 from mud bricks, sits beside a heritage **rose garden** and the original 1860 **schoolhouse** (now a quilt workshop). Across Henry St is the **Edenvale Complex**, with **tea rooms** (mains $6-15; ⊙9am-4pm) in the old homestead (1888), art and craft galleries and a machinery display in the outbuildings. On the other side of the highway, you can cross the river on foot via an old **suspension bridge**.

Peel Zoo
ZOO

(www.peelzoo.com; Sanctuary Dr, off Pinjarra Rd; adult/child $18/9; ⊙10am-4pm Mon-Fri, 9am-5pm Sat & Sun) Peacocks strut while parrots issue wisecracks as you wander around this cute little zoo, which focuses on Australian wildlife: kangaroos, wallabies, Tasmanian devils, koalas, wombats, possums, quolls, snakes and lots of native birds.

Old Blythewood Homestead
HISTORIC BUILDING

(www.ntwa.com.au; South Western Hwy; adult/child $4/2; ⊙11am-3pm Sat & Sun, closed Aug) An 1859 National Trust–owned farmhouse, furnished with antiques; about 4km south of Pinjarra.

WA Skydiving Academy
SKYDIVING

(☑1300 137 855; www.waskydiving.com.au) Tandem jumps from 6000/10,000/14,000ft for $260/340/420.

Eating

Raven Wines
CAFE

(www.ravenwines.com.au; cnr Wilson & Pinjarra Rds; small plates $10-15, cheeseboard $24; ⊙10am-5pm Wed-Sun) This chic cafe is part of a compact vineyard on the edge of town. Wine tasting and interesting small plates with an Asian or Med spin provide a welcome contrast to the occasionally chintzy heritage overkill of downtown Pinjarra.

Information

Visitor Centre (☑08-9531 1438; www.murray.wa.gov.au; Fimmel Lane; ⊙9.30am-4pm) Housed in the heritage train-station.

Getting There & Away

Pinjarra is on the **Transwa** (☑1300 662 205; www.transwa.wa.gov.au) Australind train line, with twice-daily services to Perth ($16, 1¼ hours) and Bunbury ($16, 1¼ hours).

Dwellingup

POP 550

Dwellingup is a small, forest-shrouded township with character, 100km south of Perth. Its reputation as an activity hub has been enhanced by the hardy long-distance walkers and cyclists passing through on the Bibbulmun Track and the Munda Biddi Trail respectively.

◉ Sights & Activities

Forest Heritage Centre   NATURE RESERVE
(www.forestheritagecentre.com.au; 1 Acacia St; adult/child/family $5.50/2.20/11; ⊙10am-3pm) Set within the jarrah forest, this interesting rammed-earth building takes the shape of three interlinked gum leaves. Inside are displays about the forest's flora and fauna, and a shop that sells beautiful pieces crafted by the resident woodwork artists. Short marked trails lead into the forest, including an 11m-high canopy walk. Look for the resident flock of red-tailed black cockatoos, and keep an eye out for the laidback mob of kangaroos that surprised us on our last visit.

Hotham Valley Railway   HISTORIC TRAIN
(☑08-9221 4444; www.hothamvalleyrailway.com. au) On weekends (and Tuesday and Thursday during school holidays), the Dwellingup **Forest Train** (adult/child $24/12; ⊙departs 10.30am & 2pm) chugs along 8km of forest track on a 90-minute return trip. It's usually steam driven but in summer they revert to diesel engines due to the fire risk. There's a 30-minute stopover at the end where you can take a short bushwalk. Every Saturday night and some Fridays, the **Restaurant Train** (tickets $79; ⊙departs 7.45pm) follows the same route, serving up a five-course meal in a 1919 dining car. A third option is the **Steam Ranger** (adult/child $34/17; ⊙departs 10.30am), travelling 14km via WA's steepest rail incline to Isandra Siding. Steam Ranger trains only run on Sunday from May to October.

Dwellingup Adventures   KAYAKING, RAFTING
(☑08-9538 1127; www.dwellingupadventures. com.au; 1-person kayaks & 2-person canoes per day $45; ⊙8.30am-5pm) Don't miss the opportunity to get out on the beautiful Murray River. Hire camping gear, bikes, kayaks and canoes, or take an assisted, full day, self-guided paddling tour ($90 per one-person kayak) or full-day cycling tour ($97/124/174 per one/two/three people). White-water rafting tours are available from June to October ($130 per person).

❶ Information

Visitor Centre (☑08-9538 1108; www.mur raytourism.com.au; Marrinup St; ⊙9am-3pm) Interesting displays about the 1961 bushfires that wiped out the town, destroying 75 houses but taking no lives. The centrepiece is a shiny Mack firetruck (1939).

Jarrahdale & Serpentine National Park

POP 956

Established in 1871, Jarrahdale is another old mill village, reached by a leafy 6km drive east from the South Western Hwy. The **Old Post Office** (www.jarrahdale.com; walks $5; ⊙10am-4pm Sat & Sun), built in 1896, houses a small local museum. Guided walks run by volunteers from the heritage society depart from here.

Picturesque **Millbrook Winery** (☑08-9525 5796; www.millbrookwinery.com.au; Old Chestnut Lane, signed off Jarrahdale Rd; mains $36-45; ⊙10am-5pm Wed-Sun) has a tranquil setting overlooking a small lake. Lunch bookings are recommended, especially on weekends.

The town of Jarrahdale sits on the northern fringes of **Serpentine National Park** (www.dec.wa.gov.au; per car $11; ⊙8.30am-5pm), a forested area with walking tracks, picnic areas and a leisurely 15m slide of water known as the **Serpentine Falls** (Falls Rd, off South Western Hwy). If you're not in a hurry to get somewhere, it's worth taking a pleasant detour through the park from Jarrahdale, following Kingsbury Dr to the **Serpentine Dam** before curving back to the highway.

ROCK & ROLL

At 350km from Perth, Wave Rock is rather a long day trip, and some people are disappointed by what's really a one-trick gig. However, you can spice up this trip by hunting out other, lesser-known granite outcrops and curiosities. All you need is a map and a sense of adventure. (Hint: most of the granite outcrops end in 'Rock'.) To get you started, try Kokerbin Rock, Jilakin Rock, Dragon Rocks and Yorkrakine Rock. Visitor centres en route can supply maps.

DRYANDRA TO HYDEN

A beautiful forest, rare marsupials, stunning ancient granite-rock formations, salt lakes, interesting back roads and the unique Wave Rock are the scattered highlights of this widespread farming region.

Hyden & Wave Rock

Large granite outcrops dot the area known as the Central and Southern Wheatbelts, and the most famous is the perfectly shaped, multicoloured cresting swell of **Wave Rock**. Formed some 60 million years ago by weathering and water erosion, Wave Rock is streaked with colours created by run-off from local mineral springs.

To get the most out of Wave Rock, 350km from Perth, grab the brochure *Walk Trails at Wave Rock and The Humps* from the **visitor centre** (☑08-9880 5182; www.waverock.com.au; Wave Rock; ☺9am-5pm). Park at Hippos Yawn (no fee) and follow the shady track back along the rock base to Wave Rock (1km).

Accommodation can fill quickly, so phone ahead for a spot amid the gum trees at **Wave Rock Cabins & Caravan Park** (☑08-9880 5022; www.waverock.com.au; unpowered/powered sites from $28/35, cabins from $140, cottages from $160; ✱✿).

In **Hyden** (population 190), 4km east of the rock, the '70s brick **Wave Rock Motel** (☑08-9880 5052; www.waverock.com.au; 2 Lynch St; s/d from $105/150; ✱✿) has well-equipped rooms, a comfy lounge with fireplace, and an indoor bush bistro.

If heading to/from the Nullarbor, take the unsealed direct **Hyden–Norseman Road** to save 100km or so. Look for *The Granite and Woodlands Discovery Trail* at Norseman or Wave Rock visitor centres.

❶ Getting There & Away

This area is best seen with your own vehicle, ideally on the way to somewhere else. **Transwa** (☑1300 662 205; www.transwa.wa.gov.au) runs a bus from Perth to Hyden ($51, five hours) and on to Esperance ($53, five hours) every Tuesday, returning on Thursday.

Western Travel Bug (☑08-9486 4222; www.travelbug.com.au; tours $175) offers a one-day tour, or, alternatively, you could see it as part of a six-day southwest loop with **Western Xposure** (☑08-9414 8423; www.westernxposure.com.au; tours $750)

DARLING RANGE

Commonly known as the Perth Hills, this forest-covered escarpment provides the city with a green backdrop and offers great spots for picnicking, barbecues, bushwalking and rubbing shoulders with wild kangaroos. Leafy suburbs nestle at its feet, along with a few dozen wineries.

WORTH A TRIP

DRYANDRA WOODLAND

This superb, isolated remnant of eucalypt forest 164km southeast of Perth, with its thickets of white-barked wandoo, powderbark and rock she-oak, and small populations of threatened numbats, woylies and tammar wallabies, hints at what the wheat belt was like before large-scale land clearing and feral predators wreaked havoc on the local ecosystems. It also makes a great weekend getaway, and there are numerous walking trails.

The excellent **Barna Mia Animal Sanctuary**, home to endangered bilbies, boodies, woylies and marl, conducts 90-minute after-dark torchlight tours, providing a rare opportunity to see these cute furry creatures up close. Book through **DEC** (☑weekdays 08-9881 9200, weekends 08-9881 2064; www.dec.wa.gov.au; Hough St, Narrogin; adult/child/family $14/7.50/37.50; ☺9am-4pm) for post-sunset tours on Monday, Wednesday, Friday and Saturday; book early for peak periods.

While you can hoist your tent at the pleasant **Congelin Camp Ground** (☑08-9881 9200; per person $10), Dryandra is one place you should splurge a little. The **Lions Dryandra Village** (☑08-9884 5231; www.dryandravillage.org.au; adult/child $30/15, 2-/4-/8–12-person cabins $70/90/130) is a 1920s forestry camp in the heart of the forest, offering fully self-contained, renovated woodcutters' cabins complete with fridge, stove, fireplace, en suite and nearby grazing wallabies. **Narrogin** (www.dryandratourism.org.au), serviced by Transwa buses, is 22km southeast.

Kalamunda

POP 54,700

Kalamunda is a well-heeled township on the crest of the Darling Range. The area began as a timber settlement, but it's since become a quieter residential haven close to the city (it's a 30-minute drive from Perth).

The main shopping area on Haynes St has good pubs and cafes. Nearby is **Stirk Cottage** (www.kalamundahistoricalsociety.com; Kalamunda Rd; ⊙2-4pm Sun) FREE, built of mud, saplings and shingle in 1881.

For walkers, Kalamunda is the northern terminus of the **Bibbulmun Track**, which starts near the shops and heads into the forest of **Kalamunda National Park**.

From Zig-Zag Dr, just north of Kalamunda off Lascelles Pde, there are fantastic views over Perth to the coast. The drive through the forested hills to Mundaring via Mundaring Weir Rd is also wonderful, but watch out for kangaroos.

🛈 Getting There & Away

From Perth, buses 283, 295, 296, 298 and 299 all head to Kalamunda ($4.90, 47 minutes).

Mundaring

POP 38,300

Located 35km east of Perth, Mundaring's a laid-back spot with a small artistic community. Bisected by the busy Great Eastern Hwy, the township itself isn't particularly interesting, but the **Mundaring Arts Centre** (www.mundaringartscentre.com; 7190 Great Eastern Hwy; ⊙10am-5pm Mon-Fri, 11am-3pm Sat & Sun) exhibits and sells the work of local artists.

The 16-sq-km **John Forrest National Park** (www.dec.wa.gov.au; admission per car $11), west of Mundaring, was the state's first national park. Protected areas of jarrah and marri trees are scattered about granite outcrops, waterfalls and a pool.

Immediately south of Mundaring is **Beelu National Park** (www.dec.wa.gov.au), part of a continuous swath of forest that includes Kalamunda National Park. The **Perth Hills National Parks Centre** (☑08-9295 2244; www.dec.wa.gov.au/n2n; Allens Rd, off Mundaring Weir Rd) hosts a series of kids programs with a flora-and-fauna spin. There's a good campground (adult/child $9/2), well positioned for the Bibbulmun Track, which passes nearby. A more secluded and primitive camp-

ground is available at Paten's Brook ($5 per person).

From November to April, kick back in a deckchair at the open-air **Kookaburra Cinema** (☑08-9295 6190; www.kookaburracinema.com.au; Allen Rd; adult/child $13/8), just across the road from the park centre. A little further south is **Mundaring Weir**, a dam built 100 years ago to supply water to the goldfields more than 500km to the east. The reservoir is a blissful spot, with walking trails and a well-positioned pub. Come dusk, the whole area swarms with kangaroos.

East from Mundaring and north of the Great Eastern Hwy, near Chidlow, is freshwater **Lake Leschenaultia** (⊙8.30am-dusk), a picturesque former railway dam, complete with a swimming pontoon.

🛏 Sleeping & Eating

Department of Education Hostel   HOSTEL $
(☑08-9295 0202; www.mundaringtourism.com.au; Mundaring Weir Rd; dm $25) Close to the weir, this basic hostel has a quiet bush setting, and is around 8km south of town. It's used by school groups, but there's usually room for other guests, especially if you're walking the Bibbulmun Track. Book through the Mundaring Visitors Centre, and look forward to kangaroo company at dusk.

Mundaring Weir Hotel   HOTEL $
(☑08-9295 1106; www.mundaringweirhotel.com.au; Weir Village Rd; r Mon-Thu $115, Fri-Sun $140; ☀) Overlooking the weir, this 1898 pub has bucketloads of ramshackle character. Rooms are simple but tidy, with DVD players and microwaves. The rooms also open onto an amphitheatre, which mainly functions as a beer garden but occasionally hosts concerts.

Recent performers have included Aussie icons such as Kasey Chambers and Mark Seymour.

Loose Box RESTAURANT $$$
(☑ 08-9295 1787; www.loosebox.com.au; 6825 Great Eastern Hwy; degustation $150; ⊘ 7pm-late Wed-Sat, noon-3pm Sun) A French fine-dining restaurant with provincial decor, Loose Box has such a formidable reputation that it can maintain a strictly degustation-only policy and still have people clamouring to get in. Luxury cottages are available within the grounds, so you can splash out and make a night of it (B&B $450, with meal $700 to $750).

ℹ Information

Visitor Centre (☑ 08-9295 0202; www.munda ringtourism.com.au; 7225 Great Eastern Hwy; ⊘ 9.30am-4pm Mon-Sat, 10.30am-2.30pm Sun)

ℹ Getting There & Away

You can reach Mundaring from Perth on public transport in just over an hour, by taking a train to Midland and then bus 320 ($5.80). From here it's still 6km to the weir.

Walyunga National Park

The Avon River cuts a narrow gorge through the Darling Range at **Walyunga National Park** (www.dec.wa.gov.au; admission per car $11; ⊘ 8am-5pm) in Upper Swan. Off the Great Northern Hwy (Rte 95), 40km northeast of Perth, this 18-sq-km park is a great place for hiking and picnics.

The bushwalks include a 5.2km-return walk to Syd's Rapids as well as a 1.2km Aboriginal Heritage Trail. The best trail is the 10.6km Echidna Loop, which has tremendous views over the Swan and Avon Valleys. The park has one of the largest known camp sites of the Noongar people, still in use in the late 1800s. The area may well have been occupied by Aboriginal people for more than 6000 years.

SWAN VALLEY & GUILDFORD

Perthites love to swan around this semi-rural valley on the city's eastern fringe to partake in the finer things in life: booze, nosh and the great outdoors. Perhaps in tacit acknowledgement that its wines will never compete with the state's more prestigious regions (it doesn't really have the ideal climate), the Swan Valley compensates with plenty of galleries, breweries, provedores and restaurants.

The gateway to the valley is the National Trust–classified town of Guildford, established in 1829, around the same time as Perth and Fremantle. A clutch of interesting old buildings, one housing the visitor centre, make it the logical starting place for day trippers. Guildford is only 12km from central Perth and well served by suburban trains.

History

Guildford is built on the conjunction of three rivers and was an important meeting and ceremonial place for the Wadjuk people. When the British arrived and travelled up the Swan, access to fresh water led them to establish one of their first settlements here. In 1833, four years after the colony's founding, resistance leader Yagan was shot and decapitated in the Swan Valley.

The fertile valley land was soon turned to farming. Vines were first planted in the 1830s at Houghton's but it was after the arrival of Croatian settlers (from around 1916) that the farmland was increasingly transformed into wine production.

⊙ Sights & Activities

In Guildford, the centre of town is Stirling Sq, at the intersection of Swan and Meadow Sts. The cluster of buildings opposite the square includes the **Old Courthouse** (1866), which houses the visitor centre and has interesting historical displays. In the same grounds are the **gaol** (Old Courthouse; adult/child $2/free; ⊘ 10am-2pm Wed, Fri & Sat) and **Taylor's Cottage** (1863; admission included with gaol entry). Various **heritage walks** start from here; get information from the visitor centre or download a trail card from its website. Two kilometres east is **Woodbridge House** (Ford St; adult/child $5/3; ⊘ 1-4pm Thu-Sun), an 1885 colonial mansion overlooking the river.

The following sights are in the nearby Swan Valley.

Gomboc Gallery GALLERY
(www.gomboc-gallery.com.au; 50 James Rd, Middle Swan; ⊘ 10am-5pm Wed-Sun) FREE One of WA's

best commercial galleries, surrounded by an intriguing sculpture park.

Whiteman Park PARK
(www.whitemanpark.com; ⊙8.30am-6pm) Located in Caversham in West Swan, at 26 sq km this is Perth's biggest park, with over 30km of walkways and bike paths, and numerous picnic and barbecue spots. Enter from Lord St or Beechboro Rd, West Swan.

Caversham Wildlife Park ZOO
(www.cavershamwildlife.com.au; adult/child $23/10; ⊙9am-5.30pm, last entry 4.30pm) Part of the Whiteman Park estate, this wildlife park features cassowaries, echidnas, kangaroos, koalas, echidnas, potoroos, quokkas and native birds. Say g'day to Neil, the very laidback southern hairy wombat, for us. There are also farm shows for the kids.

Bennet Brook Railway TRAIN RIDES
(www.whitemanpark.com; adult/child $8/4; ⊙11am-1pm Wed, Thu, Sat & Sun) Train rides on the Whiteman Park estate.

Tram Rides TRAM RIDES
(www.pets.org.au; adult/child $5/2.50; ⊙noon-2pm Tue & Fri-Sun) Rides on heritage trams at Whiteman Park.

Revolutions MUSEUM
(www.whitemanpark.com.au; entry by gold coin donation; ⊙10am-4pm) Museum celebrating transport in WA with horse-drawn wagons, camels, trains, boats and planes. It's located on the Whiteman Park estate.

Motor Museum of WA MUSEUM
(www.motormuseumofwa.asn.au; adult/child $10/7; ⊙10am-4pm) Vintage cars and motorbikes. Located at Whiteman Park.

✖ Eating & Drinking

In this 'Valley of Taste' eating and drinking tend to go hand in hand as many of the wineries and breweries have restaurants attached.

The Swan Valley vibe is more low-key and relaxed than that of Margaret River – don't expect grand estates. There are more than 40 vineyards, concentrated mainly along busy West Swan Rd (the road leading north from the visitor centre) and the Great Northern Hwy (running parallel to the east). There's an excellent map in the free *Food & Wine Trail Guide,* available from the visitor centre in Guildford. Tastings are usually free.

The following are all in the Swan Valley, with the exception of the Rose & Crown and Jezebelle, both in Guildford.

Margaret River Chocolate Company CHOCOLATE, CAFE $
(www.chocolatefactory.com.au; 5123 West Swan Rd, West Swan; ⊙9am-5pm) With free tastings, this chocolate shop is often mobbed by families and tour groups.

Jezebelle CAFE, TAPAS $$
(⌨08-6278 3538; www.jezebelle.com.au; 127 James St, Guildford; tapas & shared plates $10-24, breakfast $12-24; ⊙noon-late Wed-Fri, 7am-late Sat, 7am-6pm Sun) An exciting selection of WA, Spanish and Italian wines partner with interesting tapas and shared plates at Guildford's Jezebelle. Try the manchego cheese and capsicum croquettes with sweetcorn relish or chicken and rabbit paella. Leisurely weekend breakfasts are equally classy. Bookings are recommended for dinner, and it's a short walk from the Guildford train station if you're staying in Perth.

Rose & Crown PUB $$
(www.rosecrown.com.au; 105 Swan St, Guildford; mains $26-39) In Guildford, WA's oldest still-operating pub (1841) has a wonderful leafy beer garden and lots of different spaces to explore inside. Have a beer in the cellar bar, where there's a convict-built well, and, while you're there, check out the sealed-off tunnel that used to connect the hotel with the river.

Black Swan RESTAURANT, WINERY $$
(⌨08-9296 6090; www.blackswanwines.com.au; 8600 West Swan Rd, Henley Brook; mains $29-38; ⊙tastings 11am-3pm, lunch daily, dinner Wed-Sat) It's slightly ugly duckling from the outside, but inside Black Swan has an upmarket dining room with views looking over the vines to the ranges. The food is sophisticated and delicious, ranging from grilled Tasmanian salmon to top-quality eye fillet beef (the latter around $45).

Sandalford RESTAURANT $$$
(www.sandalford.com; 3210 West Swan Rd, Caversham; mains $36-45; ⊙tastings 9am-5pm, lunch noon-3pm) Sandalford has the nicest surrounds of any of the wineries, and plays host to weddings and major concerts. It's also one of the valley's big-time, long-term operators.

Lamont's   TAPAS $$
(www.lamonts.com.au; 85 Bisdee Rd, Millendon; tapas $11.50-18.50; ☺10am-5pm Thu-Sun) Now that Lamont winery's fine-dining efforts are focused in East Perth, it's just lazy tastings and tapas up here under the open sky. The wine's very good, much of it grown in its Margaret River vineyard.

★**RiverBank Estate**   MODERN AUSTRALIAN $$$
(☑08-9377 1805; www.riverbankestate.com.au; 126 Hamersley Rd, Caversham; mains $36-40; ☺tastings 10am-5pm, lunch) Our pick of the valley's restaurants, RiverBank winery is a wonderful place to while away a few hours over excellent Modern Australian cuisine. It's a little more dressed up than most other places and there's a charge for tastings if you're not dining in the restaurant, but we're willing to let that go when the food's this good. There's live jazz on the first Saturday of the month.

Dear Friends   MODERN AUSTRALIAN $$$
(☑08-9279 2815; www.dearfriends.com.au; 100 Benara Road, Caversham; degustation menu with/without wine $ 185/115, 5-course tasting menu with/without wine $ 139/89; ☺6pm-late Wed-Sat, noon-3pm Sat & Sun) Get ready for a culinary adventure at Dear Friends. Innovation and a host of international flavours are showcased in the restaurant's renowned degustation and tasting menus. Courses include air-dried ham with Swan Valley free-range yolks and locally foraged herbs, and dessert combining beetroot with wood sorrel and rich dark chocolate. Naturally, the wine list is one of WA's finest.

★**Feral Brewing Company**   CRAFT BEER
(www.feralbrewing.com.au; 152 Haddrill Rd; ☺11am-5pm Sun-Thu, till late Fri & Sat) Here's your chance to try some of Australia's finest craft beers. Head brewer Brendan Varis is regularly lauded, with his always-interesting brews including the mighty Hop Hog American Pale Ale, or Watermelon Warhead, a wheat beer infused with watermelon (!). Beer geeks definitely should sign up for a tasting paddle of six beers, and tuck into Feral's robust pub grub menu.

Mash   CRAFT BEER
(www.mashbrewing.com.au; 10250 West Swan Rd, Henley Brook; ☺11am-5pm Mon-Tue, till late Wed-Sun) A lively bar-like atmosphere and a selection of homemade lager, ales, wheat beer and cider. Interesting seasonal brews are always worth trying.

Houghton   WINERY
(www.houghton-wines.com.au; Dale Rd, Middle Swan; ☺10am-5pm) The Swan's oldest and best-known winery is surrounded by pleasant grounds, which include a jacaranda grove. There's a gallery in the cellar where bushranger Moondyne Joe was caught, and a small display of old winemaking equipment.

ℹ Information

Visitor Centre (☑08-9379 9400; www.swanvalley.com.au; Old Courthouse, cnr Swan & Meadow Sts, Guildford; ☺9am-4pm) Information and maps, plus an interesting display on local history.

ℹ Getting There & Away

Guildford falls within Zone 2 of Perth's public transport system, and it's only $4 by bus or by train on the Midland Line from Perth, East Perth or Mt Lawley station.

To get around the Swan Valley you'll need to drive or take a tour (see p56). Bikes can be hired from **Bike Hire at Brookleigh** (☑08-9296 0012; bike.hire@brookleigh.com.au; 1235 Great Northern Hwy, Brookleigh) in the north of the valley.

For Whiteman Park, catch a train on the Midland Line from Perth to Bassendean Station. Switch to a bus to Ellenbrook and get off at Lord St (bus stop 15529).

AVON VALLEY

The lush green Avon Valley – with its atmospheric homesteads featuring big verandahs, rickety wooden wagons and moss-covered rocks – was 'discovered' by European settlers in early 1830 after food shortages forced Governor Stirling to dispatch Ensign Dale to search the Darling Range for arable land. What he found was the upper reaches of the Swan River, but he presumed it was a separate river – which is why its name changes from 'the Swan' to 'the Avon' in Walyunga National Park. The valley was very soon settled, just a year after Perth was founded, and many of the historic stone buildings still stand proudly in the towns and countryside in the area.

This country traditionally belongs to the Balardung, another of the Noongar peoples.

York

POP 2100

Unrelentingly quaint, York is the most atmospheric spot in the Avon Valley and a wonderful place to while away a couple of hours on a Sunday, when it's at its liveliest. Avon Tce is lined with restored heritage buildings, and the entire town has been classified by the National Trust.

Only 97km from Perth, York is the oldest inland town in WA, first settled in 1831, just two years after the Swan River Colony. The settlers here saw similarities in the Avon Valley and their native Yorkshire, so Governor Stirling bestowed the name York.

Convicts were brought to the region in 1851 and contributed to the development of the district; the ticket-of-leave hiring depot was not closed until 1872, four years after transportation of convicts to WA ceased. During the gold rush, York prospered as a commercial centre, servicing miners who were heading to Southern Cross, a goldfields town 273km to the east. Most of its buildings date from this time.

Sights & Activities

Avon Tce is lined with **significant buildings**, such as the town hall, Castle Hotel, police station, Old Gaol & Courthouse and Settlers House. **Holy Trinity Church** (Pool St), by the Avon River, was completed in 1854 and features stained-glass windows designed by WA artist Robert Juniper, and a rare pipe organ. The **suspension bridge** across the Avon was built in 1906.

York Mill   MARKET, GALLERY

(www.theyorkmill.com.au; 13 Broome St; 10am-4pm Wed-Sun) Built in 1892, York's four-storey flour mill now houses the **Mill Cafe** (www.theyorkmill.com.au; lunch $10-18; 10am-4pm Wed-Sun) and an excellent gallery selling jarrah furniture, and art and crafts by local artisans. There are free monthly exhibitions, and occasional one-off events like medieval fayres and banquets. A bistro and craft brewery are planned for late 2013.

Residency Museum   MUSEUM

(www.yorksoc.org.au; Brook St; adult/child $4/1; 1-3pm Tue, Wed & Thu, 11am-3.30pm Sat & Sun) Built in 1858, this museum houses some intriguing historic exhibits and poignant old black-and-white photos of York.

Motor Museum   MUSEUM

(www.yorkwa.com.au/Motor.Museum; 116 Avon Tce; adult/child $9/4; 9.30am-3pm) A must for vintage-car enthusiasts.

AROUND PERTH AVON VALLEY

Avon Valley

0 — 20 km
0 — 10 miles

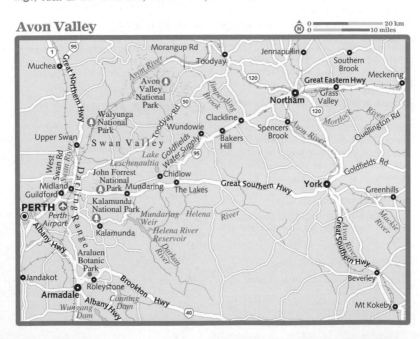

Skydive Express   SKYDIVING
(📞 08-9444 4199; www.skydive.com.au; 3453 Spencers Brook Rd; tandem jumps 10,000/14,000ft $339/399) The Avon Valley is WA's skydiving centre; the drop zone is about 3km from town.

🍴 Sleeping & Eating

York is a popular getaway destination for charm-chasing Perthites, so prices rise on the weekends. Another good place to eat is the Mill Cafe.

York Caravan Park   CARAVAN PARK **$**
(📞 08-9641 1421; york2caravan@hotmail.com; Eighth Rd; sites s/d $25/30) You can pitch your tent in a bush setting in this small park on the edge of town.

★ Faversham House   B&B **$$**
(📞 08-9641 1366; www.favershamhouse.com.au; 24 Grey St; r $120-275; ❋ 🐾) If you've ever wished you were 'to the manor born', indulge your fantasies in this grand stone mansion (1840). The rooms in the main house are large, TV-free and strewn with antiques; some have four-poster beds. All have smallish private bathrooms. The cheaper rooms are in the old servants' quarters (naturally).

Imperial Inn   BOUTIQUE HOTEL **$$**
(📞 08-9641 1255; www.imperialhotelyork.com.au; 83 Avon Tce; r $130-240; 🐾) Located in a beautiful stone heritage building, the Imperial offers zooshed-up rooms across the lawn in what might well have been the old stables. There are no TVs but there are iPod docks. Check online for good midweek discounts.

Jules Cafe   CAFE **$**
(121 Avon Tce; 🕐 8am-4pm Mon-Sat) 🍴 Putting a colourful spin on heritage York since 1990, Jules Cafe channels a Lebanese heritage for top-notch kebabs, falafel and Middle Eastern sweets. A funky new-age accent is introduced with organic, vege and gluten-free options.

ℹ️ Information

Visitor Centre (📞 08-9641 1301; www.avonvalleywa.com.au; 81 Avon Tce, Town Hall; 🕐 10am-4pm)

ℹ️ Getting There & Away

Transwa (📞 1300 662 205; www.transwa.wa.gov.au) coach routes include:
➤ GE2 (three per week) to East Perth ($16, 1½ hours), Mundaring ($13, 47 minutes), Hyden ($38, 3¼ hours) and Esperance ($78, 8½ hours)
➤ GS2 to Northam ($8, 33 minutes, six per week), Mt Barker ($53, 5¼ hours, four per week) and Albany ($58, six hours, four per week)

Northam

POP 6000

This busy commercial centre is the major town of the Avon Valley. It's a likeable place with some fine heritage buildings and pleasant cafes, but little to justify a longer stay. The railway line from Perth once ended here and miners had to make the rest of the weary trek to the goldfields by road; it now continues all the way to Sydney.

In recent years, Northam has become the hub for various Avon Valley festivals.

🎉 Festivals & Events

Avon Valley Vintage Festival VINTAGE, ANTIQUES
(ww.avonvalleywa.com.au; 🕐 late Mar-early Apr) Three days of antiques and collectables, and vintage spins on fashion, cars and bicycles.

Avon Valley Gourmet Food & Wine Festival   FOOD, WINE
(www.avonvalleywa.com.au; 🕐 early Jun) A weekend of artisan food, wine and produce from the Avon Valley and around the state.

Avon River Festival   SPORT
(www.avondescent.com.au; 🕐 early Aug) Street parade, markets and fireworks followed by the Avon Descent, a gruelling 133km whitewater event for power dinghies, kayaks and canoes.

⊙ Sights & Activities

Burlong Pool   NATURAL POOL
This picnic-ready natural pool on the Avon River is a very significant Noongar site. It is believed to be the summer home of the Wargal, the giant snakelike creature that created the waterways, and brought life to the land. It's customary to throw a handful of sand into the water out of respect. If the water stirs, keep out; otherwise all's well. Information boards recount this story and the site's history.

Follow the river southwest from the visitor centre for 3.5km. This is part of an 18km path along the river called Dorntj Koorliny (Walking Together). Otherwise, take Fitzgerald Rd, which becomes Burlong Rd, and follow it to the end.

Morby Cottage HISTORIC BUILDING
(Katrine Rd; adult/child $2/1; ⊘10.30am-4pm Sun) Built in 1836 as the home of John Morrell (founder of Northam), it now houses various family heirlooms and early Northam memorabilia.

Old Railway Station Museum MUSEUM
(Fitzgerald St; adult/child $2/0.50; ⊘10.30am-4pm Sun) This museum, housed in an 1886 National Trust–registered building, showcases railway memorabilia.

Windward Adventures BALLOONING
(☑08-9621 2000; www.ballooning.net.au; weekday/weekend flights $270/320; ⊘Apr-Oct) Sunset flights followed by a champagne breakfast.

 Eating

Cafe Yasou CAFE **$**
(www.cafeyasou.com.au; 175 Fitzgerald St; mains $11-18; ⊘8am-4pm Mon-Fri, to noon Sat) This sunny cafe serves excellent coffee, grilled haloumi and Greek salads. If you're not in a Med mood, there's a selection of sandwiches and cakes. Our pick is the Yasou Breakfast, crammed with bacon, mushrooms, tomato and feta cheese on rosti potatoes.

Riversedge Cafe CAFE **$**
(www.riversedgecafe.com.au; 1 Grey St; breakfast $10-21, lunch $13-26; ⊘8am-4pm) The verandahs of this big corrugated-iron building are a wonderful place to soak up the sun and river views.

ℹ Information

Visitor Centre (☑08-9622 2100; www.visitnorthamwa.com.au; 2 Grey St; ⊘9am-5pm Mon-Fri, to 4pm Sat & Sun) Overlooking a picturesque portion of river with fountains and a compact island. The *Experience the Avon Valley* brochure has good maps.

ℹ Getting There & Away

Transwa (☑1300 662 205; www.transwa.wa.gov.au) coach GS2 heads to East Perth ($19, 1½ hours, six per week), York ($8, 33 minutes, six per week), Mt Barker ($56, 5¾ hours, four per week) and Albany ($63, 6½ hours, four per week).

Northam is a stop on the AvonLink and Prospector lines, with trains to East Perth ($19, 1½ hours, 12 per week), Toodyay ($8, 20 minutes, 12 per week) and Kalgoorlie ($71, 5¼ hours, nine per week).

Toodyay

POP 1100

Historic Toodyay, only 85km northeast of Perth, is a popular weekend destination for browsing the bric-a-brac shops or having a beer on the verandah of an old pub. As you'd expect of a town classified by the National

---

THE MYTHOLOGY OF MOONDYNE JOE

The state of Victoria's most famous outlaw, Ned Kelly, is known for his gun battles with the law, but WA's most illustrious bushranger, Moondyne Joe, is famous for escaping. Over and over again.

Joseph Bolitho Johns (1828–1900), sent to WA for larceny, arrived in Fremantle in 1853 and was granted an immediate ticket of leave for good behaviour. This good behaviour lasted until 1861, when he was arrested on a charge of horse stealing; however, he escaped that night from Toodyay jail on the horse he rode in on, sitting snugly on the magistrate's new saddle. He was recaptured and sentenced to three years' imprisonment. Between November 1865 and March 1867 he made four attempts to escape, three of them successful. When eventually captured he was placed in a special reinforced cell with triple-barred windows in Fremantle, but in 1867 he managed to escape from the prison yard while breaking rocks. He served more time in Fremantle prison when recaptured and was conditionally pardoned in 1873. After release he worked in the Vasse district and kept his nose relatively clean, but he suffered from poor mental health later in life until his death in 1900. You can see his grave at Fremantle cemetery.

While Moondyne Joe was a criminal, these days it pays to be in the 'Moondyne Joe' business. Three books, including the latest, a prize-winning juvenile-fiction novel called *The Legend of Moondyne Joe* (Mark Greenwood), have been written about him; a Moondyne festival is held in Toodyay on the first Sunday of May; and a cave in Margaret River is named after him, as well as a pub, a caravan park and who knows what else. Let's hope he doesn't escape his final resting place and start asking for royalties...

Trust, it has plenty of charming heritage buildings. Originally known by the name Newcastle, Toodyay (pronounced '2J'), came from the Aboriginal word *duidgee* (place of plenty); the name was adopted around 1910.

◉ Sights & Activities

Connor's Mill   MUSEUM
(Stirling Tce; admission $3; ⊗9am-4pm) Start at the top of this aged flour mill (1870) and descend through three floors of chugging machinery and explanatory displays that cover the milling process, along with local history. Entry is through the neighbouring visitor centre. **St Stephen's Church** (1862), directly across the road, is also worth a look.

Newcastle Gaol   MUSEUM
(17 Clinton St; admission $3; ⊗10am-3pm) Built in the 1860s using convict labour, the gaol complex includes a courtroom, cells and stables. A gallery here tells the story of Moondyne Joe.

Coorinja   WINE TASTING
(Toodyay Rd; ⊗10am-5pm Mon-Sat) Operating continuously since the 1870s, this winery specialises in fortified wines including port, sherry, muscat and Marsala. It's 6km out of town, on the road to Perth.

✖ Festivals & Events

Moondyne Festival   HISTORICAL
(www.moondynefestival.com.au; ⊗1st Sun May) Costumed hijinks in honour of the outlaw..

Toodyay International Food Festival   FOOD
Held on the first weekend in August on the day before the Avon Descent.

Toodyay Agricultural Show   AGRICULTURE
Early October.

⊨ Sleeping & Eating

Avalon Homestead   GUESTHOUSE $
(⊘08-9574 5050; www.avalonhomestead.com.au; 381 Julimar Rd; r $145) Popular with discerning oldies, Avalon has tidy, somewhat chintzy rooms in a peaceful spot 4km out of town. The gardens are lovely, and it's a popular spot for visiting arts-and-crafts groups.

Cola Café & Museum   CAFE $
(www.colacafe.com.au; 128 Stirling Tce; snacks $10-21; ⊗9am-4.30pm) Coca-Cola memorabilia runs amok here. Order a cola spider (Coke with a scoop of ice cream) and a big burger and play 'guess the 1950s tune'.

ⓘ Information

Ye Olde Lolly Shoppe (⊘08-9574 2435; www.toodyay.com; 7 Piesse St; ⊗9am-4pm) Stock up on tourist information and fudge at the same time.

ⓘ Getting There & Away

Toodyay is a stop on the **Transwa** (⊘1300 662 205; www.transwa.wa.gov.au) AvonLink and Prospector lines, with trains to East Perth ($16, 1¼ hours, seven per week), Northam ($8, 20 minutes, 12 per week) and Kalgoorlie ($74, 5½ hours, four per week).

Avon Valley National Park

Featuring granite outcrops, forests and wonderful fauna, this **national park** (www.dec.wa.gov.au; per car $11; ⊗8am-4pm) is accessed from Toodyay and Morangup Rds. The Avon River flows through the centre of the park in winter and spring, but is usually dry at other times.

The park is the northern limit of the jarrah forests, and the jarrah and marri are mixed with wandoo woodland. Bird species include rainbow bee-eaters, honeyeaters, kingfishers and rufous treecreepers. In the understorey. honey possums and western pygmy-possums hide among the dead leaves, and skinks and geckos scuttle about.

There are **campsites** (⊘08-9574 2540; adult/child $7/2) with basic facilities (eg pit toilets and barbecues).

NEW NORCIA

POP 70

The idyllic monastery settlement of New Norcia, 132km from Perth, consists of a cluster of ornate, Spanish-style buildings set incongruously in the Australian bush. Founded in 1846 by Spanish Benedictine monks as an Aboriginal mission, the working monastery today holds prayers and retreats, alongside a business producing boutique breads and gourmet goodies.

New Norcia Museum & Art Gallery (⊘08-9654 8056; www.newnorcia.wa.edu.au; Great Northern Hwy; combined museum & town tours adult/family $25/60; ⊗10am-4.30pm) traces the history of the monastery and houses impressive art, including contemporary exhibitions and one of the country's largest collections of post-Renaissance religious art. The gift shop sells souvenirs, honeys, preserves and breads baked in the monks' wood-fired oven.

Inside the **abbey church**, try to spot the native wildlife in the sgraffito artworks that depict the Stations of the Cross. Look hard, as there's also an astronaut.

Guided two-hour **town tours** (www.newnorcia.wa.edu.au; adult/child $15/10; ⊙11am & 1.30pm) offer a look the abbey church and the frescoed college chapels; purchase tickets from the museum. At 4.30pm on Saturday afternoons, there is the opportunity to meet the monks.

New Norcia Hotel (⊉08-9654 8034; www.newnorcia.wa.edu.au; Great Northern Hwy; s/d $75/95) harks back to a more genteel time, with sweeping staircases, high ceilings, understated rooms (with shared bathrooms) and wide verandahs. An international menu ($15 to $30) is available at the bar or in the elegant dining room (where you can also nab a cooked breakfast).

Sit outside on the terrace and sample the delicious but deadly New Norcia Abbey Ale, a golden, hand-crafted, Belgian-style ale brewed especially for the abbey. Sunday is a good day to visit, either for breakfast ($20), or the popular lunchtime carvery (adult/child $19.50/14.50).

The abbey also offers lodging in the **Monastery Guesthouse** (⊉08-9654 8002; www.newnorcia.wa.edu.au; full-board suggested donation $80) within the walls of the southern cloister. Guests can also join in prayers with the monks (and males can dine with them).

WILDFLOWER WAY

Away from the coast, there are four other common routes that head north, with three running to Geraldton and the fourth, the Great Northern Hwy, disappearing into the outback and re-emerging 1600km later at Port Hedland. The Brand Hwy (Rte 1) is the least interesting for travellers, and its wildflowers can be sampled in day trips from the Turquoise Coast. Midlands Rd (Rte 116) and the Wildflower Way (Rte 115) are home to wheat silos, wildflowers and little one-pub towns; the towns are a hive of activity between August and September as minibuses full of pensioners zoom around like frantic bees hunting blossoms. Whatever the time of year, the wheat farmers have one eye on the weather and one on their crop, no doubt wondering if it will ever rain again.

❶ Getting There & Away

Transwa (⊉1300 662 205; www.transwa.wa.gov.au) runs bus services along Rte 116 on Tuesday, Thursday, Saturday and Sunday, and twice weekly (to/from Geraldton on Monday, Thursday/Tuesday and Friday) on Rte 115.

Integrity (⊉1800 226 339; www.integritycoachlines.com.au; ⊙to/from Perth Sat/Wed) runs buses weekly up the Great Northern Hwy (Rte 95).

Moora

POP 2574

Tall gums, wide streets, a pub with a wide verandah, a couple of galleries, a few B&Bs and a railway line (wheat trains only) define this agricultural service centre – a good base from which to explore the surrounding area.

The excellent **visitor centre** (⊉08-9653 1053; www.moora.wa.gov.au; Moora Railway Station; ⊙8.30am-4pm Mon-Fri; @) can supply a map of the local wildflowers and other sites including **Jingemia Cave** in Watheroo National Park. An interesting town walk takes in Moora's heritage buildings and murals.

For hundreds of WA wildflowers, visit the **Western Wildflower Farm** (www.wildflowerswa.com.au; Midlands Rd; ⊙9am-5pm Mon-Sat) **FREE**, 19km north of Moora. Morning and afternoon teas are also served. The **Wildflower Interpretative Education Centre** at the farm is a great stop if you're heading out on a wildflower pilgrimage. See the website also for information and photographs on many variants.

Moora Caravan Park (⊉0409 511 400; Dandaragan St; unpowered/powered sites $18/25, chalets $110-160) offers basic, shady sites, and some comfortable new chalets. Pay at the Gull service station. The visitor centre can arrange accommodation at well-maintained B&Bs, but you'll need a car as most are slightly out of town.

Right in town, the **Drovers Inn** (⊉08-9651 1108; cnr Dandaragan & Padbury Sts; hotel $65-85, motel $110, mains $20-34; ⊙11am-late) is a classic Aussie pub with standard rooms with shared bathrooms and counter meals. Out the back are more moderm motel rooms.

Moora's **Pioneer Bakery & Restaurant** (⊉08-9651 1277; 50 Padbury St; meals $5-20; ⊙7.30am-4pm Mon-Fri) is a great place for brekkie and pies. The best coffee (and muffins!) in town is at the **Wheatbelt Gallery** (Padbury St; ⊙9am-5pm Tue-Sat), opposite the visitor centre, while art fans can cross the tracks to **Moora Art Gallery** (☑ 0447 997 423; 95 Gardiner St; ☉ 10am-4pm Thu-Sat).

There is a supermarket and ATMs on Dandaragan and Padbury Sts.

Transwa buses go to Perth ($30, three hours) and Geraldton ($46, four hours) via Rte 116.

Wongan Hills

POP 1462

From New Norcia, take the back road via Yerecoin and you'll pass the intriguing **Lake Ninan**, a huge saltpan. Wongan Hills, with its gently undulating country and myriad verticordias, makes a pleasant change from the flat wheat-belt towns, and there are plenty of trails for bushwalkers.

The **visitor centre** (☑ 08-9671 1973; www. wongantourism.com.au; Wongan Rd, Railway Station; ☉ 9am-5pm, closed Sun Nov-Easter) has maps (and guides) for popular wildflower haunts such as **Mt Matilda** (8km return), 12km west of Wongan Hills, and **Christmas Rock** (behind the caravan park; 2km return). **Reynoldson Nature Reserve** (1km one way), 29km north of Wongan Hills, has spectacular verticordias, and you can drive to the top of **Mt O'Brien**, 11km west of Wongan Hills.

Wongan Hills Caravan Park (☑ 08-9671 1009; Wongan Rd; unpowered/powered site $19/24, cabins & chalets $70-110) has shady sites and a good kitchen.

Art deco **Wongan Hills Hotel** (☑ 08-9671 1022; www.wonganhillshotel.com.au; 5 Fenton Pl; hotel s/d $70/90, motel d $110, meals $18-32) offers classic hotel rooms, some opening onto the upstairs verandah, and modern motel rooms in a separate building. Meals are typical pub fare, including good pizzas.

There's a supermarket and bakery on Fenton Pl.

Transwa goes to Perth ($30, three hours), and Perenjori ($30, three hours) via Rte 115.

Perenjori

POP 573

Perenjori, 360km from Perth, is a pretty town surrounded by abundant wildlife and, from July to November, stunning wildflowers. The **visitor centre** (☑ 08-9973 1105; www. perenjori.wa.gov.au; Fowler St; ☉ 9am-4pm Mon-Fri Jul-Oct), also home to the **pioneer museum** (adult/child $2/0.50), has self-drive brochures including *The Way of the Wildflowers* and

Monsignor Hawes Heritage Trail. They can provide access to the beautiful **St Joseph's Church**, designed by the prolific Monsignor John Hawes.

Shady **Perenjori Caravan Park** (☑ 08-9973 1193; Crossing Rd; unpowered/powered site $20/30, chalets & eco-home $20-200) offers grassy tent sites and decent facilities.

The friendly, family-owned **Perenjori Hotel** (☑ 08-9973 1020; Fowler St; d $80) has basic pub rooms and good-value bar meals.

Transwa has services to Perth ($53, six hours) and Geraldton ($35, three hours) via Rte 115.

Morawa, Mingenew & Mullewa

The 'three Ms' form a triangle that buzzes during wildflower season but has limited appeal to travellers outside this. Most of the visitor centres close, and Port Denison-Dongara and Geraldton are only an hour away.

Each has a caravan park with tent sites, a local pub with meals and rooms, a supermarket or general store, and a Transwa bus connection several times weekly. In wildflower season, the shire may run minibuses from the visitor centres to the best sites.

Morawa and Mullewa both have distinctive churches designed by Monsignor John Hawes.

Coalseam Conservation Park (www.dec. wa.gov.au; camping per person $7), 34km northeast of Mingenew on the Irwin River, has a variety of everlastings (paper daisies), a short loop walk with interpretive signs, and ancient fossil shells embedded in the cliffs. There are dusty, unpowered camp sites at Miners, with toilets and picnic tables.

Mullewa is famous for its wreath flower, *Lechenaultia macrantha,* and holds an annual wildflower show at the end of August.

In season, the roads heading east to Yalgoo are normally carpeted in everlastings.

ⓘ Information

Mingenew Visitor Centre (☑ 08-9928 1081; ☉ 9am-5pm Jul-Sep) At Mingenew post office.

Morawa Visitor Centre (☑ 08-9971 1421; www. morawa.wa.gov.au; 34 Winfield St; ☉ Jun–mid-Oct) Note restricted months of opening.

Mullewa Visitor Centre (☑ 08-9961 1500; www.mullewatourism.com.au; cnr Jose St & Maitland Rd; ☉ 8.30am-4.30pm, closed Sat & Sun Oct-Jun; ⓐ) Information on wildflower-viewing opportunities.

SUNSET COAST

The coast road north of Perth leads to some popular spots for travellers. Within an hour's drive, Perth's outer suburbs give way to the bushland oasis of Yanchep National Park, with wonderful wildlife and walking trails.

The coastline ranges from tranquil bays at Guilderton, good for swimming and fishing, to windswept beaches at Lancelin, with excellent conditions for windsurfing and kitesurfing.

Yanchep

POP 2482

Yanchep and its close neighbour Two Rocks are effectively Perth's northernmost suburbs. The town was developed extensively during the 1980s by (now convicted fraudster) Alan Bond, and the legacy of this era includes a large marina and some dubious bits of sculpture (dolphins, a dragon and a giant Neptune).

Apart from nice beaches, the big drawcard is the woodlands and wetlands of **Yanchep National Park** (www.dec.wa.gov.au/yanchep; Wanneroo Rd; per car $11; ⊙ visitor centre 9.15am-4.30pm), home to hundreds of species of fauna and flora, including koalas, kangaroos, emus and cockatoos. The free *Wild About Walking* brochure outlines nine walking trails, from the 20-minute Dwerta Mia walk to the four-day Coastal Plain walk. Register with the park centre for longer walks.

The park features splendid caves, which can be viewed on 45-minute tours (adult/child $10/5; five per day). On weekends at 1pm and 2pm, local Noongar guides run excellent tours on Indigenous history, lifestyle and culture (adult/child $10/5), and didgeridoo and dance performances (adult/child $10/5).

Within the national park, **Yanchep Inn** (☑ 08-9561 1001; www.yanchepinn.com.au; hotel r $80, old motel r $115, new motel r $170-210; ✳) is more attractive from the outside than the inside. The inn itself has basic rooms with shared facilities and a cafe downstairs. It's more comfortable in the newer of the two motel blocks, with lake views and rammed-earth walls, but perhaps a little overpriced. Prices jump up by $25 to $55 at weekends.

To get to Yanchep by public transport, catch a train on the Joondalup line from Perth's Esplanade station to Clarkson, then catch bus 490.

Guilderton

POP 150

Some 43km north of Yanchep, Guilderton is a popular and staggeringly beautiful family-holiday spot. Children paddle safely near the mouth of the Moore River, while adults enjoy fishing and surfing on the ocean beach.

The name comes from the wreck of the *Vergulde Draeck,* part of the Dutch East India Company fleet, which ran aground nearby in 1656, reputedly carrying a treasure in guilders. Its original name was Gabbadah, meaning 'mouth of water', although many older Perthites still refer to it as Moore River.

The **Guilderton Caravan Park** (☑ 08-9577 1021; www.guildertoncaravanpark.com.au; 2 Dewar St; sites per 2 people $29-40, chalets $165) has self-contained chalets, but you'll need your own linen. There's also a cafe and general store, and a compact volunteer-run **visitor centre** (with erratic hours) next door.

Lancelin

POP 670

Afternoon offshore winds and shallows, protected by an outlying reef, make Lancelin perfect for windsurfing and kitesurfing, attracting action-seekers from around the world. In January, wind-worshippers descend for the **Lancelin Ocean Classic** (www.lancelinoceanclassic.com.au) windsurfer race, starting at Ledge Point to the south.

The coral and limestone reef, no-fishing zone and dazzling white sands also make Lancelin a great snorkelling spot, while the mountainous soft, white dunes on the edge of town are good for sandboarding.

🏃 Activities

Surfschool SURFING
(☑ 08-9444 5399, 1800 198 121; www.surfschool.com.au; 69 Casserley Way; 3-/6-hr lessons $40/75; ⊙ 8am) The main beach's gentle waves make it a good place for beginners and there are bigger breaks nearby for more experienced surfers. Three- to six-hour lessons include boards and wetsuits. There are also surf-camp packages, including lessons, transfers from Perth and accommodation.

Makanikai Kiteboarding KITEBOARDING
(☑ 0406 807 309; www.makanikaikiteboarding.com; lessons/courses from $60/200, rental per hr/day $20/60) Lessons and tuition in the fine

art of kiteboarding, and gear rental; accommodation packages are also available.

Have a Chat General Store SANDBOARDING
(☑08-9655 1054; 104 Gingin Rd; ☺7am-7pm)
Hires sandboards for $10 per two hours.

🛏 Sleeping & Eating

★**Lancelin Lodge YHA** HOSTEL $
(☑08-9655 2020; www.lancelinlodge.com.au; 10
Hopkins St; dm/d/f $30/80/98; @🛏🌐) This
laid-back hostel is well equipped and welcoming, with wide verandahs and lots of
communal spaces to hang about in. The excellent facilities include big kitchen, barbecue, wood-fire pizza oven, swimming pool,
ping-pong table, volleyball court and free
use of bikes and boogie boards.

Ledge Point Holiday Park CARAVAN PARK $
(☑1300 856 088; www.ledgepointholidaypark.com.
au; 742 Old Ledge Point Rd ; sites per 2 persons $36-
41, chalets & studios $120-230; @🌐) About 10
minutes' drive south of Lancelin, with excellent facilities and spotless accommodation
ranging from caravan and camping sites to
chalets and studios. Lots of family-friendly
attractions include pedal carts and a jumping pillow. Ledge Point's beach – good for
fishing and swimming – is around 500m
away.

Lancelin Caravan Park CARAVAN PARK $
(☑08-9655 1056; Hopkins St; sites per person $14,
on-site vans $70) Windsurfers love camping
out at this neat park – not for the facilities
and amenities, which are rudimentary, but
for the beachfront location.

Windsurfer Beach Chalets APARTMENT $$
(☑08-9655 1454; www.lancelinaccommodation.
com.au; 1 Hopkins St; d $165) Self-contained
two-bedroom chalets, near the windsurfing beach, are a good choice for groups of
friends and families (each chalet sleeps up to
six). They're functional and well equipped,
and have a sun terrace backing onto a grassy
area. The operators can also arrange accommodation in Lancelin and nearby Ledge
Point in a variety of self-contained holiday
homes.

Kombi Cafe CAFE $
(2 Robertson Rd, Ledge Point; snacks & mains $10-
13.50) Cool surfing-inspired cafe a short
drive south of Lancelin at Ledge Point. Good
coffee, lots of local information, and fish and
chips to devour on the nearby beach.

Endeavour Tavern PUB $$
(58 Gingin Rd; mains $18-34) A classic beach-front Aussie pub with a beer garden over-looking the ocean. The casual eatery serves
decent seafood, pub-grub classics and a tasty
Mediterranean platter.

🛈 Getting There & Away

Lancelin is 130km north of Perth. **Greyhound**
(☑1300 473 946; www.greyhound.com.au) has
coaches to and from East Perth ($26, 1¾ hours),
Cervantes ($28, 1½ hours), Geraldton ($54, four
hours) and Carnarvon ($156, 10½ hours).

A second bus company, **Integrity** (☑1800
226 339; www.integritycoachlines.com.au), is
now also taking advantage of the faster access
possible on the recently opened Indian Ocean
Dr. Buses leave from Lancelin Lodge YHA Sunday to Friday north to Cervantes ($15, one hour),
Jurien Bay ($18, 1¼ hours) and Geraldton ($34,
four hours). Heading south, buses travel Monday
to Saturday to Perth ($18, 1¾ hours).

TURQUOISE COAST

Stretching north of Lancelin to Port Denison, the relaxed Turquoise Coast is dotted
with sleepy fishing villages, stunning beaches, extraordinary geological formations, rugged national parks and incredibly diverse
flora. Offshore marine parks and island nature reserves provide a safe breeding habitat
for Australian sea lions and other endangered species, while crayfishing brings in the
dollars. Once somewhat isolated, the whole
area has been brought within easy reach of
Perth by the completion of the final section
of Indian Ocean Dr between Lancelin and
Cervantes.

🛈 Getting There & Away

Greyhound (☑1300 473 946; www.greyhound.
com.au) runs services to and from Perth along
Indian Ocean Dr three times per week.

Integrity (p114) runs daily along the coast
between Perth and Geraldton and overnight
twice a week to and from Exmouth.

Cervantes & Pinnacles Desert

POP 480

Heading north from Lancelin on Indian
Ocean Dr, you will pass the tiny fishing-shack villages of **Wedge Island** (http://
wedgewa.com.au) and **Grey**, where access was

previously 4WD-only along the beach. Pressure from developers and government mean the future of these communities is uncertain, and although there are no facilities for tourists, you're welcome to wander.

The laid-back crayfishing town of **Cervantes**, 198km north of Perth, makes a pleasant overnight stop for enjoying the **Pinnacles Desert** and a good base for exploring the flora of the **Kwongan**, the inland heathland of Lesueur National Park (p115) and **Badgingarra National Park**. There are also some lovely beaches on which to while away the time.

Grab a copy of the *Turquoise Coast Self Drive Map* from Cervantes' combined **post office and visitor centre** (☑08-9652 7700, freecall 1800 610 660; www.visitpinnaclescountry.com.au; Cadiz St; ☺8am-5pm; @), which also supplies accommodation and tour information. The town's general store and liquor shop are also on this strip.

Just before town, turn off for Lake Thetis, where living stromatolites – the world's oldest organisms – inhabit the shoreline. Nearby **Hansen Bay Lookout** has excellent views across the coast. In town, walkways wend along the coastline and provide beach access.

⊙ Sights & Activities

★**Nambung National Park**   NATIONAL PARK
(per car $11) Situated 19km from Cervantes, Nambung is home to the spectacular **Pinnacles Desert**, a vast, alien-like plain studded with thousands of limestone pillars. Rising eerily from the desert floor, the pillars are remnants of compacted seashells that once covered the plain and, over millennia, subsequently eroded. A loop road runs through the formations, but it's more fun to wander on foot, especially at sunset, full moon or dawn, when the light is sublime and the crowds evaporate.

Nearby **Kangaroo Point** and **Hangover Bay** make nice picnic spots with BBQs and tables. The latter has the better swimming.

Lesueur National Park   NATIONAL PARK
(per car $11) This botanical paradise, 50km north of Cervantes, contains a staggering 820 plant species, many of them rare and endemic, such as the pine banksia *(Banksia tricupsis)* and Mt Lesueur grevillea

---

KWONGAN WILDFLOWERS

Take any road inland from the Turquoise Coast and you'll soon enter the Kwongan heathlands, where, depending on the season, the roadside verges burst with native wildflowers like banksia, grevillea, hakea, calothamnus, kangaroo paw and smokebush. While Lesueur National Park is an obvious choice for all things botanical, consider some of the following options.

➡ **Badgingarra National Park** Three-and-a-half kilometres of walking trails, kangaroo paws, banksias, grass trees, verticordia and a rare mallee. The back road linking Badgingarra to Lesueur is particularly rich in flora. Obtain details from the Badgingarra Roadhouse. There's also a picnic area on Bibby Rd.

➡ **Alexander Morrison National Park** Named after WA's first botanist. There are no trails, but you can drive through slowly on the Coorow Green Head Rd, which has loads of flora along its verge all the way from Lesueur. Expect to see dryandra, banksia, grevillea, smokebush, leschenaultia and honey myrtle.

➡ **Tathra National Park** Tathra has similar flora to Alexander Morrison National Park and the drive between the two is rich with banksia, kangaroo paw and grevillea.

➡ **Coomallo Rest Area** Orchids, feather flowers, black kangaroo paws, wandoo and river red gums can be found upstream and on the slopes of the small hill.

➡ **Brand Highway (Rte 1)** The route's not exactly conducive to slow meandering, but the highway verges are surprisingly rich in wildflowers, especially either side of Eneabba.

If you're overwhelmed and frustrated by not being able to identify all these strange new plants, consider staying at **Western Flora Caravan Park** (☑08-9955 2030; wfloracp@activ8.net.au; Brand Hwy, North Eneabba; unpowered/powered sites $24/26, d $65, onsite vans $75, chalets $120) where the enthusiastic owners run free two-hour wildflower walks across their 65-hectare property every day at 4.30pm.

(*Grevillea batrachioides*). Late winter sees the heath erupt into a mass of colour, and the park is also home to the endangered Carnaby's cockatoo. An 18km circuit drive is dotted with lookouts and picnic areas. Flat-topped **Mt Lesueur** (4km return walk) has panoramic coastal views.

☞ Tours

Many Perth-based companies offer day trips to the Pinnacles.

Turquoise Coast Enviro Tours GUIDED TOURS
(☑08-9652 7047; www.thepinnacles.com.au; 59 Seville St; 3hr Pinnacles tours $60, full-day Kwongan tours $170) Cervantes local and ex-ranger Mike Newton runs morning (8am, three hours) and evening (2½ hours before sunset) Pinnacles trips, as well as a full-day Kwongan tour, including Lesueur National Park and the coast up to Leeman.

🛏 Sleeping & Eating

Watch out for school holidays, when prices surge.

★Cervantes Lodge &
Pinnacles Beach Backpackers HOSTEL $
(☑1800 245 232; www.cervanteslodge.com.au; 91 Seville St; dm $30, d with/without bathroom $130/90; @) In a great location behind the dunes, this relaxing hostel has a wide verandah, small and tidy dorms, a nice communal kitchen and a cosy lounge area. Bright, spacious en-suite rooms, some with views, are next door in the lodge.

Pinnacles Caravan Park CARAVAN PARK $
(☑08-9652 7060; www.pinnaclespark.com.au; 35 Aragon St; unpowered/powered sites from $27/32, on-site vans/cabins $50/75; ☎) Fantastic location right behind the dunes with plenty of shady, grassy sites and on-site cafe.

★Amble Inn B&B $$
(☑0429 652 401; 2150 Cadda Rd, Hill River; d spa/non-spa $165/150; ❄) High up on the heathland, about 25km east of Cervantes, this hidden gem of a B&B has beautiful thick stone walls, cool, wide verandahs and superbly styled rooms. Watch the sunset over the coast from the nearby hill with a glass of your complimentary wine.

Cervantes Holiday Homes APARTMENT $$
(☑08-9652 7115; www.cervantesholidayhomes.com.au; cnr Malaga Ct & Valencia Rd; cottages from $130; ❄) These well-equipped, fully self-contained cottages are great value, especially for groups.

Pinnacles Edge Resort RESORT $$$
(☑08-9652 7788; www.pinnaclesedgeresort.com.au; 7 Aragon St; studio/spa/2-bedroom $213/265/343; ❄ ☎ ❄) Beautifully appointed luxury rooms, the more expensive with spas and balconies, are arranged around a central pool. There's an in-house restaurant and bar, and the adjoining motel has older-style doubles from $115.

Seashells Cafe CAFE $
(☑08-9652 7060; 35 Aragon St; ⊙8am-4pm) With great coffee and the best view in town, the Seashell makes an excellent pit-stop for breakfast or that afternoon cake.

Lobster Shack SEAFOOD $$
(☑08-9652 7010; www.lobstershack.com.au; 11 Madrid St; ⊙ shop 9am-5pm, lunch 11.30am-2.30pm) Craving for crayfish? They don't come much fresher than at this lobster factory-turned-lunch spot, where a delicious grilled cray, chips and salad will set you back $25. Self-guided tours (adult/child $15/7.50) and takeaway frozen seafood are also available.

Cervantes Country Club SEAFOOD $$$
(☑08-9652 7123; Aragon St; seafood platters from $55; ⊙6-9pm) The seafood platters at this humble sporting club (shorts and sandals OK) are legendary, and include prawns, oysters, fish, calamari, crayfish (in season, extra $10), salad and mountains of chips. Bring a friend.

❶ Getting There & Away

Integrity (p114) runs daily to Perth ($26, three hours), Dongara ($28, two hours) and Geraldton ($32, three hours) with a twice-weekly overnight service to Exmouth ($162, 14 hours).

Greyhound (☑1300 473 946; www.greyhound.com.au) runs three times weekly to Perth ($37, three hours) and Dongara ($40, two hours), continuing to Broome ($380, 31 hours). Locally, both buses stop at Jurien Bay (20 minutes), Green Head (40 minutes) and Leeman (55 minutes).

Jurien Bay

POP 1500

The largest town on the Turquoise Coast is likely to become quite a lot bigger after its selection as a 'Super Town', and eligible for the 'Royalties for Regions' scheme (see p246). Home to a hefty fishing fleet and lots of big houses, it's already rather spread out; however, there's a nice long swimming beach and great snorkelling and diving opportunities. Anglers have a choice of jetties and the lengthy foreshore walkway links several pleasant parks.

Accommodation in town caters mostly for Perth families. Holiday houses and apartments can be booked via local **real estate agents.** (☑08-9652 2055; www.jurien bayholidays.com; Shop 1A, 34 Bashford Street) Plan ahead for popular **Jurien Bay Tourist Park** (☑08-9652 1595; www.jurienbaytourist park.com.au; Roberts St; unpowered/powered site $28/33; on-site van from $90; 1-/2-bedroom chalet $115/145), with its comfortable chalets right behind the beach, although the tent sites are set back against the main road. Next door, the **Jetty Cafe** (☑08-9652 1999; meals $5-17; ☺7.30am-5pm) has a great position, decent brekkies, burgers and grilled fish.

The friendly **Sandpiper Tavern** (☑08-9652 1229; cnr Roberts & Sandpiper Sts; mains $25-35; ☺lunch noon-2pm, dinner 6-9pm) has a relaxed beer garden and does all the usual pub faves. There are several takeaway shops strung along Bashford St, as well as a supermarket and ATM. Sadly, there is presently no bike hire.

Green Head & Leeman

On the way to Green Head, stop at **Grigson Lookout** for a panoramic view of the coast and Kwongan. Tiny **Green Head** (population 280) has several beautiful bays; the horseshoe-shaped **Dynamite Bay** is the most spectacular and sheltered for swimmers. There's good fishing, snorkelling, surfing and windsurfing here and at nearby **Leeman** (population 400).

★ **Sea Lion Charters** (☑08-9953 1012; http://sealioncharters.biz; 24 Bryant St, Green Head; half-day tours adult/child $120/60) offers a magical experience interacting in shallow water with playful sea lions who mimic your every move. It helps to be a good snorkeller. Wetsuits are $10 extra.

Green Head has the best sleeping and eating options with the newly opened **Centrebreak Beach Stay** (☑08-9953 1896; www. centrebreakbeachstay.com.au; Lot 402 Ocean View Dr, Green Head; dm/d/f $35/150/190, meals $14-35; ☜), complete with licensed cafe, close to Dynamite Bay. **Cool Combination Cafe** (Dynamite Bay; ☺9.30am-4pm Mon-Sat) is just behind the beach, the lovely **Seaview B&B** (☑08-9953 1487; 25 Whiteman St; per person $65) has great views, and the relaxed and shady **Green Head Caravan Park** (☑08-9953 1131; 9 Green Head Rd, Green Head; unpowered/powered sites $20/28, on-site vans from $70) will suit most campers.

Nearby, leafy **Leeman Caravan Park** (☑08-9953 1080; 43 Thomas St, Leeman; unpowered/powered sites $20/25, on-site vans $60, cabins $70-90) has lots of shade, grassy sites and a good camp kitchen all close to the dunes. Tasty meals are available all day from **Fran's Kitchen** (☑08-9953 1727; Indian Ocean Dr, Leeman; ☺6am-8pm) and there's both petrol and internet access in the village.

If you have a 4WD, **Stockyard Gully Caves** are 30km away, off the Coorow Green Head Rd, and you can explore the underground creek and caverns with a torch. Watch out for bees and bats.

Heading north on Indian Ocean Dr, unmarked side-roads lead to lonely beaches and rocky cliffs begging to be explored.

Margaret River & the Southwest Coast

Best Places to Eat

➡ Laundry Cafe (p124)

➡ Eagle Bay Brewing Co (p130)

➡ The Studio Bistro (p130)

➡ Vasse Felix (p131)

➡ Foragers Field Kitchen (p142)

Best Places to Stay

➡ Injidup Spa Retreat (p129)

➡ Old Picture Theatre Holiday Apartments (p140)

➡ Acacia Chalets (p135)

➡ Burnside Organic Farm (p133)

➡ Foragers (p140)

Why Go?

The farmland, forests, rivers and coast of the lush, green southwestern corner of Western Australia (WA) contrast vividly with the stark, sunburnt terrain of much of the state. On land, world-class wineries and craft breweries beckon, and tall trees provide shade for walking trails and scenic drives. Offshore, bottlenose dolphins and whales frolic, and devoted surfers search for – and often find – their perfect break.

Unusually for WA, distances between the many attractions are short, and driving time is mercifully limited, making it a fantastic area to explore for a few days – you will get much more out of your stay here if you have your own wheels. Summer brings hordes of visitors, but in the wintry months from July to September the cosy pot-bellied stove rules and visitors are scarce, and while opening hours can be somewhat erratic, prices are much more reasonable.

When to Go
Margaret River

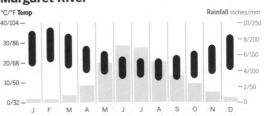

Jan Follow the party crowds from the Southbound festival to the beach.

Mar & Apr Catch surf and wine festivals in Margaret River, and the Nannup music festival.

Aug Head to empty beaches, Margaret River wineries and Busselton's film festival.

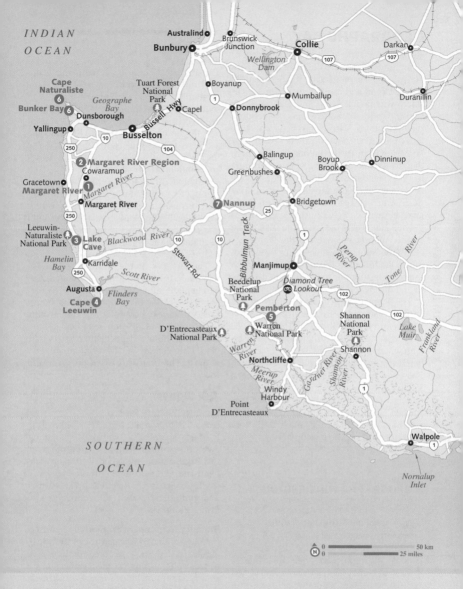

Margaret River & the Southwest Coast Highlights

1️⃣ Sampling the first-class wine, food and architecture of the vineyards of **Margaret River** (p127)

2️⃣ Getting active amid the dramatic seascapes and landscapes of the **Margaret River** (p135) region

3️⃣ Exploring the labyrinthine limestone caverns along Caves Rd, especially beautiful **Lake Cave** (p134)

4️⃣ Fronting up to the impressive coastline at Augusta's **Cape Leeuwin Lighthouse** (p136), at the confluence of the Indian and Southern Oceans

5️⃣ Sinking into the dappled depths of the karri forests surrounding **Pemberton** (p139)

6️⃣ Revelling in the wild beauty of **Cape Naturaliste** (p126) and **Bunker Bay** (p126)

7️⃣ Canoeing from the forest to the sea along the Blackwood River, starting at **Nannup** (p137)

GEOGRAPHE BAY

Turquoise waters and 30km of excellent swimming beaches are the defining features of this gorgeous bay. Positioned between the Indian Ocean and a sea of wine, the beachside towns of Busselton and Dunsborough attract hordes of holidaymakers spending their vacations with sand between their toes and a glass between their lips. It may be 230km from Perth, but once you get here the attractions are close together, certainly by WA standards. Unsurprisingly, it gets *very* busy during summer and at holiday times, when prices may rise 30% on those given here.

For 55,000 years the area from Geographe Bay to Augusta belonged to the Wardandi, one of the Noongar peoples. They lived a nomadic life linked to the seasons, heading to the coast in summer to fish, and journeying inland during the wet winter months.

The French connection to many of the current place names dates from an early-19th-century expedition by the ships *Le Géographe* and *Naturaliste*. Thomas Vasse, a crewman who was lost at sea, is remembered in the name of a village, river, inlet, Busselton bar and Margaret River winery. The latter two are particularly fitting as it's quite possible he was drunk when he was washed away. According to local Wardandi, who found and fed him, he made it to shore but later died on the beach waiting for his ship to return.

GEOGRAPHE WINE REGION

If it's wine that's lured you to the southwest, the **Geographe wine region** (www.geographewine.com.au) is the perfect primer for the glories to come. You may not have heard of it, but Geographe has 12 sq km under vines, producing 11% of the state's output in 46 wineries. The region's best-known brand is conveniently located halfway between Bunbury and Busselton. **Capel Vale** (www.capelvale.com.au; Mallokup Rd; ⏱10am-4pm) offers free tastings and a restaurant overlooking the vines, serving morning and afternoon tea and lunch. It's located off the Bussell Hwy on the opposite side of the highway from Capel village.

Bunbury

POP 66,100

The southwest's only city is remaking its image from industrial port into seaside holiday destination. It's here where the main route south from Perth branches off into the Bussell Hwy (to the Margaret River wine region) and the South Western Hwy (Rte 1, to the southern forests and south coast). It's also the southernmost stop on the train network and a hub for regional buses.

Situated 170km from Perth, Bunbury has plenty of eateries and a few interesting attractions worthy of a stop. The town centre has basically one main street (Victoria), and a few blocks to the west lies the beach. Immediately to the north, the redeveloped port features waterside restaurants.

The city lies at the western end of Leschenault Inlet. The area was named Port Leschenault after the botanist on Nicolas Baudin's ship *Le Géographe* in 1803, but in a classic case of colonial one-upmanship, Governor James Stirling renamed it Bunbury in honour of the lieutenant that he placed in charge of the original military outpost. The first British settlers arrived in 1838.

◎ Sights

Bunbury Wildlife Park   ZOO
(Prince Philip Dr; adult/child $8/5; ⏱10am-5pm) Parrots, kangaroos, wallabies, possums, owls and emus all feature. Across the road, the **Big Swamp** has good wetlands walking tracks and stops for birdwatching. Head south on Ocean Dr, turn left at Hayward St and continue through the roundabout to Prince Philip Dr.

Bunbury Regional Art Galleries   GALLERY
(www.brag.org.au; 64 Wittenoom St; ⏱10am-4pm) **FREE** Housed in a restored pink-painted convent (1897), this excellent gallery has a collection that includes works by Australian art luminaries Arthur Boyd and Sir Sidney Nolan.

St Mark's (Old Picton) Church   CHURCH
(cnr Charterhouse Cl & Flynn St, East Bunbury) Built in 1842 using wattle and daub construction, this is WA's second-oldest church.

🏃 Activities

Mangrove Boardwalk   WALKING
Mangrove Boardwalk (enter off Koombana Dr) allows you to explore the most southerly

Bunbury

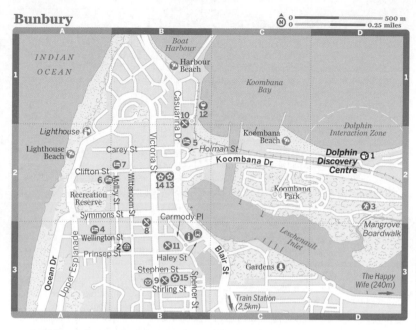

mangroves in WA, rich with more than 70 species of bird. Interpretive signs provide information about this ancient ecosystem, thought to be about 2500 years old.

Dekked Out
Adventures   KAYAKING, DOLPHIN WATCHING
(☑ 08-9796 1000; www.dekkedout.com.au; Grand Canals boat ramp, Riviera Way, Eaton; adult/student $80/60; ☺ 8.30am) Runs four-hour dolphin-spotting tours in the Collie River, Leschenault Estuary and the bay. Also hires kayaks (single per half-/full day $55/60) and sandboards ($20/30).

Tuart Forest   WALKING
This stretch lined with tall trees runs along the southern end of Ocean Dr.

🛏 Sleeping

Wander Inn Backpackers   HOSTEL $
(☑ 1800 039 032; www.bunburybackpackers.com. au; 16 Clifton St; dm $27-29, s $40-47, d $68; @ 🛜) Occupying a cheerful old blue-and-yellow house down a quiet side street between the beach and the main strip, this friendly hostel offers free basic breakfasts.

DOLPHIN DISCOVERY CENTRE

Around 60 bottlenose dolphins live in Bunbury's Koombana Bay year-round, their numbers increasing to around 260 in summer. The **Dolphin Discovery Centre** (☑ 08-9791 3088; www.dolphindiscovery.com.au; Koombana Beach; adult/child $10/5; ⊘ 9am-2pm Jun-Sep, 8am-4pm Oct-May) has a beachside zone where dolphins regularly come to interact with people in the shallows and you can wade in alongside them, under the supervision of trained volunteers. There are no guarantees of a close encounter, but these are more likely in the early mornings between November and April. Entry tickets are valid for three separate visits, a good option if you're in town for a few days.

To maximise your chances, there are **Eco Cruises** (1½hr cruise adult/child $53/35; ⊘ 11am Sat & Sun Jun-Sep, 11am & 3pm Oct-May) and **Swim Encounter Cruises** (3hr cruises $185; ⊘ 7.30am mid-Oct–Jan, 11.30am mid-Dec–Apr).

The centre also has lots of dolphin information, and tanks with lobsters and seahorses. Volunteers must commit to at least six weeks' full-time involvement.

Dolphin Retreat YHA HOSTEL $
(☑ 08-9792 4690; www.dolphinretreatbunbury.com.au; 14 Wellington St; dm/s/d $27/47/68; @ 🕾) Just around the corner from the beach, this small hostel is well located in a rabbit warren of an old house, with hammocks and a barbecue on the back verandah.

Bunbury Glade Caravan Park CARAVAN PARK $
(☑ 08-9721 3800; www.glade.com.au; Timperley Rd; 2-person sites $25-33, cabins $70-105; ✳ @ 🕾 ⊠) This spotless park is a five-minute drive from the centre of town on Blair St, the main road heading south.

The Clifton MOTEL $$
(☑ 08-9721 4300; www.theclifton.com.au; 2 Molloy St; r $150-250; 🕾) For luxurious accommodation with lots of heritage trimmings, go for the top-of-the-range rooms in the Clifton's historic Grittleton Lodge (1885). Good-value motel rooms – all recently redecorated – are also available.

Mantra APARTMENT $$
(☑ 08-9721 0100; www.mantra.com.au; 1 Holman St; apt from $209; ✳ @ 🕾 ⊠) One of the most unusual heritage conversions we've seen, the Mantra has sculpted a set of modern studios and apartments around four grain silos by the harbour. Deluxe rooms have spa baths and full kitchens.

✕ Eating

Mot's Cafe MALAYSIAN $
(17 Prinsep St, Shop 5, Central Arcade; snacks & mains $5-15; ⊘ 10am-5pm Mon-Fri, to 3pm Sat) Tasty Cocos Malay–style food from a friendly family originally from the Cocos Islands off the northwestern coast of Australia.

Benesse CAFE $
(83 Victoria St; mains $10-18; ⊘ 7.30am-5.30pm) Chic and petite, Benesse serves tasty toasties, salads, pizza and all-day breakfasts.

The Happy Wife CAFE $$
(www.thehappywife.com.au; 98 Stirling St; mains $10-20; ⊘ 6.30am-3.30pm Mon-Fri, 7.30am-2.30pm Sat) Grab a spot in the garden of this Cape Cod–style cottage just a short drive from the centre of town. Excellent home-style baking and regular lunch specials make it worth seeking out. Try the Asian-style sticky pork salad with nashi pear, cabbage salad and toasted peanuts.

Café 140 CAFE $$
(140 Victoria St; mains $12-21; ⊘ 7.30am-4.30pm Mon-Fri, 8am-2pm Sat & Sun) Hip, onto-it staff make the funky Café 140 a top spot for a leisurely Bunbury breakfast. With one of WA's best salmon omelettes, good coffee, and lots of magazines and newspapers, you can kiss goodbye to at least an hour of your travel schedule. Later in the day, gourmet burgers and grilled Turkish sandwiches are among the lunchtime stars.

Casella's SPANISH $$
(www.casellas.com.au; 1 Bonnefoi Blvd, Silos Waterfront; tapas $10-20, mains $25-40; ⊘ 11.30am-late) The bland decor hardly reinforces a colourful Iberian spirit, but a waterfront location and real skill in the kitchen more than settle the ledger. Larger meals are available – try the chicken adobado with herby roast potatoes – but the recommended Casella's experience is to settle into the huge wine list and sample a few of the authentically Spanish tapas.

☐ Drinking & Entertainment

Mash CRAFT BEER
(www.mashbrewing.com.au; 2/11 Bonnefoi Blvd;
☺11am-3pm Mon & Tue, to 9pm Wed-Sun) With
an absolute waterfront location, this modern microbrewery turns out seven regular
beers, plus always interesting seasonal con-
coctions. Our pick is the award-winning
'Freo Doctor' lager. The food (mains $18 to
$34) is OK pub grub, and Thursday's Pint &
Parma deal ($25) is good value.

Prince of Wales LIVE MUSIC
(41 Stephen St) Longstanding live-music
venue.

Grand Cinemas CINEMA
(www.moviemasters.com.au; cnr Victoria & Clifton
Sts) Blockbuster heaven.

**Bunbury Regional
Entertainment Centre** CONCERT HALL
(www.bunburyentertainment.com; Blair St) Local
and international acts.

ℹ Information

Visitor Centre (☐08-9792 7205; www.visitbun-
bury.com.au; Carmody Pl; ☺9am-5pm Mon-Sat,
10am-2pm Sun) In the historic 1904 train station.

ℹ Getting There & Around

BUS

Coaches stop at the **central bus station** (☐08-
9722 7800; Carmody Pl), or at the **train station**
(Picton Rd, Woolaston).

South West Coach Lines (☐9261 7600;
www.veoliatransportwa.com.au) runs services
to/from Perth's Esplanade Busport (2½ hours,
three daily), Mandurah (1¼ hours, daily), Busselton (1¼ hours, five daily), Dunsborough (1¾
hours, daily) and Bridgetown (1¾ hours, daily).

TransBunbury (☐9791 1955; www.veolia
transportwa.com.au) runs buses 101 (20 minutes,
seven daily) and 103 (30 minutes, five daily)
between the central bus station and train station
(both routes $2.60; no Sunday service).

Transwa (☐1300 662 205; www.transwa.
wa.gov.au) routes include the following:
➡ SW1 (12 weekly) to East Perth ($30, 3¼
hours), Mandurah ($16, two hours), Busselton
($9, 43 minutes), Margaret River ($16, two
hours) and Augusta ($24, 2½ hours)
➡ SW2 (three weekly) to Balingup ($13, 53
minutes), Bridgetown ($16, 1¼ hours) and
Pemberton ($27, 2¼ hours)
➡ GS3 (daily) to Walpole ($43, 4½ hours),
Denmark ($48, 5½ hours) and Albany ($56,
six hours)

TRAIN

Bunbury is the terminus of the **Transwa** (www.
transwa.wa.gov.au) Australind train line, with
two daily services to Perth ($30, 2½ hours) and
Pinjarra ($16, 1¼ hours).

Tuart Forest National Park

The tuart is a type of eucalypt that only
grows on coastal limestone, 200km either side of Perth, and this 20-sq-km strip
squeezed between the Bussell Hwy and the
Indian Ocean is the last pure tuart forest
left. An alternative route to Busselton from
Bunbury leads through the shade cast by
these giants, some more than 33m tall.

Turn off the highway at Tuart Dr, 4km
southwest of Capel. After driving 11km
through the forest, turn right onto Layman
Rd to find **Wonnerup House** (www.ntwa.com.
au; 935 Layman Rd; adult/child $5/3; ☺10am-4pm
Thu-Mon), a whitewashed National Trust
homestead (1859). Continue on this road
past the seaside village of Wonnerup and
then follow the coast to Busselton.

Busselton

POP 15,400

Unpretentious and uncomplicated, Busselton is what passes for the big smoke in
these parts. Surrounded by calm waters
and white-sand beaches, its outlandishly
long jetty is its most famous attraction. The
family-friendly town has plenty of diversion-
ary activities for lively kids, including sheltered beaches, water slides, animal farms
and even a classic drive-in cinema. During
school holidays, it really bustles – the population increases fourfold and accommodation prices soar.

◉ Sights & Activities

Busselton Jetty HISTORIC SITE
(☐08-9754 0900; www.busseltonjetty.com.au;
adult/child $2.50/free, return train adult/child
$11/6) Busselton's 1865 timber-piled jetty –
the longest in the southern hemisphere
(1841m) – reopened in 2011 following a
$27-million refurbishment. A little **train**
chugs along to the **Underwater Observatory** (adult/child incl train $29.50/14; ☺9am-
4.25pm), where tours take place 8m below
the surface; bookings are essential. There's
also an **Interpretive Centre** (admission free;
☺9am-5pm), an attractive building in the

style of 1930s bathing sheds, about 50m along the jetty.

ArtGeo Cultural Complex
GALLERY

(www.artgeo.com.au; 6 Queen St) Grouped around the old courthouse (1856), this complex includes tea rooms, wood turners, an artist-in-residence and the Busselton Art Society's gallery, selling works by local artists.

Old Butter Factory Museum
MUSEUM

(Peel Tce; adult/child $6/2; ⊙10am-4pm Wed-Mon) Local history.

Dive Shed
DIVING

(☑08-9754 1615; www.diveshed.com.au; 21 Queen St) Runs regular dive charters along the jetty, to Four Mile Reef (a 40km limestone ledge about 6.5km off the coast) and to the scuttled navy vessel HMAS *Swan* (off Dunsborough).

✦ Festivals & Events

Southbound
MUSIC

(www.southboundfestival.com.au; ⊙early Jan) Start off the New Year with three days of alternative music and camping – it's WA's Glastonbury, but with less mud. Recent international acts have included Hot Chip and The Hives.

CinéfestOZ
CINEMA

(www.cinefestoz.com.au; ⊙late Aug) Busselton briefly morphs into St-Tropez with this oddly glamorous festival of French and Australian cinema, including lots of Australian premieres and the odd Aussie starlet.

🛏 Sleeping

Accommodation sprawls along the beach for several kilometres either side of town; check the location if you don't have transport.

Beachlands Holiday Park
CARAVAN PARK $

(☑1800 622 107; www.beachlands.net; 10 Earnshaw Rd, West Busselton; sites per 2 people $42, chalets from $132; ▣🛜🏊) This excellent family-friendly park offers a wide range of accommodation amid shady trees, palms and flax bushes. Deluxe spa villas ($180) have corner spas, huge TVs, DVD players and full kitchens.

Blue Bay Apartments
APARTMENT $

(☑08-9751 1796; www.bluebayapartments.com; 66 Adelaide St; apt from $125; ▣) Close to the beach, these good-value self-contained apartments are bright and cheery, each with private courtyard and barbecue.

Observatory Guesthouse
B&B $$

(☑08-9751 3336; www.observatory-guesthouse.com; 7 Brown St; d $145-240; ▣) A five-minute walk from the jetty, this friendly B&B rents four bright, cheerful rooms. They're not overly big, but you can spread out on the communal sea-facing balcony and front courtyard.

Grand Mercure
RESORT $$$

(☑08-9754 9800; www.mercure.com; 553 Bussell Hwy, Broadwater; apt from $287; ▣🛜🏊) Located 6km from town, this sprawling complex of 87 flash apartments and villas is set among native vegetation. There's an exhausting array of tennis and squash courts, indoor and outdoor pools, and a small gym; or you can just lie around on the beach at the foot of the property. Check online for discounts from Sunday to Tuesday.

🍴 Eating & Drinking

★ Laundry Cafe
CAFE $$

(www.laundrycafe.com.au; 43 Prince St; shared plates $14-39) Brick walls and a honey-coloured jarrah bar form the backdrop for Margaret River beers and wines, great cocktails, and classy shared plates including panko-crumbed cuttlefish, kangaroo tataki, and a main-sized yellow duck curry. Definitely get ready to linger longer than you planned.

Coco's Thai
THAI $$

(55 Queen St; mains $16-18; ⊙5pm-late) A little place serving tasty Thai favourites and more adventurous dishes such as a delicious fish curry with apple. Loaded with fresh herbs, the prawn salad is also great.

Vasse
CAFE $$

(www.vassebarcafe.com.au; 44 Queen St; mains $17-28; ⊙9am-late) The menu mainstays are pizza and pasta, but Vasse also turns out more eclectic fare, including a special French menu for CinéfestOZ in August. Bearded Busselton hipsters make it surprisingly cosmopolitan, and there's a good spread of beers on tap.

The Goose
CAFE $$

(www.thegoose.com.au; Geographe Bay Rd; breakfast $11-24, lunch & dinner mains $29-39; ⊙7am-5pm Mon-Tue, till late Wed-Sun; 🛜) Near the jetty, this stylish cafe offers an eclectic, interesting menu and views out to sea. Between meals the Goose is open for coffee, wine and tapas ($15 to $20).

Newtown House   MODERN AUSTRALIAN $$$
($08-9755 4485; www.newtownhouse.com.au; 737 Bussell Hwy, Abbey; mains $37-42; ⊙from 10am Wed-Sat) Set amid green lawns and gardens, this early-settler residence (1851), 10km west of town, has a hefty reputation for serving up the best-quality regional ingredients. The menu changes seasonally – options could include grilled scallops or Margaret River venison – and you'll need to bring your own (BYO) wine. Bookings are recommended.

☆ Entertainment

Busselton Drive-In Outdoor Cinema   CINEMA
($ 08-9751 5638; www.busseltondrive-in.com.au; 500 Bussell Hwy, Broadwater; adult/child $15/8) Double features, under the stars. Family-friendly titles kick off at 7.30pm, followed by more grown-up flicks at around 9pm. The season starts mid-September, and note it's strictly cash only.

ℹ Information

Visitor Centre ($08-9752 5800; www.geo graphebay.com; 38 Peel Tce; ⊙9am-5pm Mon-Fri, to 4.30pm Sat & Sun)

ℹ Getting There & Around

South West Coach Lines ($08-9261 7600; www.veoliatransportwa.com.au) Runs services to/from Perth's Esplanade Busport ($35, 3¾ hours, three daily), Bunbury ($10, one hour, five daily), Dunsborough ($10, 30 minutes, three daily), Margaret River ($10, 50 minutes, three daily) and Augusta ($17, 1¼ hours, three daily).

TransBusselton ($08-9754 1666; 39 Albert St) The most useful bus is the 903 that follows the coast to Dunsborough (four daily, Monday to Saturday).

Transwa ($1300 662 205; www.transwa. wa.gov.au) Coach SW1 (12 weekly) stops at the visitor centre, heading to/from East Perth ($35, 4¼ hours), Bunbury ($9, 43 minutes), Dunsborough ($7.60, 28 minutes), Margaret River ($13, 1½ hours) and Augusta ($16, 1¾ hours).

Dunsborough

POP 3400

Smaller and less sprawling than Busselton, Dunsborough is a relaxed, beach-worshipping town that goes bonkers towards the end of November when about 7000 'schoolies' descend. When it's not inundated with drunken, squealing teenagers, it's a thoroughly pleasant place to be. The beaches are better than Busselton's, but accommodation is more limited.

The name Dunsborough first appeared on maps in the 1830s, but to the Wardandi people it was always Quedjinup, meaning 'place of women'.

🏃 Activities

Cape Dive   DIVING
($08-9756 8778; www.capedive.com; 222 Naturaliste Tce) There is excellent diving to be done in Geographe Bay, especially since the decommissioned Navy destroyer HMAS *Swan* was purposely scuttled in 1997 for use as a dive wreck. Marine life has colonised the ship, which lies at a depth of 30m, 2.5km offshore.

Naturaliste Charters   WHALE WATCHING
($ 0419 186 133; www.whales-australia.com; adult/child $80/50; ⊙10am & 2pm Sep-Dec) Two-hour whale-watching cruises from September to December. From January to March the emphasis switches to an **Eco Wilderness Tour** showcasing beaches, limestone caves with Indigenous art, and wildlife including dolphins and New Zealand fur seals. Tours also run out of Augusta.

🛏 Sleeping

There are many options for self-contained rentals in town depending on the season; the visitor centre has current listings.

Dunsborough Beachouse YHA   HOSTEL $
($08-9755 3107; www.dunsboroughbeachouse. com.au; 205 Geographe Bay Rd; dm $32-34, s/d $55/80; @ ⚡) On the Quindalup beachfront, this friendly hostel has lawns stretching languidly to the water's edge; it's an easy 2km cycle from the town centre.

Dunsborough Central Motel   MOTEL $
($08-9756 7711; www.dunsboroughmotel.com. au; 50 Dunn Bay Rd; r $120-175) Centrally located in Dunsborough town, this well-run motel is good value, especially if you can snare an online midweek discount. That means more of your travel budget to enjoy nearby wineries and breweries.

🍴 Eating & Drinking

Squid Lips   FISH & CHIPS $
(55 Dunn Bay Rd, Shop 27A, Dunsborough Centrepoint; snacks & meals $8-15; ⊙noon-2.30pm

MARGARET RIVER & THE SOUTHWEST COAST DUNSBOROUGH

RED TAILS IN THE SUNSET

Between Cape Naturaliste and Cape Leeuwin is the most southerly breeding colony of the red-tailed tropicbird (*Phaethon rubricauda*) in Australia. From September to May, look for it soaring above Sugarloaf Rock, south of Cape Naturaliste. The viewpoint can be reached by a 3.5km boardwalk from the lighthouse or by Sugarloaf Rd.

The tropicbird is distinguished by its two long, red tail streamers, which are almost twice its body length. Bring binoculars to watch this small colony soar, glide, dive and then swim with their disproportionately long tail feathers cocked up.

Tue-Sat, from 5pm daily) Rated one of WA's best fish-and-chip joints.

The Pourhouse BISTRO $$
(www.pourhouse.com.au; 26 Dunn Bay Rd; mains $19-28; ⊙4pm-late) Hip but not pretentious, with comfy couches, regular live bands, and an upstairs terrace for summer. The pizzas are excellent, and top-notch burgers come in a locally baked sourdough bun. A considered approach to beer includes rotating taps from the best of WA's craft breweries and lots of bottled surprises.

Samudra CAFE $$
(www.samudra.com.au; 226 Naturaliste Tce; mains $14-20; ⊙7.30am-4pm daily, 5.30-8pm Fri & Sat) 🌱 Featuring a funky VW Kombi coffee van, this garden cafe is one of WA's best vegetarian restaurants. Mexican, Middle Eastern and Asian flavours underpin a super-healthy menu of salads, curries, wraps and smoothies, and there are plenty of shady places to sit and read or write. Samudra also offers relaxing and reinvigorating yoga classes, as well as surfing and spa retreats.

Cape Wine Bar MODERN AUSTRALIAN $$
(www.thecapewinebar.com; 239 Naturaliste Tce; mains $24-38; ⊙4pm-late Tue-Sat) Buzzing most nights, this wine bar has a well-deserved reputation for fresh food. The seasonal menu includes dishes like crispy skin snapper or a prawn curry.

Artézen CAFE $$
(www.artezen.com.au; 234 Naturaliste Tce; mains $14-28; ⊙7am-4pm; 🖥) Funky wallpaper, good breakfasts, and packed with families and surfers at the weekend.

ℹ Information

Visitor Centre (☑08-9752 5800; www.geographebay.com; Seymour Blvd; ⊙9am-5pm Mon-Fri, 9.30am-4.30pm Sat & Sun) In the same building as the post office.

ℹ Getting There & Around

South West Coach Lines (☑08-9261 7600; www.veoliatransportwa.com.au) Services to/from Perth's Esplanade Busport ($38, 4½ hours, daily), Mandurah ($32, 3¼ hours, daily), Bunbury ($16, 1¾ hours, daily) and Busselton ($10, 30 minutes, three daily).

TransBusselton (☑08-9754 1666; www.veoliatransportwa.com.au; 39 Albert St, Busselton) Services between Dunsborough and Busselton (four daily, Monday to Saturday).

Transwa (☑1300 662 205; www.transwa.wa.gov.au) Coach SW1 (12 weekly) stops at the visitor centre, heading to/from East Perth ($38, 4½ hours), Bunbury ($13, 1¼ hours), Busselton ($7.60, 28 minutes), Margaret River ($9, 49 minutes) and Augusta ($16, 1¼ hours).

Cape Naturaliste

Northwest of Dunsborough, Cape Naturaliste Rd leads to the excellent beaches of **Meelup**, **Eagle Bay** and **Bunker Bay**, and then on to Cape Naturaliste. There are walks and lookouts along the way; pick up brochures from Dunsborough's visitor centre before heading out. Whales and hammerhead sharks like to hang out on the edge of Bunker Bay, where the continental shelf drops 75m. There's excellent snorkelling on the edge of the shelf at Shelley Cove.

Bunker Bay is also the home of **Bunkers Beach Cafe** (www.bunkersbeachcafe.com.au; Farm Break Lane; breakfast $14-24, lunch $16-34; ⊙11.30am-4pm), which serves up an adventurous menu only metres from the sand.

The **Cape Naturaliste lighthouse** (adult/child $13/7; ⊙tours every 30min 9.30am-4pm), built in 1903, can be visited on tours and there's also a free museum. Above and Below packages (adult/child $30/15), combining entry to Ngilgi Cave (p128), are also available.

MARGARET RIVER WINE REGION

✨ Festivals & Events

Telstra Drug Aware Pro   SURFING
(www.telstradrugawarepro.com; ⊘mid–late Mar)
Six-day pro-surfing competition with associated concerts and fashion shows.

**Margaret River
Wine Region Festival**   WINE, FOOD
(www.margaretriverfestival.com; ⊘mid-Apr) Five days of street carnivals, slow food and master classes.

Margaret River Gourmet Escape   WINE, FOOD
(www.gourmetescape.com.au; ⊘late Nov) From David Chang and Matt Moran to Tetsuya Wakuda, the inaugural Gourmet Escape in 2012 attracted some huge names. Look forward to four days of food workshops, tastings and demonstrations.

☞ Tours

See visitor centres for many more options. If you're feeling active, see the tours listed on p135.

Bushtucker Tours   CANOEING, WINE
(☑08-9757 9084; www.bushtuckertours.com; adult/child $90/40) Four-hour trips combine walking and canoeing up the Margaret River, and feature aspects of Aboriginal culture along with uses of flora, and a bush-tucker lunch. Winery & Brewery Tours (adult/child $90/40) run around Margaret River.

Harvest Tours   WINE, FOOD
(☑0429 728 687; www.harvesttours.com.au; adult/child $125/55) Food and wine tour with an emphasis on organic, sustainable and ethical producers. Lunch is included at Cullen Wines (p131).

Wine for Dudes   WINE TASTING
(☑0427 774 994; www.winefordudes.com; tours $90) Includes a brewery, a chocolate factory, three wineries, a wine-blending experience and lunch.

Margaret River Tours   WINE, SIGHTSEEING
(☑0419 917 166; www.margaretrivertours.com) Runs winery tours (half-/full day $80/140) and can arrange charters.

Margies Big Day Out   WINE, BEER
(☑0416 180 493; www.margaretriverbigdayout.com; tours $90) Three wineries, two breweries and lunch.

❶ Getting There & Away

Transwa (☑1300 662 205; www.transwa.wa.gov.au) Coach SW1 (12 weekly) from Perth to Augusta stops at Yallingup and Margaret River, with three coaches weekly continuing to Pemberton.

South West Coach Lines (☑08-9261 7600; www.veoliatransportwa.com.au) Buses between Busselton and Augusta (12 weekly) stop at Cowaramup and Margaret River, linking with Perth on the weekends.

Yallingup & Around

POP 1070

Beachside Yallingup is a mecca for both surfers and wine aficionados. You're permitted to let a 'wow' escape when the surf-battered coastline first comes into view. For romantic travellers, Yallingup means 'place of love' in the Wardandi Noongar tongue.

A set of beautiful walking trails follow the coast between here and **Smiths Beach**. **Canal Rocks**, a series of rocky outcrops forming a natural canal, are just past Smiths Beach.

Sights & Activities

Wardan Aboriginal Centre INDIGENOUS CULTURE
(☑08-9756 6566; www.wardan.com.au; Injidup Springs Rd, Yallingup; experiences adult/child $20/10; ⊘10am-4pm daily 15 Oct-15 Mar, closed Tue & Sat 15 Mar-15 Oct, experiences Sun, Mon, Wed & Fri) ✦ **FREE** Offers a window into the lives of the local Wardandi people. There's a gallery, an interpretive display on the six seasons that govern the Wardandi calendar (admission $5) and the opportunity to take part in various **experiences**, such as stone tool making, boomerang and spear throwing, or a guided bushwalk exploring

---

CAPE TO CAPE TRACK

Stretching from Cape Naturaliste to Cape Leeuwin, the 135km Cape to Cape Track passes through the heath, forest and sand dunes of the **Leeuwin-Naturaliste National Park** (Caves Rd), all the while providing Indian Ocean views. Most walkers take about seven days to complete the track, staying in a combination of national-park camp sites and commercial caravan parks along the way, but you can walk it in five days or break up the route into day walks.

Wardandi spirituality and the uses of various plants for food, medicine and shelter.

Ngilgi Cave   CAVING

(☑ 08-9755 2152; www.geographebay.com; Yallingup Caves Rd; adult/child $21/11; ⊙ 9.30am-4.30pm) Between Dunsborough and Yallingup, this 500,000-year-old cave is associated in Wardandi spirituality with the victory of the good spirit Ngilgi over the evil spirit Wolgine. To the Wardandi people it became a kind of honeymoon location. A European man first stumbled upon it in 1899 while looking for his horse. Formations include the white **Mother of Pearl Shawl** and the equally beautiful **Arab's Tent** and **Oriental Shawl**. Tours depart every half-hour

More adventurous caving options include the two-hour Ancient Riverbed Tour (adult/child $49/27), 2½-hour Explorer Tour (adult/child $84/52), three-hour Crystal Crawl Tour (adults only, $104) and the four-hour Ultimate Ngilgi Adventure (adults only, $149). The Above & Below ticket (adult/child $30/15) includes entry to the Cape Naturaliste Lighthouse.

Well-marked bushwalks start from here.

Yallingup Surf School   SURFING

(☑ 08-9755 2755; www.yallingupsurfschool.com) Offers 90-minute lessons for beginners ($50/125 for one/three lessons) and private coaching ($110).

🛏 Sleeping

Yallingup Beach Holiday Park CARAVAN PARK $

(☑ 08-9755 2164; www.yallingupbeach.com.au; Valley Rd; sites per 2 people $32, cabins $100-150; 🛜) You'll sleep to the sound of the surf here, with the beach just across the road.

Caves Caravan Park   CARAVAN PARK $

(☑ 08-9755 2196; www.cavescaravanpark.com.au; cnr Caves & Yallingup Beach Rds; 2-person sites $25-35, cabins $115-180; 🛜) This leafy caravan park features clean cabins and friendly management.

Wildwood Valley
Cottages & Cooking School   COTTAGES $$

(☑ 08-9755 2120; www.wildwoodvalley.com.au; 1481 Wildwood Rd; cottages from $220; 🛜) Luxury cottages trimmed by native bush are arrayed across 50 hectares, and the property's main house also hosts the Mad About Food Cooking School with Sioban and Carlo Baldini. Sioban's CV includes training with Rockpool's Neil Perry, cooking at Longrain, and

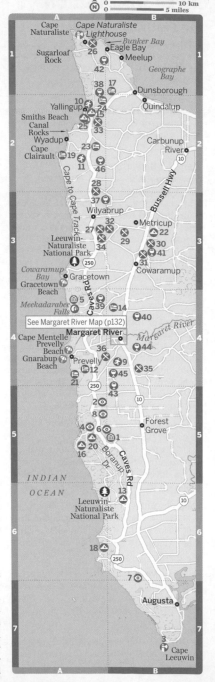

Margaret River Wine Region

Margaret River Wine Region

MARGARET RIVER & THE SOUTHWEST COAST YALLINGUP & AROUND

living in Tuscany, so the culinary emphasis is Thai or Italian. Cooking classes start at $85 per person.

Seashells Yallingup   HOTEL, APARTMENT $$
(☏ 08-9750 1500; www.seashells.com.au; Yallingup Beach Rd; d from $199; 🛜) Rooms are either in the renovated Caves House (1938) or in the adjacent modern apartments. Weekday rates are good value. It's an atmospheric spot for a drink, with live gigs on Sunday afternoon. Over summer, some of Australia's biggest touring bands sometimes drop by.

⭐ **Injidup Spa Retreat**   BOUTIQUE HOTEL $$$
(☏ 08-9750 1300; www.injidupsparetreat.com.au; Cape Clairault Rd; ste from $650; ❄🏊) 🍃 The region's most stylish and luxurious accommodation, Injidup perches atop an isolated cliff south of Yallingup. A striking carved concrete and iron facade fronts the car

park, while inside there are heated polished-concrete floors, 'eco' fires and absolute sea views. Each of the 10 suites has its own plunge pool. It's off Wyadup Rd.

Empire Retreat   SPA HOTEL $$$
(☏ 08-9755 2065; www.empireretreat.com; Caves Rd; ste $295-575; ❄🛜) Everything about the intimate Empire Retreat is stylish, from the Indonesian-inspired design to the attention to detail and service. The rooms are built around a former farmhouse, and a rustic but sophisticated ambience lingers. Check online for good packages combining accommodation and spa treatments.

Windmills Break   BOUTIQUE HOTEL $$$
(☏ 08-9755 2341; www.windmillsbreak.com.au; 2024 Caves Rd; r around $300-320; ❄@🛜🏊) Enter through the clubby lounge, which opens onto a terrace and landscaped

grounds spreading down to a lovely pool. Rooms are plush and contemporary.

 Eating & Drinking

The Studio Bistro MODERN AUSTRALIAN **$$$**
(☑08-9756 6164; www.thestudiobistro.com.au; 7 Marrinup Dr; mains $35, degustation menu with/without wine matches $125/90) 🍴 This combination art gallery and garden bistro is definitely worth seeking out. The gallery focuses on Australian artists working in all media, while the restaurant showcases subtle dishes such as pan-fried fish with cauliflower cream, radicchio, peas and crab meat. Five-course degustation menus are offered on Friday and Saturday nights. Bookings are recommended.

Wills Domain WINERY
(www.willsdomain.com.au; cnr Brash & Abbey Farm Rds; mains $28-43, shared platters $35-65; ⊙tastings 10am-5pm, lunch noon-3pm) Restaurant, gallery and wonderful hilltop views over vines.

Cowaramup & Wilyabrup
POP 988

Cowaramup (Cow Town to some) is little more than a couple of blocks of shops lining Bussell Hwy. The rustic area to the northwest, known as Wilyabrup, is where in the 1960s the Margaret River wine industry was born. This area has the highest concentration of wineries, and the pioneers (Cullen Wines and Vasse Felix) are still leading the way.

🛏 Sleeping

Taunton Farm Holiday Park CARAVAN PARK **$**
(☑1800 248 777; www.tauntonfarm.com.au; Bussell Hwy, Cowaramup; sites $37-39, cottages $110-130; 🐾) There are plenty of farm animals for the kids to meet at one of Margaret River's best family-oriented campgrounds. For caravan and tenting buffs, the amenities blocks are spotless, and also scattered about are farmstyle self-contained cottages.

BEER IS THE NEW WINE

The Margaret River region's wine credentials are impeccable, but now the area is also becoming a destination for craft-beer fans. All the following also serve bar snacks and lunch.

Eagle Bay Brewing Co (www.eaglebaybrewing.com.au; Eagle Bay Rd, Dunsborough; ⊙11am-5pm) A lovely rural outlook, interesting beers and wines served in modern, spacious surroundings, and excellent food including crisp woodfired pizzas ($20 to $24). Keep an eye out for Eagle Bay's Single Batch Specials.

Colonial Brewing Co (www.colonialbrewingco.com.au; Osmington Rd, Margaret River; ⊙11am-5pm) This modern microbrewery has great rural views, and an excellent range of authentic beers including a witbier with coriander and mandarin, and a hop-fuelled and citrusy India Pale Ale. Our favourite is the refreshing German-style Kölsch.

Bush Shack Brewery (www.bushshackbrewery.com.au; Hemsley Rd, Yallingup; ⊙10am-5pm) A small-scale brewery in a great bush setting. A healthy addition of innovation results in interesting brews like chilli beer, lemon-infused lager and strawberry pale ale.

Cheeky Monkey Brewery (www.cheekymonkeybrewery.com.au; 4259 Caves Rd, Margaret River; ⊙10am-6pm) Craft beers and ciders stand out at Margaret River's most recently opened microbrewery. Set around a pretty lake, there's also lots of room for the kids to run around. Try the Hatseller Pilsner with bold New Zealand hops.

Bootleg Brewery (www.bootlegbrewery.com.au; off Yelverton Rd, Wilyabrup; ⊙11am-6pm) More rustic than some of the area's flash new breweries, but lots of fun with a pint in the sun – especially with live bands on Saturday. Try the malty and robust Raging Bull Porter.

Cowaramup Brewing Company (www.cowaramupbrewing.com.au; North Treeton Rd, Cowaramup; ⊙11am-5pm) Modern microbrewey with an award-winning Pilsner and a moreish English-style Special Pale Ale. Four other beers and occasional seasonal brews also feature.

Noble Grape Guesthouse
B&B $$

(☑ 08-9755 5538; www.noblegrape.com.au; 29 Bussell Hwy, Cowaramup; s $135-155, d $150-190; ❋ ⦿) Noble Grape is more like an upmarket motel than a traditional B&B. Rooms offer a sense of privacy and each has a little garden courtyard as well as a microwave and DVD player. The friendly owners clearly have green fingers.

✕ Eating

Providore
DELI $

(www.providore.com.au; 448 Tom Cullity Dr, Wilyabrup; ⦿ 9am-5pm) Voted one of Australia's Top 100 Gourmet Experiences by *Australian Traveller* magazine – and, given its amazing range of artisan produce including organic olive oil, tapenades and preserved fruits, we can only agree. Look forward to loads of free samples.

Margaret Riviera
DELI $

(www.margaretriviera.com.au; Bottrill St, Cowaramup; ⦿ 10am-5pm) Gourmet food store stocking local produce including olive oils, preserves and cheeses.

Margaret River Chocolate Company
CHOCOLATE $

(www.chocolatefactory.com.au; Harman's Mill Rd; ⦿ 9am-5pm) Watch truffles being made, sample chocolate buttons, or grab a coffee.

Margaret River Dairy Company
CHEESE $

(www.mrdc.com.au; Bussell Hwy; ⦿ 9.30am-5pm) Cheese tastings at two sites on the Bussell Hwy north of Cowaramup.

Vasse Felix
RESTAURANT $$$

(☑ 08-9756 5050; www.vassefelix.com.au; cnr Caves Rd & Harmans Rd S, Cowaramup; mains $29-39; ⦿ 10am-3pm) Vasse Felix winery is considered by many to have the finest restaurant in the region, the big wooden dining room reminiscent of an extremely flash barn. The grounds are peppered with sculptures, while the gallery displaying works from the Holmes à Court collection is worth a trip in itself.

Knee Deep in Margaret River
RESTAURANT $$$

(☑ 08-9755 6776; www.kneedeepwines.com.au; 61 Johnson Rd, Wilyabrup; mains $28-38, 3-/5-course degustation $70/90; ⦿ cellar door 10am-5pm, lunch noon-3pm) ✎ Small and focused could be the motto here. Only a handful of mains are offered – crafted with locally sourced, seasonal produce – and the open-sided pavilion provides a pleasantly intimate vineyard setting. Order your food then shuffle up to the tasting counter to select its liquid companion.

Cullen Wines
RESTAURANT $$$

(☑ 08-9755 5277; www.cullenwines.com.au; 4323 Caves Rd, Cowaramup; mains $33-39; ⦿ 10am-4pm) ✎ Grapes were first planted here in 1966 and Cullen has an ongoing commitment to organic and biodynamic principles in both food and wine. It's less formal than its fancy neighbour Vasse Felix, but the food is excellent, with many of the fruit and vegetables from Cullen's own gardens.

🍷 Drinking

Margaret River Regional Wine Centre
WINE

(www.mrwines.com; 9 Bussell Hwy, Cowaramup; ⦿ 10am-7pm) A one-stop shop for Margaret River wine, with daily tastings rotating between smaller wineries without cellar doors.

Ashbrook
WINERY

(www.ashbrookwines.com.au; 448 Tom Cullity Dr, Wilyabrup; ⦿ 10am-5pm) Family-owned and -operated Ashbrook grows all of its grapes on site.

Thompson Estate
WINERY

(www.thompsonestate.com; 299 Tom Cullity Dr, Wilyabrup; ⦿ 10am-5pm) A small-scale producer with an architectural-award-winning concrete tastings and barrel room.

Margaret River
POP 4500

Although tourists usually outnumber locals, Margaret River still feels like a country town. The advantage of basing yourself here is that after 5pm, once the wineries close, it's one of the few places with any vital signs. Plus it's close to the incredible surf of Margaret River Mouth and Southside, and the swimming beaches at Prevelly and Gracetown.

Margaret River spills over with tourists every weekend and gets very busy at Easter and Christmas (book weeks, if not months, ahead). Accommodation tends to be cheaper midweek.

🛏 Sleeping

Margaret River Lodge YHA
HOSTEL $

(☑ 08-9757 9532; www.mrlodge.com.au; 220 Railway Tce; dm $31-34, r with/without bathroom $85/74; @ ⦿ ⊠) About 1.5km southwest of

MARGARET RIVER & THE SOUTHWEST COAST MARGARET RIVER

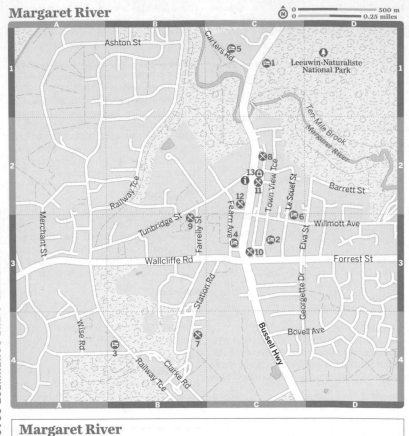

Margaret River

the town centre, this clean, well-run hostel has a pool, volleyball court and football field. Dorms share a big communal kitchen, and a quieter area with private rooms has its own little kitchen and lounge.

Margaret River Backpackers   HOSTEL **$**
(08-9757 9572; www.margaretriverbackpackers. com.au; 66 Town View Tce; dm $32-35;) Margaret River Backpackers caters mainly

to working holiday makers. Dorms are a little spartan (there are no private rooms), but there's a nice big deck out the back.

Edge of the Forest   MOTEL **$$**
(08-9757 2351; www.edgeoftheforest.com.au; 25 Bussell Hwy; r $120-180;) New owners have re-energised this motel, a pleasant stroll from Margaret River township. The six rooms have all been recently renovated

– several with a chic Asian theme – and all have new bathrooms. The leafy shared garden is perfect for an end-of-day barbecue.

Riverglen Chalets
CHALET **$$**

(🖉08-9757 2101; www.riverglenchalets.com.au; Carters Rd; chalets from $170; ▦ 🛜) Just north of town, these good-value and very comfortable timber chalets are spacious and fully self-contained, with verandahs looking onto bushland.

Prideau's
MOTEL **$$**

(🖉0438 587 180; www.prideaus.com.au; 31 Fearn Ave; r $169-229; ▦ 🛜) Centrally located, Prideau's has recently renovated units opening onto compact private courtyards. Some units have spa baths.

Vintages
MOTEL **$$**

(🖉08-9758 8333; www.vintagesmargaretriver.com. au; cnr Willmott Ave & Le Souef St; r $157-220; ▦) This spotless motel is set in tropical gardens. It's close to the centre of town, but all windows are double-glazed, so noise isn't a problem.

Burnside Organic Farm
BUNGALOW **$$$**

(🖉08-9757 2139; www.burnsideorganicfarm.com. au; 287 Burnside Rd; d $275; ▦) Rammed-earth and limestone bungalows have spacious decks and designer kitchens, and the surrounding farm hosts a menagerie of animals and organic avocado and macadamia orchards. Guests can also pick vegetables from the garden. Welcome to the perfect private retreat after a day cruising the region's wine, beer and food highlights.

🍴 Eating & Drinking

Margaret River Bakery
CAFE **$**

(89 Bussell Hwy; mains $10-18; ⊙7am-4pm Mon-Sat) 🍴 Elvis on the stereo, retro furniture and kitsch needlework 'paintings' – the MRB has a rustic, playful interior. It's the perfect backdrop to the bakery's honest home-style baking, often with a vege or gluten-free spin. Soak up the previous day's wine tasting with the legendary $13 Big Breakfast.

Blue Ginger
CAFE, DELI **$**

(www.bluegingerfinefoods.com; 31 Station Rd; mains $11-17; ⊙8am-6pm Mon-Fri, 9am-3pm Sat & Sun) Ease into the colourful, mismatched furniture on the enclosed terrace and tuck into hearty cafe fare with some adventurous twists. It's very local, crammed with regulars easing into their first coffee of the day.

Margaret River Farmers Market
MARKET **$**

(www.margaretriverfarmersmarket.com.au; cnr Tunbridge & Farrelly Sts; ⊙8am-noon Sat) 🍴 The region's organic and sustainable artisan producers come to town twice a month. Check the website for your own foodie hit list.

Morries Anytime
CAFE **$$**

(www.morries.com.au; 2/149 Bussell Hwy; mains $15-34) Settle into the clubby, cosmopolitan atmosphere of Morrie's, either for breakfast or lunch, or later at night for cocktails and tapas or dinner. Local beers from Colonial Brewing are on tap – try the refreshing Kölsch – and the menu channels European flavours with dishes like pork belly and rabbit croquettes.

Settler's Tavern
PUB **$$**

(www.settlerstavern.com; 114 Bussell Hwy; mains $15-29; ⊙11am-midnight Mon-Sat, to 10pm Sun) There's live entertainment Thursday to Sunday at Settler's, so pop in for good pub grub and a beer or wine from the extensive list. Dinner options are limited in Margaret River, and Settler's is often wildly popular with locals and visitors. Try the mammoth Seafood Deluxe with a pint of the pub's own Margaret River Pale Ale.

Must
RESTAURANT **$$$**

(🖉08-9758 8877; www.must.com.au; 107 Bussell Hwy; small plates $8-18, mains $32-38; ⊙noon-late) The sister property to one of our favourite Perth restaurants (Must Winebar), Must Margaret River doesn't disappoint. True to its location, wine bottles line the shiraz-coloured walls and dangle from the chandelier. The service here is excellent and the charcuterie plates ($28) are legendary.

🔒 Shopping

Tunbridge Gallery
INDIGENOUS ART

(www.tunbridgegallery.com.au; 101 Bussell Hwy; ⊙10am-5pm Mon-Sat, to 3pm Sun) Excellent Aboriginal art gallery, featuring mainly WA artworks.

MARGARET RIVER & THE SOUTHWEST COAST MARGARET RIVER

BEST SURF SPOTS

➡ Margaret River Mouth

➡ Southside

➡ Three Bears

➡ Yallingup

➡ Injidup Car Park

ℹ️ Information

Visitor Centre (☑08-9780 5911; www.marga retriver.com; 100 Bussell Hwy; ☺9am-5pm) Loads of information, plus displays on local wineries.

ℹ️ Getting Around

Margaret River Beach Bus (☑08-9757 9532; www.mrlodge.com.au) Minibus linking the township and the beaches around Prevelly ($10, three daily), summer only, bookings essential.

Around Margaret River

West of the Margaret River township, the coastline provides spectacular surfing and walks. **Prevelly** is the main settlement, with a few places to sleep and eat. Most of the sights are on Caves Rd or just off it.

◎ Sights & Activities

CaveWorks & Lake Cave   CAVE
(www.margaretriver.com; Conto Rd; single adult/ child $22/10; ☺9am-5pm, Lake Cave tours hourly 9.30am-3.30pm) Acting as the main ticket office for three of the region's most impressive caves (Lake, Mammoth and Jewel), CaveWorks also has excellent displays about caves, cave conservation and local fossil discoveries. There's also an authentic model cave and a 'cave crawl' experience.

Behind the centre is Lake Cave, the prettiest of them all, where limestone formations are reflected in an underground stream. The vegetated entrance to this cave is spectacular and includes a karri tree with a girth of 7m. Lake Cave is the deepest of all the caves open to the public. There are more than 300 steps down (a 62m drop) to the entrance.

Single cave tickets include entry to Cave-Works. The Grand Pass (adult/child $50/22), covering CaveWorks and all three caves, is valid for seven days, while the Ultimate Pass (adult/child $65/27) also includes Cape Leeuwin lighthouse.

CaveWorks is 20km south of Margaret River, off Caves Rd.

Mammoth Cave   CAVE
(www.margaretriver.com; Caves Rd; adult/child $22/10; ☺9am-4pm) Mammoth Cave boasts a fossilised jawbone of *Zygomaturus trilobus,* a giant wombat-like creature, as well as other fossil remains and the impressive Mammoth Shawl formation. Visits are self-guided; an MP3 audio player is provided.

Calgardup & Giants Caves   CAVES
These two self-guided caves are managed by the Department of Environment and Conservation (DEC), which provides helmets and torches. **Calgardup Cave** (www.dec. wa.gov.au; Caves Rd; adult/child $15/8; ☺9am-4.15pm) has a seasonal underground lake and is an attractive illustration of the role of the caves in the ecosystem – a stream transports nutrients to the creatures living in the cave, while tree roots hang overhead. **Giants Cave** (www.dec.wa.gov.au; Caves Rd; adult/child $15/8; ☺9.30am-3.30pm school & public holidays only), further south, is deeper and longer and has some steep ladders and scrambles.

Ellensbrook Homestead   HISTORIC BUILDING
(www.ntwa.com.au; Ellensbrook Rd; adult/child $4/2; ☺10am-4pm Sat & Sun) An intriguing National Trust property 8km northwest of Margaret River, Ellensbrook (1857) was the first home of pioneer settlers Alfred and Ellen Bussell. The Wardandi people welcomed them, gave them Noongar names and led them to this sheltered but isolated site, with its supply of fresh water.

The house is basic and more than a little ramshackle, constructed of paperbark, driftwood, timber, lime, dung and hair. Between 1899 and 1917, Edith Bussell, who farmed the property alone for many years, established an Aboriginal mission here. The children were taught to read and write, and two of them were beneficiaries of Edith's will.

A short walk leads to **Meekadarabee** ('bathing place of the moon'), a beautiful grotto set below trickling rapids and surrounded by lush bush, associated with a pair of star-crossed indigenous lovers. The grounds are open even when the house isn't.

Boranup Gallery   GALLERY
(www.boranupgallery.com; 7981 Caves Rd; ☺9.30am-5pm) Local arts and crafts, 22km south of Margaret River.

Boranup Drive   SCENIC DRIVE
This 14km diversion runs along an unsealed road through Leeuwin-Naturaliste National Park's beautiful karri forest. Near the southern end there's a lookout offering sea views.

Eagles Heritage   WILDLIFE INTERACTION
(☑08-9757 2960; www.eaglesheritage.com.au; adult/child $15/7.50; ☺10am-5pm) Housing Australia's largest collection of raptors, this centre, 5km south of Margaret River, rehabilitates many birds of prey each year. There are free-flight displays at 11am and 1.30pm.

🛏 Sleeping

Surfpoint   HOSTEL **$**
(🖉 08-9757 1777; www.surfpoint.com.au; Reidle Dr, Gnarabup; dm/d $32/105; @🛜🐕) This light and airy place offers the beach on a budget. The rooms are clean and well presented, and there's a very enticing little pool. Refurbishment aplenty was on the go when we last dropped by.

National Park Campgrounds   CAMPGROUND **$**
(www.dec.wa.gov.au; sites per adult/child $7/2) The DEC has three basic campgrounds within Leeuwin-Naturaliste National Park. **Conto Campground** (Conto Rd) has gas barbecues, toilets and running water; **Boranup Campground** (off Boranup Dr), under the tall trees off the southern end of Boranup Dr, can get damp in winter; **Point Road Campground** is only accessible by foot or 4WD from the northern end of Boranup Dr.

Llewellin's   B&B **$$**
(🖉 08-9757 9516; www.llewellinsguesthouse.com.au; 64 Yates Rd; r $198-248; 🛜) It may be a Welsh name, but the style's French provincial in the four upmarket yet homely guestrooms.

★**Acacia Chalets**   CHALET **$$$**
(🖉 08-9757 2718; www.acaciachalets.com.au; 113 Yates Rd; d $250-270; ❋) Private bushland – complete with marsupial locals – conceals three luxury chalets that are well located to explore the region's vineyards, caves and rugged nearby coastline. Limestone walls and honey-coloured jarrah floors combine for some of the area's best self-contained accommodation. Spacious decks are equipped with gas barbecues.

🍴 Eating & Drinking

Watershed Premium Wines   RESTAURANT **$$**
(www.watershedwines.com.au; cnr Bussell Hwy & Darch Rd; cafe $17-22, restaurant $38-42; ⊘10am-5pm) Famous for its 'Awakening' cabernet sauvignon, and regularly rated as one of WA's best vineyard restaurants. Dining options include an informal cafe and Watershed's classier restaurant with expansive views of a compact lake and trellised vines.

Xanadu   RESTAURANT **$$$**
(🖉 08-9758 9531; www.xanaduwines.com; Boodjidup Rd; mains $36; ⊘10am-5pm, restaurant noon-3pm) Escape into your own personal pleasure dome in the hip and chic restaurant filling Xanadu's vast space. The menu changes seasonally – we had a terrific braised-goat tortilla and confit duck – and definitely leave room for dessert.

Voyager Estate   WINERY
(🖉 08-9757 6354; www.voyagerestate.com.au; Stevens Rd; ⊘10am-5pm) The formal gardens and Cape Dutch–style buildings delight at Voyager Estate, the grandest of Margaret River's wineries. Tours are available ($25 including tastings).

Leeuwin Estate   WINERY
(🖉 08-9759 0000; www.leeuwinestate.com.au; Stevens Rd; ⊘10am-5pm) Another impressive estate, with tall trees and lawns gently rolling down to the bush. Its Art Series Chardonnay is one of the best in the country. Behind-the-scenes wine tours and tastings take place at 11am, noon and 3pm (adult/child $12.50/4). Big open-air concerts are regularly held here.

ACTIVE MARGARET RIVER

Much of the Margaret River experience is based around sybaritic pleasures, but to balance the virtue-versus-vice ledger, get active in the region's stunning scenery.

Dirty Detours (🖉 08-9758 8312; www.dirtydetours.com; tours $80) Runs guided mountain-bike rides, including through the magnificent Boranup Forest, as well as a Sip 'n' Cycle cellar-door tour. Another increasingly popular option is a mountain-biking and brewery tour. Multi-day tours are also available.

Edge Tours (🖉 0413 892 036; www.edgetours.com.au; per person from $175) Adventurous options include rock climbing, abseiling, caving and sea-kayaking.

Margaret River Climbing (🖉 0415 970 522; www.margaretriverclimbing.com.au; half-/full day $130/200) Caving, rock climbing and abseiling.

Margaret River Kitesurfing & Windsurfing (🖉 0419 959 053; www.mrkiteandsail.com.au; 2hr from $75) Instruction and gear rental.

Stella Bella
WINERY
(www.stellabella.com.au; 205 Rosabrook Rd; ⊙10am-5pm) No bells and whistles, just excellent wines with the prettiest labels in the region.

ℹ Information
National Park Information Centre (☑08-9757 7422; www.dec.wa.gov.au; Calgardup Cave, Caves Rd; ⊙9am-4.15pm)

Augusta & Around
POP 1700

Augusta is positioned at the mouth of the Blackwood River, 5km north of Cape Leeuwin, and quite separate from the main wine region. There are a few vineyards, but the vibe here is less epicurean, and more languid.

◉ Sights & Activities
Cape Leeuwin Lighthouse LIGHTHOUSE
(www.margaretriver.com; adult/child $5/3; ⊙8.45am-4.45pm) Wild and windy Cape Leeuwin, where the Indian and Southern Oceans meet, is the most southwesterly point in Australia. It takes its name from a Dutch ship that passed here in 1622. The lighthouse (1896), WA's tallest, offers magnificent views of the coastline. Tours leave every 40 minutes from 9am to 4.30pm (adult/child $17/7). Only 10 people at a time can enter, so be prepared to wait in holiday season. The Ultimate Pass (adult/child $65/27) incorporates admission to the lighthouse with Jewel, Lake and Mammoth Caves.

Jewel Cave CAVE
(www.margaretriver.com; Caves Rd; adult/child $22/10; ⊙tours hourly 9.30am-3.30pm) The most spectacular of the region's caves, Jewel Cave has an impressive 5.9m straw stalactite, so far the longest seen in a tourist cave. Fossil remains of a Tasmanian tiger (thylacine), believed to be 3500 years old, were discovered here. It's located near the south end of Caves Rd, 8km northwest of Augusta. The Grand Tour Pass (adult/child $50/22) incorporates admission to the Jewel, Lake and Mammoth Caves.

A new Jewel Cave Preservation Centre opened at Jewel Cave in 2011.

Reopened in late 2012, the nearby Moondyne Cave can be visited on the Moondyne Experience, a subterranean adventure combining overalls, hard hats and torches. The tour concludes wth lunch at the Jewel Cave, and prior booking is essential. Children must be at least 12 years of age.

Augusta Historical Museum MUSEUM
(Blackwood Ave; adult/child $3/1.50; ⊙1-3pm) Interesting local exhibits.

Blackwood River Houseboats HOUSEBOAT
(☑08-9758 0181; www.blackwoodriverhouseboats.com.au; Westbay) Take care of your accommodation, river cruise and fishing trip all at once with a houseboat holiday. They're easy to drive and available for two-night/three-day hire (weekend $950 to $1600, midweek $700 to $1150) or for weekly hire ($1900 to $2800).

Blackwood River CRUISES
(⊙Oct-May) Operators running boat trips up the Blackwood River include **Absolutely Eco River Cruises** (☑08-9758 4003; cdragon@westnet.com.au; adult/child $30/10) and **Miss Flinders** (☑0409 377 809; adult/child $40/15).

🛏 Sleeping & Eating
Baywatch Manor YHA HOSTEL $
(☑08-9758 1290; www.baywatchmanor.com.au; 9 Heppingstone View; dm $29, d with/without bathroom $93/73; @🖥) Clean, modern rooms with creamy brick walls and pieces of antique furniture. There is a bay view from the deck and, in winter, a roaring fire in the communal lounge. Some doubles have compact balconies.

Hamelin Bay Holiday Park CARAVAN PARK $
(☑08-9758 5540; www.mronline.com.au/accom/hamelin; Hamelin Bay West Rd; sites per 2 people $20-25, cabins $80-180) Absolute beachfront, northwest of Augusta, this secluded place gets very busy during holiday times.

Best Western Georgiana Molloy MOTEL $$
(☑08-9758 1255; www.augustaaccommodation.com.au; 84 Blackwood Ave; r $130-165) The decor is a little dated, but these spacious, self-contained units are standout value, each with a small garden area.

Deckchair Gourmet CAFE, DELI $
(Blackwood Ave; mains $7-16; ⊙8.30am-4pm; 🖥) Excellent coffee, delicious food and free wi-fi.

ℹ Information
Visitor Centre (☑08-9758 0166; www.margaretriver.com; cnr Blackwood Ave & Ellis St; ⊙9am-5pm)

SOUTHERN FORESTS

The tall forests of WA's southwest are simply magnificent, with towering gums (karri, jarrah, marri) sheltering cool undergrowth. Between the forests, small towns bear witness to the region's history of logging and mining. Many have redefined themselves as small-scale tourist centres where you can take walks, wine tours, canoe trips and trout- and marron-fishing expeditions.

ℹ Getting There & Away

Transwa (☎ 1300 662 205; www.transwa. wa.gov.au) coach routes include the following:

SW1 (three weekly) to Nannup and Pemberton from East Perth, Bunbury, Busselton, Margaret River and Augusta

SW2 (three weekly) to Balingup, Bridgetown, Manjimup and Pemberton from East Perth, Mandurah and Bunbury

GS3 (daily) to Balingup, Bridgetown, Manjimup and Pemberton from Perth, Bunbury, Walpole, Denmark and Albany

South West Coach Lines (☎ 08-9261 7600; www.veoliatransportwa.com.au) runs services to Nannup from Busselton (twice weekdays) and Bunbury (weekdays); and Balingup, Bridgetown and Manjimup from Bunbury, Mandurah and Perth (daily)

Nannup

POP 500

Nannup's historic weatherboard buildings and cottage gardens have an idyllic bush setting on the Blackwood River. The Noongar-derived name means 'a place to stop and rest'; it's also a good base for bushwalkers and canoeists.

Sporadic but persistent stories of sightings of a striped wolf-like animal, dubbed the Nannup tiger, have led to hopes that a Tasmanian tiger may have survived in the surrounding bush (the last known Tasmanian tiger, or thylacine, died in Hobart Zoo in 1936). Keep your camera handy and your eyes peeled!

🏃 Activities

Blackwood River Canoeing CANOEING
(☎ 08-9756 1209; www.blackwoodrivercanoeing. com; hire per day from $25) Provides equipment, basic instruction and transfers for canoeing paddles and longer expeditions. The best time to paddle is in late winter and early spring, when the water levels are up.

St John Brook Conservation Park PARK
(Barrabup Rd) A pretty spot to walk, cycle, swim and camp, 8km west of Nannup along an unsealed road.

🎊 Festivals & Events

Nannup Music Festival MUSIC
(www.nannupmusicfestival.org) Held in early March, focusing on folk and world music. Buskers are encouraged, so if you're any good, add yourself to the artists' roster.

🛏 Sleeping & Eating

Caravan Park CARAVAN PARK $
(1-/2-person sites from $15/25, cabins $66-80) This riverside caravan park is run by the visitor centre.

Holberry House B&B $
(☎ 08-9756 1276; www.holberryhouse.com; 14 Grange Rd; r $120-190; 🐕🖥) The decor might lean towards granny-chic, but this large house on the hill has charming hosts and comfortable rooms. It's surrounded by large gardens dotted with quirky sculptures (open to nonguests for $4).

Nannup Bridge Cafe CAFE $$
(1 Warren Rd; breakfast & lunch $9-18, dinner $16-38; ⏱9am-2pm Tue-Sun, 6-8pm Wed-Sat) Right opposite the tourist office, this cool-looking riverfront cafe morphs into a bistro at night. Standout dishes include the pork belly and the sticky-date pudding.

ℹ Information

Visitor Centre (☎ 08-9756 1211; www.nannup. wa.gov.au; 4 Brockman St; ⏱9am-5pm Mon-Fri, 10am-3pm Sat, 10am-1pm Sun) Check out the Nannup tiger press clippings. Housed in the 1922 police station.

Balingup & Greenbushes

It's like 1967 never ended in trippy **Balingup** (population 450), where coloured flags, scarecrows and murals of fairies and toadstools line the main street. Stop and rummage around eclectic stores such as the **Old Cheese Factory** (Nannup Rd; ⏱9.30am-4pm) and the **Tinderbox** (www.cheekyherbs.com; South West Hwy; ⏱9am-5pm) herbal remedies shop.

The **visitor centre** (☎ 08-9764 1818; www. balinguptourism.com.au; South West Hwy; ⏱10am-4pm) is on the main street, and the village's busy social hub for dogs and their owners is the **Packing Shed** (Nannup Rd; ⊘9am-4pm). Explore the heritage exhibition and try some local fruit wine.

Greenbushes (population 342) is a historic mining and timber township, 10km south of Balingup. Some splendid decaying buildings from the boom days line the road, and heritage memorabilia is dotted through town. A series of walks loop around town and out to join the Bibbulmun track; the Balingup and Bridgetown visitor centres keep walking-trail brochures.

Bridgetown

POP 2400

Lovely Bridgetwon is surrounded by karri forests and farmland, and spread around the Blackwood River. Weekends are busy, and the popular **Blues at Bridgetown Festival** (www.bluesatbridgetown.com) occurs annually on the second weekend of November.

Bridgetown's old buildings include **Bridgedale House** (Hampton St; admission by gold-coin donation; ⊘10am-2pm Sat & Sun), built of mud and clay by the area's first settler in 1862, and since restored by the National Trust.

Sleeping & Eating

Bridgetown Hotel PUB $$
(⊘08-9761 1034; www.bridgetownhotel.com.au; 157 Hampton St; r $165-265, mains $17-29; ✳) You don't expect quirky pizzas (lime and tequila, lamb and tzatziki) or large modern bedrooms with spa baths in an Australian country pub. A recent revamp has left this 1920s gem with both.

Bridgetown
Riverside Chalets RENTAL HOUSE $
(⊘08-9761 1040; www.bridgetownchalets.com. au; 1338 Brockman Hwy; chalets from $125) On a rural riverside property, 5km up the road to Nannup, these four stand-alone wooden chalets (complete with pot-bellied stoves and washing machines) sleep up to six in two bedrooms.

Nelsons of Bridgetown MOTEL $$
(⊘08-9761 1645; www.nelsonsofbridgetown.com. au; 38 Hampton St; s $95-145, d $130-195; ✳ 🏠 ✳) The central location is great, but go for the spacious newer rooms built adjacent to the 1898 Federation-style hotel.

The Cidery CAFE $
(www.thecidery.com.au; 43 Gifford Rd; mains $10-25; ⊘11am-4pm Sat-Thu, to 8pm Fri) Craft beer, cider and light lunches on outdoor tables by the river. On Friday nights from 5.30pm there's live music.

ⓘ Information

Visitor Centre (⊘08-9761 1740; www.bridg etown.com.au; 154 Hampton St; ⊘9am-5pm Mon-Fri, 10am-3pm Sat, 10am-1pm Sun; @) Includes apple-harvesting memorabilia.

Manjimup

POP 4300

Surrounded by spectacular forest, Manjimup is at the heart of WA's timber industry. For foodies it's known for something very different: truffles. During August especially, Manjimup's black Périgord truffles make their way onto top Australian menus.

ELVIS SIGHTED IN BOYUP BROOK

The pretty township of Boyup Brook (population 540), 31km northeast of Bridgetown, is the centre of country music in WA. The fantastically over-the-top **Harvey Dickson's Country Music Centre** (www.harveydickson.com.au; adult/child $8/2; ⊘9am-5pm) comes complete with a life-sized Elvis and Johnny Cash, an Elvis memorabilia room, and three 13.5m-tall guitar-playing men. It hosts regular rodeos (the big one's in October) and big-name country-music events, as well as the **Boyup Brook Country Music Festival** (www.countrymusicwa.com.au) in February. Scenic but basic **bush camping** (sites $8) is always available.

To combine country music with country critters, stay at **Nature's Guest House** (dm/cottages $20/80). Book through the **Department of Environment and Conservation** (DEC; ⊘08-9776 1207; donnelly.district@dec.wa.gov.au) in Donnelly. It's located in the 520-sq-km Perup Forest. Wildlife includes rare mammals such as the numbat, tammar wallaby and southern brown bandicoot. You'll find it south of Boyup Brook, off the Boyup Brook Cranbrook Rd.

◉ Sights & Activities

Wine & Truffle Co WINE, FOOD
(☑08-97772474; www.wineandtruffle.com.au; Seven Day Rd; mains $19-35; ⊙10am-4.30pm) To discover how the world's most expensive produce is harvested, follow your snout to the Wine & Truffle Co. Join a 2½-hour truffle hunt on Saturday or Sunday from June to August $95; book ahead), ending with breakfast of scrambled eggs with truffles. Offerings in the attached restaurant range from a truffle tasting plate to truffle fettucine.

Timber & Heritage Park PARK
(cnr Rose & Edward Sts; ⊙9am-5pm) Located in town, with a little lake, free BBQs and logging paraphernalia, including a replica of **One Tree Bridge**.

One Tree Bridge & Glenoran Pool RUINED BRIDGE
(Graphite Rd) In a forest clearing 22km from town are the remains of One Tree Bridge. It was constructed from a single karri log carefully felled to span the width of the river but rendered unusable after the floods of 1966. Adjacent is gorgeous Glenoran Pool, a popular swimming hole.

Four Aces TREES
(Graphite Rd) These four 300-plus-year-old karri trees are in a straight line; stand directly in front and they disappear into one. There's a short loop walk through the surrounding karri glade, or a 1½-hour loop bushwalking trail from the Four Aces to One Tree Bridge.

Diamond Tree Lookout LOOKOUT
Nine kilometres south of Manjimup along the South Western Hwy is this lookout. Metal spikes allow you to climb this 52m karri, and there's a nature trail nearby.

🛏 Sleeping

Diamond Forest Cottages CHALET $$
(☑08-9772 3170; www.diamondforest.com.au; 29159 South Western Hwy; chalets $180-200; ✻) South of Manjimup, before the turnoff to Pemberton, is this collection of well-equipped wooden chalets with decks, scattered around a farm. Turkeys and sheep wander around, and there's a petting zoo and daily animal-feeding for the kids.

❶ Information

Visitor Centre (☑9771 1831; www.manjimup. wa.gov.au; Giblett St; ⊙9am-5pm)

Pemberton

POP 760

Hidden deep in the karri forests, drowsy Pemberton has also taken an epicurean turn, producing excellent wine that rivals that of Margaret River for quality if not for scale. If Margaret River is WA's Bordeaux, Pemberton is its Burgundy – producing excellent chardonnay and pinot noir, among other varietals. Wine tourism isn't as developed here, with some of the better names only offering tastings by appointment. Grab a free map listing opening hours from the visitor centre.

The national parks circling Pemberton are impressive. Aim to spend a day or two driving the well-marked Karri Forest Explorer tracks, walking the trails and picnicking in the green depths.

◉ Sights & Activities

Salitage WINE TASTING
(☑08-9776 1195; www.salitage.com.au; Vasse Hwy; ⊙10am-4pm) Sailtage's pinot noir has been rated the state's best, while its chardonnay and sauvignon blanc are also very highly regarded. Hour-long vineyard tours leave at 11am; call ahead.

Pemberton Tramway TRAM RIDES
(☑08-9776 1322; www.pemtram.com.au; adult/ child $18/9; ⊙10.45am & 2pm) Built between 1929 and 1933, the route travels through lush karri and marri forests to Warren River. A commentary is provided and it's a fun – if noisy – 1¾-hour return trip.

Mountford WINE TASTING
(www.mountfordwines.com.au; Bamess Rd; ⊙10am-4pm) 🍷 The wines and ciders produced here are all certified organic, plus there's a gallery on site. It's located north of Pemberton and easily incorporated into the Karri Forest Explorer circuit.

Pemberton Wine Centre WINE TASTING
(www.marima.com.au; 388 Old Vasse Rd; ⊙noon-4pm Mon-Fri) At the very heart of Warren National Park, this centre offers tastings of local wines and can compile a mixed case of your favourites.

Pemberton Pool SWIMMING
(Swimming Pool Rd) FREE Surrounded by karri trees, this natural pool is popular on a hot day – despite the warning sign (currents, venomous snakes). They breed them tough around here.

KARRI FOREST EXPLORER

Punctuated by glorious walks, magnificent trees and picnic areas, the Karri Forest Explorer tourist drive wends its way along 86km of scenic (partly unsealed) roads through three national parks (vehicle entry $11).

Popular attractions include the **Gloucester Tree**, named after the Duke of Gloucester who visited in 1946. It's a splendid fire-lookout tree, laddered with a spiral metal stairway; if you're feeling fit and fearless, make the 58m climb to the top. The **Dave Evans Bicentennial Tree**, tallest of the 'climbing trees' at 68m, is in Warren National Park, 11km southwest of Pemberton. Its tree-house cage weighs 2 tonnes and can sway up to 1.5m in either direction in strong winds. The Bicentennial Tree one-way loop leads via **Maiden Bush** to the **Heartbreak Trail**. It passes through 250-year-old karri stands, and nearby Drafty's Camp and Warren Campsite are great for overnighting (sites per adult/child $7/2).

The enchanting **Beedelup National Park**, 15km west of town on the Vasse Hwy (Rte 104), shouldn't be missed. There's a short, scenic walk that crosses Beedelup Brook near **Beedelup Falls**. There are numerous bird species to be found in the tall trees; at ground level the red-winged fairy wren is commonly seen. North of town, **Big Brook Arboretum** features 'big' trees from all over the world.

The track loops on and off the main roads, so you can drive short sections at a time. Pick up a brochure from Pemberton's visitor centre.

Tours

Pemberton Hiking & Canoeing
HIKING, CANOEING

(☑ 08-9776 1559; www.hikingandcanoeing.com.au; half-/full day $50/100) ✐ Environmentally sound tours in Warren and D'Entrecasteaux National Parks and to the Yeagarup sand dunes. Specialist tours (wildflowers, frogs, rare fauna) are also available, as are night canoeing trips ($75) to spot nocturnal wildlife.

Pemberton Discovery Tours
DRIVING TOUR

(☑ 08-9776 0484; www.pembertondiscoverytours.com.au; adult/child $95/50) ✐ Half-day 4WD tours to the Yeagarup sand dunes and the Warren River mouth.

Donnelly River Cruises
BOAT

(☑ 08-9777 1018; www.donnellyrivercruises.com.au; adult/child $65/35) ✐ Cruises through 12km of D'Entrecasteaux National Park to the cliffs of the Southern Ocean.

🛏 Sleeping

Pemberton Backpackers YHA
HOSTEL $

(☑ 08-9776 1105; www.yha.com.au; 7 Brockman St; dm/s/d $28/62/65; @🖥) The main hostel is given over to seasonal workers, but you'll need to check in here for a room in the separate cottage (8 Dean St) that's set aside for travellers. It's cute and cosy, but book ahead as it only has three rooms, one of which is a six-person dorm.

Best Western Pemberton Hotel
HOTEL $

(☑ 08-9776 1017; www.pembertonhotel.bestwestern.com.au; 66 Brockman St; r from $115; 🖥) Attached to an classic country pub, this comfortable accommodation occupies a striking new rammed-earth and cedar extension.

Gloucester Motel
MOTEL $

(☑ 08-9776 1266; www.gloucestermotel.com.au; Ellis St; r $80-160, apt from $140; ❄) The best of the town's motels, the Gloucester also has good-value budget rooms and spacious apartments. On site is the very good Sadie's restaurant.

★ Foragers
COTTAGE $$

(☑ 08-9776 1580; www.foragers.com.au; cnr Roberts & Northcliffe Rds; cottages $160-270; ❄) ✐ Choose between very nice, simple karri cottages, or leap to the top of the ladder with the luxury eco-chalets. The latter are light and airy, with elegant, contemporary decor, eco-conscious waste-water systems and a solar-passive design. You're also right on hand to enjoy culinary treats at the adjacent Foragers Field Kitchen (p142).

Old Picture Theatre Holiday Apartments
APARTMENT $$

(☑ 08-9776 1513; www.oldpicturetheatre.com.au; cnr Ellis & Guppy Sts; apt $170-300; ❄🖥) The town's old cinema has been revamped into well-appointed, self-contained, spacious apartments with lots of jarrah detail and black-and-white movie photos. It offers terrific value for money and the guest laundry and spa are rare treats.

Pump Hill Farm Cottages   COTTAGE **$$**
(☑08-9776 1379; www.pumphill.com.au; Pump Hill Rd; d $135-270) Families love this farm property, where kids are taken on a daily hay ride to feed the animals. Child-free folk will enjoy the ambience of the private, well-equipped cottages too.

Gloucester Motel   MOTEL **$$**
(☑08-9776 1266; www.gloucestermotel.com.au; Ellis St; r $80-160, apt from $140; ✳) The best of the town's motels, the Gloucester also has good-value budget rooms and spacious apartments. On site is the very good Sadie's restaurant.

Marima Cottages   COTTAGE **$$$**
(☑08-9776 1211; www.marima.com.au; 388 Old Vasse Rd; cottages $225-245) Right in the middle of Warren National Park, these four country-style rammed-earth-and-cedar cottages with pot-bellied stoves and lots of privacy are luxurious getaways.

🍴 Eating & Drinking

The local menu specialities are trout and marron.

Holy Smoke!   SELF-CATERING **$**
(www.holysmoke.com.au; 3/19 Brockman St; snacks $5-15; ☉9am-5pm Mon-Sat) Good coffee, sourdough bread, house-smoked meat, chicken and fish. Pop in for picnic supplies.

Forest Fresh Marron   SELF-CATERING **$**
(☑0428 887 720; www.forestfreshmarron.com.au; Pump Hill Rd; ☉10am-5pm Mon-Fri, 4.30-5.30pm Sat & Sun) 🌿 Live sustainably farmed marron for sale. Transport packs – to keep the wee beasties alive for up to 30 hours – and cooking pots are also available. It's 300m left of the caravan park.

Karri Forest Explorer

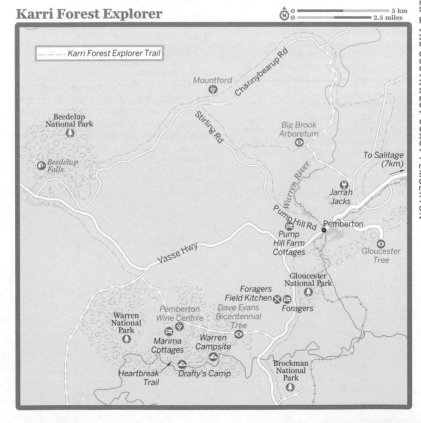

Millhouse Cafe CAFE **$$**
(Brockman St; breakfast $6-20, lunch $11-40; ⊙ 7am-5pm) Breakfast – try the breakfast crostini – and coffee are good at this old cottage with wraparound verandahs, and you can feast on local marron and trout for lunch. Local art is often displayed on the walls.

Sadie's INTERNATIONAL, INDIAN **$$**
(Ellis St; mains $25-35; ⊙ 6-9pm) Local trout and marron, and authentically good Indian curries from an authentically good Indian chef. At Gloucester Motel.

Foragers Field Kitchen INTERNATIONAL **$$$**
(✆ 08-9776 1503; www.foragers.com.au; cnr Roberts & Northcliffe Rds; dinner $55-75) Join renowned chef Sophie Zalokar at one of her regular Friday or Saturday set dinners – options could include wood-fired Italian dishes or seasonal four-course menus – or sign up for one of her cooking classes (usually across a weekend or on a Wednesday night). Check the website's events calendar for dates. Booking at least 48 hours ahead is preferred.

Jarrah Jacks CRAFT BEER
(www.jarrahjacks.com.au; Kemp Rd, Lot 2; ⊙ 9am-5pm) Wonderful vineyard views, six craft beers – try the refreshing wheat beer – and tasty food including shepherds pie, salt-and-pepper squid and daily sandwich specials.

❶ Information

DEC (✆ 08-9776 1207; www.dec.wa.gov.au; Kennedy St; ⊙ 8am-4.30pm) Has detailed information on the local parks and stocks the useful *Pemberton Bushwalks* brochure.

Visitor Centre (✆ 08-9776 1133; www.pembertonvisitor.com.au; Brockman St; ⊙ 9am-4pm; @) Includes a pioneer museum and karri-forest discovery centre. Also handles Transwa bookings.

Shannon National Park

The 535-sq-km **Shannon National Park** (entry per car/motorcycle $11/5) is on the South Western Hwy, 53km south of Manjimup. Until 1968 Shannon was the site of WA's biggest timber mill, and plants including deciduous trees from the northern hemisphere are reminders of the old settlement.

The 48km **Great Forest Trees Drive** is a one-way loop, split by the highway. Start at the park day-use area on the north of the highway. From here there's an easy 3.5km walk to the Shannon Dam and a steeper 5.5km loop to Mokare's Rock, with a boardwalk and great views. Further along, the 8km-return **Great Forest Trees Walk** crosses the Shannon River. Off the southern part of the drive, boardwalks look over stands of giant karri at **Snake Gully** and **Big Tree Grove**.

In the park's southwest, a 6km return walking track links Boorara Tree with a lookout point over Lane Poole Falls.

There is a sizeable **campground** (sites per adult/child $9/2) with showers in the spot where the original timber-milling town used to be. A self-contained bunkhouse, **Shannon Lodge** (per night $66, bond $150), is available for groups of up to eight people; book this through DEC in Pemberton.

South Coast

Includes ➡

Best Places to Eat

➡ York Street Cafe (p153)

➡ Mrs Jones (p148)

➡ Maleeya's Thai Cafe (p157)

➡ Pepper & Salt (p148)

➡ Boston Brewery (p148)

Best Places to Stay

➡ Cape Howe Cottages (p148)

➡ Beach House at Bayside (p153)

➡ Esperance B&B by the Sea (p162)

➡ Riverside Retreat (p146)

➡ 1849 Backpackers (p152)

Why Go?

Standing on the cliffs of the wild South Coast as the waves pound below is a truly exhilarating experience. And on calm days, when the sea is various shades of aquamarine and the glorious white-sand beaches lie pristine and welcoming, it's an altogether different type of magnificent. If you're seeking to get away from it all, even busy holiday periods here in the 'Great Southern' are relaxed; it's just that bit too far from Perth for the holiday hordes. Marine visitors come this way, though – the winter months bring a steady stream of migrating whales.

When you need a change from the great outdoors, Albany – the earliest European settlement in the state – has a wealth of colonial history, and towns such as Denmark and Esperance invite you to sit back with a glass of fine local wine and watch the world go by.

When to Go
Esperance

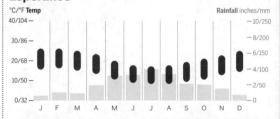

Jan The best beach weather – and it's not as hot or crowded as the west coast.

Sep Go wild for wildflowers and whales.

Dec Perfect weather for the Stirling Range and Porongurup National Parks.

South Coast Highlights

1 Walking among and above the giant tingle trees in the Valley of the Giants **Tree Top Walk** (p145)

2 Competing to see who can spot the most whales in Albany's **King George Sound** (p151)

3 Pondering our fractious human-cetacean relations at the **Whale World Museum** (p154) near Albany

4 Hiking among the tall trees and granite outcrops of **Porongurup National Park** (p156)

5 Wandering through wildflowers along the walking tracks of **Fitzgerald River National Park** (p160)

6 Marvelling at the surf-battered coast from the **Great Ocean Drive** (p162) near Esperance

7 Swimming, surfing and soaking up the sun at the squeaky-clean beaches of **Cape Le Grand National Park** (p164)

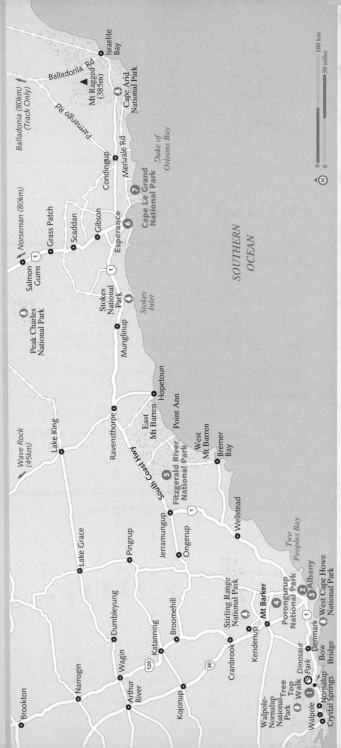

Walpole & Nornalup

The peaceful twin inlets of Walpole (population 320) and Nornalup (population 50) make good bases from which to explore the heavily forested Walpole Wilderness Area – an immense wilderness incorporating a rugged coastline, several national parks, marine parks, nature reserves and forest conservation areas – covering a whopping 3630-sq-km (an area considerably bigger than Samoa and 57 other countries). Look for *Exploring the Walpole Wilderness and Surrounding Area* pamphlet produced by the Department of Environment & Conservation (DEC).

Walpole is the bigger settlement, and the only spot in the area with mobile-phone coverage. It's here that the South Western Hwy (Rte 1) becomes the South Coast Hwy.

◉ Sights & Activities

Walpole-Nornalup
National Park   NATIONAL PARK
(www.valleyofthegiants.com.au; Valley of the Giants Tree Top Walk adult/child $12.50/5; ⊙Valley of the Giants Tree Top Walk 9am-4.15pm) The giant trees of this park include red, yellow and Rates tingle trees (all types of eucalypt or gum trees) and, closer to the coast, the red flowering gum.

In the **Valley of the Giants** the **Tree Top Walk** is Walpole's main drawcard. A 600m-long ramp rises from the floor of the valley, allowing visitors access high into the canopy of the giant tingle trees. At its highest point, the ramp is 40m above the ground. It's on a gentle incline so it's easy to walk and is even accessible by assisted wheelchair. The ramp is an engineering feat in itself, though vertigo sufferers might have a few problems; it's designed to sway gently in the breeze to mimic life in the treetops. At ground level, the **Ancient Empire** boardwalk meanders around and through the base of veteran red tingles, some of which are 16m in circumference, including one that soars to 46m.

There are numerous good walking tracks around, including a section of the **Bibbulmun Track**, which passes through Walpole to Coalmine Beach. Scenic drives include the **Knoll Drive**, 3km east of Walpole; the **Valley of the Giants Road**; and through pastoral country to **Mt Frankland**, 29km north of Walpole. Here you can climb to the summit for panoramic views or walk around the trail at its base. Opposite Knoll Drive, Hilltop Rd leads to a **giant tingle tree**; this road continues to the **Circular Pool** on the Frankland River, a popular canoeing spot. You can hire canoes from Nornalup Riverside Chalets (p146).

Midway between Nornalup and Peaceful Bay, check out **Conspicuous Cliffs**. It's a great spot for whale watching from July to November, with a boardwalk, a hilltop lookout and a steepish 800m walk to the beach.

Dinosaur World   WILDLIFE RESERVE
(www.dinosaurworld.com.au; Bow Bridge; adult/child $12/6; ⊙9.30am-4.30pm) Replica dinosaur skeletons and information boards have been added to spice up this bird and reptile park, off the South Coast Hwy at Bow Bridge. Kangaroos, lizards and snakes feature, but the parrots (most with clipped wings) are the real stars.

☞ Tours

WOW Wilderness Ecocruises   CRUISE
(☑08-9840 1036; www.wowwilderness.com.au; adult/child $40/15) ✔ The magnificent landscape and its ecology are brought to life with anecdotes about Aboriginal settlement, salmon fishers and shipwrecked pirates. The 2½-hour cruise through the inlets and river systems leaves at 10am daily; book at the visitor centre.

Naturally Walpole Eco Tours   DRIVING TOUR
(☑08-9840 1019; www.naturallywalpole.com.au) Half-day tours through the Walpole Wilderness (adult/child $75/40), and customised winery and wildflower tours.

⇙ Sleeping

Walpole Wilderness Area bush camping sites (adult/child $7/2) are located at Crystal Springs and Fernhook Falls.

Coalmine Beach   CARAVAN PARK $
(☑08-9840 1026; www.coalminebeach.com.au; Coalmine Beach Rd, Walpole; sites per 2 people $31-35, cabins $115-180; ❊@☎) You couldn't get a better location than this, under shady trees above the sheltered waters of the inlet. A new recreation room and redecorated chalets are recent improvements.

Walpole Lodge   HOSTEL $
(☑08-9840 1244; www.walpolelodge.com.au; Pier St, Walpole; dm/s/d $26/45/65; @☎) This popular place is basic, open plan and informal, with great info boards around the walls and casual, cheery owners. Ensuite rooms are excellent value.

Tingle All Over YHA

HOSTEL $

(☑08-9840 1041; www.yha.com.au; 60 Nockolds St, Walpole; dm/s/d $31/54/74; @ ☎) Help yourself to lemons and chillies from the garden of this clean, basic option near the highway. Lots of advice on local walks is on offer.

Rest Point Holiday Village

CARAVAN PARK $

(☑08-9840 1032; www.restpoint.com.au; Rest Point; sites per 2 people $22, cabins $75-115) Set on wide lawns with direct water frontage, this spacious holiday park has shade for campers and self-contained accommodation.

Nornalup Riverside Chalets

CHALET $$

(☑08-9840 1107; www.walpole.org.au/nornalupriv ersidechalets; Riverside Dr, Nornalup; chalets $110-180) Stay a night in sleepy Nornalup in these comfortable, colourful self-contained chalets, just a rod's throw from the fish in the Frankland River. The chalets are well spaced out, giving a feeling of privacy.

Riverside Retreat

CHALET $$

(☑08-9840 1255; www.riversideretreat.com.au; South Coast Hwy, Nornalup; chalets $140-200) Off the road and on the banks of the beautiful Frankland River, these spotless and well-equipped chalets are great value, with pot-bellied stoves for cosy winter warmth, and tennis and canoeing as outdoor pursuits. Frequent visits from local wildlife make Riverside Retreat a good option for families.

✗ Eating

Flaming Hot Takeaways

FAST FOOD $

(Vista St, Walpole; mains $10-15; ◷11.30am-8pm) The local chippie is a solid choice for burgers, pizza, and excellent fish and chips.

Thurlby Herb Farm

CAFE $$

(www.thurlbyherb.com.au; 3 Gardiner Rd; mains $15-20; ◷9am-4.30pm Mon-Fri) Apart from distilling its own essential oils and making herb-based products including soap and aromatherapy treatments, Thurlby serves up tasty light lunches and cakes accompanied by fresh-picked herbal teas. Try the delicious rosemary-infused scones.

Top Deck Cafe

CAFE $$

(25 Nockolds St; mains $15-27; ◷9am-8pm) Tucked away in Walpole's compact main-road shopping centre, Top Deck kicks off with breakfast, and graduates to dinner options including spinach-and-feta pie and a daily curry special. Order a glass of local wine and kick back in the sunny deck at the front.

ⓘ Information

DEC (☑08-9840 0400; www.dec.wa.gov.au; South Coast Hwy, Walpole; ◷8am-4.30pm Mon-Fri) For national-park and bushwalking information.

Visitor Centre (☑08-9840 1111; www.walpole. com.au; South Coast Hwy, Walpole; ◷9am-5pm; @)

ⓘ Getting There & Away

Transwa (☑1300 662 205; www.transwa. wa.gov.au) Bus GS3 heads daily to/from Bunbury ($43, 4½ hours), Bridgetown ($24, 3¼ hours), Pemberton ($19, 1¾ hours), Denmark ($13, 42 minutes) and Albany ($21, 1½ hours).

Denmark

POP 2800

Denmark's beaches and coastline, river and sheltered inlet, forested backdrop and hinterland have attracted a varied, creative and environmentally aware community. Farmers, ferals, fishers and families all mingle during the town's four market days each year.

Denmark was established to supply timber to the early goldfields. Known by the Minang Noongar people as Koorabup (place of the black swan), there's evidence of early Aboriginal settlement in the 3000-year-old fish traps found in Wilson Inlet.

◉ Sights & Activities

The town is located in the cool-climate Great Southern wine region and notable wineries include **Howard Park** (www.howardparkwines. com.au; Scotsdale Rd; ◷10am-4pm) and **Forest Hill** (www.foresthillwines.com.au; cnr South Coast Hwy & Myers Rd; ◷10am-5pm). The latter has an architecturally impressive tasting room and restaurant.

Surfers and anglers should head to ruggedly beautiful **Ocean Beach**. Accredited local instructor Mike Neunuebel gives **surfing lessons** (☑0401 349 854; www.southcoast surfinglessons.com.au; 2hr lessons incl equipment from $50) and hires out boards and wetsuits (per hour $20).

To get your bearings, walk the **Mokare Heritage Trail** (a 3km circuit along the Denmark River) or the **Wilson Inlet Trail** (12km return, starting at the river mouth), which forms part of the longer **Nornalup Trail**. The **Mt Shadforth Lookout** has fine coastal views, and lush **Mt Shadforth Rd**, running from town to the South Coast Hwy west of town, makes a great scenic drive. A longer pastoral loop is via **Scotsdale Rd**. Attractions include alpaca farms, wineries, cheese farms, and art-and-craft galleries.

William Bay National Park, about 20km west of town, offers sheltered swimming in gorgeous **Greens Pool** and **Elephant Rocks**, and has good walking tracks. Swing by **Bartholomews Meadery** (www.honeywine.com.au; 2620 South Coast Hwy; ⊙ 9.30am-4.30pm) for a post-beach treat of mead (honey wine) or delicious homemade honey-rose-almond ice cream ($4).

Tours

Out of Sight! DRIVING TOUR
(☑ 08-9848 2814; www.outofsighttours.com) Nature trips into the Walpole Wilderness (three hours, adult/child $90/45), West Cape Howe (six hours, adult/child $150/75) or Stirling Range (eight hours, adult/child $200/100); sightseeing around Denmark (two hours, adult/child $50/25); or sampling tours of the local wineries (full day $100). Visit its Eco-Discovery shop at the newly expanded Denmark Visitor Centre to hire canoes and bikes. In 2013 the Munda Biddi Trail was extended to Denmark, completing the trail's total of 1000km.

Denmark Wine Lovers Tour BUS TOUR, WINERY
(☑ 0410 423 262; www.denmarkwinelovers.com.au) Full-day tours taking in Denmark wineries ($95), or further afield to Porongurup or Mt Barker (price on application).

Festivals & Events

Market Days MARKET
Four times a year (early December, early and late January and Easter) Denmark hosts a colourful market day on the parkland by the river, with an unusual range of high-quality craft stalls, music and food. Accommodation rates rise on these weekends. See www.denmarkarts.com.au for relevant dates.

Festival of Voice MUSIC FESTIVAL
(www.dfov.org.au) Performances and workshops, on the early-June long weekend.

Sleeping

Blue Wren Travellers' Rest YHA HOSTEL $
(☑ 08-9848 3300; www.denmarkbluewren.com.au; 17 Price St; dm/d $27/73) Chooks live under this little timber house and everyone spoils the goofy house dog. Great info panels cover the walls, and it's small enough (just 20 beds) to

---

THE ROAD TO MANDALAY

About 13km west of Walpole, at Crystal Springs, is an 8km gravel road to **Mandalay Beach**, where the *Mandalay*, a Norwegian barque, was wrecked in 1911. As the sand gradually erodes with storms, the wreck eerily appears every 10 years or so, in shallow water that is walkable at low tide (check out the photos at Walpole visitor centre). The beach is glorious, often deserted, and accessed by an impressive boardwalk across sand dunes and cliffs. It's now part of D'Entrecasteaux National Park.

---

have a homey feel. Bikes can also be rented – $25 per day or just $15 if you're a guest – and friendly owner Graham is a whiz at bike repairs.

Denmark Ocean Beach Holiday Park CARAVAN PARK $
(☑ 08-9848 1106; www.denmarkobhp.com.au; Ocean Beach Rd; sites per 2 people $28-30, cabins $110-180; ❋ @ ⓢ) ✿ This large, long-standing complex has lots of family-friendly facilities, new kitchen and ablution blocks, and a brand-new array of stylish motel units. The surf, sun and sand of Ocean Beach are just a short stroll away, and the kids will love the giant bouncy pillow.

Denmark Rivermouth Caravan Park CARAVAN PARK $
(☑ 08-9848 1262; www.denmarkrivermouthcaravanpark.com.au; Inlet Dr; sites per 2 people $30, cabins & chalets $130-200) Ideally located for nautical pursuits, this caravan park sits along Wilson Inlet beside the boat ramp. Some of the units are properly flash, although they are quite tightly arranged. There's also a kids playground and kayaks for hire.

Riverbend Caravan Park CARAVAN PARK $
(☑ 08-9848 1107; www.riverbend-caravanpark.com.au; River Bend Lane; sites per 1/2 people from $22/26, chalets from $110) About 2km from town on a quiet stretch of river, this lovely shaded site has well-equipped cabins with private verandahs.

31 on the Terrace BOUTIQUE HOTEL $
(☑ 08-9848 1700; www.denmarkaccommodation.com.au; 31 Strickland St; r $99-115; ❋) Good-value ensuite rooms – some with compact balconies – fill this renovated corner pub in

the centre of town. Themed decor of the different rooms travels from New York to Paris via Egypt, but the ambience is classic and restrained rather than brash and showy. Compact apartments are good for families and groups up to five people.

★ **Cape Howe Cottages**   COTTAGE $$
(☑08-9845 1295; www.capehowe.com.au; 322 Tennessee Rd S; cottages $170-280; ❀) For a remote getaway, these five cottages in bushland southeast of Denmark really make the grade. They're all different, but the best is only 1½km from dolphin-favoured Lowlands Beach and is properly plush – with a BBQ on the deck, a dishwasher in the kitchen and laundry facilities.

Sensational Heights   B&B $$
(☑08-9840 9000; www.sensationalheightsbandb .com.au; 159 Suttons Rd; r $190-260; ❀🤶) Yep, it's on top of a hill (off Scotsdale Rd) and, yes, the views are sensational. It's a new house, so expect contemporary decor, shiny new fixtures, luxurious linen and very comfy beds. The pricier rooms have spa baths.

Willowleigh B&B   B&B $$
(☑08-9848 1089; www.denmarkbedandbreakfast. com.au; Kearsley Rd; r $160; ❀🤶) Enjoy the 0.8 hectares of gorgeous gardens from your conservatory or verandah at this B&B on the edge of town.

Celestine Retreat   CHALET $$$
(☑08-9848 3000; www.celestineretreat.com; 413 Mt Shadforth Rd; d $239-289; ❀) With just four spa chalets scattered on 13 hectares, there are definitely plenty of stunning views to go around at this luxury retreat. Romance is also on the agenda, with private spas, fluffy bathrobes and high-end bathroom goodies. The bright lights of Denmark are just 3km back down Mt Shadforth when you want to rejoin the real world.

Aiyana Retreat   APARTMENT $$$
(☑08-9848 3258; www.aiyanaretreat.com.au; 28 Anning Rd; apt $195-250) Three luxurious apartments, tucked down a quiet cul-de-sac; spa treatments are also available.

✕ Eating

Denmark Bakery   BAKERY $
(Strickland St; pies $5-6; ☺7am-5pm) Prize-winning and proud of it, this bakery is an institution because of its pies, and the bread is also good.

Mrs Jones   CAFE $$
(☑0467 481 878; www.mrsjonescafe.com; 12 Mt Shadforth Rd; breakfast $9-18, lunch $14-21; ☺7am-4pm) Denmark's best coffee is at this spacious spot with high ceilings and exposed beams – you can even pre-order your personal java fix by SMS. If you're not in a hurry, settle in with locals and tourists for interesting cafe fare such as Turkish eggs with roasted pumpkin, chorizo and lentils, or Asian-style duck pancakes with plum sauce.

Denmark Tavern   PUB $$
(623 South Coast Hwy; mains $25-34; ☺11am-late) Easily the best pub meals for many a mile, and a good selection of draught beers and local wines.

★ **Pepper & Salt**   MODERN AUSTRALIAN $$$
(☑08-9848 3053; www.matildasestate.com; 18 Hamilton St, Matilda's Estate; mains $35-40; ☺noon-10pm) With his Fijian-Indian heritage, chef Silas Masih's knowledge of spices and herbs is wonderfully showcased in his fresh and vibrant food. Highlights include chilli-and-coconut prawns, or the great-value tasting platter ($48), which effortlessly detours from Asia to the Middle East. Buy some wine from the adjacent Matilda's Estate before settling in for a foodies adventure. Bookings recommended.

🍷 Drinking

★ **Boston Brewery**   CRAFT BEER
(www.willoughbypark.com.au; Willoughby Park Winery, South Coast Hwy; pizzas $18-23, mains $24-32; ☺10am-7pm Mon-Thu, to 10pm Fri & Sat, to 9pm Sun) The industrial chic of the brewery gives way to an absolute edge-of-vineyard location, and wood-fired pizzas, meals and bar snacks go well with Boston's hoppy portfolio of four beers. The Willoughby Park Winery is also right on site, and there's live music from 4pm to 8pm every second Saturday.

Southern End   CRAFT BEER
(www.denmarkbrewery.com.au; 427 Mt Shadforth Rd; ☺11.30am-4.30pm Thu-Mon) Home to Denmark Brews & Ales, the Southern End Restaurant has the best views in town from a hilltop terrace. Dinner is a slightly more formal affair than lunch.

Denmark Hotel   PUB
(www.denmarkhotel.com.au; Hollings Rd) Overlooking the river, the local boozer is the hub of nocturnal activity, with live music every Friday night.

ℹ️ Information

Visitor Centre (📞 08-9848 2055; www. denmark.com.au; 73 South Coast Hwy; ⏱️ 9am-5pm) Information, accommodation bookings, and an excellent display on the local wine scene. Ask for *The Wine Lovers' Guide to Denmark* brochure and get exploring.

ℹ️ Getting There & Away

Transwa (📞 1300 662 205; www.transwa. wa.gov.au) Bus service GS3 heads daily to/from Bunbury ($48, 5½ hours), Bridgetown ($33, 4¾ hours), Pemberton ($27, 2¾ hours), Walpole ($13, 42 minutes) and Albany ($9, 42 minutes).

Albany

POP 25,200

Established shortly before Perth in 1826, the oldest European settlement in the state is now the bustling commercial centre of the southern region. Albany is a mixed bag comprising a stately and genteel decaying colonial quarter, a waterfront in the midst of sophisticated redevelopment and a hectic sprawl of malls and fast-food joints. Less ambivalent is its spectacular coastline, from Torndirrup National Park's surf-pummelled cliffs to Middleton Beach's white sands, and the calm waters of King George Sound.

The town is in an area that's seen the violence of weather and whaling. Whales are still a part of the Albany experience, but these days are hunted through a camera lens.

The Bibbulmun Track (p35) ends (or starts) here, just outside the visitor centre; the exhausted and/or exuberant comments in the walkers' log books make great reading.

History

The Minang Noongar people called this place Kinjarling (the place of rain) and believed that fighting Wargals (mystical giant serpents) created the fractured landscape. The Minang set up sophisticated fish traps on Oyster Harbour, the remains of which can still be seen.

Initial contacts with Europeans were friendly, with over 60 ships visiting between 1622 and 1826. The Minang traded crops with the early arrivals, in exchange for ship biscuits. The establishment of a British settlement here was welcomed as it regulated the behaviour of sealers and whalers, who had been responsible for kidnaps, rapes and murder of Minang people. Yet by the end of the 19th century, every shop in Albany refused entry to Aboriginal people, and control over every aspect of their lives (including the right to bring up their own children) had been lost.

For the British, Albany's raison d'être was its sheltered harbour, which made it a thriving whaling port. Later the city became a coaling station for British ships bound for the east coast, and during WWI it was the mustering point for transport ships for Australian and New Zealand troops heading for Egypt and the Gallipoli campaign.

👁️ Sights

Middleton & Emu Beaches   BEACHES
Just around the headland, east of the town centre, these beautiful beaches facing King George Sound share one long stretch of family-friendly sand. In winter, you'll often see pods of mother whales and their calves here. Head around Emu Point to Oyster Harbour for swimming pontoons and even calmer waters.

A clifftop walking track hugs much of the waterfront between the town centre and Middleton Beach. Boardwalks continue along Emu Beach.

**Western Australian
Museum – Albany**   MUSEUM
(www.museum.wa.gov.au; Residency Rd; admission by donation; ⏱️ 10am-4.30pm) This branch of the state museum is split between two neighbouring buildings. The newer Eclipse building has a kids' discovery section, a lighthouse exhibition, a gallery for temporary exhibitions and a gift shop. The restored 1850s home of the resident magistrate illuminates Minang Noongar history, local natural history and seafaring stories.

WEST CAPE HOWE NATIONAL PARK

Midway between Denmark and Albany, this 35-sq-km coastal park is a playground for naturalists, bushwalkers, rock climbers and anglers. Inland are areas of coastal heath, lakes, swamp and karri forest. With the exception of the road to Shelley Beach, access is restricted to 4WDs, mostly travelling through sand dunes, to explore the wild coast.

Camping is permitted at Shelley Beach, although campfires are banned.

SOUTH COAST ALBANY

Albany

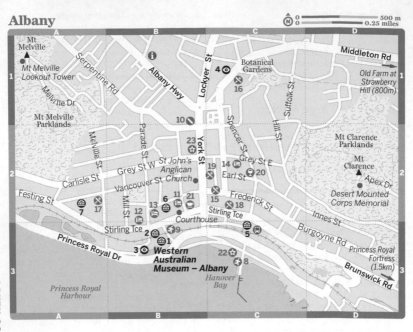

Albany

◎ Top Sights
1 Western Australian Museum
   – Albany B3

◎ Sights
2 Albany Convict Gaol B3
3 Brig Amity B3
4 Dog Rock C1
5 Old Post Office C3
6 Patrick Taylor Cottage B2
7 Vancouver Arts Centre A2

⊕ Activities, Courses & Tours
8 Albany Whale Tours C3
9 Alkoomi Wines B3
10 Southcoast Diving Supplies B1

⊜ Sleeping
11 1849 Backpackers B2
12 Albany Harbourside B2

13 Bayview Backpackers YHA B2
   Dog Rock Motel .... (see 16)
14 My Place C2

⊗ Eating
15 14 Peels Place C2
16 Lime 303 .... C1
17 Vancouver Cafe & Store A2
18 White Star Hotel C2
19 York Street Cafe C2

⊜ Drinking & Nightlife
20 Earl of Spencer C2
21 Liberté B2

⊕ Entertainment
22 Albany Entertainment
   Centre C3
23 Town Hall B2

Brig Amity   SHIP
(www.historicalbany.com.au; adult/child $5/2;
⊙9am-4pm) This full-scale replica of the brig
that carried Albany's first British settlers
from Sydney in 1826 was completed for the
city's 150th anniversary. Self-guided audio
tours bring to life the ship's history.

Town Centre   HISTORIC BUILDINGS
Near the foreshore is Albany's historic precinct. Take a stroll down Stirling Tce – noted
for its Victorian shopfronts, **Courthouse**
and **Old Post Office** – and up York St to
St John's Anglican Church and Albany's
Town Hall. A guided walking-tour brochure
is available from the visitor centre.

Patrick Taylor Cottage MUSEUM
(www.historicalbany.com.au; 39 Duke St; admission $2; ⊙ 11am-3pm) Believed to be the oldest colonial dwelling in Western Australia (WA), this 1832 wattle-and-daub cottage is packed with antiques, freaky mannequins and displays on its former residents.

Albany Convict Gaol MUSEUM
(www.historicalbany.com.au; Stirling Tce; adult/child $5/2.50; ⊙ 10am-4pm) The old gaol was built in 1851 as a hiring depot for ticket-of-leave convicts, but by 1855 most were in private employment. In 1872 the building was extended and reopened as a civil gaol, and is now a folk museum.

Old Farm at Strawberry Hill HISTORIC BUILDING
(www.ntwa.com.au; 174 Middleton Rd; adult/child $5/3; ⊙ 10am-4pm) National Trust–owned Strawberry Hill is one of the oldest farms in WA, established in 1827 as the town's government farm. The homestead (1836) features antiques and artefacts that belonged to the original owner.

Vancouver Arts Centre GALLERY
(Vancouver St; ⊙ 9am-4pm Mon-Fri, 10am-3pm Sat) Housed in a former hospital (1887), this is the centre of the city's arts community, hosting regular touring exhibitions and cultural events.

Mt Melville & Mt Clarence LANDMARK
There are more fine views over the coast and inland from the twin peaks, Mt Clarence and Mt Melville, which overlook the town. On top of Mt Clarence is the **Desert Mounted Corps Memorial**, originally erected in Port Said as a WWI memorial. It was irreparably damaged during the Suez crisis in 1956, when colonial reminders were less than popular in Egypt. This copy was made from masonry salvaged from the original.

To climb Mt Clarence follow the track accessible from the end of Grey St E, turn left, take the first turn on the right and follow the path by the water tanks. The walk is tough, but the views make it worthwhile; take a picnic and enjoy a well-earned rest at the top. By car, take Apex Dr.

Princess Royal Fortress HISTORIC SITE
(www.forts.albany.wa.gov.au; Forts Rd; adult/child $12/4.50; ⊙ 9am-5pm) As a strategic port, Albany was historically regarded as being vulnerable to attack. Built in 1893 on Mt Adelaide, this fort was initially constructed as a defence against potential attacks from the

Russians and French. The restored buildings, gun emplacements and views are interesting, and there are also poignant photos of Anzac troops leaving for Gallipoli. Forts Rd is off Marine Dr.

Dog Rock LANDMARK
On Middleton Rd, this large rock resembles a dog's head (the locals have even painted on a dog collar to reinforce the point). The Minang believed the dog had been decapitated by an angry Wargal.

🏃 Activities

Whale Watching WHALE WATCHING
After whaling ended in 1978, whales slowly began returning to the waters of Albany. They're now here to the extent that it can sometimes be hard *not* to see southern right and humpback whales near the bays and coves of King George Sound from July to mid-October. You can usually spot them from the beach, but if you fancy a closer look, both **Albany Dolphin & Whale Cruises** (☑ 0428 429 876; www.whales.com.au; adult/child $80/45; ⊙ Jul–mid-Oct) and **Albany Whale Tours** (☑ 08-9845 1068; www.albanywhaletours.com.au; Albany Waterfront Marina, cnr Princess Royal Dr & Toll Pl; adult/child $80/45; ⊙ late May–early Oct) run regular whale-watching trips in season.

Diving DIVING
Albany's appeal as a top-class diving destination grew after the 2001 scuttling of the warship HMAS *Perth* to create an artificial reef for divers; visit www.hmasperth.com.au. Its natural reefs feature temperate and tropical corals, and are home to the bizarre and wonderful leafy and weedy sea dragons. **Southcoast Diving Supplies** (☑ 08-9841 7176; www.divealbany.com.au; 84b Serpentine Rd) can show you the underwater world.

Fishing FISHING
Beach fishing at Middleton and Emu Beaches is popular, and **Spinners Charters** (☑ 08-9844 1906; www.spinnerscharters.com.au; Emu Point) run deep-sea fishing trips. **Emu Point Boat Hire** (☑ 08-9844 1562; Emu Point; ⊙ Sep-May) provides paddle boats, kayaks and motorised dinghies.

Alkoomi Wines WINE TASTING
(www.alkoomiwines.com.au; 225 Stirling Tce; ⊙ 11am-5pm Mon-Sat) Just in case you were having withdrawals from wine tasting, Frankland River's Alkoomi has set up a handy tasting room right in the middle of town.

ALBANY'S WHALING BATTLEGROUND

Talk to some Western Australians about their childhood holidays in Albany and, as well as carefree days of fishing and swimming, they're also likely to recall an almighty stench in the air and sharks circling in bloody corners of Frenchman Bay. The local whales, whose blubber created the vile smell while being melted down in pressure cookers, and whose blood spilled into water around the then Cheynes Beach Whaling Station, also appear to remember this scene far too well. It took them well over a decade to return in full strength to the waters around Albany after the last whale was hunted on 20 November 1978.

The whaling industry was gruesome in a most public way – whales were hunted, harpooned and dragged back to shore to be cut up and boiled – which is perhaps why the environmental movement managed to make its closure one of their earlier successes. It became harder for the industry to make the smell, the blood and the sight of harpooned carcasses being towed into the harbour anything but unattractive.

One of Tim Winton's earlier novels (*Shallows*, 1984), set in Albany, where Winton lived for some time as an adolescent, describes how whaling became an emotional battleground for environmentalists and the many local employees of the industry, similar to the situation in timber towns throughout the southwest in recent years. This pressure from protesters, as well as dwindling whale numbers and a drop in world whale-oil prices, sounded the death knell for the industry.

But Albany has cleverly managed to turn this now-unacceptable industry into a quaint tourist attraction, with the fascinating Whale World Museum and maritime festivals, which celebrate its rough-and-ready history on the seas. The whales who play in the surrounding waters are all the happier for it – as are the town's tourism-boosted coffers.

⚐ Tours

Kalgan Queen BOAT
(☑08-9844 3166; www.albanyaustralia.com; Emu Point; adult/child $75/40; ⊙9am Sep-Jun) Take a four-hour cruise up the Kalgan River in a glass-bottomed boat and learn about the history and wildlife of the area.

Down Under ADVENTURE TOUR
(☑08-9842 2468; www.harleytours.com.au; per 30min/hr/half-day $60/110/300) Hop on a hog and see Albany from a Harley Davidson. In addition, 'Quick Thrills' are available from Middleton Beach during the Christmas and Easter school holidays ($10).

🛏 Sleeping

★1849 Backpackers HOSTEL $
(☑08-9842 1554; www.albanybackpackers accommodation.com.au; 45 Peels Pl; dm from $25, r from $70; @🛜) Big flags from many nations provide a colourful international welcome at this well-run hostel. A huge, modern kitchen, sunny rooms and a laidback social ambience make this one of WA's best places to stay for budget travellers. Make sure you book in for 1849's free BBQ on Sunday night.

Albany Discovery Inn GUESTHOUSE $
(☑08-9842 5535; www.discoveryinn.com.au; 9 Middleton Rd, Middleton Beach; s $55, d $80-90; @🛜) Close to the beach, this guesthouse has a homey atmosphere. Guests congregate amid tropical plants in the central conservatory, and the recently refurbished rooms are colourful and individually decorated. A recent addition is an on-site cafe offering good-value evening meals ($20). Non-guests are welcome, but book ahead. Rates include a cooked breakfast.

**Middleton Beach
Holiday Park** CARAVAN PARK $
(☑08-9841 3593; www.holidayalbany.com.au; 28 Flinders Pde, Middleton Beach; sites per 2 people from $40, chalets $125-270; @🛜♨) This excellent beachfront caravan park is sheltered by high sand dunes. Book early – it's popular. Newly built spa villas are particularly flash.

Emu Beach Holiday Park CARAVAN PARK $
(☑08-9844 1147; www.emubeach.com; 8 Medcalf Pde, Emu Point; sites for 2 people from $35, chalets $130-190; ❄) Families love the Emu Beach area, and this holiday park, close to the beach, has good facilities, including a BBQ area and kids playground. Newly constructed motel units are spacious and modern.

Bayview Backpackers YHA HOSTEL $
(📞 08-9842 3388; www.bayviewbackpackers.com.
au; 49 Duke St; dm/r $28/76; @ 🛜) In a quiet
street 400m from Albany's historic centre,
this rambling backpackers has an easygoing
vibe.

Albany Harbourside APARTMENT $$
(📞 08-9842 1769; www.albanyharbourside.com.
au; 8 Festing St; d $159-219; ❄) Albany Har-
bourside's portfolio includes a brace of spa-
cious and spotless apartments on Festing
St, and three other self-contained options
arrayed around central Albany. Decor is
modern and colourful, and some apart-
ments have ocean views. For a touch of
19th-century charm, book the pretty Har-
bourside Cottage.

My Place APARTMENT $$
(📞 08-9842 3242; www.myplace.com.au; 47-61
Grey St E; r $135-175; ❄🛜) We love the tongue-
in-cheek nana-ish vibe to the studios, with
floral duvets and a trio of flying ducks on the
wall. The considerably larger one-bedroom
options aren't as kooky, but they're all clean,
central and excellent value.

Dog Rock Motel MOTEL $$
(📞 08-9841 4422; www.dogrockmotel.com.au;
303 Middleton Rd; s $115-188, d $135-208; ❄)
The renovated 'deluxe' rooms in this large
brick motel complex have a tasteful, con-
temporary feel, although we quite like the
unintentional 1970s retro chic of the older,
cheaper rooms. On site is the excellent Lime
303 restaurant, discreetly channelling the
21st century.

Beach House at Bayside BOUTIQUE HOTEL $$$
(📞 08-9844 8844; www.thebeachhouseatbayside.
com.au; 33 Barry Ct, Collingwood Park; r $249-335;
❄) Positioned right by the beach and the
golf course in a quiet cul-de-sac, midway
between Middleton Beach and Emu Point,
this modern block distinguishes itself with
absolutely wonderful service. Rates include
breakfast, afternoon tea, and evening port
and chocolates.

🍴 Eating & Drinking

Bay Merchants CAFE $
(18 Adelaide Cres, Middleton Beach; mains $10-18;
⊙6am-6pm) Just a sandy-footed stroll from
the beach, this cafe-provedore makes good
coffee, enticing cakes and to-die-for gourmet
sandwiches. The deli section has a good selection of local wines.

York Street Cafe CAFE $$
(www.184york.com; 184 York St; lunch $10-22, din-
ner $22-36; ⊙7.30am-3pm Mon-Tue, 7.30am-late
Wed-Fri. 8.30am-2.30pm Sat & Sun) The food is
wonderful at this cosmopolitan place on the
main strip. Lunch includes roasted tomato
and prosciutto salad or chicken pot pie,
while at dinner the attention turns to bistro
items like prawns with pasta and a hearty
goat tagine. It's BYO wine.

14 Peels Place CAFE $$
(14 Peels Pl; breakfast $7-21, lunch $14-22;
⊙8.30am-4pm Mon-Fri, to 1pm Sat & Sun) 🌿 A
colourful haven for in-the-know local foodies, 14 Peels Place's combo of good coffee
and cool jazz is a great way to start the day.
Browse the huge library of cookbooks while
tucking into dishes like the chilli-infused
Eggs on Fire or fluffy pancakes with berries.
Freshly baked cakes include lots of gluten-
free options.

Vancouver Cafe & Store CAFE $$
(📞 08-9841 2475; 65 Vancouver St; mains $12-25;
⊙7.30am-3.30pm) Perched above the coast,
this great little heritage cafe features bal-
cony views and delicious home baking.
More substantial lunchtime goodies include
garlic-prawn risotto or bangers and mash.
Book ahead for its music and pizza events
on Thursday nights.

White Star Hotel PUB $$
(72 Stirling Tce; mains $16-34; ⊙11am-late) With
20 beers on tap (including its own Tanglehead brews), excellent pub grub, a beer garden and lots of live music, this old pub gets
a gold star. Sunday-night folk and blues gigs
are a good opportunity to share a pint with
Albany's laidback locals.

Lime 303 MODERN AUSTRALIAN $$$
(📞 08-9845 7298; www.dogrockmotel.com.au; 303
Middleton Rd; mains $28-40; ⊙dinner 6pm-late,
tapas 5-7pm Thu & Fri) Ignore the incongruous
setting in the Dog Rock Motel, and book for
dinner at this chic Albany surprise. Highly
sophisticated for regional WA, Lime 303
showcases local produce in dishes like the
Game Plate – with barramundi, buffalo and
crocodile – and the lamb shanks with spiced
pomegranate and rosehip.

Liberté CAFE, BAR
(162 Stirling Tce, London Hotel; ⊙8.30am-5pm
Mon & Tue, till late Wed-Sat) Classy proof that
not all heritage Aussie pubs need to die a
slow death. Channelling a louche Parisian

cafe and a velvet-trimmed speakeasy, Liberté's Gallic-inspired versatility includes good coffee and cake during the day, and craft beer, potent cocktails and Med-inspired tapas later at night. It's a big hit with hip Albanians.

Earl of Spencer   PUB
(cnr Earl & Spencer Sts; mains $20-30; ⊙ 11am-late) New owners have reinvigorated Albany's oldest pub, and locals crowd in for the Earl's famous pie and a pint or hearty lamb shanks. Live bands are regular visitors on weekends, often with a jaunty Irish brogue.

☆ Entertainment

Albany Entertainment Centre   CONCERT HALL
(www.albanyentertainment.com.au; Princess Royal Dr) Vaguely reminiscent of a scaled-down Sydney Opera House in terms of its location and architectural audacity, this $58-million, 600-seat venue features Oz touring acts like Xavier Rudd and Kasey Chambers.

Town Hall   THEATRE
(www.albanytownhall.com.au; 217 York St) Has regular shows.

Orana Cinemas   CINEMA
(✆ 08-9842 2210; www.oranacinemas.com.au; 451 Albany Hwy) For the latest snog-and-shoot blockbusters.

ℹ Information

DEC (✆ 08-9842 4500; 120 Albany Hwy; ⊙ 8am-4.30pm Mon-Fri) For national-park information.

Visitor Centre (✆ 08-9841 9290; www.amazingalbany.com; Proudlove Pde; ⊙ 9am-5pm) In the old train station.

ℹ Getting There & Away

Albany Airport (ALH; Albany Hwy) is 11km northwest of the city centre. **Skywest** (✆ 1300 660 088; www.skywest.com.au) has 18 flights a week to and from Perth (70 minutes).

Transwa (✆ 1300 662 205; www.transwa.wa.gov.au) services stop at the visitor centre. These include:

➻ GS1 to/from Perth ($58, six hours) and Mt Barker ($9, 39 minutes) daily

➻ GS2 to/from Perth ($58, eight hours), Northam ($63, 6½ hours), York ($58, six hours) and Mt Barker ($9, 41 minutes) four times a week

➻ GS3 to/from Bunbury ($56, six hours), Bridgetown ($43, 4¾ hours), Pemberton ($35, 3½ hours), Walpole ($22, 1½ hours) and Denmark ($9, 42 minutes) daily

➻ GE4 to/from Esperance ($64, 6½ hours, twice weekly)

ℹ Getting Around

Loves (✆ 08-9841 1211) runs local bus services weekdays and Saturday morning. The visitor centre has information on getting to Emu Point and Middleton Beach.

Rent a car from **King Sound Vehicle Hire** (✆ 08-9841 8150; www.kingsoundcars.com; 6 Sanford Rd), **Avis** (✆ 08-9842 2833; www.avis.com.au) and **Budget** (✆ 08-9841 7799; www.budget.com.au) have agencies at the airport.

Around Albany

◉ Sights

Whale World Museum   MUSEUM
(✆ 08-9844 4019; www.whaleworld.org; Frenchman Bay Rd; adult/child $29/10; ⊙ 9am-5pm) When the Cheynes Beach Whaling Station ceased operations in November 1978, few could have guessed that its gore-covered decks would eventually be covered in tourists, craning to see whales passing within harpoon-shot of the slaughterhouse itself. The museum screens several films about marine life and whaling operations, and displays giant skeletons, harpoons, whaleboat models and scrimshaw (etchings on whalebone). Outside there's the rusting *Cheynes IV* whale chaser and station equipment to inspect. Free guided tours depart on the hour from 10am to 3pm.

Attached to the complex is the Walk on the Wild Side wildlife park. Entrance is included with admission to Whale World. Planned to open in 2013, an adjacent Biodiversity Park will include Faunatopia and Floracopia, two areas showcasing the diverse animal and plant species of the surrounding region.

Torndirrup National Park   NATIONAL PARK
(Frenchman Bay Rd) FREE Covering much of the peninsula that encloses the southern reaches of Albany's Princess Royal Harbour and King George Sound, this national park is known for its windswept, ocean-bashed cliffs. Rocks in this area have been proved to be direct matches to those in Antarctica, to which they were once joined. This is a dangerous coastline, so beware of freakish, large waves – many people have lost their lives after being swept off the rocks. **The Gap** is a natural cleft in the rock, channelling blister-

ing surf through giant walls of granite. Close by is the **Natural Bridge**, a self-explanatory landmark. Further east, the **Blowholes** can put on a show when the surf is up; it's worth the 78 steps down and back up.

Where the cliffs give way to beach, the results are just as spectacular. Steep, rocky, green-water coves such as **Jimmy Newells Harbour** and **Salmon Holes** are popular with surfers but quite scary for swimmers. You're better to head to the peninsula's sheltered side, where beautiful **Misery Beach** (a contradiction in terms) is often deserted and is an easy drive in/walk down. It's next to **Frenchman Bay**, a fine swimming beach with a shady barbecue area.

At **Stony Hill**, a short heritage trail leads around the site of an observatory station from both world wars. Keen walkers can tackle the hard 10km-return bushwalk (over five hours) over **Isthmus Hill** to **Bald Head**, at the eastern edge of the park. The views are spectacular. Whales are frequently seen from the cliffs, and the park's varied vegetation provides habitats for many native animals and reptiles.

Albany's **Wind Farm**, immediately west of the park, has a walking track winding surrounded among the 12 turbines.

Two Peoples Bay   NATURE RESERVE
(Two Peoples Bay Rd) Some 20km east of Albany, Two Peoples Bay is a scenic 46-sq-km nature reserve with a good swimming beach. From the main beach, walk east around the headland (or drive) to lovely **Little Beach**. Not much of the rest of the reserve is easily accessible and permits are required from the DEC in Albany to visit some special conservation zones. It's a significant area, home to two once-thought-to-be-extinct animals: the noisy scrub bird and Australia's rarest marsupial mammal, the Gilbert's potoroo.

The bay was named after a meeting of French and US ships here in 1803.

Around Albany

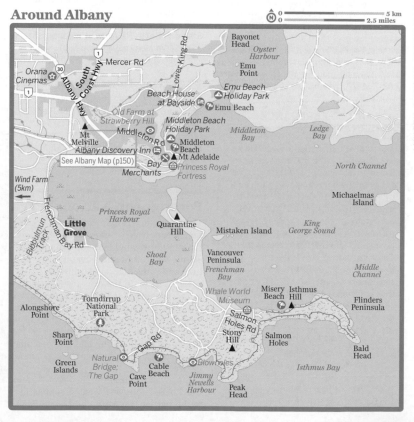

Waychinicup National Park NATIONAL PARK
(Cheyne Beach Rd; campsite adult/child $7/3)
FREE Gilbert's potoroos and noisy scrub
birds are also protected at this little national
park, east of Two Peoples Bay. Unlike at the
bay, the DEC operates a **camp site** here. It's
a beautiful spot, by the inlet of the Waychinicup River; vault toilets are provided, but no
fresh water is available.

Mt Barker

POP 1770

Mt Barker (50km north of Albany) is the
gateway to the Porongurup and Stirling
Range National Parks. It's also the hub for
the local wine industry, and **Plantagenet
Wines** (www.plantagenetwines.com; Albany Hwy;
☺10am-4.30pm) is conveniently situated in
town. Pick up the *Mt Barker Wineries* map
from the town's **visitor centre** (✆08-9851
1163; www.mountbarkertourismwa.com.au; Albany
Hwy, Railway Station), located in the railway
station. See www.mountbarkerwine.com.au.

The town has been settled since the
1830s; the 1868 convict-built police station
and gaol are preserved as a **museum** (Albany
Hwy; adult/child $5/free; ☺10am-3pm Sat & Sun).

See all 78 types and 24 subtypes of Australia's Banksia plant at the **Banksia Farm**
(✆08-9851 1770; www.banksiafarm.com.au; Pearce

ALBANY TO ESPERANCE ALTERNATIVES

The rural 480km of South Coast Hwy
(Rte 1) between Albany and Esperance
is a relatively unpopulated stretch.
Break up the first leg by taking the Albany Hwy (Rte 30) to Mt Barker, and then
head east to Porongurup. Then travel
north through the Stirling Ranges, and
turn east again through Ongerup, and
rejoin the highway at Jerramungup.
This route adds 57km to the trip.

At Ongerup, the **Yongergnow
Malleefowl Centre** (✆08-9828 2325;
www.yongergnow.com.au; adult/child $6/3;
☺10am-4pm Sat-Mon, Wed & Thu) is
devoted to the conservation of a curi-
ous endangered bird that creates huge
mounds to incubate its chicks.

Near Jerramungup is **Fitzgerald
River National Park** – base yourself
at Hopetoun or Bremer Bay. Note that
Bremer Bay is best reached by taking
the South Coast Hwy from Albany.

Rd; admission $11; ☺9.30am-4.30pm Mon-Fri Mar-
Jun, daily Aug-Nov); admission includes an
introductory talk. Also on offer are a fully
guided tour ($25), morning and afternoon
tea, and comfortable B&B accommodation
(singles/doubles from $95/150).

It's well worth heading up **Mt Barker** itself, 5km south of town, for excellent views
of the neighbouring ranges. Southwest of
Mt Barker, on the rolling grounds of the
Egerton-Warburton estate, is the exquisitely
photogenic **St Werburgh's Chapel**, built
between 1872 and 1873. The wrought-iron
chancel screen and altar rail were shaped on
the property.

A surprising sight is the authentic Mongolian yurt (felt tent) and gallery of eclectic
Mongolian and Chinese art in the grounds
of **Nomads Guest House** (✆08-9851 2131;
www.nomadsguesthousewa.com.au; 12 Morpeth St;
s/d/yurts/chalets $70/90/100/110). The own-
ers frequently play host to orphaned joeys
(baby kangaroos), so don't be surprised to
see a few temporary marsupial visitors in
the main house.

If you're stopping for lunch, try the **Old
Station Cafe** (11 Albany Hwy; mains $11-20;
☺9am-4pm Mon-Fri,10am-3pm Sun), which offers a big selection of cakes in a little cottage.

ℹ️ Getting There & Away

Transwa (✆1300 662 205; www.transwa.
wa.gov.au) operates the following bus services:
➡ GS1 to/from Perth ($51, 5½ hours) and
Albany ($9; 39 minutes) daily.

➡ GS2 to/from Perth ($51, 7¼ hours), Northam
($56, 5¾ hours), York ($53, 5¼ hours) and
Albany ($9, 41 minutes) four times a week.

Porongurup National Park

The 24-sq-km, 12km-long **Porongurup National Park** (entry per car/motorcycle $11/5) has
1100-million-year-old granite outcrops, panoramic views, beautiful scenery, large karri
trees and some excellent bushwalks.

Karris grow in the deep-red soil (known
as karri loam) of the range's upper slopes;
nurtured by run-off from the granite, this
area's karris are 100km east of their usual
range. The rich forest also supports 65 species of orchid in spring and, in September
and October, there are wildflowers among
the trees.

Bushwalks range from the 100m **Tree-in-
the-Rock** stroll (just what it sounds like)
to the harder **Hayward and Nancy Peaks**

Porongurup National Park

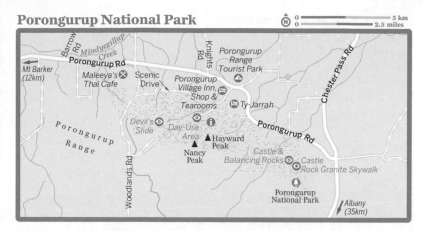

(5.5km loop). The **Devil's Slide** (5km return) is a walk of contrasts that takes you through a pass of karri forest and on to the stumpy vegetation of the granite. These walks start from the main day-use area (Bolganup Rd). The **Castle Rock Trail to Balancing Rock** (3km return) starts further east, signposted off the Mt Barker–Porongurup Rd. In 2012, the newly opened **Castle Rock Granite Skywalk** provided spectacular and more convenient access to the summit of the rock.

A very lovely 6km **scenic drive** along the northern edge of the park has great views towards the Stirling Range, which from this angle looks like a woman lying on her back. If you're driving here near dusk, take it slow and watch out for kangaroos.

Porongurup is also part of the Great Southern wine region and there are 11 wineries in the immediate vicinity.

🛏 Sleeping & Eating

There is no accommodation within the national park, but these options are close by. Eating options are very limited.

Porongurup Village
Inn, Shop & Tearooms   B&B **$**
(☑08-9853 1110; www.porongurupinn.com.au; s/d/cottages $30/60/100) This welcoming hostel-like place also serves home-cooked food (breakfast $5 to $14, lunch $16 to $18) with veggies from the organic garden. Standouts are the salmon patties and the ploughman's lunch, and there are plenty of grassy expanses and a trampoline for younger visitors.

Porongurup Range
Tourist Park   CARAVAN PARK **$**
(☑08-9853 1057; www.poronguruprangetouristpark.com.au; 1304 Porongurup Rd; sites per 2 people $30, cabins $90-110; 🖭) Tidy, with good facilities; credit cards not accepted.

Ty-Jarrah   CHALET **$**
(☑08-9853 1255; www.tyjarrah.com; 3 Bolganup Rd; 1-/2-bedroom chalets from $125/145) Located in a shady forest setting, these self-contained A-frame chalets are very cosy and comfortable. Twilight visitors include a menagerie of local marsupials.

Maleeya's Thai Cafe   THAI **$$**
(☑08-9853 1123; www.maleeya.com.au; 1376 Porongurup Rd; mains $25-30; ⊙11.30am-3pm & 6-9pm Fri-Sun) 🍴 Foodies and chefs venture all the way to Porongorup for some of WA's most authentic Thai food. Curries, soups and stir-fries all come studded with fresh herbs straight from Maleeya's garden, and other ingredients are organic and free range. Bookings recommended.

Stirling Range National Park

Ever seen a Queen of Sheba orchid or a Stirling bell? Here's your chance. Rising abruptly from the surrounding flat and sandy plains, the Stirling Range's propensity to change colour through blues, reds and purples will captivate photographers during the spectacular wildflower season from late August to early December.

Stirling Range National Park

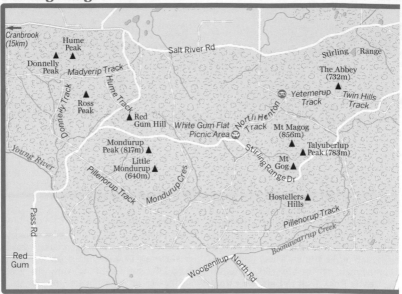

This 1156-sq-km national park consists of a single chain of peaks pushed up by plate tectonics to form a range 10km wide and 65km long. Running most of its length are isolated summits, some knobbly and some perfect pyramids, towering above broad valleys covered in shrubs and heath. Bluff Knoll (Bular Mai), at 1095m, is the highest point in the southwest.

Due to the altitude and climate there are many localised plants in the Stirlings. It is estimated that there are more than 1500 species of native plants, 80 of which are endemic. The most beautiful are the Darwinias or mountain bells, which occur only above 300m; one species may be seen in season on the Mt Talyuberlup walk.

The range was named after James Stirling, first governor of the Swan River Colony. For tens of thousands of years before that it was known as Koi Kyenunu-ruff, meaning 'mist moving around the mountains'. It's recognised by Noongar people as a place of special significance – a place where the spirits of the dead return. Every summit has an ancestral being associated with it, so it's appropriate to show proper respect when visiting here.

Park fees are charged at the start of Bluff Knoll Rd (entry per car/motorcycle $11/5).

🏃 Activities

The Stirlings are renowned for serious **bushwalking**. Keen walkers can choose from a number of high points: **Toolbrunup** (for views and a good climb; 1052m, 4km return), **Bluff Knoll** (a well-graded tourist track; 1095m, 6km return), and **Mt Hassell** (848m, 3km return) and **Talyuberlup** (783m, 2.6km return) are popular half-day walks.

Challenging walks cross the eastern sector of the range from **Bluff Knoll to Ellen Peak**, which should take three days, or the shorter traverse from **The Arrows to Ellen Peak** (two days). The latter option is a loop, but the former, from Bluff Knoll, will require a car shuttle. Walkers must be suitably experienced and equipped as the range is subject to sudden drops in temperature, driving rain and sometimes snow; register in and out of your walk with the **rangers** (☑08-9827 9230).

🛌 Sleeping & Eating

Options are very limited, so stock up on food in Mt Barker.

Stirling Range Retreat   CARAVAN PARK $
(☑08-9827 9229; www.stirlingrange.com.au; 8639 Chester Pass Rd; unpowered/powered sites per

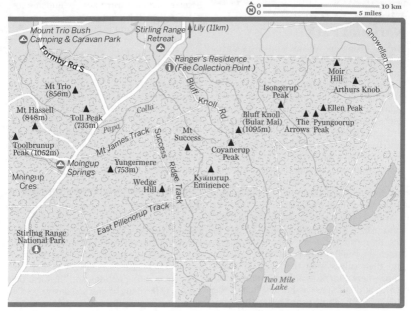

2 people $30/32, cabins $55-79, units $145-175;
❋@⚊) ⚑ Also on the park's northern
boundary, this shaded site has accommodation including campsites, simple cabins
and vans, and self-contained, rammed-earth
units. Wildflower and orchid bus tours and
walkabouts (three hours, per person $49)
are conducted from mid-August to the end
of October. The swimming pool only opens
from November to April.

Mount Trio Bush
Camping & Caravan Park   CARAVAN PARK $
(☑08-9827 9270; www.mounttrio.com.au; Salt River Rd; unpowered/powered sites per person $12/14)
Rustic bush campground on a farm property
close to the walking tracks, north of the centre of the park, has hot showers, a kitchen,
free gas BBQs and a campfire pit. Guided
walks are on offer.

Moingup Springs   CAMPGROUND $
(Chester Pass Rd; sites per adult/child $7/2) The
DEC's only campground within the park; no
showers or electricity.

The Lily   COTTAGES $$
(☑08-9827 9205; www.thelily.com.au; Chester
Pass Rd; cottages $139-169) Looking like a
16th-century Dutch farm, these cottages
12km north of the park are grouped around

a working windmill. Accommodation is
self-contained, and meals ($36) are also
available for guests at the neighbouring
restaurant (a 1924 railway-station building).
Call to enquire which nights the restaurant
is open to the public (hours vary), and to
arrange mill tours ($50, minimum of four
people).

Bremer Bay
POP 250

Edged with brilliant white sand and trans-
lucent green waters, this sleepy fishing and
holiday hamlet is 61km from the South
Coast Hwy. From July to November, the bay
is a cetacean maternity ward for southern
right whales.

The **visitor centre** (☑08-9837 4171; www.
bremerbay.com; Mary St; ⊙9am-5pm Mon-Fri; 🛜)
in the shire library also has internet access.
Holiday homes can be booked through the
visitor centre.

**Bremer Bay Beaches Resort & Tourist
Park** (☑08-9837 4290; www.bremerbaybeaches.
com.au; Wellstead Rd; sites per 2 people from $32,
cabins & chalets $115-185; ⚊) has shady camp-
sites, a well-equipped campers' kitchen and
a seasonal pizzeria. It's a 1.5km walk through
the dunes to the beach.

Fitzgerald River National Park

Midway between Albany and Esperance, this gem of a national park (entry per car/motorcycle $11/5) has been declared a Unesco Biosphere Reserve. Its 3300 sq km contains half of the orchid species in WA (more than 80, 70 of which occur nowhere else), 22 mammal species, 200 species of bird and 1700 species of plant (20% of WA's described species). It's also the blossoming ground of the royal hakea *(Hakea victoria)* and Qualup bell *(Pimelia physodes)* flowers. Wildflowers are most abundant in spring, but flowers – especially the hardy proteas – bloom throughout the year.

Walkers will discover beautiful coastline, sand plains, rugged coastal hills (known as 'the Barrens') and deep, wide river valleys. In season, you'll almost certainly see whales and their calves from the shore at **Point Ann**, where there's a lookout and a heritage walk that follows a short stretch of the 1164km **No 2 rabbit-proof fence** (built between 1904 and 1960). **Short walks** are also accessible at East Mt Barren (three hours) and West Mt Barren (two hours). For information on wilderness walks, check with the DEC rangers at **Jerramungup** (☑08-9835 5043; Quiss Rd), **Bremer Bay** (☑08-9837 1022; Murray Rd) and **East Mt Barren** (☑08-9838 3060; Hamersley Dr).

Although the park is one of the areas in southern WA least affected by the dieback fungus (a killer of native trees), precautions are in place to ensure it remains so; respect the 'no entry – dieback' signs, and clean your shoes before each walk.

The three main 2WD entry points to the park are from the South Coast Hwy (Quiss Rd and Pabelup Dr), Hopetoun (Hamersley Dr) and Bremer Bay (along Swamp and Murray Rds). This last is the prettiest route, winding through acres of flowering shrubs. All roads are gravel, and likely to be impassable after rain, so check locally before you set out.

🛏 Sleeping

Quaalup Homestead CAMPGROUND $
(☑ 08-9837 4124; www.whalesandwildflowers.com.au; Quaalup Rd; sites per person from $12, on-site vans $60, r $90-120) 🅿 Completely isolated, this 1858 homestead is secluded deep within the southern reaches of the park. Electricity is solar, so leave the gadgets behind and forget about mobile-phone coverage. Sleeping options range from a bush camp site with gas BBQs to a set of cosy units and chalets scattered around the grounds. Quaalup Rd is reached from Pabelup Dr.

DEC Campsites CAMPGROUND $
(sites per adult/child $7/2) Of the five national-park camp sites run by the DEC, only St Mary Inlet (near Point Ann) can be reached by 2WD. The two at Hamersley Inlet and the others at Whale Bone Beach, Quoin Head and Fitzgerald Inlet can only be reached by 4WD or on foot.

Hopetoun

POP 590

Once as sleepy as Bremer Bay, Hopetoun has nearly doubled in size in recent years due to the opening of a nickel mine. The beauty of the beaches hasn't changed, but there are now more eating options and the local pub fills up with young workers in dusty overalls. From the jetty at the end of the main drag (Veal St) there are wonderful views. Beside it is a child-friendly beach with a swimming pontoon.

The old train route between Ravensthorpe and Hopetoun is now a **heritage walking track**. To the west of town, separating it from Fitzgerald River National Park, is the almost landlocked **Culham Inlet** (great for fishing – especially for black bream). To the east is the scenic but in parts extremely rough **Southern Ocean East Drive**, heading to beaches with camp sites at **Mason Bay** and **Starvation Bay**. If you're in a 2WD, don't be tempted to head to Esperance this way; if you'd prefer not to double back to the highway at Ravensthorpe, take Jerdacuttup Rd (past the airport) instead.

The world's longest fence – the 1833km-long **No 1 rabbit-proof fence** – enters the sea at Starvation Bay; it starts at Eighty Mile Beach on the Indian Ocean, north of Port Hedland. The fence was built during the height of the rabbit plague between 1901 and 1907. However, the bunnies beat the fence-builders to the west side, so it wasn't as effective a barrier as hoped.

🛏 Sleeping & Eating

Hopetoun Motel & Chalet Village MOTEL $$
(☑08-9838 3219; www.hopetounmotel.com.au; 458 Veal St; r $140-200; 🖲) A very nice

rammed-earth complex with comfy beds and quality linen. A larger townhouse ($310) is also available for families.

Toun Beach Cafe CAFE **$**
(19 Veal St; pizzas $18-25, burgers $12-14; ☺8.30am-2.30pm & 5.30-8pm Tue-Sat, 8.30am-2.30pm Sun) Sit upstairs for excellent breakfasts and water views at this cool-looking cafe. Wood-fired pizzas and good burgers seal the deal.

Deck Treasures CAFE **$**
(www.gotothedeck.com.au; Veal St; ☺9am-4.30pm Mon-Fri & 9am-12.30pm Sat Sep-May; @☎) Part gift shop, part cafe, and part visitor centre with its own Southern Ocean Discovery Centre with lots of information on local wildlife. Free wi-fi and internet access too. Ask for its free self-guide driving map to the surrounding area.

Esperance

POP 9600

Esperance sits in solitary splendour on the Bay of Isles, a seascape of aquamarine waters fringed with squeaky white beaches. There's no need to fight for space here, as the town's isolation all but guarantees it. Yet Esperance has its share of devotees who will bundle up the kids for the mammoth pilgrimage from Perth, just to plug into the low-key, community-oriented vibe. In Kalgoorlie, nobody would question the wisdom of driving 390km to this, their nearest beach. For travellers taking the coastal route across the continent, it's the last sizeable town before hitting the Nullarbor wilderness.

Some of Australia's most picture-perfect beaches can be found in the even more remote national parks to the town's southeast. Out in the bay, the pristine environment of the Recherche Archipelago can be wild and windy, or turn on a calmly charming show. The archipelago's 105 islands are home to fur seals, penguins and sea birds.

History

Esperance's Indigenous name, Kepa Kurl (water boomerang), refers to the shape of the bay. Archaeological finds on Middle Island suggest that it was occupied before the last Ice Age, when it was still part of the mainland.

Esperance received its current name in 1792 when the *Recherche* and *l'Espérance* sailed through the archipelago and into the bay to shelter from a storm. In the 1820s and 1830s the Recharge Archipelago was home to Black Jack Anderson – Australia's only pirate. From his base on Middle Island he raided ships and kept a harem of Aboriginal women, whose husbands he had killed. He was eventually murdered in his sleep by one of his own men.

Although the first settlers came in 1863, it wasn't until the gold rush of the 1890s that the town really became established as a port. When the gold fever subsided, Esperance went into a state of suspended animation until after WWII.

In the 1950s it was discovered that adding missing trace elements to the soil around Esperance restored its fertility. The town has since rapidly become an agricultural centre and it continues to export grain and minerals from the region's farms and mines.

⊙ Sights & Activities

Esperance Museum MUSEUM
(cnr James & Dempster Sts; adult/child $6/2; ☺1.30-4.30pm) Glass cabinets are crammed with collections of sea shells, frog ornaments, tennis rackets and bed pans. It's absolutely charming, though, even if most of the displays wouldn't look amiss in a junk shop. Bigger items include boats, a train carriage and the remains of the USA's spacecraft *Skylab*, which made its fiery re-entry at Balladonia, east of Esperance, in 1979.

Museum Village HISTORIC BUILDING
The museum includes galleries and cafes occupying restored heritage buildings; markets are held here every second Sunday morning. Aboriginal-run Kepa Kurl Art Gallery (see boxed text, p252) has reasonably priced works by local and Central Desert artists.

Lake Warden Wetland System LAKE
Esperance is surrounded by extensive wetlands, which include seven large lakes and over 90 smaller ones. The 7.2km-return **Kepwari Wetland Trail** (off Fisheries Rd) takes in **Lake Wheatfield** and **Woody Lake**, with boardwalks, interpretive displays and good birdwatching. **Lake Monjimup**, 14km to the northwest along the South Coast Hwy, is divided by Telegraph Rd into a conservation area (to the west) and a recreation area (to the east). The conservation side has boardwalks over inky black water where it's hard to see where the paperbark trees end and their mirror image begins. The much more orderly recreation side has themed banksia,

hakea and grevillea gardens, a hedge maze and great grassy areas for throwing a ball around.

Cannery Arts Centre   GALLERY
(1018 Norseman Rd; admission by gold-coin donation; ⊙1-4pm Mon-Fri) Has artists studios, interesting exhibitions and a shop selling local artwork. For more local art, pick up the *Esperance Art Trail* brochure at the visitor centre, listing 14 stops.

Great Ocean Drive   SCENIC DRIVE
Many of Esperance's most dramatic sights can be seen on this well-signposted 40km loop. Starting from the waterfront, it heads southwest along the breathtaking stretch of coast that includes a series of popular surfing and swimming spots, including **Blue Haven Beach** and **Twilight Cove**. Stop to enjoy the rollers breaking against the cliffs from **Observatory Point** and the lookout on **Wireless Hill**. A turn-off leads to the **wind farm**, which supplies about 23% of Esperance's electricity. Among the turbines there's a walking track, which can be quite surreal when it's windy – and it often is.

The route then turns back and passes by the **Pink Lake** – or should that be the-lake-formerly-known-as-pink? Salt-tolerant algae once provided an unmistakeable rosy tint, but a storm a few years back flushed it out.

Ralph Bower
Adventureland Park   PARK
(Taylor Street Jetty; train rides $3; ⊙train rides 9am-4pm Sat & Sun May-Sep, daily Oct-Apr) FREE Popular children's playground with a miniature train.

☞ Tours

Esperance Island Cruises   BOAT
(☑08-9071 5757; www.woodyisland.com.au; 72 The Esplanade; ⊙daily late Sep-May) Tours include Esperance Bay and Woody Island in a power catamaran (half-/full day $95/150), getting close to fur seals, sea lions, Cape Barren geese and (with luck) dolphins. In January, there's a ferry to Woody Island (adult/child return $60/30).

Kepa Kurl Eco
Cultural Discovery Tours   INDIGENOUS CULTURE
(☑08-9072 1688; www.kepakurl.com.au; Museum Village) 🖉 Explore the country from an Aboriginal perspective: visit rock-art and water-holes, sample bush food and hear ancient stories (adult/child $105/90, minimum of two people).

Eco-Discovery Tours   DRIVING TOUR
(☑0407 737 261; www.esperancetours.com.au) Runs 4WD tours along the sand to Cape Le Grand National Park (half-/full day $95/165, minimum of two/four people) and two-hour circuits of Great Ocean Dr (adult/child $55/40).

Aussie Bight Expeditions   DRIVING TOUR
(☑0427 536 674; www.aussiebight.com; half/full day $90/160; ⊙Aug-Apr) Exciting and entertaining 4WD expeditions covering wildflowers and Cape Le Grand National Park. Sandboarding is available from mid-December to April. Book at the Esperance visitor centre.

Esperance Diving & Fishing   DIVING, FISHING
(☑08-9071 5111; www.esperancedivingandfishing.com.au; 72 The Esplanade) Takes you wreck diving on the *Sanko Harvest* (two-tank dive including all gear $260) or charter fishing throughout the archipelago.

🛏 Sleeping

Woody Island Eco-Stays   CAMPGROUND $
(☑08-9071 5757; www.woodyisland.com.au; sites per person $25, on-site tents $41-61, huts $140-165; ⊙late Sep-Apr; 🅿) 🖉 It's not every day you get to stay in an A-class nature reserve. Choose between leafy camp sites (very close together) or canvas-sided bush huts, a few of which have a private deck and their own lighting. Power is mostly solar, and rainwater supplies the island – both are highly valued. Count on adding on a $60 return-ferry transfer as well.

Blue Waters Lodge YHA   HOSTEL $
(☑08-9071 1040; www.yha.com.au; 299 Goldfields Rd; dm/s/d $28/50/70) On the beachfront about 1.5km from the town centre, this rambling place feels a little institutional, but the new management are friendly and it looks out over a tidy lawn to the water. Hire bikes to cycle the waterfront.

Esperance B&B by the Sea   B&B $$
(☑08-9071 5640; www.esperancebb.com; 34 Stewart St; s/d $120/170; 🅿) This great-value beachhouse features a private guest wing, and the views from the deck overlooking Blue Haven Beach are breathtaking, especially at sunset. It's just a stroll from the ocean and a five-minute drive from central Esperance.

Clearwater Motel Apartments
MOTEL $$
(☑08-9071 3587; www.clearwatermotel.com.au; 1a William St; s $110, d $140-195; ✳) The bright and spacious rooms and apartments here have balconies and are fully self-contained, and there's a well-equipped shared barbecue area. It's just a short walk from both waterfront and town.

Driftwood Apartments
APARTMENT $$
(☑0428 716 677; www.driftwoodapartments.com. au; 69 The Esplanade; apt $165-220; ✳) Each of these seven smart blue-and-yellow apartments, right across from the waterfront, has its own BBQ and outdoor table setting. The two-storey, two-bedroom units have decks and a bit more privacy.

Island View Esperance
APARTMENT $$
(☑08-9072 0044; www.esperanceapartments. com.au; 14-15 The Esplanade; apt from $200; ✳) It's easy living in these architect-designed and tastefully furnished one- to three-bedroom apartments, some with floor-to-ceiling windows overlooking the waterfront. The kitchens have all the mod cons, and there's a spacious living area.

✖ Eating & Drinking

Onshore Cafe
CAFE $
(105 Dempster St; mains $7-14; ⊘8am-6pm Mon-Fri & 9am-3pm Sat) A homewares store–cafe in a breezy modern space next to the cinema, this place serves light lunches, as well as excellent coffee, croissants and cake. The wraps and Turkish sandwiches are good value.

Taylor's Beach Bar & Cafe
CAFE $$
(Taylor Street Jetty; lunch $7-24, dinner $24-32; ⊘7am-2pm Wed, to 9pm Thu-Mon; 🛜) This attractive, sprawling cafe by the jetty serves cafe fare, tapas, seafood and salads. Locals hang out at the tables on the grass or read on the covered terrace. Sandwiches ($6.50 to $9.50) are good value if you're heading to the beach, and it's good for a glass of wine or chilled pint of Little Creatures.

Ocean Blues
CAFE $$
(19 The Esplanade; mains $22-34; ⊘9.30am-8.30pm Tue-Sat & 8am-4pm Sun) Wander in sandy-footed and order a simple lunch (burgers, salads, sandwiches, wraps) from this unpretentious eatery. Dinners are more adventurous, representing good value for the price.

Alimento
CAFE $$
(94 Dempster St; mains $13-18; ⊘7am-3pm Mon-Fri, 8am-1pm Sat, 7.30am-11.30am Sun) Excellent coffee and colourful local art feature at this centrally located cafe. Try the tasting platter with homemade hummus and warm Turkish bread, or see what's inspiring the chef for the popular 'Curry of the Day'.

Pier Hotel
PUB $$
(www.pierhotelesperance.net.au; 47 The Esplanade; mains $20-35; ⊘11.30am-late) Lots of beers on tap, wood-fired pizzas and good-value bistro meals conspire to make the local pub a firm favourite with both locals and visitors.

Coffee Cat
CAFE
(Tanker Jetty; ⊘7am-2pm Mon-Fri) WA's hippest coffee caravan also serves up yummy home-baked cakes and muffins. Grab an early-morning java to fuel you for a stroll to the end of nearby Tanker Jetty. Keep an eye out for yawning seals and sea lions also greeting the new day.

☆ Entertainment

Fenwick 3 Cinemas
CINEMA
(☑08-9072 1355; www.ausaf.com.au; 105 Dempster St) Blockbusters and arty movies.

① Information

DEC (☑08-9083 2100; 92 Dempster St) Has information on the national parks in the Esperance region.

Visitor Centre (☑08-9083 1555; www.visitesperance.com; cnr Kemp & Dempster Sts; ⊘9am-5pm Mon-Fri, to 2pm Sat, to noon Sun)

① Getting There & Away

Esperance Airport (EPR; Coolgardie-Esperance Hwy) is 18km north of the town centre. **Skywest** (☑1300 660 088; www.skywest.com.au) has

---

STOKES NATIONAL PARK

Pretty **Stokes National Park** (entry per car/motorcycle $11/5), 90km west of Esperance, is set around Stokes Inlet, known for its long beaches and rocky headlands. Most of its 107 sq km is covered in scrub and coastal heath, sheltering kangaroos and birds. You might also spot seals. It's a popular spot for anglers and there's a bush **campground** (sites adult/child $7/2), which is 2WD accessible.

one to three flights per day to and from Perth (1¾ hours).

Transwa (☑ 1300 662 205; www.transwa. wa.gov.au) services stop at the visitor centre:
➡ GE1 to/from Perth ($87, 10¼ hours, thrice weekly)
➡ GE2 to/from Perth ($87, 10 hours), Mundaring ($86, 9¼ hours), York ($78, 8½ hours) and Hyden ($53, five hours) thrice weekly
➡ GE3 to/from Kalgoorlie ($56, five hours, thrice weekly), Coolgardie ($53, 4¾ hours, weekly) and Norseman ($30, 2¼ hours, thrice weekly)
➡ GE4 to/from Albany ($62, 6½ hours, twice weekly)

❶ Getting Around

Try **Avis** (☑ 08-9071 3998; www.avis.com.au; 63 The Esplanade) or **Budget** (☑ 08-9071 2775; www.budget.com.au) at the airport. **Hollywood Car Hire** (☑ 08-9071 3144; Wood St) is the local car-rental mob.

Around Esperance

◉ Sights

Cape Le Grand National Park NATIONAL PARK
(entry per car/motorcycle $11/5, sites adult/child $9/2) An easy day tour from Esperance, Cape Le Grand National Park starts 60km to the east of town and boasts spectacular coastal scenery, turquoise water, dazzling talcum-powder-soft beaches and excellent walking tracks. It offers good fishing, swimming and camping at **Lucky Bay** and **Le Grand Beach**, and day-use facilities at gorgeous **Hellfire Bay**. Make the effort to climb **Frenchman Peak** (a steep 3km return, allow two hours), as the views from the top and through the 'eye', especially during the late afternoon, are superb.

Rossiter Bay is where the British and Aboriginal duo Edward John Eyre and Wylie fortuitously met the French whaling ship *Mississippi*, in the course of their epic 1841 overland crossing, and spent two weeks resting on board. The 15km Le Grand Coastal Trail links the bays; you can do shorter stretches between beaches.

Cape Arid National Park NATIONAL PARK
(entry per car/motorcycle $11/5, sites adult/child $7/2) At the start of the Great Australian Bight and on the fringes of the Nullarbor Plain, is Cape Arid National Park. Rugged and isolated, the park has good bushwalking, great beaches, camp sites and crazy squeaky sand.

Whales (in season), seals and Cape Barren geese are seen regularly here. Most of the park is 4WD-accessible only, although the Thomas River Rd leading to the shire camp site is accessible to all vehicles. For the hardy, there's a tough walk to the top of Tower Peak on Mt Ragged (3km return, three hours). The world's most primitive species of ant was found thriving here in 1930.

Peak Charles National Park NATIONAL PARK
FREE There are no charges to visit or camp at this granite wilderness area, 130km north of Esperance. There are only basic facilities provided (long-drop toilets); you'll need to be completely self-sufficient here.

Monkey Mia & the Central West

Best Places for Sunset

➡ Steep Point (p178)

➡ Fishermens Lookout (p167)

➡ Red Bluff (p173)

➡ Shark Bay Hotel (p179)

➡ Horrocks (p176)

Best Places to Stay

➡ Gnaraloo Station (p182)

➡ Ospreys Beach Chalet (p170)

➡ Fish & Whistle (p181)

➡ Bentwood Olive Grove (p170)

➡ Bay Lodge (p178)

Why Go?

The pristine coastline and sheltered turquoise waters of Malgana country draw tourists and marine life from around the world. Aside from Monkey Mia's famous dolphins, the submerged sea-grass meadows of World Heritage–listed Shark Bay host dugongs, rays, sharks and turtles, while rare marsupials take refuge in remote national parks. Limestone cliffs, red sand and salt lakes litter the stark interior.

Further south in the land of the Nhanda people, the gorges of Kalbarri invite adventurers to explore their depths, while above, wildflowers carpet the plains and ospreys wheel away from battered Indian Ocean cliffs as humpback whales migrate slowly southwards.

Vegies are ripening in Carnarvon as anglers and board riders check the tides, and windsurfers are waiting for the 'Doctor' (strong afternoon sea breeze) to blow. In Geraldton, the only decision to make is whether to have that second macchiato before a brisk walk along the foreshore.

When to Go

Monkey Mia

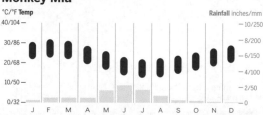

Jun & Aug The winter swells pump the breaks off Gnaraloo and Quobba.

Aug & Sep Kalbarri erupts in wildflowers.

Nov–Feb Windsurfers clutch their sails from Geraldton to Carnarvon.

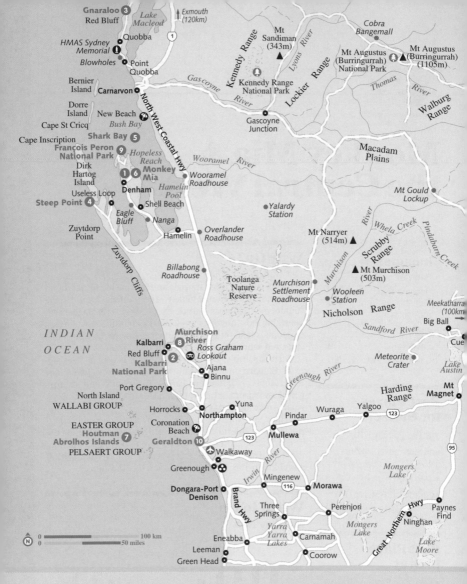

Monkey Mia & the Central West Highlights

① Watching the wild dolphins feed at **Monkey Mia** (p179)

② Canoeing through the deep gorges of **Kalbarri National Park** (p172)

③ Surfing the wild Tombstones break at **Gnaraloo** (p182)

④ Driving out to **Steep Point** (p178), the mainland's most westerly tip

⑤ Sailing out to look for dugongs in **Shark Bay** (p176)

⑥ Immersing yourself in Malgana culture on a Monkey Mia **Wula Guda Nyinda** (p179)

⑦ Diving on ancient shipwrecks at the **Houtman Abrolhos Islands** (p172)

⑧ Horse riding along the mighty **Murchison River** (p11)

⑨ Spotting marine life from a coastal walk in the **François Peron National Park** (p179)

⑩ Soaking up the coffee and culture at the museums, galleries and cafes of **Geraldton** (p168)

ⓘ Getting There & Around

AIR

Skywest (☑1300 660 088; www.skywest.com.
au) Flies regularly to Geraldton.

Skippers (☑1300 729 924; www.skippers.
com.au) Services Kalbarri, Geraldton, Shark
Bay and Carnarvon.

Qantas (☑13 13 13; www.qantas.com.au)
Perth to Geraldton daily.

BUS

Integrity (☑1800 226 339; www.integrity
coachlines.com.au) Runs a handy daily coastal
connection between Perth and Geraldton, and a
twice-weekly overnighter to Exmouth.

Greyhound (☑1300 473 946; www.greyhound.
com.au) Runs services three times weekly
between Broome and Perth along the coast.

Transwa (☑1300 662 205; www.transwa.
wa.gov.au) Runs regular buses between Perth
and Kalbarri, Geraldton and Dongara along the
Brand Hwy (Rte 1).

BATAVIA COAST

From tranquil Dongara-Port Denison to
the remote, wind-scoured Zuytdorp Cliffs
stretches a dramatic coastline steeped
in history, littered with shipwrecks and
abounding in marine life. While the region
proved the undoing of many early European
sailors, today modern fleets make the most
of a lucrative crayfish industry.

Dongara-Port Denison

POP 3100

Pretty little Dongara and Port Denison, twin
seaside towns 359km from Perth, make an
idyllic spot to break up a long drive. Surrounded by beautiful beaches, walking trails
and historic buildings, the towns have a laid-
back atmosphere that's hard to beat. Port
Denison has most of the beaches and accommodation, while Dongara's main street,
shaded by century-old figs, offers banks, internet and food options.

◎ Sights & Activities

Pick up the free *Walk Dongara Denison* brochure from the visitor centre and
choose from 12 historic or nature-based
rambles, including the **Irwin River Nature
Trail**, where you might spot black swans,
pelicans or cormorants. For $2 you can
purchase the **Heritage Trail** booklet detail-

ing a 1.6km route linking buildings such as
the 1860s **Russ Cottage** (Point Leander Dr),
with a kitchen floor made from compacted
anthills, and the landmark **Royal Steam
Flour Mill** (Brand Hwy). In the old police station, the cells of the **Irwin District Museum**
(☑08-9927 1404; admission $2.50; ◎10am-noon
Mon-Sat) hold crusty historical displays.

Denison Beach Marina brims with boats
that haul crayfish, the towns' livelihood,
while sunsets are dazzling from nearby
Fishermens Lookout.

🛏 Sleeping & Eating

Note that public and school holidays attract
a surcharge.

There is a supermarket, cafes and takeaways on Moreton Tce and a good bakery
on Waldeck St in Dongara; the **Port Store**
(☑08-9927 1030; 52 Point Leander Dr; ◎7.30am-
6pm) in Port Denison has most necessities.

Dongara Backpackers   HOSTEL $
(Breeze Inn; ☑08-9927 1332; www.dongaraback
packers.com.au; 32 Waldeck St, Dongara; dm/d/f
$30/85/130) The cheapest beds in town look
onto a leafy garden at this popular backpackers, which has stylish doubles, rustic
dorms (in a vintage railway carriage) and
free bike hire for guests.

Dongara Tourist Park   CARAVAN PARK $
(☑08-9927 1210; www.dongaratouristpark.com
.au; 8 George St, Port Denison; unpowered/pow-
ered sites $25/33, 1-/2-bedroom cabins $105/145;
❄🖥) The best camping option has shaded,
spacious sites behind South Beach. The two-
bed cabins on the hill have great views, and
there's a lush pergola for dining outdoors.

Port Denison Holiday Units   APARTMENTS $$
(☑08-9927 1104; www.portdenisonholidayunits
.com.au; 14 Carnarvon St, Port Denison; d $110-120;
❄🖥) These spotless, spacious, self-catering
units, some with views, are just a block from
the beach.

Priory Hotel   GUESTHOUSE $
(☑08-9927 1090; www.prioryhotel.com.au; 11
St Dominics Rd, Dongara; r $70-130; ❄@🖥)
There's a touch of *Picnic at Hanging Rock*
about this leafy former nunnery and ladies
college with its period furniture, polished
floorboards, black-and-white photos and
wide verandahs. Sundays bring roasts and
wood-fired pizza (mains $20 to $32), several
nights offer live music, and steaks are avail-
able every evening.

Little Starfish
CAFE $

(📞0448 344 215; White Tops Rd, Port Denison; mains $6-18; ⊘8am-4pm Wed-Mon) Hidden away in the South Beach car park, this casual snack shack offers coffee, jaffles, winter soups and summer salads.

Dongara Hotel Motel
AUSTRALIAN, ASIAN $$

(📞08-9927 1023; www.dongaramotel.com.au; 12 Moreton Tce, Dongara; mains $20-40; ⊘breakfast, lunch & dinner; 🛜) Locals love the Dongara's legendary servings of fresh seafood, steaks and 'Asian Corner' curries, *mie goreng* and *phàt thai*. The motel rooms (doubles $130), popular with corporates, are adequate if not flash.

ℹ Information

Moreton Tce has several banks with ATMs.
Telecentre (CRC; 📞08-9927 2111; 11 Moreton Tce; ⊘8.30am-4.30pm Mon-Fri; @)
Visitor Centre (📞08-9927 1404; www.irwin. wa.gov.au; 9 Waldeck St, Dongara; ⊘9am-5pm Mon-Fri, to noon Sat)

ℹ Getting There & Around

Dongara-Port Denison is accessible via the Brand Hwy, Indian Ocean Dr or Midlands Rd (Rte 116).

Greyhound has services to Broome ($356, 29 hours, Monday, Wednesday and Friday) and Perth ($60, five hours, Wednesday, Friday and Sunday). Transwa runs daily to Perth ($53, five hours) and Geraldton ($13, one hour). runs daily to Perth ($49, five hours) and Geraldton ($16, one hour) and twice weekly overnight to Exmouth ($149, 12 hours). Buses arrive/depart from the visitor centre.

For a taxi, call 📞9927 1555.

Geraldton

POP 39,000

Capital of the midwest, sun-drenched 'Gero' is surrounded by excellent beaches offering myriad aquatic opportunities – swimming, snorkelling, surfing and, in particular, wind and kite surfing. The largest town between Perth and Darwin has huge wheat-handling and fishing industries that make it independent of the fickle tourist dollar, and seasonal workers flood the town during crayfish season. Still a work in progress, Gero blends big-city sophistication with small-town friendliness, offering a strong arts culture, a blossoming foodie scene and some great local music.

◉ Sights

★ Western Australian Museum
MUSEUM

(📞08-9921 5080; www.museum.wa.gov.au; 1 Museum Pl; admission by donation; ⊘9.30am-4pm) At one of the state's best museums, intelligent multimedia displays relate the area's natural, cultural and indigenous history. The Shipwreck Gallery documents the tragic story of the *Batavia*, while video footage reveals the sunken HMAS *Sydney II*. Enquire about **sailing open days** held on the long-boat moored behind the museum.

Cathedral of St Francis Xavier Church
CHURCH

(📞08-9921 3221; www.geraldtondiocese.org.au; Cathedral Ave; ⊘tours 10am Mon & Fri, 4pm Wed) Arguably the finest example of the architectural achievements of the multi-skilled Monsignor John Hawes. The cathedral's striking features include imposing twin towers with arched openings, a central dome, Romanesque columns and boldly striped walls.

Geraldton Regional Art Gallery
GALLERY

(📞08-9964 7170; 24 Chapman Rd; ⊘10am-4pm Tue-Sat, from 1pm Sun) **FREE** Featuring an excellent permanent collection, including paintings by Norman Lindsay and Elizabeth Durack, this gallery also presents provocative contemporary work and regular touring exhibitions.

Old Geraldton Gaol Craft Centre
HISTORIC BUILDING

(📞08-9921 1614; Bill Sewell Complex, Chapman Rd; ⊘10am-4pm Mon-Sat) The crafts are secondary to the gloomy cells that housed prisoners from 1858 to 1986, and the historic documents that detail their grim circumstances.

HMAS Sydney II Memorial
MONUMENT

(Mt Scott; tours free; ⊘tours 10am) Commanding the hill overlooking Geraldton is this memorial commemorating the 1941 loss of the *Sydney* and its 645 men after a skirmish with the German raider *Kormoran*.

🏃 Activities

With all that beachfront it's no surprise most activities are water based, but landlubbers can take heart from Geraldton's excellent network of bike paths, including the 10km-long coastal route from **Tarcoola Beach to Chapman River**. Grab the *Local Travelsmart Guide* from the visitor centre.

Geraldton

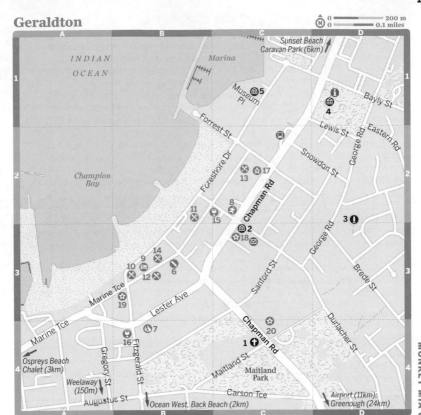

Geraldton

◎ Sights
1 Cathedral of St Francis Xavier
Church...................C4
2 Geraldton Regional Art Gallery...........C3
3 HMAS Sydney II Memorial...............D2
4 Old Geraldton Gaol Craft Centre..........D1
5 Western Australian Museum...........C1

◆ Activities, Courses & Tours
6 Batavia Coast Dive Academy..............B3
7 G-Spot Xtreme......................B4
8 Revolutions.......................C2

◉ Sleeping
9 Foreshore Backpackers...............B3

◈ Eating
10 Culinary HQ.......................B3

11 Go Health
Lunch Bar......................B2
12 Provincial.......................B3
13 Saltdish.......................C2
14 Topolinis Caffe....................B3

◉ Drinking & Nightlife
15 Freemasons
Hotel.......................C2
16 Vibe.......................B4

◈ Entertainment
17 Breakers Bar......................C2
18 Camel Bar.......................C3
19 Orana Cinemas.....................B3
20 Queens Park
Theatre.......................C4

GREENOUGH

Located 24km south of Geraldton, the rural area of historic Greenough makes for a pleasant overnight alternative. Historic sights such as the **Central Greenough Historical Settlement** (☑08-9926 1084; www.centralgreenough.com; Brand Hwy; adult/child $6/3, cafe meals $7-28; ⊗9am-5pm, shorter hours Feb-Mar), with its handful of 19th-century buildings, and the **Pioneer Museum** (www.greenough-pioneer-museum.com; Phillips Rd; adult/child $4.50/free; ⊗9.30am-3.30pm) detail early settler life and offer a chance to stretch the legs, although the area's main attractions are its excellent food and lodgings.

Bentwood Olive Grove (☑08-9926 1196; www.bentwood.com.au; Brand Hwy; d from $120; ✸) has a long connection to gourmet food, though its focus is now on accommodation, with a beautiful stone cabin sleeping six, and more rooms slated. WWOOFers (Willing Workers on Organic Farms) are welcome and there are lovely gardens to wander through and enjoy.

You can almost picture horse-drawn coaches pulling up to the **Hampton Arms Inn** (☑08-9926 1057; www.hamptonarms.com.au; Company Rd; s/d $75/95; ⊗ Tue-Sun, meals Wed-Sun), built in 1863. It features period bedrooms (some with fireplaces), a cluttered bookshop crammed with rare titles, a formal dining room (mains $12 to $34)and a cosy, well-stocked bar.

While away the days swimming and fishing at **Double Beach Holiday Park** (☑08-9921 5845; www.doublebeach.com.au; 4 Hull St, Cape Burnery; unpowered/powered sites $25/30, cabins $100-140), with its quiet, shady sites and great BBQ pergola. It's located behind the dunes at the mouth of the Greenough River.

The Transwa daily service to Geraldton will drop you on the Brand Hwy.

Bikes can be hired from **Revolutions** (☑08-9964 1399; 1/27 Chapman Rd; bike hire per day $20; ⊗9am-5.30pm Mon-Fri, to noon Sat).

G-Spot Xtreme WINDSURFING
(☑08-9965 5577; www.gspotxtreme.com.au; 241a Lester Ave; hire per day windsurfers $100, paddleboards $100, electric bikes $25) You can hire or buy windsurfing and paddleboard equipment here.

Batavia Coast Dive Academy DIVING
(☑08-9921 4229; www.bcda.com.au; 153 Marine Tce; local dives with/without equipment $140/100) Offers open-water courses (full PADI $630) and a range of diving trips, including chartered trips to the Abrolhos (from $300 per person per day).

Midwest Surf School SURFING
(☑0419 988 756; http://surf2skool.com; lessons from $60, board hire $30) Ever wanted to surf but don't know how? Courses run from absolute beginners to advanced at Geraldton's back beach.

KiteWest KITEBOARDING
(☑0449 021 784; www.kitewest.com.au; coaching per hr from $80) Kitesurfing courses and 4WD camping tours.

🛏 Sleeping

Expect price hikes during school and public holidays.

Foreshore Backpackers HOSTEL $
(☑08-9921 3275; 172 Marine Tce; dm/s/d $30/45/65; @) Shambolic, rambling and oozing character, this central hostel is full of hidden nooks, sunny balconies and world-weary travellers. Recently renovated and under new management, it's still the best place to find a job, lift or travel buddy. Discounts apply for longer stays.

Sunset Beach Holiday Park CARAVAN PARK $
(☑1800 353 389; www.sunsetbeachpark.com.au; Bosley St; powered sites $35, cabins $100-152) About 6km north of the CBD, Sunset Beach has roomy, shaded sites just a few steps from a lovely beach, and an ultramodern camp kitchen with the biggest plasma TV on the entire coast.

★ **Ospreys Beach Chalet** COTTAGE $$
(☑0447 647 994; enerhkalm@gmail.com; 40 Bosuns Cr, Point Moore; for 2 persons from $145) 🐾 Both ospreys and beach are near this sustainably restored cottage, which began life as a proof-of-concept project. Rainwater tanks and solar panels complement recycled

materials in a restoration that doesn't skimp on comfort. There are plenty of outdoor areas and the rear native garden is a gem.

★**Weelaway**   B&B **$$**
(☑08-9965 5232; www.weelaway.com.au; 104 Gregory St; r $100-145, 2-bedroom cottages $175; 🐾) Weelaway offers exquisitely decorated rooms in a heritage-listed house dating from 1862. There are formal lounge rooms, shady wide verandahs and a well-stocked library, and it's all within walking distance of the centre of town.

Ocean West   APARTMENTS **$$**
(☑08-9921 1047; www.oceanwest.com.au; 1 Hadda Way; 1-/3-bedroom apt from $135/215; ❋🐾❤) Don't let the '60s brick put you off; these fully self-contained units have all been tastefully renovated, making them one of the better deals in town. The wildly beautiful back beach is just across the road.

✖ **Eating**

Geraldton has great food options including Asian, takeaways, coffee lounges, bakeries and supermarkets. Free BBQs and picnic tables dot the foreshore.

Go Health Lunch Bar   CAFE **$**
(☑08-9965 5200; 122 Marine Tce; light meals around $10; ⊙8.30am-3pm Mon-Fri, to 1pm Sat; 🐾) Vegetarians can rejoice at the choice of fresh juices and smoothies, excellent espresso, healthy burritos, lentil burgers, focaccias and other light meals from this popular lunch bar in the middle of the mall.

Culinary HQ   CAFE **$**
(☑08-9964 8308; culinaryhq@westnet.com.au; 202 Marine Tce; lunch $8-13, cooking class $95; ⊙9am-5pm Mon-Fri) An eclectic gourmet menu changes weekly at this fledgling providore and includes soups, baguettes and cooked meals that are also available for takeaway – perfect for that hostel or campervan reheat. Phone ahead for the Thursday-evening cooking class.

★**Saltdish**   CAFE **$$**
(☑08-9964 6030; 35 Marine Tce; breakfasts $6-20, lunches $18-30; ⊙7.30am-2.30pm Mon-Sat; 🐾) The hippest cafe in town offers innovative, contemporary brekkies, light lunches and industrial-strength coffee, and screens films in its courtyard on summer evenings. Try the Spanish omelette or coconut lime chicken. BYO.

Provincial   MODERN AUSTRALIAN **$$**
(☑08-9964 1887; www.theprovincial.com.au; 167 Marine Tce; tapas $8-12, pizza $24-30, mains $28-42; ⊙5.30pm-late, lunch Fri-Sun, breakfast Sat & Sun) Stencil art adorns this atmospheric wine bar serving up tapas, wood-fired pizzas and Mod Oz/Mediterranean–inspired dishes like pork belly with pine nuts, goats cheese tortellini or angel-hair pasta with crab meat. Live music Friday nights.

Topolinis Caffe   ITALIAN **$$**
(☑08-9964 5866; 158 Marine Tce; mains $22-36; ⊙8.30am-late; 🐾) This home-style licensed bistro is perfect for an afternoon coffee, cake and wi-fi, a preshow bite, or just a relaxed family feed. The $34 dinner-and-movie deal (Sunday to Thursday) and Monday half-price pasta are popular.

🍷 **Drinking & Nightlife**

Freemasons Hotel   PUB
(☑08-9964 3457; www.freemasonshotel.com.au; cnr Marine Tce & Durlacher St; ⊙11am-late) The heritage-listed Freo has been serving beer to thirsty travellers since the 1800s. Nowadays it's a popular hangout, with live music, DJs and open-mic and trivia nights complemented by a good range of bar meals ($16 to $33; try the sizzling stones!). There's also a small number of budget rooms (with/without ensuite $100/50).

Vibe   CLUB
(☑08-9921 3700; 38-42 Fitzgerald St; ⊙from 11pm Thu-Sun) Expect all the usual nightclub action of DJs, chill rooms and dance floors.

☆ **Entertainment**

Live-music options include **Breakers** (☑08-9921 8924; 41 Chapman Rd; ⊙from 9pm), **Camel Bar** (☑08-9965 5500; 20 Chapman Rd, Geraldton), Provincial and Freemasons. There's also a **cinema** (☑08-9965 0568; www.oranacinemas.com.au; cnr Marine Tce & Fitzgerald St; tickets $16) and **theatre** (☑08-9956 6662; cnr Cathedral Ave & Maitland St).

❶ **Information**

The best free wi-fi in town is at the **library** (☑08-9956 6659; library.cgg.wa.gov.au; 37 Marine Tce; wi-fi 1st hr free; ⊙from 9am Tue-Sat, from 1pm Sun & Mon; @🐾). There are several banks with ATMs along Marine Tce.

Sun City Books & Internet Corner (☑08-9964 7258; 49 Marine Tce; ⊙9am-5pm Mon-Fri, to 1pm Sat; @) Lots of terminals and a decent selection of books.

HOUTMAN ABROLHOS ISLANDS

Better known as 'the Abrolhos', this archipelago of 122 coral islands, 60km off the coast of Geraldton, is home to some amazing wildlife, including sea lions, green turtles, carpet pythons, over 90 seabird species and the Tammar wallaby. Much of the flora is rare, endemic and protected, and the surrounding reefs offer great diving thanks to the warm Leeuwin Current, which allows tropical species such as *Acropora* (staghorn) coral to flourish further south than normal.

These gnarly reefs have claimed many ships over the years, including the ill-fated *Batavia* (1629) and *Hadda* (1877), and you can dive on the wreck sites, as well as follow a number of self-guided dive trails (see the WA Fisheries *Abrolhos Islands Information Guide* for details). Because the general public can't stay overnight, divers (and surfers) normally need a multi-day boat charter. If you're content with a day trip, where you can bushwalk, picnic, snorkel or fish, then flying is your best bet.

Batavia Coast Dive Academy (p170) can help you get a boat together. Those wanting to fly could try the following operators.

Shine Aviation Services (☑ 9923 3600; www.shineaviation.com.au; 90min/full-day tours $175/240)

Geraldton Air Charter (☑ 08-9923 3434; www.geraldtonaircharter.com.au; Brierly Terminal, Geraldton Airport; half-/full-day tours $230/250)

Visitor Centre (☑ 08-9921 3999; www.geraldtontourist.com.au; Bill Sewell Complex, Chapman Rd; ☺ 9am-5pm Mon-Fri, 10am-4pm Sat & Sun) One of the best around, with lots of great info sheets and helpful staff who'll book accommodation, tours and transport.

ℹ Getting There & Around

AIR

SkyWest and Qantas both fly daily to/from Perth. Skippers flies direct to/from Carnarvon several times weekly. The airport is 12km from Marine Tce.

BUS

Integrity coaches service Perth ($54, six hours) daily via the coast and run twice weekly to Carnarvon ($99, six hours) and Exmouth ($135, 11 hours). Transwa has daily inland services to Perth ($61, six hours) and thrice weekly to Kalbarri ($27, two hours). There's also a twice-weekly service to Meekatharra ($73, seven hours). Greyhound runs three times weekly to Perth ($65, six hours) and north to Carnarvon ($105, six hours) and Broome ($350, 27 hours). All long-distance buses leave from the old railway station (Greyhound from the rear). **Transgeraldton** (☑ 08-9923 2225; www.buswest .com.au) operates eight routes to local suburbs.

Batavia Tickets (☑ 08-9964 8881; www.bataviatickets.com.au; old railway station; ☺ 8am-4.30pm Mon-Fri, to 9.30am Sat) Sells tickets for the long-distance buses departing outside.

TAXI

Call ☑ 1300 008.

Kalbarri

POP 2000

Magnificent red-sandstone cliffs border the Indian Ocean. The beautiful Murchison River snakes through tall, steep gorges before ending treacherously at Gantheaume Bay. Wildflowers line paths frequented by kangaroos, emus and thorny devils, while whales breach just offshore, and rare orchids struggle in the rocky ground. To the north, the towering line of the limestone Zuytdorp Cliffs remains aloof, pristine and remote.

Kalbarri is surrounded by stunning nature, and there's great surfing, swimming, fishing, bushwalking, horse riding and canoeing near town and in Kalbarri National Park. While the vibe is mostly low key, school holidays see Kalbarri stretched to the limit.

◉ Sights & Activities

Kalbarri National Park

With its magnificent river red gums and Tumblagooda sandstone, rugged **Kalbarri National Park** (admission per car $11) contains almost 2000 sq km of wild bushland, stunning river gorges and savagely eroded coastal cliffs. There's abundant wildlife, including 200 species of birds, and spectacular wildflowers between July and November.

A string of lookouts dot the impressive coast south of town and the easy **Bigurda Trail** (8km one way) follows the clifftops between Natural Bridge and Eagle Gorge;

from July to November you may spot migrating whales. Closer to town are **Pot Alley**, **Rainbow Valley**, **Mushroom Rock** and **Red Bluff** – the last being accessible via a walking trail from Kalbarri (5.5km one way).

The river gorges are east of Kalbarri, 11km down Ajana Kalbarri Rd to the turn-off, and then 20km unsealed to a T-intersection. Turn left for lookouts over **The Loop** and the superb **Nature's Window** (1km return). Bring lots of water for the unshaded **Loop Trail** (8km return). Turning right at the T leads to **Z-Bend** with a breathtaking lookout (1.2km return) or you can continue steeply down to the gorge bottom (2.6km return). Head back to Ajana Kalbarri Rd and travel a further 24km before turning off to **Hawk's Head**, where there are great views and picnic tables, and **Ross Graham lookout**, where you can access the river. It's possible to hike 38km from Ross Graham to The Loop in a demanding four-day epic, but be warned: there are no marked trails and several river crossings.

Other Attractions

Kalbarri has a network of cycle paths along the foreshore, and you can ride out to **Blue Holes** for snorkelling, **Jakes Point** for surfing and fishing, and **Red Bluff Beach**, 5.5km away. Any of the lookouts along the coast are perfect for watching the sunset. Look for wildflowers along Siles Rd, River Rd and out near the airport; the visitor centre publishes regular wildflower updates in season.

Kalbarri Wildflower Centre   GARDENS
(☑08-9937 1229; adult/child $5/2, tours $10; ☺9am-1pm Wed-Mon Jun-Oct, tours 10am) Stroll 1.8km along a labelled wildflower trail, or take a guided tour. There's a small cafe on site. The gardens are located off Ajana Kalbarri Rd.

Pelican Feeding   WILDLIFE WATCHING
(☑08-9937 1104; ☺8.45am) **FREE** Kalbarri's most popular attraction.

Kalbarri Boat Hire   CANOEING
(☑08-9937 1245; www.kalbarriboathire.com; Grey St; kayak/canoe/surf cat/powerboat per hr $15/15/45/50) If it goes in the water, then these guys hire it out. They also run four-hour breakfast and lunch canoe trips down the Murchison (adult/child $65/45). You'll find them on the waterfront.

Kalbarri Abseil   CANYONING
(☑08-9937 1618; www.abseilaustralia.com.au; half-day abseil year round/full-day canyoning tours Apr-Nov only $80/135) Abseil into the sheer gorges of Kalbarri National Park, then float along the bottom on inner tubes.

Kalbarri Sandboarding   SANDBOARDING
(☑08-9937 2377; www.sandboardingaustralia.com. au; adult/child $80/70) Muck around on sand dunes, then go for a snorkel on these fun half-day tours.

Kalbarri Adventure Tours   CANOEING
(☑08-9937 1677; www.kalbarritours.com.au; adult/child $90/70) Combine canoeing, bushwalking and swimming around the park's Z-Bend/Loop area.

Big River Ranch   HORSE RIDING
(☑08-9937 1214; www.bigriverranch.net; 90min trail rides $85) Track through the beautiful Murchsion River floodplain on horseback. All experience levels catered for, and the overnight rides are the highlight. Camping (sites per person $10, powered sites $25) and rustic bunkhouse rooms (from $25 per person) are available. Off Ajana Kalbarri Rd.

 Tours

Here's a selection; the visitor centre has a full list and arranges bookings.

Kalbarri Air Charter   SCENIC FLIGHTS
(☑08-9937 1130; www.kalbarriaircharter.com.au; 62 Grey St; flights $65-300) Offers 20-minute scenic flights over the coastal cliffs, and longer flights over gorges, the Zuytdorp Cliffs, Monkey Mia and the Abrolhos Islands.

Kalbarri Wilderness Cruises   CRUISES
(☑08-9937 1601; kalbarricruises@westnet.com.au; adult/child $44/22) Runs popular two-hour licensed nature cruises along the Murchison.

Reefwalker Adventure Tours   WHALE WATCHING
(☑0417 931 091; www.reefwalker.com.au; adult/child $85/55) A chance to get up close to those migrating humpbacks (from July to November). Also runs ocean fishing and sightseeing tours.

Sleeping

There's a lot of choice, but avoid school holidays, when prices skyrocket. The visitor centre is your friend.

Kalbarri Backpackers   HOSTEL $
(☑08-9937 1430; www.yha.com.au; cnr Woods & Mortimer Sts; dm/d $29/77, bike hire $20; @☀☒)

MONKEY MIA & THE CENTRAL WEST KALBARRI

Kalbarri

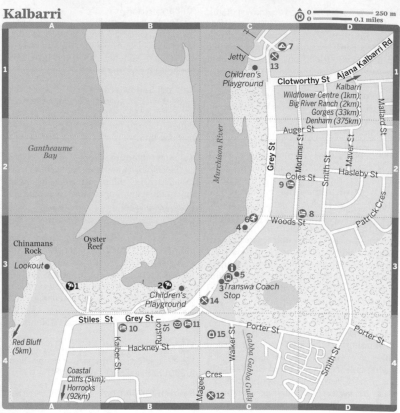

Kalbarri

⊙ Sights
1 Chinamans Beach.................................A3
2 Swimming Beach B3

⊙ Activities, Courses & Tours
3 Kalbarri Air Charter C3
4 Kalbarri Boat Hire C3
5 Kalbarri Wilderness Cruises C3
6 Pelican Feeding C3

⊟ Sleeping
7 Anchorage Caravan Park C1
8 Kalbarri Backpackers D2
9 Kalbarri Reef Villas..............................C2

10 Pelican Shore Villas.............................B4
   Pelican's Nest ....(see 8)
11 Ray White Kalbarri
   Accommodation Service B4

⊗ Eating
   Angies Cafe....................................(see 11)
12 Finlay's Fresh Fish BBQ C4
13 Gorges Café C1
14 Kalbarri Motor Hotel C3

ⓐ Shopping
15 Marudi Designs....................................C4
   The Art Place ....(see 15)

This nice, shady hostel with a decent pool and BBQ is one block back from the beach. Bikes are available and staff also handle the shuttle out to the Greyhound stop on the highway at Binnu ($41).

Anchorage Caravan Park   CARAVAN PARK $
(☑08-9937 1181; www.kalbarrianchorage.com.au; cnr Anchorage Lane & Grey St; powered sites $34, cabins with/without bathroom $100/70; ⊛) The best option for campers, Anchorage has roomy, shaded sites overlooking the river mouth.

⭐ Pelican's Nest · MOTEL $$

(☑ 08-9937 1430; www.pelicansnestkalbarri.com.au; 45-47 Mortimer St; d $100-140; ❄@❄) Adjoining Kalbarri Backpackers, the Nest has a selection of neat motel-style rooms (some with kitchenettes), and excellent facilities.

Pelican Shore Villas · APARTMENTS $$

(☑ 08-9937 1708; www.pelicanshorevillas.com.au; cnr Grey & Kaiber Sts; villas $136-188; ❄❄❄) These beautiful manicured town houses have all the mod cons, and the best view in town.

Kalbarri Reef Villas · APARTMENTS $$

(☑ 08-9937 1165; www.reefvillas.com.au; cnr Coles & Mortimer Sts; units $130-180; ❄❄❄) One block behind the foreshore, these fully self-contained two-storey, two-bedroom apartments face onto a palm-filled garden.

Ray White Kalbarri Accommodation Service · ACCOMMODATION SERVICES $$$

(☑ 08-9937 1700; www.kalbarriaccommodation.com.au; Kalbarri Arcade, 44 Grey St; houses per week from $460) Has a wide range of self-contained apartments and houses.

✕ Eating

Supermarkets and takeaways are at the shopping centres; bistros are at the taverns.

Angies Cafe · CAFE $

(☑ 08-9937 1738; Shop 6, 46 Grey St; meals $8-20; ⊙8am-4pm) Great little cafe offering fresh, tasty meals with a good selection of salads.

⭐ Gorges Café · CAFE $$

(☑ 08-9937 1200; Marina Complex, Grey St; meals $8-25; ⊙7am-5pm Mon & Wed-Fri, to 2pm Sat & Sun) Ask at this airy cafe for its Morning Cure and you won't be disappointed; it serves up wonderful breakfasts and lunches, just opposite the jetty.

Kalbarri Motor Hotel · PUB $$

(☑ 08-9937 1400; 50 Grey St; pizzas $22, mains $22-45) A cut above normal pub fare, with gourmet wood-fired pizzas, 'wok-of-the-day' and stand-out local seafood. Also has clean, basic rooms (doubles $105).

Finlay's Fresh Fish BBQ · SEAFOOD $$

(☑ 08-9937 1260; 24 Magee Cres; mains $15-30; ⊙5.30-8.30pm Tue-Sun) You'll either love it or hate it, but you'll certainly always remember your no-frills BBQ fish dinner at this Kalbarri institution, where the huge portions of fish come with lashings of (usually, but not always) tongue-in-cheek abuse.

🛍 Shopping

Marudi Designs · ARTS & CRAFTS

(☑ 0487 419 820; Shop 2, 51 Hackney St; ⊙9am-4pm) Fully indigenous owned and run gallery showcasing local Nhanda arts and crafts. Behind the tavern.

The Art Place · ARTS & CRAFTS

(Shop 3, 51 Hackney St; ⊙10am-4pm Wed-Sun) Quirky gallery featuring local artists, glassblowers, jewellers and photographers. Behind the tavern.

ℹ Information

There are ATMs at the shopping centres on Grey and Porter Sts.

Kalbarri Community Resource Centre (☑08-9937 1933; Hackney St; ⊙9am-3pm Mon-Fri; @) Fax and internet.

Book Nook (☑08-9937 2676; ⊙10am-5pm Mon-Fri, to 4pm Sat & Sun; @) Internet and secondhand books.

Visitor Centre (☑1800 639 468; www.kalbarri.org.au; Grey St; ⊙9am-5pm Mon-Sat) Great wildflower and activities info; also can book accommodation and tours. Internet is available at the library next door.

> **OFF THE BEATEN TRACK**
>
> ### WOOLEEN STATION
>
> Well and truly off the beaten track at roughly 200km from the closest asphalt, **Wooleen Station** (☑08-9963 7973; www.wooleen.com.au; Murchison; camp sites $25, d $170, homestead full board per person $190; ⊙Apr-Oct) 🌿 is a historic pastoral lease reinventing itself as an ecotourism destination. The emphasis is on conservation and land regeneration, trying to undo decades of erosion and degradation due to outdated farming practices. There's a variety of accommodation from dusty camp sites to an all-meals-included room in the heritage-listed homestead, but space is strictly limited, so book first before making that long drive. Wooleen is always looking for workers, and backpackers are welcome.
>
> Head north from Mullewa on the Carnarvon Mullewa Rd or east on the Butchers Track just north of Billabong Roadhouse.

HORROCKS & PORT GREGORY

The tiny seaside villages of Horrocks and Port Gregory, 92km and 68km south of Kalbarri, respectively, are as quiet as they come. Horrocks, the smaller and prettier of the two, has several accommodation options including the laid-back **Horrocks Beach Caravan Park** (08-9934 3039; www.horrocksbeachcaravanpark.com.au; sites $24-32, cabins $75-90;), right behind the dunes, and the nearby bargain, **Beachside Cottages** (08-9934 3031; www.northamptonaccommodation.com.au/horrocks_beachside_cottages.htm; 5 Glance St; d $75-85). Port Gregory, on the far side of the mysterious Pink Lakes, and with a fringing reef, is great for fishing and snorkelling. **Port Gregory Caravan Park** (08-9935 1052; www.portgregorycaravanpark.com.au; powered sites $32, cabins $85-115) is your best choice.

Getting There & Around

Skippers flies to Perth, Shark Bay and Carnarvon several times weekly.

Getting to/from Perth ($76, nine hours) and Geraldton ($27, two hours) by bus is easiest with Transwa at the visitor centre. Heading to/from points further north, Greyhound stops at Binnu on the highway, 77km away – arrange a shuttle from the YHA (p173). From Binnu you can reach Overlander Roadhouse (for Monkey Mia, $52, two hours), Coral Bay ($106, eight hours) and Broome ($325, 26 hours). Integrity passes through Ajana on the way to Exmouth ($126, 10 hours).

Kalbarri Auto Centre (08-9937 1290) rents out 4WDs and sedans from $60 per day. Both bikes and scooters can be hired from **Kalbarri Air Charter** (08-9937 1130; 62 Grey St; bikes half-/full day $10/20, scooters half-/full day $45/85), and bikes are also available from the YHA and the **entertainment centre** (08-9937 1105; 15 Magee Cres). For a taxi, call 0419 371 888.

SHARK BAY

The World Heritage–listed area of Shark Bay, stretching from Kalbarri to Carnarvon, consists of more than 1500km of spectacular coastline, containing turquoise lagoons, barren finger-like peninsulas, hidden bays, white-sand beaches, towering limestone cliffs and numerous islands. It's the westernmost part of the Australian mainland, and one of WA's most biologically rich habitats, with an array of plant and animal life found nowhere else on earth. Lush beds of seagrass and sheltered bays nourish dugongs, sea turtles, humpback whales, dolphins, stingrays, sharks and other aquatic life. On land, Shark Bay's biodiversity has benefited from Project Eden, an ambitious ecosystem-regeneration program that has sought to eradicate feral animals and reintroduce endemic species. Shark Bay is also home to the amazing stromatolites of Hamelin Pool.

The Malgana, Nhanda and Inggarda peoples originally inhabited the area, and visitors can take indigenous cultural tours to learn about country. Shark Bay played host to early European explorers and many geographical names display this legacy. In 1616, Dutch explorer Dirk Hartog nailed a pewter dinner plate (now in Amsterdam's Rijksmuseum) to a post on the island that now bears his name. Dirk Hartog Island is WA's largest.

Getting There & Away

Shark Bay airport is located between Denham and Monkey Mia. Skippers flies to Perth six times weekly, with some return flights via Kalbarri.

The closest Greyhound and Integrity approach is the Overlander Roadhouse, 128km away on the North West Coastal Hwy. **Shark Bay Car Hire** (0427 483 032; www.carhire.net.au; 65 Knight Tce, Denham; shuttle $67, car/4WD hire per day $95/185) runs a connecting shuttle (book ahead!).

Overlander Roadhouse to Denham

Twenty-nine kilometres along Shark Bay Rd from the Overlander Roadhouse is the turn-off for **Hamelin Pool** (not nearby Hamelin Station!), a marine reserve that contains the world's best-known colony of stromatolites. These coral-like formations consist of cyanobacteria almost identical to organisms that existed 3.5 billion years ago, and, through their use of photosynthesis, are considered largely responsible for creating our current atmosphere, paving the way for more complex life. There's an excellent boardwalk with information panels, best seen at low tide.

The nearby 1884 Telegraph Office (admission $5.50; ⊘ check at shop) houses a fascinating museum containing possibly the only living stromatolites in captivity. The Postmasters Residence is also the office for the tiny Hamelin Pool Caravan Park (☑ 08-9942 5905; Hamelin Pool; unpowered/powered sites $22/27) and serves Devonshire teas, pies and ice creams.

Along the road you pass the turn-off for Hamelin Station (☑ 08-9948 5145; www.hame linstationstay.com.au; sites per person $12, s/d/f $60/90/120), which has lovely rooms in converted shearers' quarters, top-class amenities and somewhat arid camp sites. There's great bird life at the nearby waterhole.

As Shark Bay Rd swings north, you'll pass the turn-off for Useless Loop (a closed salt-mining town), Edel Land and Steep Point, the Australian mainland's most westerly tip.

The dusty former sheep station Nanga Bay Resort (☑ 08-9948 3992; www.nanga bayresort.com.au; Nanga Bay; unpowered/powered sites $25/30, dongas/motel r/huts/villas $50/165/180/250; ❄ ❄) has a range of accommodation. The Fishermens Huts, which sleep four to six people, have good views, but some of the other options are a little depressing.

Inside the vermin-proof fence, and 55km from the Hamelin turn-off, is the road to deserted Shell Beach, where tiny cockle shells, densely compacted over time, were once quarried as building material for places like the Old Pearler Restaurant in Denham.

You'll pass turn-offs to bush camp sites before reaching Eagle Bluff, which has clifftop views overlooking an azure lagoon. You may spot turtles, sharks or manta rays.

Denham

POP 1500

Beautiful, laid-back Denham, with its aquamarine sea and palm-fringed beachfront, makes a great base for trips to the surrounding Shark Bay Marine Park, nearby François Peron and Dirk Hartog Island National Parks, and Monkey Mia, 26km away.

Australia's westernmost town originated as a pearling base, and the streets were once paved with pearl shell. Knight Tce, the now-tarmac main drag, has everything you will need.

◉ Sights & Activities

★ Shark Bay World Heritage Discovery Centre   MUSEUM
(☑ 08-9948 1590; www.sharkbayvisit.com; 53 Knight Tce; adult/child $11/6; ⊘ 9am-5pm Mon-Fri, 10am-4pm Sat & Sun) Informative and evocative displays of Shark Bay's ecosystems, marine and animal life, indigenous culture, early explorers, settlers and shipwrecks.

Ocean Park   AQUARIUM
(☑ 08-9948 1765; www.oceanpark.com.au; Shark Bay Rd; adult/child $20/12; ⊘ 9am-5pm) Superbly located on a headland just before town, this family-run aquaculture farm features an artificial lagoon where you can take a 60-minute guided tour to observe feeding sharks, turtles, stingrays and fish. The licensed cafe has sensational views, and it also conducts full-day 4WD tours with bushwalks and snorkelling to François Peron National Park ($180) and Steep Point ($350).

Little Lagoon   LANDMARK
Little Lagoon, 4km from town, is a pleasant picnic spot with tables and barbecues; you can walk, drive or cycle there. Don't be surprised if an emu wanders by.

◉ Tours

Aussie Off Road Tours   DRIVING TOUR
(☑ 0429 929 175; www.aussieoffroadtours.com.au) Culture, history, wildlife and bush tucker feature in these excellent indigenous-owned and -operated 4WD tours, including twilight wildlife ($90), full-day François Peron National Park ($189) or Shell Beach/Hamelin ($200), overnight camping in François Peron ($300) and overnight to Steep Point ($390).

ⓘ SEASIDE BUSH CAMPING
Shark Bay shire offers a choice of four coastal bush camp sites, Goulet Bluff, Whalebone, Fowlers Camp and Eagle Bluff, all 20km to 40km south of Denham in the area known as South Peron. To camp here, you must first obtain a permit ($10 per vehicle) from the Shark Bay visitor centre (p179). While this is easily arranged via phone (if yours has any reception), in practice it's better to scope the sites first, then get the permit. There are no facilities and a one-night limit applies to the whole area.

WAY OUT WEST IN EDEL LAND

The Australian mainland's westernmost tip is **Steep Point**, just below Dirk Hartog Island. It's a wild, wind-scarred, barren clifftop with a beauty born of desolation and remoteness. The **Zuytdorp Cliffs** stretch away to the south, the limestone peppered with blowholes, while leeward, bays with white sandy beaches provide sheltered camp sites. The entire area is known as **Edel Land**, soon to become a national park. Anglers have been coming here for years to go game fishing off the towering cliffs, but few tourists make the 140km rough drive down a dead-end road.

Access to the area is via Useless Loop Rd, and is controlled by the **Department of Environment and Conservation** (DEC; ☑08-9948 3993; entry permit per vehicle $11, sites per person $7). There is a ranger station at **Shelter Bay**, with camping nearby; at Steep Point (rocky and exposed); and at **False Entrance** to the south. Sites are strictly limited and must be booked in advance. You'll need a high-clearance 4WD as the road deteriorates past the Useless Loop turn-off (approximately 100km from Shark Bay Rd). Tyres should be deflated to 20psi. Ensure you bring ample water and enough fuel to return to the Overlander Roadhouse (185km) or Denham (230km). During winter, a barge runs from Shelter Bay to **Dirk Hartog Island** (bookings essential). The website www.sharkbay.org.au has all the details and downloadable permits. Hire-car companies will not insure for this road, though (expensive) tours can be arranged from Denham. The drive is pure adventure; Steep Point is probably more easily reached by boat, but then that's not the Point, is it?

Shark Bay Scenic Flights   SCENIC FLIGHTS
(☑0417 919 059; www.sharkbayair.com.au) Offers various scenic flights, including 15-minute Monkey Mia flyovers ($59) and a sensational 40-minute trip over Steep Point and the Zuytdorp Cliffs ($175). Ask if the planned Dirk Hartog Island fly/drive tour to Cape Inscription is running, as this would be as spectacular. Planes are also available for one-way charters to/from the Overlander Roadhouse ($140).

Shark Bay Coaches & Tours   TOUR
(☑08-9948 1081; www.sbcoaches.com; bus/quad bike $80/$90) Half-day bus tours to all key sights and two-hour quad-bike tours to Little Lagoon.

🛏 Sleeping & Eating

Denham has accommodation for all budgets, and some places offer long-stay discounts and/or school-holiday surcharges. There's a pub, a supermarket, a bakery, cafes and takeaways on Knight Tce.

★Bay Lodge   HOSTEL $
(☑08-9948 1278; www.baylodge.info; 113 Knight Tce; dm/d from $26/68; ✳@🌊) Every room at this YHA hostel has its own en suite, kitchenette and TV/DVD player. Ideally located across from the beach, it also has a great pool, a large common kitchen, and a shuttle bus to Monkey Mia.

Denham Seaside Tourist Village   CARAVAN PARK $
(☑1300 133 733; www.sharkbayfun.com; Knight Tce; sites unpowered/powered/with bathroom $30/37/45, d cabins $80, 1-/2-bedroom chalets $125/135; ✳) This lovely, shady park on the water's edge is the best in town, though you will need to borrow the drill for your tent pegs. Cover up at night against the insects and ring first if arriving after 6pm.

Oceanside Village   CABINS $$
(☑1800 680 600; www.oceanside.com.au; 117 Knight Tce; cabins $160-200; ✳🌐🌊) These neat self-catering cottages with sunny balconies are perfectly located directly opposite the beach.

Tradewinds   APARTMENTS $$
(☑1800 816 160; www.tradewindsdenham.com.au; Knight Tce; units $140-160; ✳) Spacious, fully self-contained, modern units right across from the beach.

Ray White   ACCOMMODATION SERVICES $$
(☑08-99481323; www.raywhitesb.com; Knight Tce; flats per night $100-240; ⊘8am-5pm Mon-Fri, 9am-noon Sat) Looking for a self-contained flat? These guys usually have a list of everything available in town.

★Old Pearler Restaurant   SEAFOOD $$$
(☑08-9948 1373; 71 Knight Tce; meals $30-49; ⊘dinner Mon-Sat) Built from shell bricks, this

atmospheric nautical haven serves fantastic seafood. The exceptional platter features local snapper, whiting, cray, oysters, prawns and squid – all grilled, not fried. BYO.

Ocean Restaurant CAFE **$$**
(www.oceanpark.com.au; Shark Bay Rd; mains $19-32; ☺9am-5pm; 🐾) The most refined lunch in Shark Bay also comes with the best view. Inside Ocean Park, overlooking turquoise waters, you can choose from mouth-watering tapas, all-day brekkies or tantalising local seafood dishes. Fully licensed.

Drinking

Shark Bay Hotel PUB
(☑08-9948 1203; www.sharkbayhotelwa.com.au; 43 Knight Tce; ☺10am-late) Sunsets are dynamite from the beer garden of the mainland's most westerly pub (dinner $22 to $38).

ℹ Information

There are ATMs at Heritage Resort and Shark Bay Hotel, and internet access at the **CRC** (☑08-9948 1787; 67 Knight Tce; @) and post office.
Department of Environment & Conservation (☑08-9948 1208; www.dec.gov.au; 61-63 Knight Tce; ☺8am-5pm Mon-Fri) Park passes and information.
Shark Bay Home Page (www.sharkbay.org.au) Great information, interactive maps and downloadable permits.
Shark Bay Visitor Centre (☑08-9948 1590; www.sharkbayvisit.com; 53 Knight Tce; ☺9am-5pm Mon-Fri, 10am-4pm Sat & Sun) The very informative staff handle accommodation and tour bookings and issue bush-camping permits for South Peron. Located in the foyer of the Shark Bay World Heritage Discovery Centre.

François Peron National Park

Covering the whole peninsula north of Denham is an area of low scrub, salt lakes and red sandy dunes, home to the rare bilby, mallee fowl and woma python. There's a scattering of rough **camp sites** (per person $7) alongside brilliant white beaches, all accessible via 4WD (deflate tyres to 20psi). Don't miss the fantastic **Wanamalu Trail** (3km return), which follows the cliff top between Cape Peron and Skipjack Point, from where you can spot marine life in the crystal waters below. Those with 2WD can enter only as far as the old **Peron Homestead**, where there's a short 'lifestyle' walk around

the shearing sheds, and an artesian-bore hot tub to soak in. Park entry is $11 per vehicle. Tours start at around $180 from Denham or Monkey Mia, but if there's a group of you, consider hiring your own 4WD from Denham for the same price.

Monkey Mia

Watching the wild dolphins turning up for a feed each morning in the shallow waters of **Monkey Mia** (adult/child/family $8/3/16), 26km northeast of Denham, is a highlight of every traveller's trip to the region. Don't be put off by the resort vibe – once you see these beautiful, intelligent mammals up close you'll forget about everything else. Watch the way they herd fish upside down, trying to trap them against the surface. The pier makes a good vantage point. The first feed is around 7.45am, but you'll see them arrive earlier, and hang around after the session, as the dolphins commonly come a second, and sometimes even a third time.

Monkey Mia Visitors Centre (☑08-9948 1366; ☺8am-4pm) has a good range of publications, information and tours.

You can **volunteer** to work full time with the dolphins for between four and 14 days; it's popular, so apply several months in advance and specify availability dates, though sometimes there are last-minute openings. Contact the **volunteer coordinator** (☑08-9948 1366; monkeymiavolunteers @westnet.com.au).

☞ Tours

Wula Guda Nyinda
Aboriginal Cultural Tours INDIGENOUS CULTURE
(☑0429 708 847; www.wulaguda.com.au; 90min tours adult/child from $50/25) Learn 'how to let country talk to you' on these amazing bushwalks led by local Aboriginal guide Darren 'Capes' Capewell. You'll pick up some local Malgana language and identify bush tucker and indigenous medicine. The evening 'Didgeridoo Dreaming' tours (adult/child $60/30) are magical. There are also 'Saltwater Dreaming' kayak tours (adult half-/full day $120/165).

Aristocat II CRUISE
(☑1800 030 427; www.monkey-mia.net; 1/2½hr tours $45/80) Cruise in comfort on this large catamaran, and you might see dugongs, dolphins and loggerhead turtles. You'll also stop off at the **Blue Lagoon Pearl Farm**.

Wildsights   ADVENTURE TOUR

(☑1800 241 481; www.monkeymiawildsights.com.
au) On the small *Shotover* catamaran you're
close to the action; 2½-hour wildlife cruises
start from $79. There are also 1½-hour sun-
set cruises ($39) and full-day 4WD trips to
François Peron National Park ($195); dis-
counts are available for multiple trips.

🛏 Sleeping & Eating

Monkey Mia is a resort and not a town, so
eating and sleeping options are limited to the
Monkey Mia Dolphin Resort. Self-catering
is a good option.

Monkey Mia Dolphin Resort   RESORT $$$

(☑1800 653 611; www.monkeymia.com.au; tent
sites per person $15, van sites from $39, dm/d
$30/89, garden units $223, beachfront villas $315;
🟦@🛜🏊) Although the location is stun-
ning, trying to cater for all markets, includ-
ing campers, backpackers, package and top-
end tourists, is never a great idea. The staff
are friendly, and the backpacker 'shared en
suites' are good value, but the same can't be
said of the top-end rooms. This place gets
seriously crowded and at times sounds like
a continuous party. The restaurant has sen-
sational water views but bland, overpriced
meals, while the backpacker bar has cheaper
food and liquored-up backpackers.

ℹ Getting There & Away

There is no public transport to Monkey Mia from
Denham. If you stay at Bay Lodge in Denham,
you can use its shuttle but it only runs alternate
days. Your other options are hiring a car or
bicycle.

GASCOYNE COAST

This wild, rugged, largely unpopulated
coastline stretches from Shark Bay to Nin-
galoo, with excellent fishing, and waves
that attract surfers from around the world.
Subtropical Carnarvon, the region's hub, is
an important fruit- and vegetable-growing
district, and farms are always looking for
seasonal workers. The 760km Gascoyne
River, WA's longest, is responsible for all
that lushness, though it flows underground
for most of the year. Inland, the distances
are huge and the temperatures high; here
you'll find the ancient eroded rocks of the
Kennedy Range, as well as massive Mt Au-
gustus (Burringurrah).

Carnarvon

POP 9000

On Yinggarda country at the mouth of the
Gascoyne River, fertile Carnarvon, with its
fruit and vegetable plantations and thriv-
ing fishing industry, makes a pleasant stop-
over between Denham and Exmouth. This
friendly, vibrant town has quirky attrac-
tions, a range of decent accommodation,
well-stocked supermarkets and great local
produce. The tree-lined CBD exudes a tropi-
cal feel, and the palm-fringed waterfront is
a relaxing place to amble. The long picking
season from March to January ensures plen-
ty of seasonal work. Floods devastated the
area in December 2010 and many businesses
are still recovering.

⊙ Sights & Activities

Established jointly with NASA in 1966, the
OTC Dish (Mahony Ave) at the edge of town
tracked Gemini and Apollo space missions,
as well as Halley's Comet, before closing in
1987. Stage One of the small but fascinating
**Carnarvon Space and Technology Mu-
seum** (Mahony Ave; admission $5; ⊙10am-3pm)
is nearby.

Carnarvon's luxuriant plantations along
North and South River Rds provide a large
proportion of WA's fruit and veg; grab the
Gascoyne Food Trail (www.gascoynefood.
com.au) brochure from the visitor centre.
Bumbak's (☑08-9941 8006; 449 North River
Rd; 1hr tours $8.80; ⊙shop 9am-4pm Mon-Fri,
tours 10am Mon, Wed & Fri Apr-Oct) offers tours
and sells a variety of fresh and dried fruit,
preserves and yummy home-made ice
cream. Check out the delicious produce at
the **Gascoyne Arts, Crafts & Growers
Market** (Civic Centre car park; ⊙8-11.30am Sat
May-Oct).

You can walk or ride 2.5km along the old
tramway to the **Heritage Precinct** on Bab-
bage Island, once the city's port. **One Mile
Jetty** (admission tram/walking $7/4; ⊙9am-
4.30pm) provides great fishing and views;
walk or take the vintage tram to the end.
The nearby **Lighthouse Keepers Cottage**
(Heritage Precinct; ⊙10am-1pm) has been pains-
takingly restored; don't miss the view from
the top of the creaky water tower in the **Rail-
way Station Museum** (⊙9am-5pm).

Gwoonwardu Mia (☑08-99411989; gahcc@
gahcc.com.au; 146 Robinson St; ⊙10am-3pm Mon-
Fri), built to depict a cyclone, represents the
five local Aboriginal language groups and

houses a cultural centre, art gallery, interpretive garden and the hospitality-training Yallibiddi Café.

September to March windsurfers head to Pelican Point, while novice (or advanced) kiteboarders can learn some new skills from Kitemix (☑ 0400 648 706; www.kitemix.com; lessons per hr from $80; ☺ Sep-Mar).

The last weekend of October sees the town taken over by desert riders competing in the gruelling 511km **Gascoyne Dash** (Gassy Dash; www.gasdash.com).

The palm-lined **walking path** along the side of the Fascine (the body of water at the end of Robinson St) is a pleasant place for a wander, especially at sunset.

🛏 Sleeping

Most accommodation, including numerous caravan parks, is spread out along the 5km feeder road from the highway. Try to arrive before 6pm.

★ Fish & Whistle   HOSTEL $
(☑ 08-9941 1704; 35 Robinson St; dm/s $30/45, motel r $99; ❄ @) Travellers love this big, breezy backpackers with its wide verandahs, bunk-free rooms, enormous communal spaces, excellent kitchen and happy vibe. There are air-con motel rooms out the back, discounts for longer stays and the revamped Port Hotel serving decent beer downstairs. The owners can help guests find seasonal jobs, and provide transport to work every day ($25 per week).

Capricorn Holiday Park   CARAVAN PARK $
(☑ 08-9941 8153; www.capricornholidaypark. com.au; 1042 North West Coastal Hwy; sites d $36, cabins $120; ❄ 🛜 ≋) Out on the highway, this peaceful, friendly park has lots of shade, a covered pool, grassy sites and lovely bougainvillea.

Coral Coast Tourist Park   CARAVAN PARK $
(☑ 08-9941 1438; www.coralcoasttouristpark. au; 108 Robinson St; powered sites $35, cabins $75-155, bicycles half-/full day $10/15; ❄ 🛜 ≋) This pleasant, shady park, with tropical pool and grassy sites, is the closest to the town centre. There's a variety of well-appointed cabins, a decent camp kitchen, and bicycles for hire.

Carnarvon Central
Apartments   APARTMENTS $$
(☑ 08-9941 1317; www.carnarvonholidays.com; 120 Robinson St; 2-bedroom apt $135; ❄) These neat,

fully self-contained apartments are popular with business travellers.

Hospitality Inn   MOTEL $$
(Best Western; ☑ 08-9941 1600; www.carnarvon. wa.hospitalityinns.com.au; 6 West St; d/f $169/199) The best of the motels in town. Rooms are clean and quiet and there's a nice on-site restaurant (meals $19 to $42).

🍴 Eating

The 2010 floods nobbled the fine-dining scene, and most eateries reverted to standards like burgers and steaks. Hopefully all that great produce will lure the chefs back. Otherwise, hit the markets and cook your own on the free BBQs along the Fascine and at Baxter Park. Knight Tce has takeaways and some early-opening cafes.

Morel's Orchard   MARKET $
(☑ 08-9941 8368; 486 Robinson St; ☺ 8.30am-5.30pm) A great selection of local fresh fruit and vegetables, as well as natural fruit ice creams.

Yallibiddi Café   CAFE $$
(☑ 08-9941 3127; 146 Robinson St; mains $10-20; ☺ 9am-3pm Mon-Fri) This training cafe was previously doing great things with bush tucker but now seems content to churn out roo burgers and chicken satays.

Hacienda Crab Shack   SEAFOOD $$
(☑ 08-9941 4078; Small Boat Harbour; ☺ 9am-4pm, shorter hr Sun) Got an esky? Then fill it with freshly steamed crabs, prawns, mussels, shucked oysters and fish fillets from this fishmonger.

Waters Edge   MODERN AUSTRALIAN $$
(☑ 08-9941 1181; www.thecarnarvon.com.au; 121 Olivia Tce; mains $25-46; ☺ 6-9pm Tue-Sat) Perfectly situated to capture the sunset over the Fascine, the restaurant out the back of the Carnarvon Hotel has a good selection of seafood and steaks. It also has clean, basic rooms (singles/doubles $65/80).

🛍 Shopping

Books & Stuff   BOOKS
(☑ 08-9941 2265; 2 Robinson St; ☺ 10am-1pm Mon-Fri) An eclectic collection of new, old and local books, with a nice 'reading' courtyard. BYO coffee.

ℹ Information

There's a post office on Camel Lane and ATMs on Robinson St.

MONKEY MIA & THE CENTRAL WEST CARNARVON

Visitor Centre (☑08-9941 1146; www.car narvon.org.au; Civic Centre, 21 Robinson St; ☺9am-5pm Mon-Fri, to noon Sat; ⊛) Very helpful, with information, maps, local books and produce.

❶ Getting There & Around

Skippers flies daily to Perth, and less often to Geraldton, Shark Bay and Kalbarri.

Greyhound buses head to Perth ($175, 13 hours), Broome ($293, 21 hours) and Coral Bay ($37, three hours) three times per week. Integrity runs twice weekly to Exmouth ($79, four hours), Geraldton ($99, six hours) and Perth ($144, 12 hours). All buses depart from the visitor centre.

Bikes can be hired from Coral Coast Tourist Park (p181).

For a taxi, call ☑131 008.

Point Quobba to Gnaraloo Bay

While the North West Coastal Hwy heads inland, the coast north of Carnarvon is wild, windswept and desolate, a favourite haunt of surfers and fisherfolk. Not many make it this far, but those who do are rewarded by huge winter swells, high summer temperatures, relentless winds, amazing marine life, breathtaking scenery and some truly magical experiences.

Turn down Blowholes Rd, 12km after the Gascoyne bridge, then proceed 49km along the sealed road to the coast. The **blowholes** (waves spraying out of limestone chimneys during a big swell) are just left of the T-intersection. **Point Quobba**, 1km further south, has beach shacks, excellent fishing, some gritty **camp sites** (sites $5.50), and not much else.

Heading right from the T onto dirt, after 8km you'll come across a lonely little cairn staring out to sea, commemorating HMAS *Sydney II*. Two kilometres further is **Quobba Station** (☑9948 5098; www.quobba.com.au; unpowered/powered sites $11/13.50, cabins per person $25-60), with plenty of rustic accommodation, a small store and legendary fishing.

Still on Quobba, 60km north of the homestead, **Red Bluff** (☑08-9948 5001; www.quobba.com.au; unpowered sites per person $12, shacks per person from $20, bungalows/safari retreats $170/$345) is a spectacular headland with a wicked surf break, excellent fishing and the southern boundary of Ningaloo Marine Park. Accommodation comes in all forms, from exposed camp sites and palm shelters, to exclusive upmarket safari tents with decking and superb views. Red Bluff's first shark attack happened in 2012.

The jewel, however, is at the end of the road around 150km from Carnarvon: **Gnaraloo Station** (☑08-9942 5927; www.gnaraloo.com; unpowered sites per person $20, cabins d $130-210; ☎)✐. Surfers from around the world come every winter to ride the notorious **Tombstones**, while summer brings turtle monitoring and windsurfers trying to catch the strong afternoon sea breeze, the 'Carnarvon Doctor'. There's excellent snorkelling close to shore and the coastline north from **Gnaraloo Bay** is eye-burningly pristine. You can stay in rough camp sites next to the beach at **3-Mile**, or there's a range of options up at the homestead, the nicest being stone cabins with uninterrupted ocean views – great for spotting migrating whales (June to November) and sea eagles. Gnaraloo is dedicated to sustainability and has implemented a number of visionary environmental programs. The station is always looking for willing workers, and there's such a nice vibe happening that many folk come for a night and end up staying months. Who could blame them?

Coral Coast & the Pilbara

Best Places to Eat

➡ Whalers (p191)
➡ Karijini Eco Retreat (p201)
➡ Ningaloo Health (p191)
➡ Silver Star (p203)
➡ Samson Beach Bistro (p198)

Best Places to Swim

➡ Turquoise Bay (p194)
➡ Coral Bay (p186)
➡ Fern Pool (p199)
➡ Deep Reach Pool (p198)
➡ Hamersley Gorge (p199)

Why Go?

Lapping on the edge of the Indian Ocean, the shallow, turquoise waters of the Coral Coast nurture a unique marine paradise. World Heritage–listed Ningaloo Reef is one of the very few places you can swim with the world's largest fish, the gentle whale shark. Lonely bays, deserted beaches and crystal-clear lagoons offer superb snorkelling and diving among myriad sea life including humpback whales, manta rays and loggerhead turtles. Development is low-key, towns few and far between, and seafood and sunsets legendary.

Inland, miners swarm like ants over the high, eroded ranges of the Pilbara, while ore trains snake down to a string of busy ports stretching from Dampier to Port Hedland. But hidden in the hills are two beautiful gems – Karijini and Millstream-Chichester National Parks, home to spectacular gorges, remote peaks, deep tranquil pools and abundant wildlife.

When to Go
Exmouth

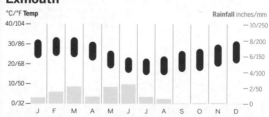

Apr–Jul Whale shark season – don't miss the swim of a lifetime.

Sep & Oct Karijini's gorges warm up and wildflowers blanket the ranges.

Nov–Mar Ningaloo is full of turtle love, eggs and hatchlings.

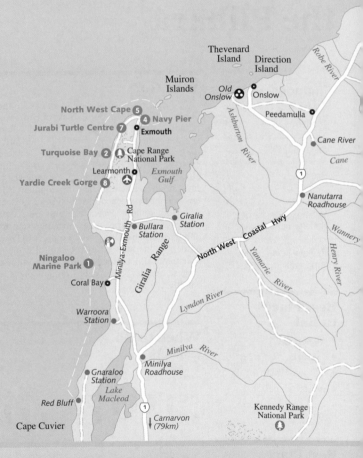

100 km
50 miles

INDIAN
OCEAN

Montebello Islands
Conservation Park

Barrow
Island

Thevenard
Island

Direction
Island

Robe River

Muiron
Islands

Old
Onslow

Onslow

Peedamulla

North West Cape ⑤

Navy Pier ④

Jurabi Turtle Centre ⑦

Exmouth

Cane River

Cane

Turquoise Bay ②

Cape Range
National Park

Ashburton River

Learmonth

Exmouth
Gulf

Nanutarra
Roadhouse

Yardie Creek Gorge ⑧

Giralia
Station

Wannery

North West Coastal Hwy

Bullara
Station

Giralia Range

Yannarie River

Henry River

Ningaloo
Marine Park ①

Minilya-Exmouth Rd

Lyndon River

Coral Bay

Warroora
Station

Minilya River

Gnaraloo
Station

Minilya
Roadhouse

Lake
Macleod

Red Bluff

Kennedy Range
National Park

Cape Cuvier

Carnarvon
(79km)

Coral Coast & the Pilbara Highlights

① Swimming with whale sharks in **Ningaloo Marine Park** (p193)

② Snorkelling over marine life at **Turquoise Bay** (p194)

③ Descending to the 'centre of the earth' on a gorge tour of **Karijini National Park** (p198)

④ Scuba diving off the **Navy Pier** at Point Murat (p192),

one of the world's finest shore dives

⑤ Watching the annual humpback-whale migration at the **North West Cape** (p194)

Cape Keraudren
Eighty Mile
Beach (103km)
Poissonnier Point
American Silver
Star Railcar
Cape Thouin
Port
Hedland
Pardoo
Station
Pardoo
Roadhouse
10
Great Northern Hwy
1
South Hedland
Indee Station
Turner River
Yule River
95
Great Northern Hwy
Shaw River
Marble
Bar
Coongan River
Burrup
Peninsula
Dampier
Archipelago
Hearson
Cove
Point Samson
Wickham
Dampier
Cossack
Karratha
Roebourne
Karratha
Roadhouse
Whim
Creek
The Pilbara
Peawah River
Fortescue
River Roadhouse
Python Pool
Mt Herbert (366m)
Yandeyarra
Aboriginal Land
Hillside Rd
Fortescue River
Pannawonica
Millstream-Chichester
National Park
Millstream
Homestead &
Crossing Pool
HI Railway Rd
(Permit Required)
Mt Florance Station
Chichester Range
Nullagine (5km)
Duck River
River
Hamersley
Hamersley
Gorge
Range
Karijini
Visitor Centre
Karijini Gorges 3
Munjina
(Auski)
Roadhouse
Boolgeeda Creek
Jarndunmunha
(Mt Nameless)
(1128m)
Tom
Price
Punurrunha
(Mt Bruce)
(1235m)
95
Hardey River
Beasley River
Mt Tom Price
(1072m)
Karijini
National Park
9
Juna
Downs
Mt Meharry
(1249m)
Eagle Rock
Falls
Range
Ophthalmia
Creek
Paraburdoo
Newman
Mt Newman
(1057m)
Capricorn
Roadhouse
Seven Mile
Creek
Ashburton
Downs
Turee Creek
Angelo River
Tunnel Creek
Edmund River
Lyons River
Cobra
Bangemall
Dooley
Downs
Ashburton River
Kumarina Roadhouse
(30km); Meekatharra
(248km)
Mt Augustus
(Burringurrah)
National Park
Mt Augustus (Burringurrah) (1105m)
Mt Augustus Outback Tourist Resort
Meekatharra (311km)
Eithel River
Collier Range
Collier Range
National Park

6 Cooling off in an idyllic
waterhole at **Millstream-
Chichester National Park**
(p198)
7 Tracking turtles on remote
beaches and becoming a

certified 'turtle guide' at the
Jurabi Turtle Centre (p192)
8 Spotting rare black-
flanked rock wallabies on a
cruise into stunning **Yardie
Creek Gorge** (p195)

9 Peak bagging on the
state's highest peaks in
Karijini National Park (p198)
10 Enjoying a real coffee in the
1930s **American Silver Star
Railcar** in Port Hedland (p203)

ℹ️ Getting There & Around

AIR

The following airlines service the Coral Coast and the Pilbara.

Airnorth (📞1800 627 474; www.airnorth.com.au)

Alliance Airlines (📞1300 780 970; www.allianceairlines.com.au) Perth to Karratha.

Qantas (📞13 13 13; www.qantas.com.au)

Skywest (📞1300 660 088; www.skywest.com.au)

Virgin Australia (📞13 67 89; www.virginaustralia.com)

BUS

Greyhound (📞1300 473 946; www.greyhound.com.au) runs three times weekly between Broome and Perth along the coast.

Integrity (📞1800 226 339; www.integritycoachlines.com.au) runs weekly between Perth and Port Hedland via Newman on the inland Great Northern Hwy and twice weekly to Exmouth on the coastal route.

CORAL COAST

Coral Bay

POP 255

Beautifully situated just north of the Tropic of Capricorn, the tiny seaside village of Coral Bay is one of the easiest locations to access the exquisite Ningaloo Marine Park. Consisting of only one street and a sweeping white-sand beach, the town is small enough to enjoy on foot, making it popular with families. It's also a great base for outer-reef activities like scuba diving, fishing and whale watching (June to November), and tourists flock here in the winter months to swim with whale sharks (April to July) and manta rays.

Development is strictly limited, so expect higher prices for food and accommodation. Exmouth, 118km away, has more options. There are ATMs at the shopping centre and the Peoples Park grocer, and internet access at some of the tour outlets and Fins Cafe. The town is chockers from April to October.

◉ Sights & Activities

Keep to the southern end of **Bills Bay** when swimming; the northern end (Skeleton Bay) is a breeding ground for reef sharks. There's good snorkelling in the bay, and it's even better at **Purdy Point**; walk 500m south along the coast until you see the 8km/h marker, then drift with the current back to the bay. You can hire snorkel gear anywhere in town.

Fish feeding occurs on the beach at 3.30pm every day and sunsets are sublime from the lookout above the beach car park.

Ningaloo Kayak Adventures KAYAKING
(📞08-9948 5034; www.ningalookayakadventures.com; 2/3hr tours $50/70) Various length kayak tours with snorkelling are available from the main beach. You can also hire a glass-bottom canoe ($25 per hour), wetsuit and snorkelling gear ($15 per day).

Ningaloo Reef Dive DIVING
(📞08-9942 5824; www.ningalooreefdive.com) This PADI and eco-certified dive crew offers snorkelling with whale sharks ($390, late March to July) and manta rays ($150, all year), half-day reef dives ($170) and a full range of dive courses (from $380).

Ningaloo Marine Interactions SNORKELLING
(📞08-9948 5190; www.mantaraycoralbay.com.au; 2hr/half-/full day $75/170/210; ☀️Jun-Oct, manta rays all year) 🖉 Informative and sustainably run tours to the outer reef include whale watching, manta-ray interaction and wildlife spotting with snorkelling.

🧭 Tours

Popular tours from Coral Bay include swimming with whale sharks, spotting marine life (whales, dolphins, dugongs, turtles and manta rays), coral viewing from glass-bottom boats, and quad-bike trips. Tour operators have offices in the shopping centre and caravan parks; the following is only a small selection.

Coral Bay Ecotours BOAT TOUR
(📞08-9942 5885; www.coralbayecotours.com.au; 1/2/3hr $39/54/75, all day $140) 🖉 Eco-certified and carbon-neutral tours include glass-bottom boat cruises with snorkelling, and all-day wildlife-spotting trips with manta-ray interaction. Scenic flights are also available.

Coral Coast Tours DRIVING TOUR
(📞0427 180 568; www.coralcoasttours.com.au; half-day 4WD adult/child $135/78, snorkelling 2/3hr $55/75) Explore the wildlife along the rugged 4WD coastal tracks of Warroora Station, or try your hand at Blo Karting (sand yachting) on nearby salt lakes ($50 per hour). It also runs reef tours and offers airport transfers ($80), continuing on to Exmouth ($100).

STATION STAYS

If you're sick of cramped caravan parks and want to escape the hordes, or just stay somewhere a little more relaxed and off the beaten track, consider a station stay. Scattered around the Coral Coast are a number of sheep and cattle stations (some former, some still working) that offer varying styles of accommodation – it may be an exquisite slice of empty coast or a dusty spot in the home paddock, a basic room in the shearers' quarters or a fully self-contained, air-conditioned cottage.

Don't expect top-notch facilities; in fact, a lot of sites don't have any at all. Power and water are at a premium, so the more self-sufficient you are, the more you will enjoy your stay – remember, you're getting away from it all. What you will find is loads of wildlife, stars you've never seen before, oodles of space, some fair-dinkum outback and an insight into station life.

Some stations offer wilderness camping away from the main homestead (usually by the coast) and you'll need a 4WD for access and a chemical toilet. These places tend to cater for fisher-types with boats and grey nomads who stay by the week.

Some stations only offer accommodation during the peak season (April to October).

➤ **Warroora** (🖉 08-9942 5920; www.warroora.com; Minilya Exmouth Rd; camping per day/week $7.50/37.50, r per person $30, cottages $130) Offers wilderness camp sites along the coast and cheap rooms in the shearers' quarters as well as a self-contained cottage and homestead. It's 47km north of Minilya.

➤ **Bullara** (🖉 08-9942 5938; www.bullara-station.com.au; Burkett Rd; camping $12, tw/d/cottages $100/130/220; ☺ Apr-Oct) Has four queen and two twin-share rooms in renovated shearers' quarters, unpowered camping and a communal kitchen (BYO food). Also runs half-day station tours ($110). It's 70km north of Coral Bay.

➤ **Giralia** (🖉 08-9942 5937; www.giraliastation.com.au; Burkett Rd; camping per person $10, budget s/d $60/70, 4-person cottages $160, homestead r $260; ❄ ✉) Well set up for travellers, with a bush-camping area (some powered sites) and kitchen, budget rooms with shared bathroom, a family cottage and air-conditioned homestead rooms with breakfast and dinner included. The coast is 40 minutes away by 4WD. Meals and liquor are available. It's 110km north of Coral Bay.

Sail Ningaloo SAILING
(🖉 1800 197 194; www.sailningaloo.com.au; 3-day tours from $1700; ☺ Mar-Dec) The fully cashed-up can select from a number of multi-day reef-sailing cruises aboard the catamaran *Shore Thing*.

🛏 Sleeping & Eating

Avoid school holidays and book well ahead for peak season (April to October). Holiday houses can be rented online from www.coralbay.org, starting from $950 per week.

The shopping-centre **bakery** (Robinson St; ☺ 6.30am-5.30pm) is the best option for early risers and vegetarians with its muesli and salad rolls. Seriously consider self-catering, as eating out is expensive.

Peoples Park Caravan Village CARAVAN PARK $
(🖉 08-9942 5933; www.peoplesparkcoralbay.com; sites unpowered $36, powered $42-52, 1-/2-bedroom cabins $240/260, hilltop villas $285; ❄) This excellent park offers grassy, shaded sites

and a variety of fully self-contained cabins. Friendly staff keep the modern amenities and spacious camp kitchen spotless, and it's the only place with freshwater showers. The hilltop villas have superb views, there are plenty of BBQs scattered around, and internet access is available at nearby Fins Cafe.

Ningaloo Club HOSTEL $
(🖉 08-9948 5100; www.ningalooclub.com; Robinson St; dm $27-30, d with/without bathroom $120/95; ❄ @ ✉) Popular with the party crowd, this friendly, vibey hostel is a great place to meet people, and boasts a central pool, a well-equipped kitchen and a bar featuring live music. The rooms could be cleaner, and forget about sleeping before the bar closes. It also sells bus tickets (coach stop outside) and discounted tours.

Ningaloo Reef Resort RESORT $$$
(🖉 1800 795 522; www.ningalooreefresort.com.au; d/apt from $216/276, penthouses $385; ❄ @ 🛜 ✉) Among palms just above the

beach, this resort has a combination of well-appointed motel-style rooms and larger apartments, with garden or ocean views. It's also the local pub, with happy hours (Tuesday and Friday) and live-music Thursday attracting a crowd. Shades restaurant (mains $13 to $45) delivers predictable fare.

Fins Cafe   INTERNATIONAL $$
(☑08-9942 5900; Peoples Park; dinner mains $28-36; ☺breakfast, lunch & dinner; @) Book ahead for dinner at this intimate, outdoor BYO cafe with its ever-changing blackboard menu showcasing local seafood, Asian-style curries and Mediterranean–Oz fusion dishes.

Reef Cafe   ITALIAN $$
(☑08-9942 5882; mains $21-36; ☺6pm-late) While this licensed family-friendly bistro features seafood and steaks, most people come for its pizzas and gelato.

❶ Getting There & Away

Coral Bay is 1144km north of Perth and 152km south of Exmouth, off the Minilya–Exmouth Rd.

Both Qantas and Skywest fly into Exmouth's Learmonth Airport, 118km to the north; most Coral Bay resorts can arrange a private shuttle on request.

Integrity coaches run twice weekly to Perth ($176, 15 hours) and Exmouth ($45, 90 minutes). Greyhound buses run between Perth ($198, 16 hours) and Broome ($265, 19 hours) three times weekly.

Exmouth

POP 2500

Exmouth began life during WWII as a US submarine base, though the town didn't flourish until the 1960s with the establishment of the Very Low Frequency (VLF) communications facility at the North West Cape. Fishing (especially prawns) and oil and gas exploration commenced, and both industries are still thriving – the flares of gas platforms are visible from Vlamingh Head at night.

With the protection of pristine Ningaloo Reef, tourism now accounts for the bulk of all visitors, many coming to see the magnificent and enigmatic whale sharks (April to July). Peak season (April to October) sees this laid-back town stretched to epic proportions, but don't be put off, as it's still the perfect base to explore nearby Ningaloo Marine and Cape Range National Parks. Alternatively, just relax, wash away the dust after a long road trip and enjoy the local wildlife;

emus walking down the street, 'roos lounging in the shade, lizards ambling across the highway and corellas, galahs and ringnecks screeching and swooping through the trees.

Exmouth is at the western end of the Pilbara's 'cyclone alley', and in 1999 Cyclone Vance caused widespread devastation, reaching wind speeds of 267km/h. Once hailed as 'New Broome' (the marina development that stalled during the 2009 global financial crisis is showing signs of life again), with Rio Tinto's successful application to billet its FIFO workers in local accommodation, hopefully the town won't become 'New Karratha'.

◉ Sights & Activities

Exmouth is flat, hot and sprawling, with most of the attractions outside town and no public transport. **Town Beach** is an easy 1km walk east, though swimmers and anglers usually head to **Bundegi Beach**, 14km north in the shadow of the VLF antenna array. A set of cycle paths ring the town and continue out to the Harold E Holt Naval Base (HEH), where you can follow the road on to Bundegi; watch out for dingos! Bikes can be hired from **Exmouth Minigolf** (☑08-9949 4644; www.exmouthminigolf.com.au; Murat Rd; bike/kayak/snorkel gear per day $20/50/10; ☺9am-5pm).

The **sewerage works** (Willersdorf Rd) and **golf course** (Willersdorf Rd) are good places for birdwatching, while turtle volunteering (see boxed text, p190) is popular from November to January. From April to October a Sunday crafts market runs in the mall area.

Snorkellers and divers head to Ningaloo Marine Park or the Muiron Islands. Try to find the informative Department for Environment and Conservation (DEC) book *Dive and Snorkel Sites in Western Australia*. Several dive shops in town offer PADI courses.

Surfers flock to Dunes (p192) on the western cape during winter, while in the summer months windsurfing and kiteboarding are popular.

Ningaloo Kite & Board   KITEBOARDING
(☑08-9949 2770; www.ningalooexcape.com.au; 16 Nimitz St; 2hr lessons $200; ☺10am-1pm Mon-Sat) Talk to the experts about the best windsurfing and kiteboarding locations, book a lesson or even buy a secondhand kite.

Capricorn Kayak Tours   KAYAKING
(☑0427 485 123; www.capricornseakayaking.com.au; half-/1-/2-/5-day $89/169/665/1650) Capri-

Exmouth

Map labels:

Bundegi Beach (14km); Cape Range National Park (38km)

Willersdorf Rd

Murdoch Park Golf Course

Sewerage Works

Exmouth Gulf

Truscott Cres

Krait St, Lyon St, Lockwood St, Fyfe St, Payne St, Maidstone Cres, Kennedy St, Carpenter St, Christie St, Lefroy St, Nimitz St, Huston St, Polias St, Carter Rd, Reid St, Pellew St, Maley St, Murat Rd

Novotel Ningaloo Resort (600m)

Warne St

Airport (35km); Coral Bay (150km)

Welch St

Exmouth

◉ Sights
1 Town Beach C3

◉ Activities, Courses & Tours
2 Exmouth Minigolt B2
3 Ningaloo Kite & Board B2

🛏 Sleeping
4 Exmouth Cape Holiday Park B2
Exmouth Holiday Accommodation/Ray White .... (see 11)
5 Exmouth Ningaloo Caravan & Holiday Resort B2
6 Ningaloo Lodge B2
7 Potshot Hotel Resort B1

✗ Eating
8 Ningaloo Health A1
Pinocchio .... (see 5)
Whalers Restaurant .... (see 8)

🍸 Drinking & Nightlife
9 Grace's Tavern B2
10 Potshot Hotel B1

🛍 Shopping
11 Exmouth Shopping Centre A1

ℹ Information
12 Department of Environment & Conservation B2
13 Visitor Centre B2

ℹ Transport
14 Integrity Coach Stop B2

corn offers single- and multi-day kayaking and snorkelling tours along the lagoons of Ningaloo Reef.

Ningaloo Whaleshark-N-Dive DIVING
(☎1800 224 060; www.ningaloowhalesharkndive.com.au) Offers daily dives to Lighthouse Bay ($165) and the Muiron Islands ($200) as well as longer liveaboard tours to the Mui-

ron and Montebello Islands. Currently holds the exclusive licence to Navy Pier ($145). Dive courses also available from introductory ($215) to full PADI ($600).

☞ Tours

Adventure tours from Exmouth include swimming with whale sharks, wildlife spotting, diving, sea kayaking, fishing and surf charters, and coral viewing from glass-bottom boats. Some companies only operate during peak season. Check conditions carefully regarding 'no sighting' policies and cancellations.

Outside the whale-shark season, tours focus on manta rays. You need to be a capable snorkeller to get the most out of these experiences. It's normally 30% cheaper if you don't swim. Also be wary of snorkelling on what may essentially be a dive tour – the action may be too deep. Most ocean tours usually depart from Tantabiddi on the western Cape and include free transfers from Exmouth. Here is just a selection of operators – see the visitor centre for a full list.

Kings Ningaloo Reef Tours WILDLIFE
(☑ 08-9949 1764; www.kingsningalooreeftours.com.au; snorkeller/observer $385/285) Longtime player Kings still gets rave reviews for its whale-shark tours. It's renowned for stay-ing out longer than everyone else, and has a 'next available tour' no-sighting policy.

Ningaloo Ecology Cruises CRUISE
(☑ 1800 554 062; www.ningalootreasures.com.au; 1/2½hr $40/60) Has one-hour glass-bottom boat trips (April to October), and longer 2½-hour trips (all year) including snorkelling.

WestTreks DRIVING TOUR
(☑ 08-9949 2659; www.westtreksafaritours.com.au; night/half-/full-day 4WD tours $90/$110/$199) Caves, canyons, a boat cruise and snorkelling are only part of these full-day 4WD tours that traverse the Cape Range to the west coast. Perfect for those without their own transport; shorter tours also available.

Montebello Island Safaris CRUISE
(☑ 0419 091 670; www.montebello.com.au; ☺ Apr-Oct) Has a permanent houseboat moored at the Montebello Islands where you can dive, snorkel, surf and fish to your heart's content on a six-night tour.

NINGA TURTLE GUIDES

Between November and March each year, volunteer turtle-monitoring programs run up and down the coast, providing an amazing experience for those with time to spare. You'll be working at strange hours during the hottest season in remote areas with little comfort, but seeing these magnificent creatures up close, knowing that you're actively taking part in their conservation, is incredibly satisfying. Applications usually open around August, but check individual program timelines.

Exmouth volunteers need to commit to a five-week period and be prepared to spend most of that time at a remote base. Days start at sunrise with five hours' work collecting data on turtle nesting, habitat and predation, then the rest of the day is free to enjoy the surroundings. Volunteers pay around $1300 (depending on funding), which covers all equipment, meals, transport from Exmouth and insurance. Accommodation is usually in tents or swags at a Department of Environment and Conservation (DEC) research station or remote beach. See the **Ningaloo Turtle Program** (NTP; www.ningalooturtles.org.au) website for more information.

If you enjoy interaction of the human kind, consider the NTP's Turtle Guide Program. You will need to complete at least the first module of the Exmouth TAFE formal training course, Turtle Tour Guiding, before commencing at the Jurabi Turtle Centre (p192) and this course gains credits towards a Certificate III in Tourism. The JCT plays an important role in minimising the disturbance to nesting turtles and hatchlings by educating tourists and supervising interaction during the breeding period.

Port Hedland volunteers can apply for **Pendoley Environmental's** (www.penv.com.au) tagging program, which works alongside the oil and gas industry at sites like Barrow Island. Typical placements are for 17 days with all expenses covered, there's a strict selection process and you'll be working mostly at night with minimal free time. The environmental group **Care for Hedland** (☑ 0439 941 431; www.careforhedland.org.au) also runs volunteer monitoring programs, and training sessions kick off in November.

Science graduates (any discipline) prepared to commit for six months can apply to Gnaraloo Station's **Turtle Conservation Program** (GTCP; www.gnaraloo.com), where all food, accommodation, transport and training are supplied, and volunteers work at the world's third-largest loggerhead rookery.

🛏 Sleeping

Accommodation is limited; book ahead, especially in peak season (April to October).

Exmouth Ningaloo

Caravan & Holiday Resort   CARAVAN PARK $
(☑08-9949 2377; www.exmouthresort.com; Murat Rd; unpowered/powered sites $38/48, dm/d $39/80, chalets $200; ❄️🛜🏊) Across from the visitor centre, this friendly, spacious park has grassy sites, self-contained chalets, four-bed dorms, an on-site restaurant and even a pet section. If you're tenting, this is your best bet.

Exmouth Cape Holiday Park   CARAVAN PARK $
(Blue Reef Backpackers; ☎1800 621 101; www.aspenparks.com.au; cnr Truscott Cres & Murat Rd; sites unpowered/powered/with bathroom $35/49/76, dm/d $32/100, cabin d $130-297; ❄️@🏊) The Cape offers van sites with their own en suites, as well as four-bed dorms, budget twins and a host of different cabin options. There's a good camp kitchen and an excellent pool. The few unpowered tent sites are rather cramped.

Ningaloo Lodge   GUESTHOUSE $$
(☎1800 880 949; www.ningaloolodge.com.au; Lefroy St; d $140; ❄️🛜🏊) These clean, tastefully appointed motel rooms are one of the better deals, with a modern communal kitchen, barbecue, shady pool and free wi-fi.

Potshot Hotel Resort   RESORT $$
(☑08-9949 1200; www.potshotresort.com; Murat Rd; dm/d $30/70, motel d $120, studios $225, apt from $245; ❄️@🛜🏊) A town-within-a-town, this bustling resort has seven-bed dorms, standard motel rooms, luxury Osprey apartments and several bars, catering for all comers. The backpacker rooms can be noisy.

Exmouth Holiday

Accommodation/Ray White   RENTAL HOUSES $$
(☑08-9949 1144; www.exmouthholidays.com.au; 3 Kennedy St; per week from $600; ❄️) Ray White has a wide range of weekly rentals, from fibro shacks to double-storey mansions.

Novotel Ningaloo Resort   RESORT $$$
(☑08-9949 0000; www.novotelningaloo.com.au; Madaffari Dr; d/apt from $275/355; ❄️🛜🏊) In the marina, the Novotel Ningaloo is at the pointy end of sophistication (and expense) in Exmouth. The tastefully designed rooms are spacious and well equipped and all include balconies.

🍴 Eating & Drinking

There's a supermarket, a bakery and several takeaways at **Exmouth Shopping Centre** (Maidstone Cres).

Grace's Tavern (☑08-9949 1000; Murat Rd; ☺dinner) and **Potshot Hotel** (☑08-9949 1200; Murat Rd; ☺dinner) are your drinking options and both serve decent pub meals.

Ningaloo Health   CAFE $
(☑08-9949 1400; www.ningaloohealth.com.au; 3A Kennedy St; mains $7-19; ☺7.30am-4pm) Breakfasts start with a bang at this tiny cafe – try the chilli eggs on blue vein toast with jalapenos, or a bowl of Vietnamese *pho* (beef-and-rice-noodle soup). The less brave can dive into a berry-pancake stack, bircher muesli or a detox juice. NH also offers light lunches, salads, smoothies, takeaway picnic hampers (great for a day trip to Cape Range National Park) and the best coffee around.

★**Whalers Restaurant**   SEAFOOD $$
(☑08-9949 2416; www.whalersrestaurant.com.au; 5 Kennedy St; mains lunch $8-24, dinner $29-40; ☺9am-2pm & 6pm-late) Delicious Creole-influenced seafood is the star attraction at this Exmouth institution. Sit back on the leafy verandah and share a seafood tasting plate with soft-shell crab and local prawns, or try the signature New Orleans gumbo. Non-fishheads can hook into char-grilled kangaroo or Mexican fajitas. The lunch menu is more bistro-like.

Pinocchio   ITALIAN $$
(☑08-9949 2577; Murat Rd; mains $16-35; ☺6-9pm) Located inside the Exmouth Ningaloo Caravan Park, this licensed alfresco *ristorante* is popular with locals and travellers alike. Families are well catered for, there's a pleasant deck by the pool, and the tasty pasta and pizza servings are huge.

Mantaray's Bar & Brasserie   INTERNATIONAL $$$
(☑08-9949 0000; www.novotelningaloo.com.au; Madaffari Dr; mains lunch $16-28, dinner $36-44; ☺lunch & dinner; 🛜) Novotel Ningaloo's in-house restaurant is the perfect place for a long, lazy waterside lunch with local, quality ingredients, affordable dishes and the best view in town.

🔒 Shopping

Exmouth Shopping Centre   SHOPPING CENTRE
(Maidstone Cres) The centre includes several dive shops, a gift shop and a surf and camping store.

❶ Information

Internet access is available at the **library** (🖵 08-9949 1462; 22 Maidstone Cres; ⊙ 8.30am-4pm Mon-Thu, to noon Sat; @), **Exmouth Diner** (Maidstone Cr; free with $5 minimum purchase; ⊙ 4.30-8.30pm; 🛜), Potshot (p191) and the dive shops.

Department of Environment & Conservation (DEC; 🖵 08-9947 8000; www.dec.wa.gov.au; 20 Nimitz St; ⊙ 8am-5pm Mon-Fri) Supplies maps, brochures and permits for Ningaloo, Cape Range and Muiron Islands, including excellent wildlife guides. Can advise on turtle volunteering.

Cape Conservation Group (www.ccg.org.au) Website listing environmental projects around the cape.

Visitor Centre (🖵 08-9949 1176; www.exmouthwa.com.au; Murat Rd; ⊙ 9am-5pm Mon-Sat, to 1pm Sun) Tour bookings, bus tickets, accommodation service and parks information.

❶ Getting There & Away

Exmouth's Learmonth Airport is 37km south of town. Both Qantas and Skywest fly to Perth daily. Skywest also flies direct to Broome on Sunday (April to October). The **airport shuttle** (🖵 08-9949 4623; $25) meets all flights.

Integrity coaches run to Perth twice weekly ($200, 17 hours) via Coral Bay ($45, 90 minutes). Greyhound no longer visits Exmouth, so if you're heading north it's easiest to depart from Coral Bay via the charter shuttle (p186; $100, two hours). Buses leave from the visitors centre.

Red Earth Safaris (🖵 1800 501 968; www.redearthsafaris.com.au) offers a weekly Perth express departing from Exmouth 7am Sunday (one way $200, 30 hours) with an overnight stop.

❶ Getting Around

Allens (🖵 08-9949 2403; rear 24 Nimitz St) Cars start from $60 per day with 150 free kilometres; Budget, Avis and Europcar also have agents.

Exmouth Boat & Kayak Hire (🖵 0438 230 269; www.exmouthboathire.com; kayaks per day $50) Tinnies (small dinghies) or something larger (including a skipper!) can be hired from $150 per day.

Exmouth Camper Hire (🖵 08-9949 4050; www.exmouthcamperhire.com.au; 16 Nimitz St; 4 days from $600) Camper vans with everything you need to spend time in Cape Range National Park, including solar panels.

Scooters2go (🖵 08-9949 4488; www.scooters2go.com.au; cnr Murat Rd & Pellew St; per day/week $80/$175) You only need a car licence for these 50cc scooters, which are much cheaper by the week.

Around Exmouth

Heading north past HEH, the **VLF antenna array** dominates the cape's northern tip, and was once the tallest structure in the southern hemisphere.

Keep straight at the Yardie Creek turn-off for **Bundegi Beach**, 14km north of Exmouth, where clear, sheltered waters mean pleasant swimming, snorkelling and fishing.

There's great diving at nearby **Bundegi Reef**, but even better slightly north under the **Navy Pier** at Point Murat (named for Napoleon's brother-in-law by French explorers). Rated one of the world's best shore dives, there's a bewildering array of marine life including nudibranchs, scorpion fish, moray eels and reef sharks. As it's on defence territory, you'll need to join a tour; the exclusive licence rotates regularly among Exmouth dive shops.

Turn back onto Yardie Creek Rd and head west for the best beaches. Take the first right, signposted **'Mildura Wreck'**, to the end to see the 1907 cattle ship that ran aground on the reef. Along the way are turn-offs leading to ruggedly beautiful **Surfers Beach** (Dunes).

Ideally located just south of Dunes, **Ningaloo Lighthouse Caravan Park** (🖵 08-9949 1478; www.ningaloolighthouse.com; Yardie Creek Rd; unpowered/powered sites $29/35, cabins $95, bungalows $125, lighthouse/lookout chalets $150/245; ❄ ⛱) has cliff-top chalets with fantastic views and shady sites for mere mortals.

It's hard to miss the hilltop **Vlamingh Head Lighthouse** (1912), where spectacular views of the entire cape make it a great place for whale spotting and watching sunsets.

Nearby is the excellent **Jurabi Turtle Centre** (JTC; Yardie Creek Rd). Visit by day to read about the turtle life cycle, and obtain the DEC pamphlet *Marine Turtles in Ningaloo Marine Park*. Return at night to observe nesting turtles and hatchlings (November to March), remembering to keep the correct distance and never to shine a light or camera flash directly at any animal. Those people who have more time can volunteer to become a 'turtle tracker'. See the **Ningaloo Turtle Program** (NTP; www.ningalooturtles.org.au) website to obtain more information.

Fantastic beaches continue down the western side of the cape, such as clothing-optional **Mauritius Beach**, 21km from Exmouth, and the snorkelling favourites of

North West Cape

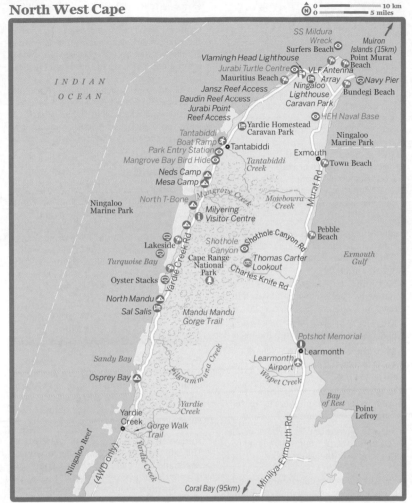

Lakeside (54km), **Turquoise Bay** (65km) and **Oyster Stacks** (69km).

The entrance to Cape Range National Park (p195) is at 40km and camp sites are allocated here (when open). At 53km you'll find the **Milyering visitor centre** (☑08-9949 2808; Yardie Creek Rd; ☉9am-3.45pm), which serves Ningaloo Marine Park and Cape Range National Park. You can buy tickets here for the Yardie Creek cruise and hire snorkelling gear ($10). Experienced 4WD-ers can check road conditions for the rough coastal track continuing south to Coral Bay.

Ningaloo Marine Park

Recently extended and World Heritage listed, the Ningaloo Marine Park now protects the full 300km length of the exquisite Ningaloo Reef, from Bundegi Reef on the eastern tip of the peninsula to Red Bluff on Quobba Station far to the south.

Ningaloo is Australia's largest fringing reef, and in places only 100m offshore. It's this accessibility, and the fact that it's home to a staggering array of **marine life**, that makes it so popular. Sharks, manta rays, humpback

ℹ CAPE RANGE & NINGALOO CAMP SITES

Try to check out the different camping areas a day before if possible, or use the **DEC website** (www.dec.wa.gov.au/campgrounds). Shade, size and shelter are more important than closeness to the beach. Neds Camp (18 sites) and Osprey Bay (20 sites) are the largest campgrounds, while North T-Bone (three sites) and North Mandu (five sites) are the smallest. Milyering visitor centre (p193) also has a poster showing the different beaches. During peak season there's normally a camp host residing at each site.

whales, turtles, dugongs and dolphins complement more than 500 species of fish.

There are excellent marine activities to enjoy year-round:

➡ **November to March** Turtles – three endangered species nestle and hatch in the dunes.

➡ **March** Coral spawning – an amazing event seven days after the full moon.

➡ **Mid-March to July** Whale sharks – the biggest fish on the planet arrive for the coral spawning.

➡ **May to November** Manta rays – present all year round; their numbers increase dramatically over winter and spring.

➡ **June to November** Humpback whales – breed in the warm tropics then head back south to feed in the Antarctic.

Over 220 species of hard **coral** have been recorded in Ningaloo, ranging from bulbous brain corals found on bommies, to delicate branching staghorns and the slow-growing massive coral. While less colourful than soft corals (normally found in deeper water on the outer reef), the hard corals have incredible formations. Spawning, where branches of hermaphroditic coral simultaneously eject eggs and sperm into the water, occurs after full and new moons between February and May, but the peak action is usually six to 10 days after the March full moon.

It's this spawning that attracts the park's biggest drawcard, the solitary speckled **whale shark** (*Rhiniodon typus*). Ningaloo is one of the few places in the world where these gentle giants arrive like clockwork each year to feed on plankton and small fish, making it a mecca for marine biologists and visitors alike. The largest fish in the world, the whale shark can weigh up to 21 tonnes, although most weigh between 13 and 15 tonnes, and reach up to 18m long. They can live for 70 years.

Upload your amazing whale-shark pics to **Ecocean** (www.whaleshark.org), which will identify and track your whale shark. To learn more about Ningaloo's denizens, grab a copy of the DEC's *The Marine Life of Ningaloo Marine Park & Coral Bay*.

🏃 Activities

Most travellers visit Ningaloo Marine Park to **snorkel**. Stop at Milyering visitor centre (p193) for maps and information on the best spots and conditions. Check its tide chart and know your limits, as the currents can be dangerous. The shop next to the park office sells and rents snorkelling equipment ($10 per day, $15 overnight). The following are the most popular snorkelling spots.

Lakeside   SNORKELLING
Walk 500m south along the beach from the car park, then snorkel out with the current before returning close to your original point.

Oyster Stacks   SNORKELLING
These spectacular bommies are just metres offshore, but you need a tide of at least 1.2m and sharp rocks make entry/exit difficult. If you tire, don't stand on the bommies; look for some sand.

Turquoise Bay   SNORKELLING
The Bay Snorkel Area is suitable for all skill levels and provides myriad fish and corals just off the beach to the right of the bay car park. Stronger swimmers will want to head to the Drift Snorkel Area: 300m south along the beach from the Drift car park, swim out for about 40m then float face down. The current will carry you over coral bommies and abundant sea life. Get out before the sandy point, then run back along the beach and start all over! Beware of strong currents and don't miss the exit point or you'll be carried out through the gap in the reef.

Lighthouse Bay   SCUBA DIVING
There's great scuba diving at Lighthouse Bay at sites like the Labyrinth, Blizzard Ridge and Mandu Wall. Check out the DEC book *Dive and Snorkel Sites in Western Australia* for other ideas.

Cape Range National Park

The jagged limestone peaks and gorges of rugged 510-sq-km **Cape Range National Park** (per car $11) offer relief from the otherwise flat, arid expanse of the North West Cape, and are rich in wildlife, including the rare black-flanked rock wallaby, five types of bat and over 200 species of bird. Spectacular deep canyons cut dramatically into the range, before emptying out onto the wind-blown coastal dunes and turquoise waters of Ningaloo Reef.

The main park access is via Yardie Creek Rd. Several areas in the east are accessible from unsealed roads off Minilya–Exmouth Rd, south of Exmouth. Milyering visitor centre (p193) has comprehensive natural and cultural displays, maps and publications.

◉ Sights & Activities

On the east coast, 23km south of Exmouth, the scenic and at times incredible **Charles Knife Rd** climbs dramatically above the canyon of the same name. The road follows the knife-edge ridge up through rickety corners and you'll need frequent stops to take make the most of the breathtaking views. A rough track continues to **Thomas Carter lookout**, where (in the cooler months) you can walk the 8km **Badjirrajirra loop trail** through spinifex and rocky gullies; be aware that there's no shade or water. Under no circumstances attempt this during summer.

Don't miss beautiful **Shothole Canyon** (turn-off 16km south of Exmouth), with its colourful walls, pretty picnic area and plenty of exploration options.

On the west coast, spot migratory birds at the **Mangrove Bay Bird Hide**, 8km from the entrance station. **Mandu Mandu Gorge** is a pleasant but dry walk (3km return) from a car park 20km south of the Milyering visitor centre.

Much nicer is the 2km return walk to **Yardie Creek Gorge** with its permanent water, sheer cliffs and excellent views. You can take the relaxing one-hour **Yardie Creek Cruise** (☑08-9949 2808; adult/child $25/12; ⊙11am daily) up the short, sheer gorge to spot rare black-flanked rock wallabies.

Only experienced 4WD-ers should contemplate the hazardous Yardie Creek crossing (low tide only!), and the sandy coastal track that continues south to Coral Bay.

🛌 Sleeping

A string of sandy, compact **camp sites** (per person $7) line the coast within the park. Facilities and shade are minimal, though most have toilets and some shelter from prevailing winds. To avoid long peak-season queues (from 7am!) at the park entrance station, consider pre-booking a site (at least 48 hours ahead) through the DEC. Only certain sites can be booked online; the rest are allocated upon arrival at the entrance station (not the visitor centre!) – ask for a generator-free site if you're after peace and quiet.

Yardie Homestead Caravan Park CARAVAN PARK $
(☑08-9949 1389; www.yardie.com.au; Yardie Creek Rd; unpowered/powered sites $26/30, d $75, cabins $110, chalets $180; ☀) Located just outside the park boundary, this former sheep station caters mainly for anglers, though travellers are also welcome and there are some nice grassy tent sites. There's a range of cabins (most require a security bond) plus a pool, shop and camp kitchen.

SURFING THE CAPE

The big swells arrive on the North West Cape between July and October. Dunes (p192) has a popular reef break accessible from the first car park. **Lighthouse Bombie**, a couple of kilometres south, is further out and a bit more challenging. Beginners should continue south down the cape to **Wobiri Access**, where the waves are gentler and surf classes are sometimes held.

Serious surfers should consider getting a few mates together for a boat charter to the outer reef and the **Muiron Islands**, where there are countless breaks and no one to ride them. You can camp on **South Muiron** with a permit from Exmouth DEC (p192). Your charter fee should include all meals, accommodation (onboard or camping) and fishing and snorkelling gear. Charters may be arranged from both Exmouth and Coral Bay, but check with the Exmouth visitor centre first, as the owner may have just sailed off for the Mentawais. You could try **Ningaloo Fusion Charters** (☑0438 993 284; www.ningaloofusioncharters.com).

Sal Salis   LUXURY WILDERNESS $$$
(☎1300 790 561; www.salsalis.com; wilderness tent s/d $1088/1450; ☺Mar-Dec) Want to watch that flaming crimson Indian Ocean sunset from between 500-threadcount pure cotton sheets? Pass the Chablis! For those who want their camp without the cramp, there's a minimum two-night stay, three gourmet meals a day, a free bar (!) and the same things to do as the couple over the dune in the pop-up camper.

THE PILBARA

Dampier to Roebourne

Most travellers skip this mining-services section of the coast as there's not much to see, unless you like huge industrial facilities. Accommodation is ludicrously overpriced and almost impossible to find thanks to the resources boom and the flood of FIFO (fly-in, fly-out) workers. House prices and rents are among the highest in the country, and huge suburbs of donga (small, transportable buildings) are springing up on town outskirts to handle the overflow. However, the area has good transport, well-stocked supermarkets and useful repair shops.

⚒ Festivals

Red Earth Arts Festival   ARTS
(www.reaf.com.au; ☺Sep) An annual celebration of music, theatre and visual arts spread across the towns of the Pilbara coast.

Dampier

Dampier is the region's main port. Spread around King Bay, it overlooks the 42 pristine islands of the **Dampier Archipelago**, and supports a wealth of marine life in its coral waters, but heavy industry has blighted Dampier's shores. The nearby **Burrup Peninsula** contains possibly the greatest number of rock-art petroglyphs on the planet but is under threat from continued industrial expansion (see www.burrup.org.au). The most accessible are at Deep Gorge near Hearson Cove, where you can also view the Staircase to the Moon (see boxed text, p210); you'll need a 4WD for the rest of the peninsula.

🛏 Sleeping

Dampier Transit Caravan Park   CARAVAN PARK $
(☎08-9183 1109; The Esplanade; unpowered/powered sites $18/22) Has a handful of grassy sites overlooking the water.

Karratha

Most travellers bank, restock, repair stuff and get out of town before their wallet ignites.

From behind the visitor centre, the **Jaburara Heritage Trail** (3.5km one way) takes visitors through significant traditional sites and details the displacement and eventual extinction of the Jaburara people. Bring plenty of water and start early.

🛏 Sleeping & Eating

Accommodation prospects are dire in Karratha; try to stay at beautiful Point Samson instead. Otherwise, search online for last-minute deals. Due to FIFO, weekends are usually cheaper than midweek.

The shopping centre has most things you'll need, including ATMs, takeaway food and supermarkets. The JavaVan coffee, in the visitor centre car park, is the best in town.

Pilbara Holiday Park   CARAVAN PARK $
(☎08-9185 1855; www.aspenparks.com.au; Rosemary Rd; powered sites $40, motel/studio d $229/220; ❄@≋) Neat and well run with good facilities.

All Seasons Karratha   HOTEL $$$
(☎08-9185 1155; www.accorhotels.com.au; Searipple Rd; d from $309; ❄@☞≋) This hotel has pleasant rooms with data ports (15 minutes free), several bars, a pool and an outdoor bistro.

Karratha Sushi Bar   JAPANESE $
(☎08-9183 8789; Balmoral Rd; ☺10am-9pm) Sick of pub grub? Try the excellent sushi.

ℹ Information

Karratha Visitor Centre (☎08-9144 4600; www.pilbaracoast.com; Karratha Rd; ☺9am-5pm Mon-Fri, 10am-1pm Sat & Sun, shorter hr Nov-Apr; @) Has good local info, supplies Hamersley Iron (HI) road permits, books tours (including to mining infrastructure) and may be able to find you a room.

ℹ Getting There & Away

Karratha is exceptionally well connected. Virgin, Qantas and Alliance all fly daily to Perth, while Qantas also offers weekly direct flights to most

MT AUGUSTUS (BURRINGURRAH) NATIONAL PARK

In Wajarri country, the huge monocline of **Mt Augustus** (Burringurrah; 1105m), twice as large as Uluru and a good deal more remote, rises 717m above the surrounding plains. There are several walking trails and Aboriginal rock-art sites to explore, including the superb summit trail (12km return, six hours). In a 2WD it's a rough, unsealed 450km from Carnarvon via Gascoyne Junction or 350km from Meekatharra. With a 4WD there are at least three other routes including a handy back door to Karijini via Dooley Downs and Tom Price. All of these routes see little traffic, so be prepared for the worst. There's no camping in the park, though you can stay at nearby dusty **Mt Augustus Tourist Park** (☑08-9943 0527; www.mtaugustustouristpark.com; unpowered/powered sites $22/33, donga d $88, units $176; ❄). Worth a look 60km to the west is the historic **Cobra Bangemail Inn** (☑08-9943 9565; sites per person $15, d $160). If you get to Gascoyne Junction and decide to give up, nearby **Bidgemia Station** (☑08-9943 0501; caunt@harboursat.com.au; Gascoyne Junction; sites per person $15, shearers quarters $65) offers shearers quarters and shady camping.

other capitals. Airnorth flies to Broome (with a Darwin connection) and Port Hedland weekly.

Greyhound coaches run to Perth ($286, 22 hours), Port Hedland ($61, three hours) and Broome ($168, 11 hours) three times weekly.

Roebourne

Roebourne, 40km east of Karratha, is the oldest (1866) Pilbara town still functioning, and sits on Ngaluma country. It's home to a large Aboriginal community; Yindjibarndi is the dominant language group. There are some beautiful old buildings, including the old gaol, which houses the **visitor centre** (☑08-9182 1060; www.pilbaracoast.com/towns/roebourne-visitor-centre; Queen St; ◷9am-4pm Mon-Fri, to 3pm Sat & Sun, shorter hr Nov-Apr) and museum. Don't miss the mineral display in the courtyard.

Roebourne has a thriving indigenous art scene, and you'll pass the odd gallery on the highway. See www.roebourneart.com.au for more details.

Cossack

The scenic ghost town of Cossack, at the mouth of the Harding River, was previously the district's main port but was usurped by Point Samson and then eventually abandoned. Many of the historic bluestone buildings date from the late 1800s; there's a 6km **Heritage Trail** around the town that links all the major sites (pick up the brochure from Roebourne visitor centre). Attractions include the self-guided **Social History Museum** (adult/child $2/1; ◷9am-4pm), and the pioneer **cemetery** with a tiny Japanese section dating from Cossack's pearling days. Past the cemetery, **Reader Head Lookout**

has great views of the river mouth and the Staircase to the Moon (see boxed text, p210).

🛏 Sleeping

Cossack Budget Accommodation   GUESTHOUSE **$$**
(☑08-9182 1190; www.roebourne.wa.gov.au/cossack.aspx; d with/without air-con $110/90; ❄) There are five basic rooms in this atmospheric old police barracks. BYO food.

Point Samson

Point Samson is a small, industrial-free seaside village, home to great seafood and clean beaches, making it the nicest place to stay in the area. There's good **snorkelling** off Point Samson, and the picturesque curved beach of Honeymoon Cove.

🛏 Sleeping & Eating

Samson Beach Caravan Park   CARAVAN PARK **$**
(☑08-9187 1414; Samson Rd; powered sites $39) A tiny park in lovely, leafy surrounds, close to the water and tavern. Bookings are essential in school holidays.

The Cove   CARAVAN PARK **$**
(☑08-9187 0199; www.thecovecaravanpark.com.au; Macleod St; sites $49.50, 1-/2-bedroom units $240/310) It's a bit 'van city', but the modern, clean facilities complement a great location an easy walk to all attractions.

Samson Beach Chalets   COTTAGES **$$$**
(☑08-9187 0202; www.samsonbeach.com.au; Samson Rd; chalets $250-600; ❄🛜🏊) Offers beautifully appointed self-contained chalets (various sizes) just a short walk from the beach. There's a shady pool, free wi-fi and in-house movies.

Samson Beach Bistro SEAFOOD $$
(☑08-9187 1435; mains $11-44; ☺11am-8.30pm daily, closed 2-5pm Mon-Fri) Serves up great seafood on a shady deck overlooking the ocean. Underneath the pub.

Millstream-Chichester National Park

Among the arid, spinifex-covered plateaus and basalt ranges between Karijini and the coast, the tranquil Millstream waterholes of the Fortescue River form cool, lush oases. Lovely **Crossing Pool** (sites per person $7; ☒), with palms, pelicans and gas barbecues, makes an idyllic camp site, though some may prefer the larger **Milliyanha Campground** (sites per person $7), with its camp kitchen and nearby visitor centre. **Murlamunyjunha Trail** (7km, two hours return) links both areas and features interpretive plaques by the traditional Yindjibarndi owners.

Once the station homestead, the unmanned **visitor centre** (☑08-9184 5144; ☺8am-4pm) houses historical, ecological and cultural displays; as a lifeline for flora and fauna during dry spells, the park is one of the most important indigenous sites in WA. The nearby lily- and palm-fringed **Jirndar-wurrunha Pool** is especially significant and swimming is not permitted.

You can swim at **Deep Reach Pool** (Nhangganggunha), believed to be the resting place of the Warlu (the creation serpent) and the shady tables and barbecues are perfect for a lazy picnic.

In the park's north are the stunning breakaways and eroded mesas of the **Chichester Range**. Don't miss the amazing panorama from the top of Mt Herbert (the viewpoint is a 10-minute walk from the car park) and on the road to Roebourne. You can continue walking to McKenzie Spring (4.5km, one hour return). Lower down the range, **Python Pool** is worth a look, though check for algal bloom before diving in; the pool is linked to Mt Herbert by the Chichester Range Camel Trail (16km, six hours return).

Karijini National Park

Arguably one of WA's most magnificent destinations, **Karijini National Park** (per car $11) reveals itself slowly. Ragged ranges, upthrust and twisted by nature, glow in the setting sun. Wedge-tailed eagles soar above grey-green spinifex and goannas shelter under stunted mulga. Kangaroos and wildflowers dot the plains, criss-crossed by deep, dark chasms emitting the enticing sound of distant water.

While the narrow, breathtaking gorges, with their hidden, sculptured pools are Karijini's biggest drawcard, the park is also home to a wide variety of fauna and flora, with an estimated 800 plant species, including some 50 varieties of wattle (acacia). Dragon lizards scurry over stones, rock wallabies cling to sheer cliffs, and endangered olive pythons lurk on the far side of pools. The park also contains the state's three highest peaks: Mt Meharry, Mt Bruce and Mt Frederick.

Banyjima Dr, the park's main thoroughfare, connects with Karijini Dr at two entrance stations. The eastern access is sealed to the visitor centre and Dales Gorge, while the rest of the park is unsealed. Take extra care driving as tourist rollovers are common. Avoid driving at night.

Choose walks wisely, dress appropriately and never enter a restricted area without a

❶ TOM PRICE & NEWMAN

Bookending Karijini National Park are the neat, company-built mining towns of Tom Price and Newman. Newman, to the east on the Great Northern Hwy, is the larger of the two, with better transport and accommodation options, although it's a lot further from Karijini. Both have good (ie air-con) supermarkets, fuel and excellent visitor centres, which can book you on mine tours if huge holes are your thing. The local libraries have internet access, and Newman's caravan parks are OK for a tent.

Newman Visitor Centre (☑08-9175 2888; www.newman-wa.org; Fortescue Ave; ☺8am-5pm, closed Sun Jan) Ask for its mud-map of local sights.

Tom Price Visitor Centre (☑08-9188 1112; www.tompricewa.com.au; Central Rd; ☺8.30am-5pm Mon-Fri, to 12.30pm Sat & Sun, shorter hr Nov-Apr) Can supply HI road permits and also books tours.

Karijini National Park

Unsealed roads can vary from excellent to impassable, depending on many factors

certified guide. Avoid the gorges during and after rain, as flash flooding does occur.

◉ Sights & Activities

Scenic **Dales Gorge** and its campground are 19km from the eastern entrance. A short, sharp descent leads to **Fortescue Falls**, behind which a leafy stroll upstream reveals the beautiful **Fern Pool**; head downstream from Fortescue Falls to picturesque **Circular Pool**; ascend to **Three Ways Lookout** and return along the cliff top.

Wide **Kalamina Gorge**, 24km from the visitor centre, has a small tranquil pool and falls with easy access suitable for families. Joffre Falls Rd leads to stunning **Knox Gorge**, passing the lookout over the spectacular **Joffre Falls**. Knox Gorge has several nice swimming holes, fringed by native figs, while in **Joffre Gorge** the frigid pools are perennially shaded.

Weano Rd junction is 32km from the visitor centre, and the **Eco Retreat** is nearby. The final 13km to the breathtaking **Oxers Lookout** can be rough, but it's worth it for the magnificent views of the junction of Red, Weano, Joffre and Hancock Gorges some 130m below.

A steep descent into **Hancock Gorge** (partly on ladders) will bring you first to the sunny **Amphitheatre**, then along the slippery **Spider Walk** to the sublime **Kermits Pool**. On the other side of the car park, a rough track winds down to the surreal **Handrail Pool** in the bowels of **Weano Gorge**. Swimming in these pools is a magical experience, but obey all signs and don't even think about entering a restricted area

Hamersley Gorge   SWIMMING
In Karijini's northwest corner, off Nanutarra-Wittenoom Rd, this makes a pleasant stopover if you're heading north towards the

JOURNEY TO THE CENTRE OF THE EARTH

The instructor sits down in the Water Slide, pushes off, then disappears. I hear a splash echo from below. He's done this a thousand times. I haven't done it once, and I'm next.

We're in the depths of Karijini's Knox Gorge. It's 35°C 'upstairs', but the water in the gorge is freezing, and while we're all in summer wetsuits, everybody's shivering. The day started early when our guides, Dan and Pete, kitted us out with wetsuits, gorge slippers, harnesses, helmets and inner tubes. A short, sunny stroll down from Knox Lookout brought our small group to a pool ringed by native figs, where we practised paddling. A quick 'jump test' off a 2m rock to check we won't 'choke' at the first obstacle (the one I'm staring at), and we were off into the restricted zone, with the gorge shrinking rapidly to a single body width.

I sit down, give the thumbs up, and push off and over a 4m drop into an enclosed plunge pool. An involuntary scream and I'm underwater. It's scary and exhilarating; I'd love to do it again, but once over the edge, there's no way back. Soon we're all down, and floating in the Styx-like water, and Dan sets up the 8m abseil into the next pool. Light falls in narrow shafts as sheer walls tower overhead.

Eventually we escape shady Knox into the sun at the bottom of Red Gorge and warm our bodies on a nearby 'beach'. Soon we're back on our inner tubes, this time for a sunny, relaxed paddle across long, tranquil pools. We pass the entrance to Weano Gorge, a 40m-high waterfall, on the way to our lunch spot at Junction Pool, 130m below Oxers Lookout. As we munch sandwiches, we watch a rock wallaby bounding around halfway up the vertical face, seemingly oblivious to the sheer drop only centimetres away.

Joffre Gorge leads off darkly to the south, but we head into Hancock Gorge, and a tight, steep, slippery climb beside a cascade leading through The Centre of the Earth to Garden Pool. Sublime and sobering, Regans Pool (named after a local SES volunteer who died during a rescue) is next and as Pete lays in the rope for the climb above the pool, the rest of us float silently, lost in our thoughts.

The climb is the last hurdle as we ascend steeply, doubly clipped into the anchor rope. A short traverse and we're out of the restricted area into Kermits Pool, and our final swim. The Spider Walk holds no challenge and soon we're through the sunny Amphitheatre and up the exit ladders to the car park. We've been out all day, and it's been one action-packed, adrenalin-charged adventure.

Steve Waters

coast. Idyllic swimming holes and a waterfall lie only minutes from the car park.

Punurrunha   WALKING
(Mt Bruce) Gorged out? Go and grab some altitude on WA's second-highest mountain (1235m), a superb ridge walk with fantastic views all the way to the summit. Start early, carry lots of water and allow five hours (the route's 9km return). The access road is off Karijini Dr opposite the western end of Banyjima Dr.

☞ Tours

To fully appreciate the magical quality of Karijini's gorges, consider an accredited adventure tour through the restricted areas.

★ West Oz
Active Adventure Tours   ADVENTURE TOUR
(☑ 0438 913 713; www.westozactive.com.au; Karijini Eco Retreat; 1-/3-/5-day tours $245/$745/1450;

⊘ Apr-Nov) Offers action-packed day trips through the restricted gorges and combines hiking, swimming, floating on inner tubes, climbing, sliding off waterfalls and abseiling. All equipment and lunch provided. Also offers longer all-inclusive multi-day tours with airport pickups and a Ningaloo option.

Lestok Tours   BUS TOUR
(☑ 08-9188 1112; www.lestoktours.com.au; tours $155) Offers full-day outings to Karijini from Tom Price.

🛏 Sleeping & Eating

Dales Gorge   CAMPGROUND
(sites adult/child $7/2) Though somewhat dusty, this large DEC campground offers shady, spacious sites with nearby toilets and picnic tables. Forget tent pegs – you'll be using rocks as anchors.

Karijini Eco Retreat RESORT
(☑ 08-9425 5591; www.karijiniecoretreat.com.
au; sites $35, tent d low/high season $177/315) ✐
This 100% indigenous-owned retreat is a
model for sustainable tourism, and the attached bar and restaurant has fantastic food
(mains $32 to $38), including the best barra
within light years. Campers get hot showers
and the same rocks as elsewhere in the park.
Peak-season astronomy tours are popular
($30, two hours). Things are cheaper in
summer when the retreat winds down and
temperatures soar.

ⓘ Information

Visitor Centre (☑ 08-9189 8121; Banyjima
Dr; ☻ 9am-4pm Apr-Oct, from 10am Nov-Mar)
Indigenous managed with excellent interpretive
displays highlighting Banyjima culture and park
wildlife, good maps and walks information, a
public phone and great air-con.

ⓘ Getting There & Away

There's no public transport. The closest airports
are at the mining towns of Paraburdoo (101km
southwest) and Newman (201km southeast).
Integrity coaches stop at Munjina (Auski) Roadhouse on Thursday (northbound) and Friday
(southbound). Munjina is the best place to wait
for a lift.

Port Hedland

POP 16,000

Port Hedland ain't the prettiest place. Con-
fronted by its railway yards, iron-ore stock-
piles, salt mountains, furnaces and massive
deepwater port, the average tourist might
instinctively floor the accelerator. Yet Hedland is not just another bland prefab Pilbara
town. With a heritage spanning over 115
years, it's been battered by cyclones, plun-
dered by pearlers and bombed by the Japanese – it's even hosted royalty.

Iron ore plays a huge part in the town's
fortunes, and Port Hedland is riding the
current resources boom. While this pushes
up prices and squeezes accommodation,
it's also sparked a renaissance. Old pubs
are being renovated, the art and cafe (real
coffee!) scenes are expanding, fine dining
is flourishing, cocktail and tapas bars are
sprouting and cycle paths are spreading
along the foreshore. Just don't mind the
red dust.

◉ Sights & Activities

Collect the excellent *Port Hedland Cultural
& Heritage Sites* brochure from the visitor
centre and take a self-guided tour around
the CBD, or hire a bicycle and meander
along the **Richardson Street Bike Path** to
a cold beer at the Yacht Club (p203).

Between November and February **flat-
back turtles** nest on nearby beaches. Check
at the visitor centre for volunteer options.

Goode St, near Pretty Pool, is handy to observe Port Hedland's Staircase to the Moon
(see boxed text, p210).

★ **Courthouse Gallery** GALLERY
(☑ 08-9173 1064; www.courthousegallery.com.au;
16 Edgar St; ☻ 9am-4pm Mon-Fri, to 2pm Sat & Sun)
More than a gallery, this leafy arts HQ is the
centre of all goodness in Hedland. Inside are
stunning local contemporary and indigenous exhibitions, while the shady surrounds
host sporadic craft markets. If something is
happening, these folks will know about it.

Marapikurrinya Park PARK
(end of Wedge St) The visitor centre publishes
shipping times for the ridiculously large
tankers passing by. After dark, the park's
Finucane Lookout provides a view into
BHP Billiton's smouldering Hot Briquetted
Iron plant on Finucane Island.

Pretty Pool FISHING, PICNIC SPOT
A popular fishing and picnicking spot (beware of stonefish), 7km east of the town
centre.

☞ Tours

BHP Billiton IRON-ORE PLANT
(adult/child $26/20; ☻ 9.30am Mon, Wed & Fri)
This popular iron-ore plant tour departs
from the visitor centre.

🛏 Sleeping

As in most mining towns, finding a room in
Hedland isn't easy or cheap, and weekends
are cheaper than midweek. If you haven't
booked well ahead, the visitor centre may be
able to help.

There are supermarkets, cafes and take-
aways at both the **Boulevard** (cnr Wilson &
McGregor Sts) and **South Hedland** (Throssell
Rd) shopping centres.

Cooke Point Caravan Park CARAVAN PARK $$
(☑ 08-9173 1271; www.aspenparks.com.au; cnr
Athol & Taylor Sts; powered sites $52, d without

CORAL COAST & THE PILBARA PORT HEDLAND

bathroom $150, unit d from $320; ✱ 🛜 🛎) You might be able to snag a dusty van or tent site here, but the other options are usually full. There's a nice view over the mangroves and the amenities are well maintained.

Esplanade Hotel RESORT **$$$**
(📞 08-9173 9700; www.theesplanadeporthedland. com.au; 2-4 Anderson St; d Fri-Sun from $295, Mon-Thu from 495; ✱ @ 🛜) Previously one of the roughest pubs in Port Hedland, the 'Nard'

OFF THE BEATEN TRACK

CHRISTMAS & COCOS (KEELING) ISLANDS

Christmas Island

A mountainous lump of bird poo in the Indian Ocean, not far from Java, Christmas Island (population 1600) was originally settled in 1888 by guano (phosphate) miners, which is still the main economic activity. Its people are a mix of Chinese, Malays and European-Australians, a blend reflected in the island's food, languages and customs. In recent years, CI has gained notoriety as the number-one destination for illegal asylum-seeker boats, causing an influx of government workers.

Don't be put off, as nature here is stunning and more than half the island remains protected as **CI National Park**. Tall rainforest covers the plateau, and a series of limestone cliffs and terraces attract rare and endemic sea birds. A network of trails runs through the park, and it's possible to camp at **Dolly Beach**. CI is famous for the spectacular annual migration in November-December of millions of **red land crabs** marching from the forest down to the coast to breed, covering everything in sight. On the edge of the **Java Trench**, diving is superb all year, and snorkelling on the fringing reefs is popular during the Dry. The Wet (December to March) brings a swell and decent surf.

While the island is keen to shake off the detention-centre vibe and encourage tourists, the reality is that most facilities are overtaken by government contractors. Hopefully the situation will change. CI is one hour behind Perth (WST; Western Standard Time).

Christmas Island Tourism (📞 08-9164 8382; www.christmas.net.au) Your best bet to sniff out a room, car, boat, airport transfer and whatever else is happening on CI.

Cocos (Keeling) Islands

Situated 2750km west of Perth are the Cocos (Keeling) Islands (population 650), a necklace of 27 idyllic, low-lying islands around a blue lagoon that inspired Charles Darwin's theory of coral-atoll formation. CKI was settled by John Clunies-Ross in 1826 and his family remained in control of the islands and their Malay workers until 1978, when CKI became part of Australia's Indian Ocean territories. Today about 550 Malays and 100 European-Australians live on **Home** and **West Islands**. It's a very low-key place in which to walk, snorkel, dive, fish, windsurf, birdwatch and relax. While most people come on a package, you can visit independently, and camping is allowed at Scout Park on West Island, and on **Direction** and **South Islands**. You will need to bring all your own gear. Bring lots of cash as there are no ATMs, though some places accept credit cards. CKI is 90 minutes behind WST.

Cocos-Keeling Islands (📞 08-9162 6790; www.cocos-tourism.cc) Great CKI website includes accommodation, tours and activities.

Cocos Dive (📞 08-9162 6515; www.cocosdive.com; per day from $210) Able to arrange single dives, week-long packages or SSI courses.

Getting There & Away

Virgin flies from Perth to both islands several times weekly. Prices start at around $500 for either island, and at $220 between the two. There's also a return charter flight on Saturday from Kuala Lumpur to CI, bookable through **Island Explorer Holidays** (📞 1300 884 855; www.islandexplorer.com.au). Twitchers could consider an all-inclusive tour of both islands from **Birding Tours Australia** (📞 02-4927 1808; www.birdingtours. com.au; 14-day tours $3800; 🕒 Feb-Mar & Nov-Dec). Australian visa requirements apply, and Australians should bring their passports.

OFF THE BEATEN TRACK

MARBLE BAR

Marble Bar, population 196, and a long way off everybody's beaten track, has burnt itself into the Australian psyche as the country's hottest town, when back in 1921 the mercury didn't dip below 37.8°C (100°F) for 161 consecutive days. The town is (mistakenly) named after a bar of jasper beside a pool on the Coongan River, 5km southwest.

Most days there's not much to do. You can pore over the minerals at the **Comet Gold Mine** (☑ 08-9176 1015; Hillside Rd; admission $3; ☺ 9am-4pm), 8km out of town on the Hillside Rd, or you can prop at the bar and have a yarn with Foxie at the **Iron Clad Hotel** (☑ 08-9176 1066; 15 Francis St; d $120). This classic outback pub offers comfy motel rooms, decent meals and a welcome to budget travellers.

But come the first weekend in July, the town swells to 10 times its normal size for a weekend of drinking, gambling, fashion crime, country music, nudie runs and horse racing known as the Marble Bar Cup. The **caravan park** (☑ 08-9176 1569; 64 Contest St) overflows and the Iron Clad is besieged as punters from far and wide come for a bit of an outback knees-up.

The **shire office** (☑ 08-9176 1008) runs a weekly bus service to Port Hedland and Newman (via Nullagine) and provides tourist information. If you're heading south, the easiest route back to bitumen is the lonely but beautiful Hillside Rd.

is now an exclusive 4.5-star resort with fully clothed staff, sumptuous though hideously expensive doubles, à la carte dining ($24 to $48; from 6pm) and popular all-you-can-eat buffets ($42).

🍴 Eating & Drinking

★**Silver Star**   CAFE **$$**
(☑ 0411 143 663; Edgar St; breakfast $12-18, lunch $18-24; ☺ 8am-2pm daily, tapas from 6pm Fri & Sat) Possibly the coolest cafe in the Pilbara, this 1930s American Silver Star railcar serves up decent coffee, brekkies and burgers in the original observation lounge. A tapas selection ($40 per head) is available Friday and Saturday evenings.

Port Hedland Yacht Club   BAR
(☑ 08-9173 1198; Sutherland St; ☺ Thu-Sun) Grab a cold one, find a table in the shade and enjoy the view at the yachties' brand-new premises. Sadly, the food doesn't match the surroundings.

ℹ Information

There are ATMs along Wedge St and in the Boulevard shopping centre. Internet access is available at the visitor centre, the **library** (☑ 08-9158 9378; Dempster St; ☺ 9am-5pm Mon-Fri, 10am-1pm Sat; @) and the **Seafarers Centre** (☑ 08-9173 1315; www.phseafarers.org; cnr Wedge & Wilson Sts; ☺ 9am-9pm).
Visitor Centre (☑ 08-9173 1711; www.phvc. com.au; 13 Wedge St; ☺ 9am-4pm Mon-Fri,

10am-2pm Sat; @) Newly refurbished, the centre sells bus tickets, publishes shipping times, arranges iron-ore plant tours, and helps with accommodation and turtle monitoring (November to February). Check here for bicycle hire.

ℹ Getting There & Away

Virgin and Qantas both fly to Perth daily, and on Tuesday Qantas also flies direct to Brisbane and Melbourne. Skywest offers handy weekend Bali flights as well as flights to Broome and Perth weekly. Airnorth heads to Broome (Tuesday and Friday) with a Darwin connection, and Karratha (Friday).

Greyhound coaches run to Perth ($258, 26 hours) and Broome ($87, eight hours) three times weekly. Integrity departs from Perth Wednesday using the quicker ($232, 22 hours) inland route via Newman, returning Friday. Both depart from the visitor centre and South Hedland shopping centre.

ℹ Getting Around

The airport is 13km from town; **Airport Shuttle Service** (☑ 08-9173 4554; per person $22) meets every flight, while **Hedland Taxis** (☑ 08-9172 1010) charge around $35. **Hedland Bus Lines** (☑ 08-9172 1394) runs limited weekday services between Port Hedland and Cooke Point (via the visitor centre) and on to South Hedland ($3.50). **McLaren Hire** (☑ 08-9140 2200; www.rawhire.com.au) offers a large range of rental 4WDs. Rent scooters from **Port Hedland Scooter Hire** (☑ 0450 481 765; www.phsh.com. au; from $45 per day).

Broome & the Kimberley

Best Cafes

➡ Whale Song (p216)
➡ 12 Mile (p213)
➡ Wild Mango (p227)
➡ Five Rivers (p225)
➡ Jila Gallery (p219)

Best off the Beaten Track Locations

➡ Middle Lagoon (p216)
➡ Mornington Wilderness Camp (p221)
➡ Mitchell Falls (p223)
➡ Duncan Road (p222)
➡ Kalumburu (p221)

Why Go?

Australia's last frontier is a wild land of remote, spectacular scenery spread over huge distances, with a severe climate, a sparse population and minimal infrastructure. Larger than 75% of the world's countries, the Kimberley is hemmed by impenetrable coastline and unforgiving deserts. In between lie vast boab-studded spinifex plains, palm-fringed gorges, desolate mountains and magnificent waterfalls. It is a true adventure: each dry season a steady flow of explorers search for the real outback along the Gibb River Road.

Aboriginal culture runs deep, from the Dampier Peninsula, where neat communities welcome visitors to country, to distant Mitchell Plateau, where ancient Wandjina and Gwion Gwion stand vigil over sacred waterholes.

Swashbuckling Broome (home to iconic Cable Beach, camel-tinged sunsets and amber-hued watering holes) and practical Kununurra (with its irrigation miracle) bookend the region.

When to Go
Broome

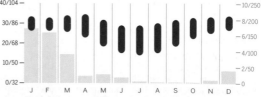

Apr Fly over thundering Mitchell and King George Falls.

May Broome's at its greenest right before the tourist tide.

Sep & Oct Hit Purnululu and the Gibb River Road as the season winds down.

ℹ️ Getting There & Around

AIR

The following airlines service Broome and the Kimberley.

Airnorth (☎1800 627 474; www.airnorth.com.au)

Qantas (☎13 13 13; www.qantas.com.au)

Skippers (☎1300 729 924; www.skippers.com.au) Flies between Broome, Derby, Halls Creek and Fitzroy Crossing.

Skywest (☎1300 660 088; www.skywest.com.au)

Slingair (Heliwork; ☎1800 095 500; www.slingair.com.au) Runs helicopters and fixed-wing sightseeing tours across the Kimberley.

Virgin Australia (☎13 67 89; www.virginaustralia.com.au)

BUS

Greyhound (☎1300 473 946; www.greyhound.com.au) Runs three times weekly Broome to Perth and daily Broome to Darwin.

BROOME REGION

Port Hedland to Broome

The Big Empty stretches from Port Hedland to Broome, as the highway skirts the Great Sandy Desert. It's 609km of willy-willies and dust and not much else. There are only two roadhouses, Pardoo (148km) and Sandfire (288km), so keep the tank full. The coast, wild and unspoilt, is never far away.

🛏️ Sleeping

The following places are all packed from May to September.

Eighty Mile Beach
Caravan Park   CARAVAN PARK **$**
(☎08-9176 5941; www.eightymilebeach.com.au; unpowered/powered sites $32/37, cabins $180; 🛜)
Popular with fishermen and 250km from Port Hedland, this shady, laid-back park backs onto a beautiful white-sand beach. Turtles nest November to March.

Port Smith Caravan Park   CARAVAN PARK **$**
(☎9192 4983; www.portsmithcaravanpark.com.au; unpowered/powered sites $30/35, dongas d $75, cabins $175) There's loads of wildlife at this caravan park situated on a tidal lagoon, 487km from Port Hedland.

Barn Hill Station   ACCOMMODATION **$**
(☎08-9192 4975; www.barnhill.com.au; unpowered sites $20, powered sites $25-30, cabins from $100)
A working cattle station, 490km from Port Hedland, with its own 'mini-Pinnacles'.

Broome

POP 16,000

Like a paste jewel set in a tiara of natural splendours, Broome clings to a narrow strip of red pindan on the Kimberley's far-western edge, at the base of the pristine Dampier Peninsula. Surrounded by the aquamarine waters of the Indian Ocean and the creeks, mangroves and mudflats of Roebuck Bay, this Yawuru country is a good 2000km from the nearest capital city.

Broome's cemeteries are a stark reminder of its pearling heritage, which claimed the lives of many Japanese, Chinese, Malay and Aboriginal divers. Today, Broome's pearls are still exported around the world, produced on modern sea farms.

Cable Beach, with its luxury resorts, hauls in the tourists during the Dry (April to October), with romantic notions of camels, surf and sunsets. Magnificent, sure, but there's a lot more to Broome than postcards, and tourists are sometimes surprised when they scratch the surface and find pindan just below.

Broome's centre is Chinatown, on the shores of Roebuck Bay, while Cable Beach and its resorts are 6km west on the Indian Ocean. The airport stretches between the two; the port and Gantheaume Point are 7km south.

The Dry's a great time to find casual work, in hospitality or out on the pearl farms. In the Wet, it feels like you're swimming in a warm, moist glove, and while many places close or restrict their hours, others offer amazingly good deals as prices plummet.

Each evening, the whole town pauses, collective drinks in mid-air, while the sun slips slowly seawards.

👁️ Sights & Activities

◉ Cable Beach Area

⭐ **Cable Beach**   BEACH
(Map p208) The state's most famous landmark offers turquoise waters and beautiful, white sand curving away to the sunset.

Broome & the Kimberley Highlights

1 Taking a camel ride at sunset along Broome's **Cable Beach** (p205)

2 Learning about traditional culture with Aboriginal communities on the pristine **Dampier Peninsula** (p216)

3 Tackling the notorious **Gibb River Road** (p220) in a 4WD adventure

4 Flying over the stunning **Mitchell and King George Falls** (p226) after the Wet

5 Riding the wild **Horizontal Waterfalls** (p220)

6 Losing yourself among the ancient beehive domes of **Purnululu National Park** (p224)

7 Canoeing the mighty **Ord River** (p225) in a three-day self-guided epic

8 Immersing yourself in indigenous art at **Aboriginal art cooperatives** (p218)

9 Trekking through the bowels of the earth at **Tunnel Creek National Park** (p223)

10 Following the Lurujarri Song Cycle on the **Lurujarri Dreaming Trail** (p209) to James Price Point and beyond

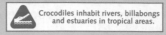
Crocodiles inhabit rivers, billabongs and estuaries in tropical areas.

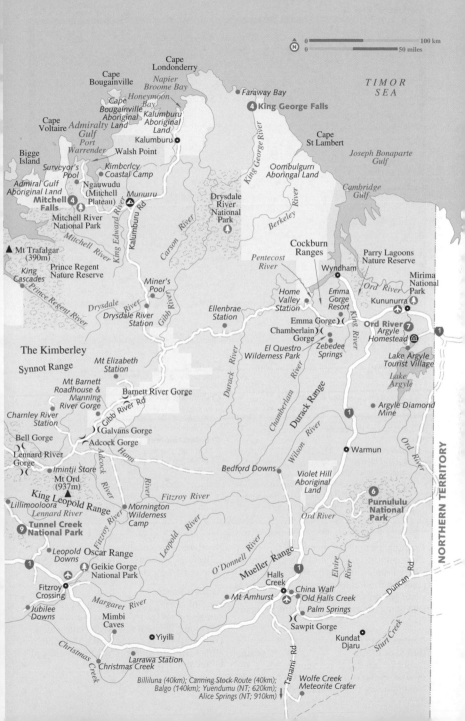

Cable Beach

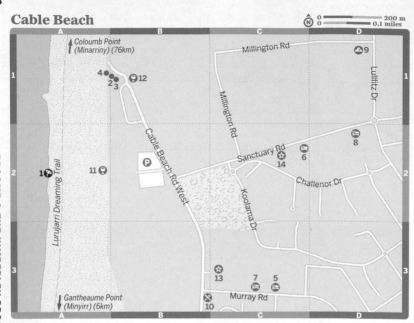

Cable Beach

◎ Sights
1 Cable Beach A2

◎ Activities, Courses & Tours
2 Broome Camel Safaris B1
3 Red Sun Camels B1
4 Ships of the Desert A1

◎ Sleeping
5 Bali Hai Resort & Spa C3
6 Beaches of Broome C2
7 Broome Beach Resort C3
8 Cable Beach Backpackers D2
9 Tarangau Caravan Park D1

◎ Eating
10 Cable Beach General Store B3

◎ Drinking & Nightlife
11 Broome SLSC A2
12 Sunset Bar & Grill B1

◎ Entertainment
13 Diver's Tavern C3
14 ZeeBar C2

Clothing is optional north of the rocks, while south, walking trails lead through the red dunes of **Minyirr Park**, a spiritual place for the Rubibi people. Cable Beach is synonymous with camels, and an evening ride along the sand is a highlight for many visitors.

Gantheaume Point & Dinosaur Prints   LANDMARK
Beautiful at dawn or sunset when the pindan cliffs turn scarlet, this peaceful lookout holds a 135-million-year-old secret. Nearby lies one of the world's most varied collections of **dinosaur footprints**, impossible to find except at very low tides.

Reddell Beach   BEACH
For a blistering sunset without the tourists, camels or 4WDs, pull into any of the turn-offs along Kavite Rd between Gantheaume Point and the port and watch the pindan cliffs turn into molten lava above wild and lonely Reddell Beach.

Lurujarri Dreaming Trail WALKING
(☑Frans 0423 817 925; www.goolarabooloo.org
.au; ⊙May-Jul) This 82km song cycle follows
the coast north from Gantheaume Point
(Minyirr) to Coulomb Point (Minarriny).
The Goolarabooloo organise a yearly guided
nine-day trip ($1600), staying at traditional
camp sites. Independent walkers should
first check with the Goolarabooloo for route
conditions as water is scarce.

◉ Chinatown Area

A number of cemeteries testify to Broome's
multicultural past; the most striking is the
Japanese Cemetery (Frederick St), with 919
graves (mostly those of pearl divers), while
Chinese (Frederick St) and **Muslim** (Frederick
St) cemeteries are nearby. There's a small **pioneer cemetery** (Map p212) by Town Beach
overlooking the bay.

Town Beach is fine for a dip if it's not
stinger season, and the port jetty is good for
fishing and whale watching.

Sun Pictures HISTORIC BUILDING
(Map p212; ☑08-9192 1077; www.sunpictures.com
.au; 27 Carnarvon St; adult/child/family $16.50/
11.50/55, History Tours per person $5; ⊙tours
10.30am & 1pm Mon-Fri) Sink back in a canvas
deckchair in the world's oldest operating
picture gardens and enjoy the latest movies. The history of the Sun building is the
history of Broome itself – don't miss the informative **History Tours**.

Broome Museum MUSEUM
(Map p212; ☑08-9192 2075; www.broomemuseum
.org.au; 67 Robinson St; adult/child $5/1; ⊙10am-
4pm Mon-Fri, to 1pm Sat & Sun Jun-Sep, to 1pm
daily Oct-May) Discover Cable Beach and Chinatown's origins as you examine pearling
history and WWII bombing in this quirky
museum.

★Short Street Gallery GALLERY
(Map p212; ☑08-9192 2658; www.shortstgallery.com
.au; 7 Short St; ⊙10am-5pm Mon-Fri, to 2pm Sat)
Broome's oldest gallery is now an artist-run
space, though several curated exhibitions
still run each year. Its studio at 3 Hopton St,
Old Broome, holds a stunning collection of
canvases.

⛓ Tours

Camels

It's a feisty business, but at last count there
were three camel-tour operators running at
Cable Beach offering similar trips.

Broome Camel Safaris CAMEL TOUR
(Map p208; ☑0419 916 101; www.broomecamelsafa
ris.com.au; 30min afternoon rides $25, 1hr sunset
rides adult/child $70/55) Alison, the only fe-
male camel-tour operator in Broome, offers
afternoon and evening trips.

Red Sun Camels CAMEL TOUR
(Map p208; ☑1800 184 488; www.redsuncamels.com
.au; 40min morning rides adult/child $55/35, 1hr
sunset rides $75/55) Red Sun runs both morn-
ing and sunset tours, with a shorter trip at
4pm (30 minutes, $30).

Ships of the Desert CAMEL TOUR
(Map p208; ☑08-9192 2958; www.shipsofthedesert
.com.au; 40min morning rides adult/child $50/30,
1hr sunset rides $70/50) The original camel-
tour company offers morning and sunset
trips, and a shorter afternoon option (30
minutes, $30).

Not Camels

There's a million of them; head to the visitor
centre for the full selection.

Kujurta Buru INDIGENOUS CULTURE
(☑08-9192 1662; www.kujurtaburu.com.au; adult/
child from $77/39; ⊙Tue, Thu & Sun) Nagula
half-day tours explore Yawuru culture and

OFF THE BEATEN TRACK

WWII FLYING BOAT WRECKS

On a very low tide it's possible to walk
out across the mudflats from Town
Beach to the **wrecks** (Map p212) of
Catalina and *Dornier* flying boats attacked by Japanese 'Zeroes' during
WWII. The planes had been evacuating
refugees from Java and many still had
passengers aboard. Over 60 people
and 15 flying boats (mostly Dutch and
British) were lost. Only six wrecks are
visible, with the rest in deep water.

Start walking an hour before low
tide, and head roughly southeast for
1.5km (about 30 minutes). Wear appropriate footwear – the mud's sticky and
can hide sharp objects, not all of them
inanimate. Watch out for other marine
hazards like jellyfish and check with
the visitor centre for tide times. The
museum also has a handy brochure. Or
just take the **hovercraft** (☑08-9193
5025; www.broomehovercraft.com.au; 1hr
adult/child $111/80, sunset/flying boat
$159/101).

STAIRCASE TO THE MOON

The reflections of a rising full moon, rippling over low-tide-exposed mudflats, create the optical illusion of a golden stairway leading to the moon. Between March and October, full moons see Broome buzzing with everyone eager to see the spectacle. At Town Beach there's a lively evening market with food stalls, and people bring their fold-up chairs, although the small headland at the end of Hamersley St has a better view. While Roebuck Bay parties like nowhere else, this phenomenon happens across the Kimberley and Pilbara coasts – anywhere with some east-facing mudflats. Other good viewing spots are One Arm Point at Cape Leveque, Cooke Point in Port Hedland, Sunrise Beach at Onslow, Hearson Cove near Dampier and the lookout at Cossack. Most visitor centres publish the dates on their websites.

country, including spear throwing and bush tucker tasting.

Broome Adventure Company　KAYAKING
(☑ 1300 665 888; www.broomeadventure.com.au; 3/4hr trips $70/90) Glide past turtles on these eco-certified coastal kayaking trips.

Astro Tours　ASTRONOMY TOUR
(☑ 0417 949 958; www.astrotours.net; adult/child $75/45) Fascinating after-dark two-hour stargazing tours, held just outside Broome. Self-drive and save $10.

**Kimberley Dreamtime
Adventure Tours**　INDIGENOUS CULTURE
(☑ 0447 214 681; www.kimberleydreamtimeadven tures.com.au; 1-/2-day cultural tours $299/492; ⊘ year round) Immerse yourself in Nyikina culture and learn bush skills on these amazing tours to Mt Andersen on the Fitzroy River. Longer tours and camel treks also available.

Kimberley Birdwatching　BIRDWATCHING
(☑ 08-9192 1246; www.kimberleybirdwatching.com .au; 3/5/10hr tours $100/150/290) Join ornithologist George Swann on his informative Broome nature tours. Overnight trips are also available.

★☆ Festivals & Events

Dates (and festivals!) vary from year to year. Check with the visitor centre and consult the community website (p215).

Staircase to the Moon　MOON FESTIVAL
(⊘ Mar-Oct) A festival of three magical nights each month at the full moon.

Gimme Fest　MUSIC FESTIVAL
(www.goolarri.com; ⊘ May) Showcasing the best of indigenous music.

Kullari NAIDOC Week　INDIGENOUS CULTURE
(www.goolarri.com; ⊘ late Jun–mid-Jul) Celebration of Aboriginal and Torres Strait Islander culture.

Environs Annual Art Auction　ART FESTIVAL
(www.environskimberley.org.au; ⊘ Jul) Annual environment fundraiser auctioning work by local and indigenous Kimberley artists.

Broome Race Round　HORSE RACING
(www.broometurfclub.com.au; ⊘ Jul/Aug) Kimberley Cup, Ladies Day and Broome Cup are when locals and tourists frock up and party hard.

Corrugated Lines　WRITING FESTIVAL
(http://broome.wa.au/events/corrugated-lines; ⊘ Aug) A three-day festival of the written word.

Opera Under the Stars　OPERA FESTIVAL
(www.operaunderthestars.com.au; ⊘ Aug) Opera al fresco; one night only at the Cable Beach Amphitheatre.

Shinju Matsuri Festival of the Pearl　PEARLS
(www.shinjumatsuri.com.au; ⊘ Aug or Sep) This homage to the pearl includes a week of parades, food, art, concerts, fireworks and dragon-boat races.

Mango Festival　MANGOES
(⊘ last weekend Nov) A celebration of the fruit in all its forms.

⊨ Sleeping

Accommodation is plentiful, but either book ahead or be flexible. If you're travelling in a group, consider an apartment. Prices plummet in the Wet.

Kimberley Klub　HOSTEL $
(Map p212; ☑ 08-9192 3233; www.kimberleyklub. com; 62 Frederick St; dm $26-33, d $95-135; ✳@🛜🏊) Handy to the airport, this big, laid-back tropical backpackers is a great place to meet other travellers. Features in-

clude poolside bar, games room, massive kitchen, an excellent noticeboard and organised activities most nights.

Tarangau Caravan Park
CARAVAN PARK $

(☑ 08-9193 5084; www.tarangaucaravanpark.com; 16 Millington Rd; unpowered/powered sites $34/42) A quieter alternative to often noisy Cable Beach caravan parks, Tarangau has pleasant grassy sites 1km from the beach, though at times it can be overly officious.

Cable Beach Backpackers
HOSTEL $

(Map p208; ☑ 1800 655 011; www.cablebeachback packers.com; 12 Sanctuary Rd; dm $30, d $85; ✲ @ 🛜 🕾) Within splashing distance of Cable Beach, this relaxed place has a lush tropical courtyard, swimming pool, big communal kitchen and bar.

Roebuck Bay Caravan Park
CARAVAN PARK $

(Map p212; ☑ 08-9192 1366; www.roebuckbaycp. com.au; 91 Walcott St; unpowered sites d $28-40, powered sites d $37-50, on-site van d $90) Right next to Town Beach, this shady, popular park has several camp-site options, though the sandflies can be menacing.

★ Beaches of Broome
HOSTEL $$

(Map p208; ☑ 1300 881 031; www.beachesofbroome .com.au; 4 Sanctuary Rd, Cable Beach; dm $32-45, motel d $140-180; ✲ @ 🛜 🕾) More resort than hostel; spotless, air-conditioned rooms are complemented by shady common areas, poolside bar and a modern self-catering kitchen. Dorms come in a variety of sizes, and the motel rooms are beautifully appointed. Scooter hire available.

★ Old Broome Guesthouse
GUESTHOUSE $$$

(Map p212; ☑ 08-9192 6106; www.oldbroomeguest house.com.au; 64 Walcott St; s/d $265/285; ✲ 🛜 🕾) Exotically appointed rooms with a Southeast Asian aesthetic surround a shady common area and leafy pool. High ceilings, sunken baths, an immaculate common kitchen and drooping palms create a tropical Eden.

Bali Hai Resort & Spa
RESORT $$$

(Map p208; ☑ 08-9191 3100; www.balihairesort. com; 6 Murray Rd, Cable Beach; d $298-525; ✲ 🛜 🕾) Lush and tranquil, this beautiful small resort has gorgeously decorated studios and villas, each with individual outside dining areas and open-roofed bathrooms. The emphasis is on relaxation, and the on-site spa offers a range of exotic therapies. The off-season prices are a bargain.

Broome Beach Resort
APARTMENTS $$$

(Map p208; ☑ 08-9158 3300; www.broomebeach resort.com.au; 4 Murray Rd, Cable Beach; 1-/2-/3-bed apt $300/340/375; ✲ 🛜 🕾) Great for families and groups. Large, modest apartments surround a central pool within easy walking distance of Cable Beach.

🍴 Eating

Be prepared for 'Broome prices' (exorbitant), 'Broome time' (when it should be open but it's closed) and surcharges: credit cards, public holidays, bad karma. Service can fluctuate wildly, as most staff are just passing through. Most places close in the Wet.

The back lanes of Chinatown, especially around **Johnny Chi Lane**, have cheap weekday lunch options. All pubs and resorts have in-house restaurants; some are good value, at others you're just paying for the view.

Self-caterers can enjoy well-stocked supermarkets and bakeries at Paspaley and Boulevard Shopping Centres and **Yuen Wing** (Map p212; ☑ 08-9192 1267; 19 Carnarvon St; ⊙ 8.30am-5.30pm Mon-Fri, to 2pm Sat & Sun), an Asian grocery.

Cable Beach General Store
CAFE $

(Map p208; ☑ 08-9192 5572; www.cablebeachstore .com.au; cnr Cable Beach & Murray Rds; ⊙ 6am-8.30pm daily; @ 🛜) Cable Beach unplugged – a typical Aussie corner shop with coffee, pancakes, barra burgers, pies, internet and no hidden charges. You can even play a round of mini-golf (adult/child/family $7/5/20) and there's internet access ($4 per hour).

ℹ CHEAP SUNDAY BRUNCH

The cheapest Sunday brunch at Cable Beach also has the best view. In a time-honoured Australian tradition you can support the local **Broome Surf Life Saving Club** (SLSC; Map p208; ☑ 08-9193 7327; www.broomeslsc.com; Cable Beach foreshore; sausage sangers $2; ⊙ bar 5-7pm Wed, Fri & Sun, sausages morning Sun) by buying a 'snag sanger'. Your $2 secures one barbecued sausage on a piece of white bread, possibly with onions, definitely with a choice of sauce (tomato or HP). Sit on the grass, munch away and stare at that Indian Ocean. The club also runs a 'members-only' bar some evenings, and they're pretty relaxed as to who's a member.

Central Broome

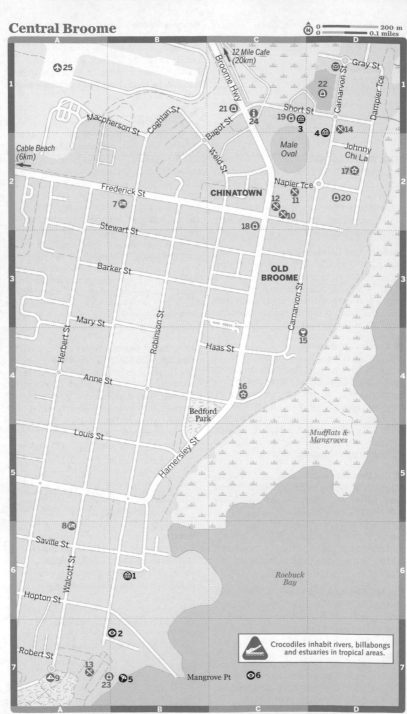

N

0   200 m
0   0.1 miles

12 Mile Cafe
(20km)

Gray St

Broome Hwy

Carnarvon St

Dampier Tce

Macpherson St

Coghlan St

Bagot St

Short St

25

22

21

24

19

3

4   14

Cable Beach
(6km)

Weld St

Male
Oval

Johnny
Chi La

17

Frederick St

CHINATOWN

Napier Tce

12

11

7

10

20

Stewart St

18

Barker St

OLD
BROOME

Robinson St

Carnarvon St

Mary St

Haas St

15

Herbert St

Anne St

16

Louis St

Bedford
Park

Hamersley St

Mudflats &
Mangroves

8

Saville St

Walcott St

1

Hopton St

Roebuck
Bay

2

Robert St

13

23   5

9

Mangrove Pt   6

Crocodiles inhabit rivers, billabongs
and estuaries in tropical areas.

Central Broome

★ **12 Mile Cafe**   CAFE **$$**
(☑ 08-9192 8552; 12milecafe@westnet.com.au; 53 Yamashita Rd, 12 Mile; mains $16-30; ⊙8am-4pm Thu-Mon dry season, Sat & Sun wet season) 🌿 Out among the shady mango plantations of 12 Mile, lovely Asian flavours are fused with local organic produce, sending vegoes to instant heaven, kids to smoothie and pikelet bliss and crusty old hippies to cake nirvana. Reduce, reuse, recycle...

★ **Aarli**   TAPAS **$$**
(Map p212; ☑ 08-9192 5529; 2/6 Hamersley St, cnr Frederick St; tapas $13-19, pizzas $20, fish by weight; ⊙8am-late Dry) Meaning 'fish' in Bardi, Aarli cooks up some of the most inventive and tasty titbits in Broome. The Med-Asian fusion tapas are excellent with a cold beer or chilled wine, and the pizzas are simple and scrumptious, but you really want to share the signature baked whole fish because it is superb – just check the price first!

Noodlefish   ASIAN **$$**
(Map p212; ☑ 08-9192 1697; 6 Hamersley St, cnr Fred-erick St; mains $21-36; ⊙6-9pm Tue-Sat) This quirky al-fresco BYO is doing fantastic contemporary Asian dishes using classic Kimberley ingredients. Get there early, because you can't book, and it's cash-only.

Azuki   JAPANESE **$$**
(Map p212; ☑ 08-9193 7211; 1/15 Napier Tce; sushi $8-10, mains $19-36; ⊙11am-2pm, 6-9pm Mon-Fri, dinner Sat) Enjoy the exquisite subtlety of authentic Japanese cuisine at this tiny BYO, from the takeaway fresh sushi rolls to the wonderfully tasty bento boxes.

Town Beach Cafe   CAFE **$$**
(Map p212; ☑ 08-9193 5585; Robinson St; breakfast $11-20, lunch $18-24; ⊙7.30am-2pm Tue-Sun, from 6pm Fri & Sat) With a great view over Roebuck Bay, the al-fresco tables of the Town are an ideal spot for an early brekkie.

Wharf Restaurant   SEAFOOD **$$$**
(☑ 08-9192 5800; Port of Pearls House, Port Dr; mains $20-42; ⊙11am-11pm) Settle back for a long, lazy seafood lunch with waterside ambience and the chance of a whale sighting. OK, it's pricey, but the wine's cold, the sea stunning and the chilli blue swimmer crab sensational. Just wait until after 2pm before ordering oysters.

🍷 Drinking & Entertainment

Check the gig guide on www.broome.wa.au. Avoid wandering around late at night, alone and off your dial; it's not as safe as it may seem.

Tides Garden Bar   BAR
(Map p212; ☑ 08-9192 1303; www.mangrovehotel. com.au; 47 Carnarvon St) The Mangrove Resort's casual outdoor bar is perfect for a few early bevvies while contemplating Roebuck Bay. Decent bistro meals, half-price oysters (5.30pm to 6.30pm) and live music (Thursday to Sunday) complement excellent Staircase to the Moon viewing.

Broome

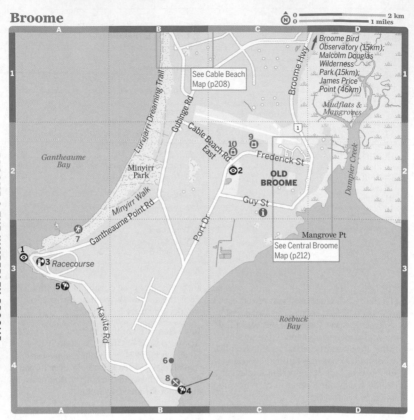

Broome

⊙ Sights
1 Gantheaume Point & Dinosaur
  Prints..A3
2 Japanese, Chinese & Muslim
  Cemeteries.................................C2
3 Lighthouse.....................................A3
4 Port...B4
5 Reddell Beach...............................A3

⊕ Activities, Courses & Tours
6 Hovercraft Tours..........................B4

7 Lurujarri Dreaming Trail.................A3

⊗ Eating
8 Wharf Restaurant.........................B4

⊚ Shopping
9 Boulevard Shopping Centre.............C2
10 Kimberley Camping & Outback
  Supplies.......................................C2

Sunset Bar & Grill　　　　BAR
(Map p208; ☑ 08-9192 0470; Cable Beach
Resort, Cable Beach Rd) Arrive around 4.45pm,
grab a front-row seat, order a drink and
watch the show – backpackers, package
tourists, locals, camels and a searing Indian
Ocean sunset shaded by imported coconut
palms.

Roebuck Bay Hotel　　　　PUB
(Map p212; ☑ 08-9192 1221; www.roebuckbayhotel
.com.au; 45 Dampier Tce; ☉ noon-late) Party central, the Roey's labyrinthine bars offer sports
on TV, live music, DJs, cocktails and wet
T-shirts until the wee hours.

Matso's Broome Brewery   PUB
(Map p212; ☑08-9193 5811; www.matsos.com.au; 60 Hamersley St; ☺music 3-6pm Sun) Get a Smokey Bishop into you at this casual backpackers pub and kick back to live music on the verandah. Bring something for the sandflies.

Diver's Tavern   LIVE MUSIC
(Map p208; ☑08-9193 6066; www.diverstavern.com .au; Cable Beach Rd; ☺noon-midnight) Diver's pumps most nights. Don't miss Wednesday jams and the Sunday Session.

ZeeBar   COCKTAIL BAR
(Map p208; ☑08-9193 6511; www.zeebar.com.au; 4 Sanctuary Rd; ☺6pm-late) This stylish bar and bistro near Cable Beach mixes up tasty cocktails, great tapas and DJs. Tuesday is trivia night.

🛍 Shopping

The old tin shanties of Short St and Dampier Tce are chock-full of extraordinary indigenous art, beautiful, expensive jewellery and cheap, tacky souvenirs.

Gecko Gallery   INDIGENOUS ART
(Map p212; ☑08-9192 8909; www.geckogallery. com.au; 9 Short St; ☺10am-6pm Mon-Fri, to 2pm Sat & Sun Dry, shorter hr Wet) Gecko specialises in East Kimberley and Western Desert art, including canvases, prints and etchings.

Kimberley Bookshop   BOOKS
(Map p212; ☑08-9192 1944; www.kimberleybook shop.com.au; 4 Napier Tce; ☺9am-5pm Mon-Fri, 10am-2pm Sat) Extensive range of books on Broome and the Kimberley.

Kimberley Camping & Outback Supplies   OUTDOOR EQUIPMENT
(☑08-9193 5909; www.kimberleycamping.com.au; cnr Frederick St & Cable Beach Rd) Camp ovens, jaffle irons and everything else you need for a successful expedition.

Magabala Books   BOOKS
(Map p212; ☑08-9192 1991; www.magabala.com; 1 Bagot St; ☺9am-4.30pm Mon-Fri) Indigenous publishers with selection of novels, social history, biographies and children's literature.

Courthouse Markets   MARKET
(Map p212; Hamersley St; ☺mornings Sat, additional Sun Apr-Oct) Local arts, crafts, music and general hippie gear.

ℹ Information

The hostels, **Fongs** (29 Saville St) and Yuen Wing (p211); all have great noticeboards.

INTERNET ACCESS
Broome Community Resource Centre (CRC; ☑08-9193 7153; 40 Dampier Tce; per hr $5; ☺9am-5pm Mon-Fri, to noon Sat; @ ⓦ) Cheap printing and wi-fi.

Galactica DMZ Internet Café (☑08-9192 5897; 4/2 Hamersley St; per hr $5; ☺10am-8pm; @ ⓦ) The usual geek stuff; behind Macca's.

INTERNET RESOURCES
Broome Community Website (www.broome .wa.au) Gig guide and what's on.

Environs Kimberley (www.environskimber ley.org.au) Latest environmental issues and projects across the Kimberley.

Chunes of Broome (www.chunesofbroome. com.au) Online Kimberley music and DVDs.

PERMITS
Department of Indigenous Affairs (DIA; ☑1300 651 077; www.dia.wa.gov.au) Apply online for free permits to visit Aboriginal communities. Processing usually takes three days.

TOURIST INFORMATION
Broome Visitor Centre (Map p212; ☑08-9195 2200; www.broomevisitorcentre.com.au; Male Oval, Hamersley St; ☺8.30am-5pm Mon-Fri, to 4.30pm Sat & Sun Dry, shorter hr Wet) On the roundabout entering town. Good info on road conditions, Staircase to the Moon, dinosaur footprints, WWII wrecks and tide times; can book most things.

ℹ Getting There & Away

Virgin and Qantas fly daily to Perth, and Qantas also has seasonal direct flights to eastern capitals. Airnorth flies daily to Darwin (except Saturday) and Kununurra, and to Karratha and Port Hedland twice weekly (Tuesday and Friday). Skywest flies daily to Perth, and to Darwin and Exmouth during the Dry. It also has a handy weekly connection to Bali (via Port Hedland). Skippers flies to Fitzroy Crossing, Halls Creek and Port Hedland four times weekly.

Greyhound buses leave the visitor centre daily for Darwin, and Tuesday, Thursday and Saturday for Perth. The local Derby bus (p219) leaves on Monday, Wednesday and Friday. Broome is a popular destination for **car pooling** (www .findalift.com.au).

ℹ Getting Around

Town Bus Service (☑08-9193 6585; www .broomebus.com.au; adult/child $3.50/1.50, day pass $10) links Chinatown with Cable Beach every hour (7.10am to 6.23pm year-round), plus half-hourly (8.40am to 6.40pm) from May to mid-October. Under 16s ride free with an adult.

No rental-car company offers unlimited kilometres. Local operator **Broome Broome** (☑ 08-9192 2210; www.broomebroome.com .au; cars/4WDs/scooters from $63/153/40) has cars, 4WDs and scooters. **Britz** (☑ 08-9192 2647; www.britz.com; 10 Livingston St) hires out campervans and 4WD Toyota Land Cruisers (from $176 per day) – essential for the Gibb River Road.

Broome Cycles (☑ 08-9192 1871; www .broomecycles.com.au; 2 Hamersley St, Chinatown; per day/week $24/84, deposit $50; ◷ 8.30am-5pm Mon-Fri, to 2pm Sat) has locations in Chinatown and **Cable Beach** (☑ 0409 192 289; Old Crocodile Park car park, Cable Beach; ◷ 9am-noon May-Oct). For a taxi, try **Broome Taxis** (☑ 13 10 08) or **Chinatown Taxis** (☑ 1800 811 772).

Around Broome

◉ Sights

Malcolm Douglas
Wilderness Park
WILDLIFE RESERVE

(☑ 08-9193 6580; www.malcolmdouglas.com .au; Broome Hwy; adult/child/family $35/25/95; ◷ 2-5pm daily, from 10am Dry) Visitors enter through the jaws of a giant crocodile at this 30-hectare animal refuge 16km northeast of Broome. The park is home to dozens of crocs (feedings 3pm), as well as kangaroos, cassowaries, emus, dingos, jabirus and numerous birds.

Broome Bird Observatory
WILDLIFE RESERVE

(☑ 08-9193 5600; www.broomebirdobservatory .com; Crab Creek Rd; admission by donation, camping per person $15, donga s/d $50/85, chalets $165; ◷ 8am-5pm) On Roebuck Bay, 25km from Broome, this amazing bird observatory is a vital staging post for hundreds of migratory species, some travelling over 12,000km. Tours range from an excellent two-hour walk ($70) to a five-day all-inclusive course ($1290). Self-guided trails, accommodation and binoculars are available. The unsealed access road can close during the Wet.

Dampier Peninsula

Stretching north from Broome, the red pindan of the Dampier Peninsula ends abruptly above deserted beaches, secluded mangrove bays and cliffs burnished crimson by the setting sun. This country is home to the thriving indigenous settlements of the Ngumbarl, Jabirr Jabirr, Nyul

Nyul, Nimanburu, Bardi, Jawi and Goolarabooloo peoples.

Access is by 4WD, along the largely unsealed 215km-long Cape Leveque Rd. Visiting Aboriginal communities requires both a DIA (p215) permit and one from the community (there are exceptions), payable at the office on arrival. Communities can close suddenly, so always book ahead from the Broome Visitor Centre (p215). Look for the booklet *Ardi – Dampier Peninsula Travellers Guide*. You should be self-sufficient, though limited supplies are available.

On Cape Leveque Rd, turn left after 14km onto Manari Rd, and head north along the spectacular coast. There are **bush camping sites** (no facilities) at Barred Creek, Quandong Point, James Price Point and Coulomb Point, where there is a **nature reserve**. Conventional vehicles should make it to **James Price Point**, the Kimberley's foremost environmental battleground, where there are plans to construct a large LNG facility. See it in its pristine state while you still can.

Back on Cape Leveque Rd, it's 110km to **Beagle Bay** (☑ 08-9192 4913), notable for the extraordinarily beautiful mother-of-pearl altar at Beagle Bay church, built by Pallottine monks in 1918. There's no accommodation, but fuel is available (weekdays only). Contact the office on arrival.

★**Middle Lagoon** (☑ 08-9192 4002; www .middlelagoon.com.au; unpowered/powered sites $30/40, beach shelter d $50, cabins d $140-240), 180km from Broome and surrounded by empty beaches, is superb for swimming, snorkelling, fishing and doing nothing. There's plenty of shade and bird life, and the cabins are great value, though the access road is terrible. Other options include quiet **Gnylmarung Retreat** (☑ 0429 411 241; http://gnylmarung.org.au; sites per person $20, bungalows from $90) and upmarket **Mercedes Cove** (☑ 08-9192 4687; www.mercedescove.com. au; eco tents/air-con cabins $150/300). Don't miss **Whale Song Cafe** at nearby Munget, overlooking exquisite Pender Bay. This ecocafe serves fabulous mango smoothies, lovingly made pizzas and the best coffee on the peninsula. There's a tiny bush campground with stunning views, a funky outdoor bathroom and not a caravan in sight.

Between Middle Lagoon and Cape Leveque, **Lombadina** (☑ 08-9192 4936; www.lom badina.com; entry per car $10, s/d $80/150, cabin 4-person $200-260; ◷ office 8am-noon, 1-4pm Mon-Fri), 200km from Broome, is a beautiful tree-fringed village offering various tours (minimum of three people) including fishing, whale watching, 4WDing, mudcrabbing, kayaking and walking. There are lodge-style rooms and self-contained cabins, but no camping. Fuel is available weekdays; lovely artifacts are for sale at the Arts Centre.

Tiny **Chile Creek** (✐ 08-9192 4141; www.chile creek.com; sites per person $16.50, bush bungalows $100, 4-person safari tents $185), 7km from Lombadina down a disintegrating track, offers basic bush camp sites, modern ensuite safari tents and renovated bungalows, all just a short stroll to a lovely beach. Ask Roma if she's running her legendary cultural tours.

Cape Leveque is spectacular, with gorgeous white beaches and stunning red cliffs. Ecotourism award-winner **Kooljaman** (✐ 08-9192 4970; www.kooljaman.com.au; per car $10, unpowered/powered sites d $38/43, dome tents $65, cabins with/without bathroom d $170/145, safari tents d $275; 🐾) offers grassy camp sites, driftwood beach shelters, hilltop safari tents with superb views, and stuffy budget tents. There's a minimum two-night stay, and the place is packed from June to October. The BYO **restaurant** (✐ 08-9192 4970; mains $29-38, BBQ packs $22-26; ⊘ 11.30am-1.30pm & 6pm-late Apr-Oct) opens for lunch and dinner, or you can order a BBQ pack.

If you prefer less bling, a couple of outstations offer camp sites between Cape Leveque and One Arm Point. **Goombading** (✐ 0457 138 027; unpowered/powered sites per person $15/20), with fantastic water views, is very relaxed. Hosts Unja and Jenny are keen to share Bardi culture, and offer spear-making, fishing and crabbing tours.

You can't camp at **Ardiyooloon** (One Arm Point; per person $10), but you can visit this neat community with a well-stocked store, fuel, a barramundi hatchery and great fishing and swimming with views of the Buccaneer Archipelago.

A handful of other outstations offer camping, fishing and crabbing opportunities. **Chomley's Tours** (✐ 08-9192 6195; www .chomleystours.com.au; 1-/2-day tours $260/490) has several day and overnight tours (including mudcrabbing) on the peninsula, plus one-way transfers (from $110). **Kujurta Buru** (✐ 08-9192 1662; www.kujurtaburu.com.au) has transport Sunday, Tuesday and Thursday from Broome to Beagle Bay ($95) and Lombadina, Kooljaman and Ardiyooloon (all $155), returning the same day.

THE KIMBERLEY

Derby
POP 5000

Late at night while Derby sleeps, the boabs cut loose and wander around town, marauding mobs flailing their many limbs in battle against an army of giant, killer crocpeople emerging from the encircling mudflats... If only.

There are crocs hiding in the mangroves, but you're more likely to see birds, over 200 different varieties, while the boabs are firmly rooted along the two main parallel drags, Loch and Clarendon Sts. Derby, sitting on King Sound, is the departure point for tours to the Horizontal Waterfalls and Buccaneer Archipelago, and the western terminus of the Gibb River Rd (GRR). It is also West Kimberley's administrative centre, and the asylum seeker detention facility at nearby RAAF Curtin brings in hordes of contractors.

⊙ Sights & Activities

The visitor centre's excellent town map lists every conceivable attraction.

★**Norval Gallery**   GALLERY
(Loch St; ⊘varies) Kimberley art legends Mark and Mary Norval have set up an exciting gallery-cafe in an old tin shed on the edge of town. Featuring striking artworks, exquisite jewellery, decent coffee and 5000 vinyl records (brought out on themed nights), any visit here is a delight to the senses.

Wharefinger Museum   MUSEUM
(admission by donation) Grab the key from the visitor centre and have a peek inside the nearby museum, with its atmospheric shipping and aviation displays.

Jetty   LANDMARK
Check out King Sound's colossal 11.5m tides from the circular jetty, 1km north of town, a popular fishing, crabbing, bird-spotting and staring-into-the-distance haunt. Yep, there are crocs in the mangroves.

Kimberley School of the Air   SCHOOL
(Marmion St; admission $5) Fascinating look at how school is conducted over the radio for children on remote stations. Tour times vary, so check with the visitor centre first.

KIMBERLEY ART COOPERATIVES

Indigenous art of the Kimberley is unique. Encompassing powerful and strongly guarded Wandjina, prolific and puzzling Gwion Gwion (Bradshaws), bright tropical coastal x-rays, subtle and sombre bush ochres and topographical dots of the western desert, every work sings a story about country.

To experience it firsthand, visit some of these Aboriginal-owned cooperatives; most are accessible by 2WD:

➜ **Mowanjum Art & Culture Centre** (🖉 08-9191 1008; www.mowanjumarts.com; Gibb River Rd, Derby; ⊙ 9am-5pm daily Dry, closed Sat & Sun Wet) Just 4km along the Gibb River Rd, Mowanjum artists recreate Wandjina and Gwion Gwion images in this incredible gallery shaped like their artwork.

➜ **Waringarri Aboriginal Arts Centre** (🖉 08-9168 2212; www.waringarriarts.com.au; 16 Speargrass Rd; ⊙ 8.30am-4.30pm Mon-Fri, 10am-2pm Sat Dry, weekdays only Wet) This excellent Kununurra gallery-studio hosts local artists working with ochres in a unique abstract style. It also represents artists from Kalumburu.

➜ **Warmun Arts** (🖉 08-9168 7496; www.warmunart.com; Great Northern Hwy, Warmun; ⊙ 9am-4pm Mon-Fri) Between Kununurra and Halls Creek, Warmun artists create beautiful works, using ochres to explore Gija identity. Phone first from Warmun Roadhouse for a verbal permit.

➜ **Laarri Gallery** (🖉 08-9191 7195; yiyilischool@activ8.net.au; Yiyilli; ⊙ 8am-4pm school days) This tiny not-for-profit gallery in the back of the community school has interesting contemporary-style art detailing local history. It's 120km west of Halls Creek and 5km from the Great Northern Hwy. Phone ahead.

➜ **Mangkaja Arts** (🖉 08-9191 5833; www.mangkaja.com; 8 Bell Rd , Fitzroy Crossing; ⊙ 11am-4pm Mon-Fri) A Fitzroy Crossing gallery where desert and river tribes interact, producing unique acrylics, prints and baskets.

➜ **Yaruman Artists Centre** (🖉 08-9168 8208; Kundat Djaru) Sitting on the edge of the Tanami, 162km from Halls Creek, Yaruman has acrylic works featuring the many local soaks (waterholes). The weekly mail run from Kununurra stops here (Ringer Soak).

➜ **Yarliyil Gallery** (🖉 08-9168 6723; www.yarliyil.com.au; Great Northern Hwy, Halls Creek; ⊙ 9am-4.30pm Mon-Fri) Great new Halls Creek gallery showcasing talented local artists as well as some of the Ringer Soak mob.

➜ **Warlayirti Artists Centre** (🖉 08-9168 8960; www.balgoart.org.au; Balgo; ⊙ 9am-5pm) This centre, 255km down the Tanami Track, is a conduit for artists around the area and features bright acrylic dot-style as well as lithographs and glass. Phone first to arrange an entry permit.

Old Derby Gaol   HISTORICAL BUILDING
(Loch St) Along with the **Boab Prison Tree** (7km south), this old gaol is a sad reminder of man's inhumanity to man.

Bird Hide   BIRDWATCHING
There's a bird hide in the wetlands (aka sewerage ponds) at the end of Conway St.

Joonjoo Botanical Trail   WALKING
This 2.3km trail, opposite the GRR turn-off, has neat interpretive displays from the local Nyikina people.

🕝 Tours

The Horizontal Waterfalls are Derby's top draw and most cruises also include the natural splendours of remote King Sound and the Buccaneer Archipelago. There are many operators to choose from (see the visitor centre for a full list). Most tours only operate during peak season.

**Horizontal Falls Seaplane
Adventures**   SCENIC FLIGHTS
(🖉 08-9192 1172; www.horizontalfallsadventures.com.au; 6hr tours from Derby/Broome $695/745) Flights to Horizontal Falls include a speedboat ride through the falls. There's also an overnight-stay option (ex-Derby) for $845.

Bush Flight   SCENIC FLIGHTS
(🖉 08-9193 2680; www.bushflight.com.au; flights from $352) Scenic tours of the Horizontal Waterfalls and the Buccaneer Archipelago – you can look but not touch.

One Tide Charters
CRUISES

(☑08-9193 1358; www.onetide.com; 5-12 days $3200-7680) Offers eco-certified all-inclusive multiday 'sea safaris' with overnight camping on remote beaches, a ride through the Horizontal Waterfalls, mudcrabbing, fishing and freshwater swimming on exotic islands.

Derby Bus Service
BUS TOUR, CAMPING

(West Kimberley Tours/Windjana Tours; ☑08-9193 1550; www.derbybus.com.au; day tours $150, camping tours per day from $200) The local bus company runs a full-day tour to Windjana Gorge and Tunnel Creek National Parks, and tailored two- to seven-day Kimberley camping trips.

🎊 Festivals & Events

Boab Festival
MUSIC, CULTURE

(www.derbyboabfestival.org.au; ☺ Jul) Derby goes off with concerts, mud footy, horse and mudcrab races, poetry readings, art exhibitions and street parades. Try to catch the Long Table dinner out on the mudflats.

🛏 Sleeping & Eating

Any decent accommodation is normally full of contract workers. Try the visitor centre, but if you're heading to/from the Gibb, consider stopping at Birdwood Downs Station (20km) instead.

There are several takeaways and cafes along Loch and Clarendon Sts.

Kimberley Entrance
Caravan Park
CARAVAN PARK $

(☑08-9193 1055; www.kimberleyentrancecaravanpark.com; 2 Rowan St; unpowered/powered sites $32/38) You'll always find room here, though not all sites are shaded. There's a nice outdoor area with tables, although expect lots of insects this close to the mudflats.

Spinifex Hotel
RESORT $$

(☑08-9191 1233; www.spinifexhotel.com.au; Clarendon St; dongas/motel r $160/250; ❄@❄) Rising phoenix-like from the ashes of the old Spini, this sleek new resort has corporate-class rooms (some with kitchenettes) and an on-site restaurant.

★ Desert Rose
B&B $$$

(☑08-9193 2813; 4 Marmion St; d $250; ❄) It's worth booking ahead for the best sleep in town: spacious, individually styled rooms with a nice shady pool, leadlight windows

and a sumptuous breakfast. Host Anne is a font of local information.

Boab Inn
PUB $$

(☑08-9191 1044; www.derbyboabinn.com; Loch St; lunches $16-18, dinners $22-39; @❄) Excellent counter meals and free wi-fi make this the lunch stop of choice. The motel-style rooms (doubles $225) are clean, comfortable and normally booked out.

Jila Gallery
ITALIAN $$

(☑08-9193 2560; 18 Clarendon St; pizzas $19-25, mains $19-35; ☺10am-2pm & 6pm-late Tue-Fri, 6pm-late Sat) Great wood-fired pizzas, shady al-fresco dining and wonderful cakes are the highlights of this friendly trattoria.

Catch
SEAFOOD $$

(☑08-9191 2664; Jetty; meals $18-25; ☺10am-9pm) Gloriously overlooking the jetty, Catch offers (mainly) seafood meals that are quite reasonable, though quality can fluctuate. Takeaway is also available.

Sampey Meats
BUTCHER $

(☑08-9193 2455; 59 Rowan St; ☺7am-5pm Mon-Fri, to noon Sat) Homemade jerkies, biltong and cryovaced roasts, all ready for the Gibb.

ℹ Information

The supermarkets and ATMs are on Loch and Clarendon Sts.

DARC (http://darcinc.wordpress.com) Online resource listing everything arty going down in Derbs.

Derby Visitor Centre (☑1800 621 426; www.derbytourism.com.au; 30 Loch St; ☺8.30am-5pm Mon-Fri, 9am-4pm Sat & Sun) Recently relocated, this super-helpful centre has the low-down on road conditions, accommodation, transport and tour bookings.

Library (Clarendon St; ☺closed Sun; @) Internet; first five minutes free.

ℹ Getting There & Away

Skywest heads to Perth Monday to Friday. Skippers flies to Broome, Fitzroy Crossing and Halls Creek several times weekly. There's an **airport shuttle** (☑08-9193 2568; per person $30) to/from Curtin.

Greyhound buses to Darwin ($350, 25 hours) and Broome ($68, two hours) stop at the visitor centre.

Derby Bus Service (☑08-9193 1550; www.derbybus.com.au; one way/return $50/80; ☺Mon, Wed & Fri) runs to Broome three times weekly, leaving early and returning the same day.

For a taxi, call ☑13 10 08.

BROOME & THE KIMBERLEY GIBB RIVER ROAD

Gibb River Road

Cutting a brown swathe through the scorched heart of the Kimberley, the legendary Gibb River Road ('the Gibb' or GRR) provides one of Australia's wildest outback experiences. Stretching some 660km between Derby and Kununurra, the largely unpaved GRR is an endless sea of red dirt, big open skies and dramatic terrain. Rough, sometimes deeply corrugated side roads lead to remote gorges, shady pools, distant waterfalls and million-acre cattle stations. Rain can close the road any time and permanently during the Wet. This is true wilderness with minimal services, so good planning and self-sufficiency are vital.

Several pastoral stations offer overnight accommodation from mid-April to late October; advance bookings are essential during the peak period of June to August. Hema Maps' *Kimberley Atlas & Guide* provides the best coverage, while visitor centres sell copies of *The Gibb River & Kalumburu Road Guide* ($5).

A high-clearance 4WD (such as a Toyota Land Cruiser) is mandatory, with two spare tyres, tools, emergency water (20L minimum) and several days' food in case of breakdown. Britz (p216) in Broome is a reputable hire outfit. Fuel supplies are limited and expensive, most mobile phones won't work, and temperatures can be life-threatening. Broome and Kununurra are best for supplies.

For just a sniff of outback adventure, try the 'tourist loop' along the GRR from Derby onto Fairfield Leopold Downs Rd to Windjana Gorge and Tunnel Creek National Parks, then exit onto the Great Northern Hwy near Fitzroy Crossing.

 Tours

Western Xposure   DRIVING TOUR
(☑08-9414 8423; www.westernxposure.com.au; 7 days $1795) Runs seven-day and longer camping trips through the GRR.

Kimberley Wild Expeditions   DRIVING TOUR
(☑1300 738 870; www.kimberleywild.com.au) A consistent award winner. Tours from Broome range from one- ($250) to nine-day GRR ($2050).

Kimberley Adventure Tours   DRIVING TOUR
(☑1800 083 368; www.kimberleyadventures.com .au) Runs between Broome and Darwin including the GRR and Purnululu National Park ($1825, nine days).

ℹ Information

Try the online resources listed below and the Derby and Kununurra visitor centre sites.

For maps, take Hema's *Kimberley Atlas & Guide* ($35) or *Regional Map – The Kimberley* ($10).

Department of Environment & Conservation (DEC; www.dec.wa.gov.au) Park permits, camping fees, info. A Holiday Pass ($40) works out cheaper if visiting more than three parks in one month.

Mainroads Western Australia (MRWA; ☑138 138; www.mainroads.wa.gov.au; ⊙24hr) Highway and GRR conditions.

Online Resources (www.gibbriverroad.net)

Shire of Derby/West Kimberley (☑08-9191 0999; www.sdwk.wa.gov.au) Provides side road conditions.

Shire of Wyndham/East Kimberley (☑08-9168 4100; www.swek.wa.gov.au) Kalumburu/Mitchell Falls road conditions.

HORIZONTAL WATERFALLS

One of the most intriguing features of the Kimberley coastline is the phenomenon known as 'horizontal waterfalls'. Despite the name, the falls are simply tides gushing through narrow coastal gorges in the Buccaneer Archipelago, north of Derby. What creates such a spectacle are the huge tides, often varying up to 11m. The water flow reaches an astonishing 30 knots as it's forced through two narrow gaps 20m and 10m wide – resulting in a 'waterfall' reaching 4m in height.

Many tours leave Derby (and some from Broome) each Dry, by air, sea or a combination of both. It's become de rigueur to 'ride' the tide change through the gorge on a high-powered speedboat, but this is risky at best, and accidents have occurred. Scenic flights are the quickest and cheapest option, and some seaplanes will land and transfer passengers to a waiting speedboat for the adrenalin hit. If you prefer to be stirred, not shaken, then consider seeing the falls as part of a longer cruise through the archipelago. Book tours at Derby and Broome visitor centres.

KALUMBURU

The road to Kalumburu deteriorates quickly after the Mitchell Plateau turn-off and eventually becomes very rocky. You'll need a permit from the DIA (p215) to visit Kalumburu and a visitors pass (valid for seven days) on entry from the **Kalumburu Aboriginal Community** (KAC; ✆ 08-9161 4300; www.kalumburu.org; per car $50). Kalumburu is a picturesque mission nestled beneath giant mango trees and coconut palms with two shops and **fuel** (⊙ 7.30-11.30am & 1.30-4.30pm Mon-Fri). Ask around if you need any repairs. There's some interesting rock art nearby, and the odd WWII bomber wreck. You can stay at the **Kalumburu Mission** (✆ 08-9161 4333; kalumburumission@bigpond.com; sites per person $20, donga s/d $120/175), which has a small **museum** (admission $10; ⊙ 8.30-10.30am), or obtain a permit from the KAC office to camp at **Honeymoon Bay** (✆ 08-9161 4378) or **McGowan Island** (✆ 08-9161 4748; www.mcgowanisland.com.au), 20km further out on the coast – the end of the road. Alcohol is banned at Kalumburu.

Derby to Wyndham & Kununurra

The first 100-odd kilometres of the GRR from Derby are sealed.

After only 4km, Mowanjum Art & Culture Centre (see boxed text, p251), with its striking Wandjina and Gwion Gwion images, is well worth a stop. Nine kilometres further, 2000-hectare **Birdwood Downs Station** (✆ 08-9191 1275; www.birdwooddowns.com; camping $13, savannah huts per person incl breakfast & dinner $135) offers rustic savannah huts and dusty camping. WWOOFers are welcome and it's also the **Kimberley School of Horsemanship**, with lessons, riding camps and trail rides (two-hour sunset rides $99).

At the 40km mark, a rough track heads left 12km to several bush camp sites on the **May River**. Windjana Gorge turn-off arrives at the 119km mark – your last chance to head back to the highway. The scenery improves after crossing the Lennard River into Napier Downs Station as the ancient **King Leopold** ranges loom straight ahead. Just after Inglis Gap is the turn-off (a rough 50km) to the remote **Mt Hart Wilderness Lodge** (✆ 08-9191 4645; sites per person $18, r per person incl dinner & breakfast $200; ⊙ dry season) with grassy camp sites, pleasant gorges, swimming and fishing holes. Seven kilometres past the Mt Hart turn-off brings the narrow **Lennard River Gorge** (3km return walk).

March Fly Glen, at the 204km mark, despite its name, is a pleasant, shady picnic area ringed by pandanus. Don't miss stunning **Bell Gorge**, 29km down a rough track, with a picturesque waterfall and popular plunge pool; you can camp at **Silent Grove** (adult/child $11/2). Refuel (diesel only) and grab an ice cream at **Imintji Store** (✆ 08-

9191 7471; ⊙ 7am-4.30pm dry season, shorter hours wet season), your last chance for supplies. Next door is **Over the Range Repairs** (✆ 08-9191 7887; ⊙ 8am-5pm dry season), where Neville is your best, if not only, hope of mechanical salvation on the whole Gibb.

Part of the Australian Wildlife Conservancy, the superb **Mornington Wilderness Camp** (✆ 08-9191 7406; www.awc.org.au; entry fee per vehicle $25, sites adult/child $17.50/8, safari tents incl full board s/d $315/540; ⊙ dry season) is as remote as it gets, lying on the Fitzroy River, a very rough, incredibly scenic 95km drive south of the Gibb's 247km mark. Nearly 400,000 hectares are devoted to conserving the Kimberley's endangered fauna and there's excellent canoeing, birdwatching and bushwalking. Choose from shady camp sites or spacious, raised tents with verandahs. The bar and restaurant offer picnic hampers and the best cheese platter this side of Margaret River.

Just 4km past Mornington's turn-off is the entrance to historic **Charnley River Station** (✆ 08-9191 4646; www.charnleyriverstation.com; camp sites d $35, rondavels & guesthouse incl full board s/d $230/310, day visit $20) and its alluring gorges. Grassy camp sites come with hot showers, or you can opt for full board up at the homestead. Meals and home-grown vegies are available.

Beautiful **Galvans Gorge**, with waterfall, swimming hole, rock wallabies and Wandjina art, is the most accessible of all gorges, less than 1km from the road. Fuel up at **Mt Barnett Roadhouse** (✆ 08-9191 7007; ⊙ 8am-5pm), at the 300km point, and get your camping permit if choosing to stay at **Manning River Gorge** (per person $20), 7km behind the roadhouse. The campground is often full of travellers waiting for fuel but at least there's a good swimming hole and even

DUNCAN ROAD

Snaking its way east from Halls Creek before eventually turning north and playing hide and seek with the Northern Territory border, Duncan Rd is the Kimberley's 'other' great outback driving experience. Unsealed for its entire length (445km), it receives only a trickle of travellers compared to the GRR, but those who make the effort are rewarded with stunning scenery, beautiful gorges, tranquil billabongs and breathtakingly lonely camp sites.

Technically it's no harder than the Gibb, and while there are several creek and river crossings, the fords are concrete lined and croc free. It also makes a nice loop if you've come down the Great Northern Hwy to Purnululu and want to return to Kununurra and/or the NT. There are no services on the entire Duncan, so carry fuel for at least 500km and watch out for road trains. Enquire at Halls Creek or Kununurra visitor centres about road conditions.

hot showers. Better still are the free bush camp sites at **Barnett River Gorge**; turn off 29km from the roadhouse – they're several kilometres down a sandy track.

Further up the Gibb (at the 338km mark) is the turn-off to **Mt Elizabeth Station** (✆08-9191 4644; www.mountelizabethstation.com; sites per person $15, s/d incl breakfast & dinner $170/340; ☺dry season), one of the few remaining private leaseholders in the Kimberley. Peter Lacy's 200,000-hectare property is a good base for exploring the nearby gorges, waterfalls and indigenous rock art; don't miss the 4WD tag-along tour ($50). Wallabies frequent the camp site, and the homestyle three-course dinners ($45) hit the spot.

At 406km you reach the Kalumburu turnoff. Head right on the GRR, and pull into atmospheric **Ellenbrae Station** (✆08-9161 4325; sites per person $15, bungalow d $155) for fresh scones and quirky bungalows. The GRR continues through spectacular country, crossing the mighty Durack River and, at 579km, providing panoramic views of the Cockburn Ranges, Cambridge Gulf and Pentecost River.

The privations of the Gibb are left behind after pulling into amazing **Home Valley Station** (✆08-9161 4322; www.homevalley.com

.au; sites adult/child $17/5, eco tents for 4 people $190, homestead d from $250; ✳@☎☎☎), an indigenous hospitality training resort with a superb range of luxurious accommodation. There are excellent grassy camp sites and motel-style rooms, a fantastic open bistro, tyre repairs and activities including trail rides, fishing and cattle mustering.

At 589km cross the infamous **Pentecost River**. Take care: water levels are unpredictable and saltwater crocs lurk nearby. Slightly further is 400,000-hectare **El Questro Wilderness Park** (✆08-9169 1777; www.elquestro .com.au; 7-day park permit $20; ☺dry season), a vast former cattle station with scenic gorges (Amelia, El Questro) and Zebedee thermal springs (mornings only). Boat tours explore **Chamberlain Gorge** (adult/child $64/34; ☺ tours 3pm) or hire your own boat ($70). There are shady camp sites and air-con bungalows at **El Questro Station Township** (sites per person $20-25, bungalow d from $329; ✳) and also an outdoor bar and upmarket **steakhouse** (mains $28-42). There are a million activities, but you'll pay for most of them.

The rest of the GRR is sealed. Ten kilometres along is El Questro's **Emma Gorge Resort** (safari cabin d from $289; ☺dry season; ✳), where a 40-minute walk reaches a sublime plunge pool and waterfall, one of the prettiest in the whole Kimberley. The resort has an open-air bar and restaurant, though the non-air-con cabins are stuffy and overpriced.

At 630km you cross King River and at 647km you finally hit the highway – turn left for Wyndham (48km) and right for Kununurra (53km).

Devonian Reef National Parks

Three national parks with three stunning gorges were once part of a western 'great barrier reef' in the Devonian era, 350 million years ago. Windjana Gorge and Tunnel Creek National Parks are accessed via Fairfield Leopold Downs Rd (linking the Great Northern Hwy with the Gibb River Rd), while Geikie Gorge National Park is just northeast of Fitzroy Crossing.

The walls of beautiful **Windjana Gorge** (per car $11) soar 100m above the Lennard River, which surges in the Wet but is a series of pools in the Dry. Scores of freshwater crocodiles lurk along the banks. Bring plenty of water for the 7km return walk from the **campground** (per person $10).

Sick of the sun? Then cool down underground at **Tunnel Creek** (per car $11, no camping), which cuts through a spur of the Napier Range for almost 1km. It was famously the hideout of rebel Jandamarra. In the Dry, the full length is walkable by wading partly through knee-deep water; watch out for bats and take good footwear and a strong torch. Aboriginal paintings exist at both ends and a two-hour **tour** (☎08-9191 5355; www.bungoolee.com.au; adult/child $50/20) is available.

Not to be missed, magnificent **Geikie Gorge** (⊙Apr-Dec) is 22km north of Fitzroy Crossing. The self-guided trails are sandy and hot, but the **DEC** (☎08-9191 5121; 1hr tour adult/child $30/7.50; ⊙various cruises from 8am May-Oct) runs daily cruises. Local Bunuba guides introduce indigenous culture and bush tucker on the amazingly informative cruises run by **Darngku Heritage Tours** (☎0417 907 609; www.darngku.com.au; adult/child 2hr $65/55, 3hr $80/65, half-day $160/$128; ⊙Apr-Dec). A shorter one-hour cruise (adult/child $30/5) operates during the shoulder season (April and October to December).

Fitzroy Crossing to Halls Creek

Gooniyandi, Bunuba, Walmatjarri and Wangkajungka people populate the small settlement where the Great Northern Hwy crosses the mighty Fitzroy River. There's little reason to stay other than its good access to the Devonian Reef national parks. Check out Mangkaja Arts (see boxed text, p218) with its unique acrylics, and the exquisite glass and ceramics of **Dr Sawfish** (⊙8.30am-4.30pm Mon-Fri, shorter hours Sat & Sun), next to the tyre guy (whom you'll probably need).

Camping and rooms are available at the atmospheric **Crossing Inn** (☎08-9191 5080; www.crossinginn.com.au; Skuthorpe Rd; unpowered/powered sites $26/30, r from $180; ❄@) and across the river at the upmarket **Fitzroy River Lodge** (☎08-9191 5141; www.fitzroyriverlodge.com.au; Great Northern Hwy; camping per person $15, tent d $155, motel d $199, meals $20-34; ❄@📶≋), which also offers decent counter meals. There's a new, well-stocked supermarket, and the **visitor centre** (☎08-9191 5355; www.sdwk.wa.gov.au; ⊙8.30am-4.30pm Mon-Fri year round, plus 9am-1pm Sat in dry season) and bus stop are just off the highway.

One of the Kimberley's best-kept secrets is the vast subterranean labyrinth of **Mimbi Caves**, 90km southeast of Fitzroy Crossing. Located within Mt Pierre Station, on Gooniyandi land, the caves house a significant collection of Aboriginal rock art and some of the most impressive fish fossils in the southern hemisphere. Aboriginal-owned **Girloorloo Tours** (adult/child $80/40; ⊙Tue-Sat Apr-Sep) operates trips, including an introduction to local Dreaming stories, bush tucker and

WORTH A TRIP

MITCHELL FALLS & DRYSDALE RIVER

In the Dry, Kalumburu Rd is normally navigable as far as **Drysdale River Station** (☎08-9161 4326; www.drysdaleriver.com.au; sites $10-15, d $150; ⊙8am-5pm Apr-Dec), 59km from the GRR, where fuel, meals and accommodation are available, and you can check ongoing conditions. Scenic flights to Mitchell Falls operate April to September (from $400 per person).

The Ngauwudu (Mitchell Plateau) turn-off is 160km from the GRR, and within 6km a deep, rocky ford crosses the King Edward River, formidable early in the season. Another 2km brings pleasant, shady **Munurru Campground** (adult/child $7/2), with excellent nearby rock art. Many people prefer to camp here and visit Mitchell Falls as a day trip. From the Kalumburu Rd it's a rough 87km, past lookouts and forests of *livistona* palms to the dusty camping ground at **Mitchell River National Park** (entry per vehicle $11, camping adult/child $7/2).

Leave early if walking to **Mitchell Falls** (Punamii-unpuu). The easy trail (8.6km return) meanders through spinifex, woodlands and gorge country, dotted with Wandjina and Gwion Gwion rock-art sites, secluded waterholes, lizards, wallabies and brolga. The falls are stunning, whether trickling in the Dry, or raging in the Wet (when only visible from the air). You can swim in the long pool above the falls, but swimming in the lower pools is strictly forbidden because of their cultural importance to the Wunambal people. Most people will complete the walk in three hours.

DON'T MISS

PURNULULU NATIONAL PARK & BUNGLE BUNGLE RANGE

Looking like a packet of half-melted Jaffas, the World Heritage–listed **Purnululu National Park** (per car $11; ☉Apr-Dec) is home to the incredible ochre and black striped 'beehive' domes of the Bungle Bungle Range.

The distinctive rounded rock towers are made of sandstone and conglomerates moulded by rainfall over millions of years. Their stripes are the result of oxidised iron compounds and algae. To the local Kidja people, *purnululu* means sandstone, with Bungle Bungle possibly a corruption of 'bundle bundle', a common grass. Whitefellas only 'discovered' the range during the mid-1980s.

Over 3000 sq km of ancient country contains a wide array of wildlife, including over 130 bird species. **Kungkalahayi Lookout** has a fine view of the range. Look for tiny bats high on the walls above palm-fringed **Echidna Chasm** (a one-hour return walk) in the north, but it's the southern area comprising aptly named **Cathedral Gorge** (a 45-minute return walk) that's most inspiring. Remote and pristine **Piccaninny Gorge** is best experienced as an overnight round trip (30km return); check with the park's visitor centre for details. The restricted gorges in the northern park can only be seen from the air.

Rangers are based here April to December and the park is closed outside this time. The turn-off is 53km south of Warmun and you'll need a high-clearance 4WD for the 52km twisting, unsealed road to the visitor centre. There are five deep, permanent creek crossings, so allow 2½ hours. **Kurrajong Camp Site** (☉May-Sep) and **Walardi Camp Site** (☉Apr-Dec) have fresh water and toilets (sites per person $11). Book online via the DEC (p194), allowing at least 48 hours' notice. Alternatively, **Mabel Downs Station** (Bungle Bungle Caravan Park; ☎08-9168 7220; www.bunglebunglecaravanpark.com.au; tent sites/powered sites $30/45, safari tents with/without en suite $225/120) offers camping just 1km from the highway (outside the park). Don't expect much privacy: tents are jammed between choppers and ridiculously long trailers. Various tours are available.

Tours

Most Kimberley tour operators include Purnululu in multi-day tours. See p226 for tours operating from Kununurra. You can also pick up tours at Warmun Roadhouse, Halls Creek and Mabel Downs. Helicopters will get you closer than fixed-wing flights.

East Kimberley (☎08-9168 2213; www.eastkimberleytours.com.au; tours from $180) Has a wide range of tours from both Kununurra and Warmun.

Sling Air (☎1800 095 500; www.slingair.com.au; 18/30/48min flights $225/299/495) Runs helicopter flights from Bellburn airstrip in the park, as well as fixed-wing flights from Warmun and Kununurra.

Bungle Bungle Expeditions (☎08-9168 7220; www.bunglebungleexpeditions.com.au; bus day/overnight $250/695, helicopter from $250) Various 4WD bus and helicopter tours run from the caravan park on Mabel Downs, near the highway.

---

traditional medicines. Book through Fitzroy Crossing or Halls Creek visitor centres.

Nearby **Larrawa Station** (☎08-9191 7025; Great Northern Hwy; sites $20, s with/without meals $120/70), halfway between Fitzroy Crossing and Halls Creek, makes a pleasant overnight stop, with hot showers, basic camp sites, and shearers rooms. Another 30km towards Halls Creek brings Yiyilli with its Laarri Gallery (see boxed text, p218).

On the edge of the Great Sandy Desert, Halls Creek is a small town with communities of Kija, Jaru and Gooniyandi people.

The excellent **visitor centre** (☎08-9168 6262; www.hallscreektourism.com.au; Great Northern Hwy; ☉8am-5pm; @) books tours to the Bungles and tickets for Mimbi Caves. Check email next door at the **Community Resource Centre** (☉8.15am-3.45pm Mon-Fri) and across the highway, Yarliyil Gallery (see boxed text, p218) is definitely worth a look.

The **Kimberley Hotel** (☎08-9168 6101; www.kimberleyhotel.com.au; Roberta Ave; r from $172, restaurant mains $16-42; ❄☎☒) is your best lunch option and you can find a bed there or at **Best Western** (☎08-9168 9600;

www.bestwestern.com.au; d $260; 🔆 🐾). There's a caravan park, but you're better off heading out of town.

Skippers flies from Fitzroy Crossing and Halls Creek to Broome, and Greyhound passes through daily.

Wyndham
POP 900

A gold-rush town fallen on leaner times, Wyndham is scenically nestled between rugged hills and Cambridge Gulf, some 100km northwest of Kununurra. Sunsets are superb from the spectacular **Five Rivers Lookout** on Mt Bastion (325m) overlooking the King, Pentecost, Durack, Forrest and Ord Rivers entering Cambridge Gulf.

A giant 20m croc greets visitors entering town, but you might see the real thing if **Wyndham Crocodile Farm** (✆08-9161 1124; Barytes Rd; ☉ feeding time 11am) is open. The port precinct also contains a small **museum** (✆08-9161 1857; Old Courthouse, Port Precinct; ☉ 10am-3pm daily Dry) and the **Wyndham Town Hotel** (✆08-9161 1202; O'Donnell St; d $143, meals $18-38; 🔆) with its legendary meals and overpriced rooms.

In town, **Five Rivers Cafe** (✆08-9161 2271; 12 Great Northern Hwy; meals $6-16; ☉ 6am-3pm daily, from 7am Sat & Sun) serves up great coffee, breakfasts and huge burgers, while laid-back **Wyndham Caravan Park** (✆08-9161 1064; Baker St; unpowered/powered sites $25/30, donga d $70; 🔆) offers grassy, shady camp sites.

Greyhound drops passengers 56km away at the Victoria Hwy junction. Internet is available at the **Telecentre** (CRC; ✆08-9161 1166; www.wyndham.crc.net.au; 26 Koojarra Rd; ☉ 8am-4pm Mon-Fri; @), and Tuesday/Wednesdays' mail-run flights might get you to Kununurra.

For a taxi, call ✆0408 898 638.

Kununurra
POP 6000

Kununurra, on Miriwoong country, is a relaxed town set in an oasis of lush farmland and tropical fruit and sandalwood plantations, thanks to the Ord River irrigation scheme. With good transport and communications, excellent services and well-stocked supermarkets, it's every traveller's favourite slice of civilisation between Broome and Darwin.

Kununurra is also the departure point for most of the tours in the East Kimberley, and with all that fruit, there's plenty of seasonal work. Note that there's a 90-minute time difference with the NT.

◉ Sights & Activities

Across the highway from the township, **Lily Creek Lagoon** is a mini-wetlands with amazing bird life, boating and freshwater crocs. **Lake Kununurra** (Diversion Dam) has pleasant picnic spots and great fishing. Groups could consider hiring their own 'barbie' boat from **Kununurra Self Drive Hire Boats** (✆0409 291 959; Lakeside Resort; per hr from $88).

Self-guided two- or three-day canoe trips run from Lake Argyle along the scenic **Ord River** to Kununurra, overnighting at desig-

Purnululu National Park

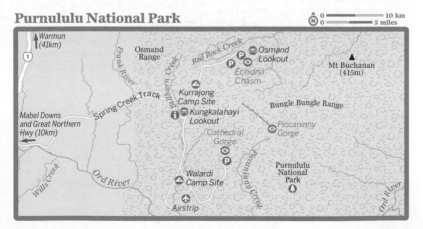

WORTH A TRIP

PARRY LAGOONS NATURE RESERVE

This beautiful Ramsar-listed wetland, 15km from Wyndham, teems in the Wet with migratory birds arriving from as far away as Siberia. There's a bird hide and boardwalk at **Marlgu Billabong** (4WD) and an excellent view from **Telegraph Hill**. Back on the highway, steep steps lead down to the **Grotto**, a deep, peaceful pool in a small gorge, perfect for a quiet dip.

Surrounded by nature reserve, tranquil **Parry Creek Farm** (☑08-9161 1139; www.parrycreekfarm.com.au; unpowered/powered sites $34/37, r $125, cabins $210; ❋ ≋), with grassy camp sites, attracts hordes of wildlife. Comfy rooms and air-con cabins are connected by a raised boardwalk above a billabong for easy bird spotting. The licensed cafe serves excellent baked barramundi, wood-fired pizzas and other gourmet delights.

nated riverside camp sites. Canoes, camping equipment and transport are provided, while you supply your own food and sleeping bag. You can choose to paddle the whole way back, bail out along the way, or take an extra day.

Don't miss the excellent Waringarri Aboriginal Arts centre (p218) on Speargrass Rd, opposite the road to **Kelly's Knob**, a popular sunset viewpoint.

Mirima National Park   NATIONAL PARK
(per car $11) A stunning area of rugged sedimentary formations like a mini-Bungle Bungles. The eroded gorges of Hidden Valley are home to brittle red peaks, spinifex, boab trees and abundant wildlife. Several walking trails lead to lookouts, and early morning or dusk are the best times for sighting fauna.

Red Rock Art Gallery   GALLERY
(☑08-9169 3000; 50 Coolibah Dr; ☺10am-4pm Mon-Fri) If you're lucky, you might see indigenous artists in action at this excellent gallery showcasing ochres from the East Kimberley.

Kununurra Historical Society Museum   MUSEUM
(Coolibah Dr; admission by gold-coin donation) Old photographs and newspaper articles document the history of Kununurra, including the story of a wartime Wirraway aircraft crash and subsequent recovery mission. The museum is opposite the country club exit.

Big Waters   CANOEING
(☑1800 650 580; www.bigwaters.com.au; 3 days $185) Self-guided overnight canoe trips on the Ord River.

Go Wild   CANOEING, ADVENTURE SPORTS
(☑1300 663 369; www.gowild.com.au; 3-day canoe trips $180) Guide yourself down the Ord by canoe on a three-day trip, or join a group caving ($200), abseiling (from $150) or bushwalking (from $40).

Yeehaa Trail Rides   HORSE RIDING
(☑0417 957 607; yeehaa7@hotmail.com; Boab Park, Old Darwin Rd; per hr from $60) Various-length bush rides and tuition to suit all levels.

☞ Tours

Kununurra Cruises   CRUISE
(☑08-9168 1718; www.thebbqboat.com.au; adult/child $95/45) Popular sunset 'BBQ Dinner' cruises on Lily Creek Lagoon and the Ord River. BYO drinks.

Triple J Tours   CRUISE
(☑08-9168 2682; www.triplejtours.net.au; adult/child one way $165/125, return $150/115) Triple J cruises along the 55km Ord River between Kununurra and Lake Argyle Dam.

Shoal Air   SCENIC FLIGHTS
(☑08-9169 3554; www.shoalair.com.au; per person from $295) Various flights around the Bungles, Cambridge Gulf, Kalumburu and majestic Mitchell and King George Falls.

⇤ Sleeping

There's a great variety of accommodation to choose from, and the more it costs, the more of a discount you'll get in the Wet. Watch out for mozzies if you're camping near the lake.

Hidden Valley Tourist Park   CARAVAN PARK $
(☑08-9168 1790; www.hiddenvalleytouristpark .com; 110 Weaber Plains Rd; unpowered/powered sites $24/30, cabin d $125; ❀ ☎ ≋) Under the looming crags of Mirima National Park, this excellent little park has nice grassy sites and is popular with seasonal workers. The self-contained cabins are good value.

Kimberley Croc Backpackers HOSTEL **$**
(☑1300 136 702; www.kimberleycroc.com.au; 120 Konkerberry Dr; dm $27-33, d $89-125; ✴@🛜🏊) Close to the action, this slick, modern YHA has a large pool and BBQ area and excellent kitchen facilities. It also runs the nearby **Kimberley Croc Lodge** (dm per week $160) for seasonal workers.

Freshwater APARTMENTS **$$**
(☑1300 729 267; www.freshwaterapartments.net.au; 19 Victoria Hwy; studio/1-/2-/3-bedroom apt $218/249/304/399; ✴🛜🏊) At Freshwater, Kununurra's newest rooms feature exquisite fully self-contained units with exotic open-roofed showers.

Lakeview Apartments APARTMENTS **$$**
(☑08-9168 0000; www.lakeviewapartments.net; 31 Victoria Hwy; 1-/2-/3-bedroom apt $230/280/380; ✴🛜🏊) Across from Lily Creek Lagoon, these spacious, self-contained apartments have all mod cons, fully equipped kitchens, free wi-fi and cable. There's a weekend minimum two-night stay.

🍴 Eating

The big resorts all have restaurants offering similar dining experiences. There are two well-stocked supermarkets and several takeaways. Most places keep shorter hours during the Wet, and you'll struggle finding lunch after 2pm.

★ Wild Mango CAFE **$**
(☑08-9169 2810; 20 Messmate Way; breakfasts $9-23, lunches $6-13; ⊙7.30am-4pm Mon-Fri, 8am-1pm Sat & Sun; 🛜) 🖋 The hippest, healthiest feed in town, with curry wraps, mouthwatering pancakes, chai smoothies, real coffee, gelato and free wi-fi. The entrance is in Konkerberry Dr.

Kimberley Asian Cuisine ASIAN **$**
(☑08-9169 3698; 75 Coolibah Dr; mains $7-22; ⊙10am-2pm & 5-10pm daily) Ask any local and they'll tell you this quality Asian (next to the visitor centre) is one of the best feeds in town.

Ivanhoe Cafe CAFE **$$**
(☑0427 692 775; Ivanhoe Rd; mains $11-20; ⊙8am-4pm Tue-Fri, to 2pm Sat & Sun) Grab a table under the leafy mango trees and tuck into tasty wraps, salads and burgers, all made from fresh, local produce.

★ PumpHouse MODERN AUSTRALIAN **$$$**
(☑08-9169 3222; www.ordpumphouse.com.au; Lakeview Dr; lunches $18-30, dinners $33-42; ⊙11.45am-1.45pm & 6pm-late Wed-Fri, from 8am Sat & Sun, dinner only Tue; 🛜) Idyllically situated on Lake Kununurra, the PumpHouse creates succulent dishes featuring quality local ingredients. Watch the catfish swarm should a morsel slip off the verandah. Or just have a beer and watch the sunset. There's an excellent wine list to enjoy and free wi-fi.

🛍 Shopping

Artlandish INDIGENOUS ART
(☑08-9168 1881; www.aboriginal-art-australia.com; cnr Papuana St & Konkerberry Dr; ⊙9am-4.30pm Mon-Fri, to 1pm Sat) Features a stunning collection of Kimberley ochres and Western Desert acrylics to suit all price ranges.

Kununurra Markets MARKET
(Whitegum Park; ⊙8am-noon Sat dry season) The Kununurra Markets are located in the park opposite the visitor centre; stalls feature local crafts and produce.

WORTH A TRIP

LAKE ARGYLE

Enormous Lake Argyle, where barren red ridges plunge spectacularly into the deep blue water of the dammed Ord River, is Australia's second-largest reservoir. Holding the equivalent of 18 Sydney Harbours, it provides Kununurra with year-round irrigation, and important wildlife habitats for migratory waterbirds, freshwater crocodiles and isolated marsupial colonies. You can drive across the dam wall, take a **boat tour** (☑08-9168 7687; www.lakeargylecruises.com; adult/child morning $70/45, afternoon $155/90, sunset $85/50) or just amble nearby. **Lake Argyle Village** (☑08-9168 7777; www.lakeargyle.com; Lake Argyle Rd; unpowered/powered sites $28/35, cabins $139-199, units from $299; ✴@🏊) offers a range of accommodation and incredible views, especially from its infinity pool. Nearby, the original **Argyle Homestead** (☑08-9167 8088; adult/child $4/1; ⊙8am-4pm Apr-Oct) has been turned into a museum.

Bush Camp Surplus OUTDOOR EQUIPMENT
(☑ 08-9168 1476; cnr Papuana St & Konkerberry Dr)
The best camping gear between Broome and
Darwin.

ℹ Information

There are ATMs near the supermarkets and
a 24-hour laundromat at the **BP roadhouse**
(Messmate Way). Several cafes have free wi-fi;
otherwise try the **library** (☑ 08-9169 1227;
Mangaloo St; ☉ from 8am, closed Sun; @) or
CRC (☑ 08-9169 1868; Coolibah Dr; per hr $6;
☉ 8am-5pm Mon-Fri, 9am-1pm Sat; @ 🛜).
DEC Office (☑ 08-9168 4200; Lot 248) Ivanhoe Rd; ☉ 8am-4.30pm Mon-Fri) Parks information and permits.
Visitor Centre (☑ 1800 586 868; www.visitku
nunurra.com; Coolibah Dr; ☉ 8.30am-4.30pm
Mon-Fri, 9am-1pm Sat & Sun Apr-Oct, shorter
hours Nov-Mar) Check here for accommodation, tours, seasonal work and road conditions.

ℹ Getting There & Around

Airnorth flies to Broome and Darwin daily, and
to Perth on Saturday. Skywest departs for
Perth daily, Broome thrice weekly and Darwin
on Monday.

Greyhound has daily buses to Darwin ($191, 13
hours) and Broome ($237, 13 hours) that stop
at the BP roadhouse. Destinations include Halls
Creek ($86, four hours), Fitzroy Crossing ($181,
seven hours), Derby ($212, 10 hours) and Kath-
erine ($129, eight hours).

Avis (☑ 08-9168 1999), **Budget** (☑ 08-9168
2033) and **Thrifty** (☑ 1800 626 515) rental cars
are available.

For a taxi, call ☑ 13 10 08.

Understand
Perth & West
Coast Australia

Perth & West Coast Australia Today

Welcome to the engine room of the Australian economy, a boom town where nature's resources are driving ongoing growth and expansion (p245). Perth is rapidly developing into an international city – further enhancing the population's existing independent streak – and the urban landscape is being transformed by heritage restorations and audacious town planning. And in the remote mining regions that drive the economy, there are glimmers of hope that the benefits of this latest fiscal gold rush may be slightly more equitably spread.

Best on Film

Rabbit-Proof Fence (2002) Three Aboriginal girls trek through the WA desert to be reunited with their families.

Japanese Story (2003) A touching film that's set in the Pilbara and equal parts romance and thriller.

Gallipoli (1981) Young men from rural WA enlist to fight as Anzac soldiers in the ill-fated Gallipoli campaign.

Mad Bastards (2010) Shot in the Kimberley and featuring Indigenous issues and a great soundtrack.

Best in Print

Cloudstreet (Tim Winton, 1991) A chronicle of post-WWII working-class families sharing a house in Perth.

Sand (John Kinsella and Robert Drewe, 2010) Poetry and prose exploring the role of sand in the Australian psyche.

Tales from Outer Suburbia (Shaun Tan, 2008) Beautifully illustrated short stories – for kids – with quirky reimaginings of Australian suburbia.

That Deadman Dance (Kim Scott, 2011) Novel exploring the 19th-century interactions between settlers, whalers and the indigenous Noongar people of Albany.

A Confident Western Capital

Just a few decades ago, Perth was definitely in the shadow of east-coast Australia's major cities, but, fuelled by the energy and economics of the mining boom, it's now a contemporary city on the rise. There's an almost tangible confidence and verve to the city's population, keen to look westwards for both recreation and reward. Bali is firmly entrenched as the state's favourite holiday destination – it's even emerging as a residential option for FIFO ('fly in, fly out') mining workers – and the 21st-century mega economies of China, India and Indonesia are huge markets for WA's resources and agricultural sectors.

Evidence of the city's impetuous growth includes newly sprawling suburbs, with oversized homes squeezed onto compact plots, and front gardens punctuated with shiny boats, flash utes, and other blokey indicators of ongoing injections of mining money. With so many cars in circulation, transport to these emerging satellite suburbs can be slow going, and the need for ongoing investment to keep Perth's much-admired rail system up to scratch is another hot topic. A $1-billion light-rail system to link Perth's northern suburbs to the CBD is projected to open in 2018. Other major civic works in progress include Perth's City Link Project and the development of Elizabeth Quay to *finally* reintroduce the CBD to the river (see boxed text, p51).

Another 'finally' moment is the restoration of many of the heritage buildings along St George's Terrace in the city's west end that were proudly constructed during much earlier mining booms. The emergence of new eating and drinking precincts and boutique hotels is an overdue dynamic in a city blighted sometimes in recent history by showy modern architecture.

Spreading the Success?

As in other parts of Australia, Aboriginal communities in WA struggle on, many mired in disadvantage, and a form of unspoken segregation between white Australians and Aboriginal Australians appears to exist.

Divisions persist, but the search for petroleum and gas has brought mining companies and Aboriginal groups to the negotiating table in deals brokered, both successfully and unsuccessfully, for mining companies to set up shop on traditional Aboriginal lands.

In the far north region of the Kimberley, one of the biggest planned developments is a $35-billion liquefied natural gas (LNG) project at James Price Point near Broome. Following the striking of a $1.5-billion compensation deal with the Kimberley Land Council (KLC) – representing members of the local Aboriginal Goolarabooloo and Jabirr Jabirr peoples – other members of the Goolarabooloo people have lodged a claim with the Western Australia Supreme Court to overturn the state government's compulsory acquisition of the site. Opponents of the acquisition contend that the KLC was placed under 'improper pressure' by the state government, and the ongoing legal machinations are powerful proof that negotiations between traditional Aboriginal landowners, the government and resource companies are seldom straightforward.

The rise of Indigenous recruitment agencies has increased the number of Aboriginal workers in the resources sector. The mine owners benefit from a reduced need for costly FIFO workers, and the local Aboriginal population benefits from education and employment opportunities.

Football Crazy

Western Australia has two teams in the AFL: the Fremantle Dockers and the West Coast Eagles. The Dockers (often just 'Freo') were only founded in 1995 but have already built a very strong following. They've traditionally enjoyed a working-class underdog image, but with another strong finals showing in 2012, the underdog moniker is starting to look slightly out of date. With key players like skipper Matthew Pavlich, an AFL premiership crown can't be too far away. Watch this space.

Founded in 1986, the West Coast Eagles currently play at Subiaco Oval (aka Patersons Stadium), but when – or maybe if – a new stadium is built across the river at Burswood, they'll be moving there for the 2018 season. Like expansion teams in other codes – come on down, the Melbourne Storm NRL team – they've enjoyed considerable success in their short history, and have already won three premierships, the last in 2006. Like Freo, the Eagles also reached the finals in the 2012, but just missed out on a Grand Final berth.

Now if only they could get started on that new footie stadium...

POPULATION: **2.19 MILLION**

POPULATION GROWTH: **3.1%**

AREA: **2,529,875 SQ KM**

GDP: **AU$2.17 BILLION**

GDP GROWTH: **4.3%**

UNEMPLOYMENT: **3.5%**

if Perth were 100 people

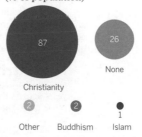

65 would be born in Australia
11 would be born in the UK
3 would be born in New Zealand
21 would be born elsewhere

belief systems
(% of population)

87 Christianity

26 None

2 Other

2 Buddhism

1 Islam

population per sq km

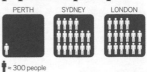

PERTH   SYDNEY   LONDON

= 300 people

History

Today Western Australia (WA), the largest state in the country, is also the most sparsely populated, being home to less than 10% of the population.

Many of the first ships to bring convicts to WA were whalers. Human cargo would be unloaded and then the ships continued whaling.

The story of Western Australia's history is one of hardship, boom, bust, and boom again. Human history started some 40,000 years ago, when the first people are thought to have arrived – although some argue that this could have occurred as long as 65,000 years ago.

Dirk Hartog is considered the first European explorer to land on the shores of WA (as a record of his journey he displayed a pewter plate on an island in Shark Bay in 1616, now known as Dirk Hartog Island).

The British set up a military base in Albany, in the south of the state, in 1826. Perth was then founded in 1829, when Captain James Stirling declared all surrounding land property of King George IV.

In 1829 immigrants led by Stirling arrived in the territory of the Noongar people, sparking controversy between the two groups. Conflict with the indigenous population continued, notably in the Battle of Pinjarra (1834), when some 25 Aboriginal people and one European were killed.

WA began its economic transformation with the discovery of gold in the 1880s and the inception of the nickel boom in the early 1960s, albeit thwarted by the two world wars and the Depression. Riches from the mines at Mt Newman, Tom Price and Kalgoorlie, among several others, dovetailed into the economic bubble of the 1980s, which burst when WA Inc (as the dealings among select businessmen and state politicians came to be known) was discovered to have lost $600 million in public money. Ever enterprising, it was not long, however, before the state was soon back on its feet, enjoying untrammelled economic mining growth and development by 2010.

First Arrivals

People first arrived on the northern shores of Australia at least 40,000 years ago. As they began building shelters, cooking food and telling each other tales, they left behind signs of their activities. They left layers of

TIMELINE	40,000 years ago	Up to 6000 years ago	1616
	First humans arrive on the shores of Australia.	Aboriginal communities from northwestern Australia trade and interact with Macassan fishermen from Sulawesi.	Dutch explorer Dirk Hartog lands on an island in Shark Bay, marking his visit with a pewter plate on which he inscribed a record of his visit.

carbon – the residue of their ancient fires – deep in the soil. Piles of shells and fish bones mark the places where these people hunted and ate. And on rock walls across WA they left paintings and etchings, some thousands of years old, which tell their stories of the Dreaming, that spiritual dimension where the earth and its people were created, and the law was laid down.

Contrary to popular belief, these Aboriginal people, especially those living in the north, were not entirely isolated from the rest of the world. Until 6000 years ago, they were able to travel and trade across a bridge of land that connected Australia to New Guinea. Even after white occupation, Aboriginal people of the northern coasts regularly hosted Macassan fishermen from Sulawesi, with whom they traded and socialised.

When European sailors first stumbled on the coast of 'Terra Australis', the entire continent was occupied by hundreds of Aboriginal groups, living in their own territories and maintaining their own distinctive languages and traditions. The fertile Swan Valley around Perth, for example, is the customary homeland of about a dozen groups of Noongar people, each speaking a distinctive dialect.

The prehistory of Australia is filled with tantalising mysteries. In the Kimberley, scholars and amateur sleuths are fascinated by the so-called Bradshaw paintings. These enigmatic and mystical stick figures are thousands of years old. Because they look nothing like the artwork of any other Aboriginal group, the identity of the culture that created them is the subject of fierce debate.

Meanwhile there are historians who claim the Aboriginal people's first contact with the wider world occurred when a Chinese admiral, Zheng He, visited Australia in the 15th century. Others say that Portuguese navigators mapped the continent in the 16th century.

Early Dutch Exploration

These are intriguing theories. But most authorities believe that the first man to travel any great distance to see Aboriginal Australia was a Dutchman named Willem Janszoon. In 1606, he sailed the speedy little ship *Duyfken* out of the Dutch settlement at Batavia (modern Jakarta) to scout for the Dutch East India Company, and found Cape York (the pointy bit at the top of Australia), which he thought was an extension of New Guinea.

Ten years later, another Dutch ship, the *Eendracht*, rode the mighty trade winds across the Atlantic, bound for the 'spice islands' of modern Indonesia. But the captain, Dirk Hartog, misjudged his position, and stumbled onto the island (near Gladstone) that now bears his name. Hartog inscribed the details of his visit onto a pewter plate and nailed it to a

FOUNDATIONS

The founding of Perth is most famously depicted in George Pitt Morison's painting *The Foundation of Perth* (1829). It is often erroneously credited as an authentic record of the ceremony rather than a historical reconstruction.

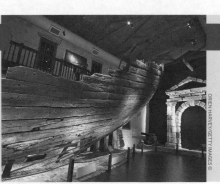

1629
Debauchery, rape and murder break out while the *Batavia* is shipwrecked at the Houtman Abrolhos Islands. All crew but two are subsequently executed at senior merchant Francisco Pelsaert's behest.

1697
Willem de Vlamingh replaces Hartog's plate with his own.

ORIEN HARVEY/GETTY IMAGES ©

➤ *Batavia* wreck, Western Australian Museum (p168)

CONVICTS

post. In 1697, the island was visited by a second Dutch explorer, named Willem de Vlamingh, who swapped Hartog's plate for one of his own.

Other Dutch mariners were not so lucky. Several ships were wrecked on the uncharted western coast of the Aboriginal continent. The most infamous of these is the *Batavia*. After the ship foundered in the waters off modern Geraldton in 1629, the captain, Francis Pelsaert, sailed a boat to the Dutch East India Company's base at Batavia. While his back was turned, some demented crewmen unleashed a nightmare of debauchery, rape and murder on the men, women and children who had been on the ship. When Pelsaert returned with a rescue vessel, he executed the murderers, sparing only two youths whom he marooned on the beach of the continent they knew as New Holland. Some experts believe the legacy of these boys can be found in the sandy hair and the Dutch-sounding words of some local Aboriginal people. The remains of the *Batavia* and other wrecks are now displayed at the Western Australian Museum in Geraldton and in the Fremantle Shipwreck Galleries, where you can also see de Vlamingh's battered old plate.

The Dutch were businessmen, scouring the world for commodities. Nothing they saw on the dry coasts of this so-called 'New Holland' convinced them that the land or its native people offered any promise of profit. When another Dutchman named Abel Tasman charted the western and southern coasts of Australia in 1644, he was mapping not a commercial opportunity but a maritime hazard.

The British (Finally) Claim the West Coast

Today the dominant version of Australian history is written as though Sydney is the only wellspring of Australia's identity. But when you live in WA, history looks very different. In Sydney, white history traditionally begins with Captain James Cook's epic voyage of 1770, in which he mapped the east coast. But Cook creates little excitement in Albany, Perth or Geraldton – places he never saw.

Cook's voyage revealed that the eastern coastline was fertile, and he was particularly taken with the diversity of plant life at the place he called 'Botany Bay'. Acting on Cook's discovery, the British government decided to establish a convict colony there. The result was the settlement of Sydney in 1788 – out of which grew the great sheep industry of Australia.

By the early 19th century, it was clear that the Dutch had no inclination to settle WA. Meanwhile, the British were growing alarmed by the activities of the French in the region. So on Christmas Day 1826, the British army warned them off by establishing a lonely military outpost at Albany, on the strategically important southwestern tip of the country.

Built by convicts, the Fremantle Arts Centre was once a lunatic asylum and then a poorhouse, or 'women's home'. Today this Gothic building is a thriving arts centre well worth a visit.

1826	1829	1829	1834
The British army establishes a military post in Albany, on the southern coast.	Led by Captain James Stirling, a boatload of free immigrants land in the territory of the Noongar people.	Governor Stirling declares all surrounding Aboriginal lands to be the property of King George IV. Perth is founded.	The Battle of Pinjarra occurs after Stirling leads a punitive expedition against the Noongar. It is thought that 25 Aboriginal people are shot, with Stirling's camp suffering one fatality.

The Founding of Perth

The challenge to Aboriginal supremacy in the west began in 1829, when a boatload of free immigrants arrived with all their possessions in the territory of the Noongar people. This group was led by Captain James Stirling – a swashbuckling and entrepreneurial naval officer – who had investigated the coastal region two years earlier. Stirling had convinced British authorities to appoint him governor of the new settlement, and promptly declared all the surrounding Aboriginal lands to be the property of King George IV. Such was the foundation of Perth.

Stirling's glowing reports had fired the ambitions of English adventurers and investors, and by the end of the year, 25 ships had reached the colony's port at Fremantle. Unlike their predecessors in Sydney, these settlers were determined to build their fortunes without calling on government assistance and without the shame of using convict labour.

Frontier Conflict

As a cluster of shops, houses and hotels rose on the banks of the Swan River, settlers established sheep and cattle runs in the surrounding country. This led to conflict with the Aboriginal people, following a pattern which was tragically common throughout the Australian colonies. The Aboriginal people speared sheep and cattle – sometimes for food, sometimes as an act of defiance. In the reprisals that resulted, people on both sides were killed, and by 1832 it was clear that the Aboriginal people were organising a violent resistance. Governor Stirling declared that he would retaliate with such 'acts of decisive severity as will appal them as people for a time and reduce their tribe to weakness'.

In October 1834 Stirling showed he was a man of his word. He led a punitive expedition against the Noongar, who were under the leadership of the warrior Calyute. In the Battle of Pinjarra, the governor's forces shot, according to one report, around 25 Aboriginal people and suffered one fatality themselves. This display of official terror had the desired effect. The Noongar ended their resistance and the violence of the frontier moved further out.

The Deployment of Convicts

Aboriginal resistance was not the only threat to the survival of this most isolated outpost of the British Empire. The arid countryside, the loneliness and the cost of transport also took their toll. When tough men of capital could make a fortune in the east, there were few good reasons to struggle against the frustrations of the west, and most of the early settlers left. Two decades on, there were just 5000 Europeans holding

Kim Scott's *Benang* (1999), which won the Miles Franklin Award in 2000, is a confronting but rewarding read about the assimilation policies of the 20th century and the devastating effect they had on Aboriginal Australia.

1840–41	1850	1860s	1880s–90s
An Aboriginal man called Wylie and explorer Edward Eyre make a staggering journey across the Nullarbor Plain to Albany.	Shiploads of male convicts start to arrive in Fremantle. They go on to build key historical buildings such as Fremantle prison, Government House and Perth Town Hall.	With no democracy, a network of city merchants and squatters exercises control over the colony.	Gold changes everything. The first discoveries are in the Kimberley and the Pilbara, followed by massive finds in Coolgardie and Kalgoorlie.

GALLIPOLI

out on the western edge of the continent. Some of the capitalists who had stayed began to rethink their aversion to using cheap prison labour.

In 1850 – just as the practice of sending British convicts to eastern Australia ended – shiploads of male convicts started to arrive in Fremantle harbour.

Exploration & Gold

Meanwhile, several explorers undertook journeys into the remote Aboriginal territories, drawn in by dreams of mighty rivers and rolling plains of grass 'further out'. Mostly their thirsty ordeals ended in disappointment. But the pastoralists did expand through much of the southwestern corner of WA, while others took up runs on the rivers of the northwest and in the Kimberley.

Perhaps the most staggering journey of exploration was undertaken by an Aboriginal man called Wylie and the explorer Edward Eyre, who travelled from South Australia, across the vast, dry Nullarbor Plain, to Albany.

By the 1880s, the entire European population of this sleepy western third of Australia was not much more than 40,000 people. In the absence of democracy, a network of city merchants and large squatters exercised political and economic control over the colony.

The great agent of change was gold. The first discoveries were made in the 1880s in the Kimberley and the Pilbara, followed by huge finds in the 1890s at Coolgardie and Kalgoorlie, in hot, dry country 600km inland from Perth. So many people were lured by the promise of gold that the population of the colony doubled and redoubled in a single decade. But the easy gold was soon exhausted, and most independent prospectors gave way to mining companies who had the capital to sink deep shafts. Soon the miners were working not for nuggets of gold but for wages. Toiling in hot, dangerous conditions, these men banded together to form trade unions, which remained a potent force in the life of WA throughout the following century.

The Great Pipeline to Kalgoorlie

The year 1890 also saw the introduction of representative government, a full generation after democracy had arrived in the east. The first elected premier was a tough, capable bushman named John Forrest, who borrowed courageously in order to finance vast public works to encourage immigrants and private investors. He was blessed with the services of a brilliant civil engineer, CY O'Connor. O'Connor oversaw the improvement of the Fremantle harbour, and built and ran the state's rail system. But O'Connor's greatest feat was the construction of a system of steam-powered pumping stations along a mighty pipeline to drive water uphill,

Largely set in WA, *Gallipoli* (1981, directed by Peter Weir, screenplay by David Williamson) is an iconic Australian movie exploring naivety, social pressure to enlist and, ultimately, the utter futility of this campaign.

1890	1890	1893	1901
The state's first trade unions are formed by three men. Unions exert a substantial influence for the following century.	Representative government is formed. Bushman John Forrest is the first elected premier.	Inception of the Education Act, which allows white parents to bar Aboriginal children from schools. What follows is a policy of removal of 'half-caste' children from their parents.	WA and the other colonies are federated to form the nation of Australia.

from Mundaring Weir near Perth to the thirsty goldfields around distant Kalgoorlie.

By the time Forrest opened the pipeline, O'Connor was dead. His political enemies had defamed him in the press and in parliament, falsely accusing him of incompetence and corruption. On 10 March 1902, O'Connor rode into the surf near Fremantle and shot himself. Today, the site of his anguish is commemorated by a haunting statue of him on horseback, which rises out of the waves at South Beach.

Ironically, just as the water began to flow, the mining industry went into decline. But the 'Golden Pipeline' continues to supply water to the mining city of Kalgoorlie, where gold is once again being mined, on a Herculean scale unimaginable a century ago. Today you can visit the No 1 Pump Station at Mundaring Weir and follow the Golden Pipeline Heritage Trail as a motorist from Perth to Kalgoorlie, where you can visit the rather astonishing Super Pit.

The Stolen Generations

At the turn of the century, the lives of many Aboriginal people became more wretched. The colony's 1893 Education Act empowered the parents of white schoolchildren to bar any Aboriginal child from attending their school, and it was not long before Aboriginal people were completely excluded from state-run classrooms. The following decade, the government embarked on a policy of removing so-called 'half-caste' children from their parents, placing them with white families or in government institutions. The objective of the policy was explicit. Full-blood Aboriginal people were to be segregated, in the belief that they were doomed to extinction, while half-caste children were expected to marry whites, thereby breeding Aboriginal people out of existence. These policies inflicted great suffering and sorrow on the many Aboriginal people who were recognised in the 1990s as 'the stolen generations'.

Wars & the Depression

On 1 January 1901, WA and the other colonies federated to form the nation of Australia. This was not a declaration of independence. This new Australia was a dominion within the British Empire. It was as citizens of the empire that thousands of Australian men volunteered to fight in the Australian Imperial Force when WWI broke out in 1914. They fought in Turkey, Sinai and in Europe – notably on the Somme. More than 200,000 of them were killed or wounded over the terrible four years of the war. Today, in cities and towns across the state you will see war memorials that commemorate their service.

Though mining, for the time being, had ceased to be an economic force, farmers were developing the lucrative WA wheat belt, which they

1902	1914	1933	1939
Following false accusations of incompetence and corruption, CY O'Connor, engineer of the great pipeline from Perth to Kalgoorlie, takes his own life at a Fremantle beach.	Over 200,000 are killed or wounded in WWI.	Two-thirds of the voting population votes to secede from the rest of the country. Although never enacted, secession remains topical.	WWII begins. Several towns in WA's north, including Broome, are bombed during the war. Fremantle is turned into an Allied naval base, and a US submarine-refuelling base is established at Exmouth.

cultivated with the horse-drawn stump-jump plough, one of the icons of Australian frontier farming. At the same time, a growing demand for wool and beef and the expansion of dairying added to the state's economic growth.

Nevertheless, many people were struggling to earn a living – especially those ex-soldiers who were unable to shake off the horrors they had endured in the trenches. In 1929, the lives of these 'battlers' grew even more miserable when the cold winds of the Great Depression blew through the towns and farms of the state. So alienated did West Australians feel from the centres of power and politics in the east that, in 1933, two-thirds of them voted to secede from the rest of Australia. Although the decision was never enacted, it expressed a profound sense of isolation from the east that is still a major factor in the culture and attitudes of the state today.

In 1939, Australians were once again fighting a war alongside the British, this time against Hitler in WWII. But the military situation changed radically in December 1941 when the Japanese bombed the American fleet at Hawaii's Pearl Harbor. The Japanese swept through Southeast Asia and, within weeks, were threatening Australia. Over the next two years they bombed several towns in the north of the state, including Broome, which was almost abandoned.

It was not the British but the Americans who came to Australia's aid. As thousands of Australian soldiers were taken prisoner and suffered in the torturous Japanese prisoner-of-war camps, West Australians opened their arms to US servicemen. Fremantle was transformed into an Allied naval base for operations in the Indian Ocean, while a US submarine-refuelling base was established at Exmouth. In New Guinea and the Pacific, Americans and Australians fought together until the tide of war eventually turned in their favour.

When *Australia II* won the America's Cup in 1983, Australian Prime Minister Bob Hawke opined, 'Any boss who sacks a worker for not turning up today is a bum'.

Postwar Prosperity

When the war ended, the story of modern Western Australia began to unfold. Under the banner of 'postwar reconstruction', the federal government set about transforming Australia with a policy of assisted immigration, designed to populate Australia more densely as a defence against the 'hordes' of Asia. Many members of this new work force found jobs in the mines, where men and machines turned over thousands of tonnes of earth in search of the precious lode. On city stock exchanges, the names of such Western Australian mines as Tom Price, Mt Newman and Goldsworthy became symbols of development, modernisation and wealth. Now, rather than being a wasteland that history had forgotten, the west was becoming synonymous with ambition, and a new spirit of capitalist pioneering. As union membership flourished, labour and

1963	1967	1970	1979
Development of the gargantuan Ord River Irrigation Scheme to fertilise the desert.	Australia's Indigenous Aboriginal people are recognised as Australian citizens and granted the right to vote.	The Indian Pacific train completes its first trans-continental journey from Sydney to Perth.	The Skylab space station crashes in the state's remote southeastern sector. Remnants are now at the Esperance Museum.

WESTERN AUSTRALIA IN BLACK & WHITE

Like other Aboriginal Australians in the rest of the country, the 70,000 or so who live in WA are the state's most disadvantaged group. Many live in deplorable conditions; outbreaks of preventable diseases are common, and infant-mortality rates are higher than in many developing countries. Indigenous employment in the resources sector is slowly increasing, but the mining boom has not alleviated indigenous social and economic disadvantage to any large degree.

In 1993, the federal government recognised that Aboriginal people with an ongoing association with their traditional lands were the rightful owners, unless those lands had been sold to someone else.

Despite this recognition, the issue of racial relations in WA remains a problematic one, and racial intolerance is still evident in many parts of the state.

capital entered into a pact to turn the country to profit. In the Kimberley, the government built the gigantic Ord River Irrigation Scheme, which boasted that it could bring fertility to the desert – and which convinced many Western Australians that engineering and not the environment contained the secret of life.

There was so much country, it hardly seemed to matter that salt was starting to poison the wheat belt or that mines scoured the land. In 1952 the British exploded their first nuclear bomb on the state's Monte Bello Islands. And when opponents of the test alleged that nuclear clouds were drifting over Australia, the government scoffed. The land was big – and anyway, we needed a strong, nuclear-armed ally to protect us in the Cold War world.

This spirit of reckless capitalism reached its climax in the 1980s when the state became known as 'West Australia Inc' – a reference to the state in operation as a giant corporation in which government, business and unions had lost sight of any value other than speculation and profit. The embodiment of this brash spirit was an English migrant named Alan Bond, who became so rich that he could buy anything he pleased. In 1983 he funded a sleek new racing yacht called *Australia II* in its challenge for the millionaire's yachting prize, the America's Cup. Equipped with a secret – and now legendary – winged keel, the boat became the first non-American yacht to win the race. It seemed as though everyone in Australia was cheering on the day Bond held aloft the shining silver trophy.

But in the 1990s, legal authorities began to investigate the dealings of Alan Bond, and of many other players in West Australia Inc. Bond found himself in court and spent four years in jail after pleading guilty to Australia's biggest corporate fraud.

Once bankrupt and convicted of corporate fraud, Alan Bond's wealth was estimated at $265 million by *Business Review Weekly* in 2008.

1980s	1983	1987
The state becomes known as WA Inc, a reference to its image as a giant corporation intent on speculation and profit.	'Bondie' (Alan Bond) funds the racing yacht *Australia II*, which wins the America's Cup with its secret winged keel. Bond is later jailed for corporate fraud.	Sleepy Fremantle is transformed for Australia's first defence of America's Cup. Australia loses 5-0 to the United States.

ANDREW WATSON/GETTY IMAGES ©

➡ *Australia II* racing yacht

The State Today

WA's mining boom of the early 21st century continues to make the state one of the most dynamic parts of the country. The populations of Perth and key mining areas like the Pilbara are growing faster than east-coast Australia, with many of the state's total population of 2.4 million originally born overseas. There are substantial South African and British communities in Perth, and many New Zealanders and Irish immigrants are taking advantage of employment opportunities in the mining and resources sector. In the case of the Kiwis, they are the ultimate in mobile FIFO ('fly in, fly out') workers, some making the seven-hour flight back home to New Zealand between contracts.

Despite occasional warnings of a slow-down in the Chinese and Indian economies fuelling the mining boom, there's still plenty of optimism in the resources sector. However, the benefits are not spread equally, and for many Perth and WA residents not earning a mine worker's salary, the high costs of accommodation and eating out can be a struggle. WA's high prices, the global financial crisis and a strong Australian dollar have all conspired to put a dampener on the tourism sector, with the north of the state particularly hard hit.

With the huge economies of Asia in close proximity – Indonesia and Vietnam are also being touted as the next countries to drive growth in the mining and agricultural sectors – WA's future remains inexorably linked to the resources under the state's red earth. Huge new developments are planned for the Kimberley region, and even areas around Exmouth and Ningaloo are potentially being dragged into a mining way of life.

Welcome to Australia's biggest environmental battleground of the 21st century.

1990s	1995	1998	2000s
Aboriginal rock art (the Bradshaw paintings), featuring distinctive stick-like images, possibly the earliest figurative painting, is found in the Kimberley. The stolen generations are formally recognised.	The Fremantle Dockers join the Australian Football League.	One of Australia's most infamous trade union battles is waged in Fremantle between the Maritime Union and Patrick Corporation (a stevedore company).	Unparalleled economic growth due to the mining boom.

Local Produce & Wineries

**Regional produce and local wines are the highlights of Western Australia (WA), and lei-
surely, outdoor eating is best experienced in the vineyard restaurants of the Margaret
River, the Porongurups, Denmark and the Swan Valley. Select spots up north – Geraldton, Broome, Kununurra, Exmouth – include a few local gems.**

Local Beer

WA's leading working-class beers are Emu Bitter (EB) and Swan Draught.
They're both pretty bland, so focus instead on exploring the craft-beer
scene. In Fremantle, and the southwest in particular, local microbreweries abound, and the Swan Valley is also a top spot.

In Fremantle, visit the Sail & Anchor and the Monk for blackboards
full of ever-changing brews. Freo also has the iconic Little Creatures, now
owned by a multi-national company but still tasting great with its hoppy
Pale Ale.

In the Swan Valley, the best craft breweries are Feral Brewing Company and Mash Brewing, and Mash also has locations in Bunbury and
Rockingham.

Continuing south, the Margaret River region is emerging as a craft-
beer hot spot – see our picks on p130 – and Denmark's Boston Brewing
Company and Pemberton' Jarrah Jacks are also worth visiting. In Albany,
there's the excellent Tanglehead Brewery at the White Star Hotel, and
good beers and ciders are crafted at the Cidery in Bridgetown.

Up north, the only craft brewery you'll find is Matso's in Broome.
EB and Swan are surprisingly difficult to find, and Carlton, XXXX and
Tooheys dominate the mainstream market.

Australian beer has a higher alcohol content than British or American
beers. Standard beer is around 5% alcohol (midstrength is around 3.5%,
light 2% to 3%).

The Wine Indus-
try Association of
Western Australia
(www.winewa.
asn.au) runs
wine courses for
consumers and
the industry.

Wine & the Cellar Door

Wine is a big deal, with the focus firmly on the quality end of the market.
For example, the Margaret River region produces only 3% of Australia's
grapes but accounts for over 20% of the country's premium wines.

The first wineries began in the southwest in the 1960s, and Vasse Felix
was a notable early player. Because the southwest has always focused on
low-yield, quality output, it wasn't as influenced by the problems of over-
supply that beset the Australian wine industry in 2005 and 2006. Fortui-
tous combinations of rain and warm weather also produced consistently
excellent Margaret River vintages from 2007 to 2011.

Aside from Margaret River, other key winery regions are the Swan
Valley, the Great Southern (Frankland, the Porongurups, Denmark, Mt
Barker) region, Pemberton, and the Peel and Geographe regions. These
all uphold WA's reputation as a world-class wine producer.

**Organic &
Sustainable**

*Perth's City Farm
Market (p64)*

*Margaret River
Farmers Market
(p133)*

*Cullen Wines
(p131)*

Samudra (p126)

Providore (p131)

Local Produce & Wineries

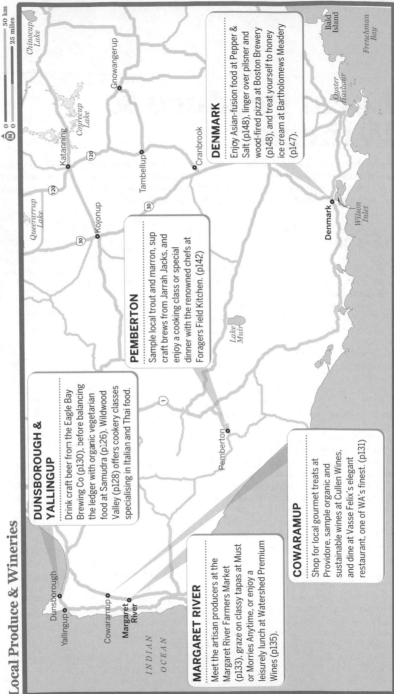

DENMARK

Enjoy Asian-fusion food at Pepper & Salt (p148), linger over pilsner and wood-fired pizza at Boston Brewery (p148), and treat yourself to honey ice cream at Bartholomews Meadery (p147).

PEMBERTON

Sample local trout and marron, sup craft brews from Jarrah Jacks, and enjoy a cooking class or special dinner with the renowned chefs at Foragers Field Kitchen. (p142)

DUNSBOROUGH & YALLINGUP

Drink craft beer from the Eagle Bay Brewing Co (p130), before balancing the ledger with organic vegetarian food at Samudra (p126). Wildwood Valley (p128) offers cookery classes specialising in Italian and Thai food.

COWARAMUP

Shop for local gourmet treats at Providore, sample organic and sustainable wines at Cullen Wines, and dine at Vasse Felix's elegant restaurant, one of WA's finest. (p131)

MARGARET RIVER

Meet the artisan producers at the Margaret River Farmers Market (p133), graze on classy tapas at Must or Morries Anytime, or enjoy a leisurely lunch at Watershed Premium Wines (p135).

MARGARET RIVER'S FOUNDING FIVE

Five top wineries compose the cornerstone of Margaret River.

➡ **Cape Mentelle** Makes consistently excellent cabernet sauvignon and a wonderful example of sauvignon blanc semillon.

➡ **Cullen Wines** (p131) Still in the family, producing superb chardonnay and excellent cabernet merlot while adhering to sustainable winemaking principles.

➡ **Leeuwin Estate** (p135) Stylish cellar door, a highly regarded restaurant, and put chardonnay on the map in Australia with its Art Series.

➡ **Moss Wood** Makes a heady semillon, a notable cabernet sauvignon and a surprising pinot noir.

➡ **Vasse Felix** (p131) Must-see winery with a renowned restaurant.

Margaret River

WA's best wineries are in Margaret River, 250km (3½ hours' drive) southwest of Perth. The climate is defined by cooling ocean breezes, producing Margaret River's distinctively elegant and rich wines.

Margaret River also produces many blends of semillon and sauvignon blanc grapes. These very popular fruity wines are not Margaret River's very best, but they are often the most affordable. Cape Mentelle, Cullen Wines and Lenton Brae all make good examples. Cullen Wines is also renowned for its organic and sustainable approach to winemaking.

Swan Valley

The Swan Valley may once have aspired to take on mighty Margaret River, but now the region's true merit lies in its proximity to Perth and its small clutch of winery-restaurants – not the wines per se. It's hotter than down south, so leisurely outdoor-dining opportunities are better. You can also travel from Perth along the Swan River to the Sandalford Winery.

Houghton Wines is the area's best winery, and the Houghton Classic White, a blend of white-wine grapes that tastes like a mix of tropical, zesty fruits, is the Swan Valley's most ubiquitous wine. Others of note include Lamont Wines and Sandalford. Best for lunch are Riverbank Estate and Lamont's (tapas only).

Peel & Geographe Regions

Because the Peel region starts about 70km south of Perth, it's often hot, dry and rugged. Much like the Swan Valley, wine here is not generally considered of great significance. Millbrook Winery, relatively close to Perth, is excellent for lunch, with a verandah right beside the vines.

Further south, in the slightly cooler Geographe region, are wineries of varying quality, and many people come to visit Capel Vale. This winery has a 30-year history of winemaking excellence, particularly with chardonnay, shiraz and, more recently, merlot. Willow Bridge Estate also produces well-priced wines, with its whites attracting attention.

Great Southern & Pemberton

The Great Southern region will never challenge Margaret River's pre-eminence among wine-touring regions – Margaret River is so spectacularly beautiful – but it nevertheless produces good-quality wines. Wine tourism here is not as developed, and that can be a good thing. Shiraz, cabernet sauvignon, riesling and sauvignon blanc do especially well.

The region stretches from the southeast town of Frankland, further southeast to Albany, and then west again to Denmark. Mt Barker, in the

---

Best Margaret River Winery Restaurants

Cullen Wines
(p131)

Knee Deep in Margaret River
(p131)

Leeuwin Estate
(p135)

Vasse Felix (p131)

Watershed Premium Wines
(p135)

TOURS

Wine for Dudes (p127) has excellent wine tours led by a winemaker. It also visits craft breweries around Margaret River.

LOCAL PRODUCE & WINERIES WINE & THE CELLAR DOOR

ESSENTIAL CELLAR-DOOR STOPS

A second set of wineries that remain standouts:

➡ **Devil's Lair** Small, cosy, stylish cellar door with top-of-the-line chardonnay and cabernet.

➡ **Happs** Impressive wines, including the Three Hills range.

➡ **Pierro** Powerful chardonnay and sauvignon blanc.

➡ **Voyager Estate** (p135) Great wines, and an elegant cellar door and restaurant.

➡ **Xanadu** (p135) Broad range, decent cellar door and restaurant.

middle, is 350km southeast of Perth. The Great Southern's wines are full of flavour and power, and have a sense of elegance – try the peppery shiraz.

In Frankland, Alkoomi is still a family-run business, and produces great cabernet sauvignon and riesling. Ferngrove produces an honest chardonnay, an excellent shiraz and a brilliant cabernet sauvignon–shiraz blend called 'the Stirlings'. Frankland Estate is one of the key wineries that has helped revitalise riesling.

There are more wineries southwest of Frankland, in Mt Barker, and among the nearby Porongurup range. Riesling and shiraz are consistently great performers here; also try the lean, long-flavoured cabernet sauvignon. Two of the best are Forest Hill (try its cabernet sauvignon) and Plantagenet Wines, the area's best winery.

Further south, in Denmark and Albany, are some of Australia's most esteemed wine names. Howard Park, the area's standout, has superb cabernet sauvignon, riesling and chardonnay. West Cape Howe is a straightforward winery that's excellent value, and Wignall's Wines is noted for its pinot noir.

Travelling east of Margaret River in the direction of the Great Southern wine region, you'll hit the Pemberton–Manjimup area (280km due south of Perth). Pemberton is a beautiful, undulating area home to forests of the area's famous karri trees, and its cool-ish climate produces cooler wine styles – pinot noir, merlot and chardonnay, in particular. Excellent producers in Pemberton are Salitage Wines and Smithbrook Wines. Salitage is a large, stylish winery and the wines back it up. Try one of the winery tours. Smithbrook Wines has excellent merlot.

For information and tasting notes about Western Australian wines, and to shop online for reds and whites, visit www.mrwines.com.

Boom Town: Mining & the Environment

If you fly into Perth, you'll notice one thing straight away. The fly-in, fly-out 'FIFO' lifestyle is not only ubiquitous but now the norm. Large clutches of workers nonchalantly board their flights to remote mines and oil and gas plants every few hours. Some will be wearing their fluorescent orange or yellow 'high-vis' vests, required attire on site and perhaps an understated badge of honour at the airport.

1970s
Environmentalists take on and defeat the Albany whaling industry.

1980s
Clashes with loggers over the old-growth jarrah, karri and wandoo forests in the southwest.

2000s
Development of a $200-million marina resort at Ningaloo Reef is prevented.

Today
Controversy over a liquefied natural gas (LNG) refinery at the Kimberley's James Price Point.

How It All Got Started

Really, mining is old news – this is a frontier land founded on mining money. Although in the 1800s Western Australia (WA) was once quietly focused on acquiring more modest fortunes from wheat, meat and wool, gold was discovered in Coolgardie in 1892, and in Kalgoorlie in 1893. And so the transformation to riches began. Today, gold mining is still going strong, albeit with incrementally diminishing returns. In Kalgoorlie you can visit the Super Pit, an open-pit gold mine the size of 35 football fields sunk 360m into the ground. Copper, nickel, oil and gas are also a steady source of state income, with uranium mining (slated for Wiluna, in the midwest) a current aspiration.

But iron ore is today's multi-billion-dollar blockbuster industry. Karara mine in the midwest, for example, sits on just under $100 billion worth of iron ore. All this magnetite dug up out of the ground, later to become iron ore, is expected to generate $3 billion per year in export revenue for the next 30 years. Most of it will go to China.

Of course, foreign investment is big business. And while such major investment has now been criticised for exposing the state to the twisting fortunes of the Chinese economy, the boom would never have occurred without it. For an iron-ore mine, for example, about $1 billion must be available up front just to develop the extraction machinery. These biscuits are just too big for the Australian economy alone.

Life on the Mines

The source of the state's affluence remains outside many travellers' field of view. Take the Pilbara gold-mining town of Telfer, for instance, considered the most remote town in WA. Life here is altogether different to that in the leafy western suburbs of Perth. For Telfer is less traditional country town (with main street, two quiet pubs, maybe a community town hall) and more giant mine plus attendant camp, purpose-built for its hundreds of workers.

The Birth of the Mobile Workforce

In efforts to accommodate a work force that periodically grows and shrinks, Telfer has been dismantled and rebuilt a few times by mining companies over the years. But then in the mid-1990s it was discovered that it was cheaper to simply fly the entire work force in and out rather than continually build and reconstruct permanent accommodation. Under the new plan, those flown in would work for a sustained period of time (say four weeks), then have a week or two off back home – in Perth or over east. The company would then be able to draw from a broader, more skilled labour force, and workers would no longer need to contemplate the unattractive lifestyle of living permanently in the middle of nowhere. As this business model was adopted across the state, the FIFO work culture was born.

Setting Up Camp

The FIFO lifestyle is perhaps no more apparent than in Karratha, once a sleepy, nondescript town but today infamous for its bulging FIFO population, expensive food and severe accommodation shortages. Woodside, a major oil and gas producer, has set up camp here, exploring for gas off the north coast. The pace of expansion was so speedy, in fact, that there wasn't time to build brick-and-tile homes for the workers. And so today in Karratha, bolted on to the original small town centre, are a number of suburbs composed of 'dongas' – makeshift, moveable, one-man accommodation units. A typical donga in Gap Ridge, the main suburb, has a single bed, a TV, a shower and a toilet carved into a shipping-container-like box-home. Meals are taken in the 'wet mess' (much like a mess hall).

Karratha locals have for some time been voicing concerns that an entire FIFO population parties in their town without regard for the community. Places like Gap Ridge are home to an almost entirely young, moneyed, male population, and this has created a pattern of influx and change in Karratha that is echoed in other mining towns across the state. Many labourers are away from home and family, and have considerable funds to sink into beer and good times.

Such social shifts have not gone unnoticed by politicians, including Premier Colin Barnett. One initiative rolled out since the peak of the boom is 'Royalties for Regions' – putting money back into regional areas like Karratha, which had not been able to easily build much-needed infrastructure despite the boom. Mobile-phone coverage is now being expanded on the remote highways.

Work Hard, Play Hard

Drinking has long been part of Australian culture, but FIFO workers off the clock focus particularly keenly on playing hard. Throughout the global financial crisis (or 'GFC' in Australian parlance), letting off steam over a few beers simply continued apace for many. But by late 2012, dropping iron-ore and nickel prices had started to reduce the number of nights out on the town: jobs had been shed. And it is perhaps those who hold the mantra 'work hard, play hard' most closely to their hearts who have been found to be most vulnerable to shakes in the economy. Many young workers have limited education and have been earning big sums from a young age. For some, the upkeep of their lifestyle (jet skis, cars, houses) has always been contingent on a mining salary that did not waver. When it does, there may be no Plan B.

Field Guide to the Birds of Australia is full colour, splendidly detailed, accessible and portable. This endlessly fascinating reference, Pizzey and Knight's claim to fame, is in its 8th edition.

Tim Flannery's *The Future Eaters* is a highly readable overview of evolution in Australasia, covering the last 120 million years of history, with thoughts on how the environment has shaped Australasia's human cultures.

You're In or You're Out

Aboriginal Australian employment is very low within the mining indus-try. Some argue that training programs for Aboriginal Australians – at-tempts to settle Australia's most disadvantaged into the western work-ing life – have not proved effective. Mining magnate Andrew 'Twiggy' Forrest (whom Forbes labelled Australia's richest man in 2010) in 2008 boldly promised support for 50,000 jobs for Aboriginal Australians. This government-backed program is also one of the most high-profile attempts by a key mining figure to not only change employment pat-terns but also speak frankly about the lack of opportunity afforded to Aboriginal communities across the state. Just how the 50,000 jobs will be effectively taken up in the long term is yet to be determined, and that will be the tricky bit. By late 2012, fours years after the program was developed, some 10,000 positions had been taken up.

It is now more widely acknowledged that the gap between the re-source boom–driven 'haves' and 'have-nots' is real and ever increasing, with signs of economic strain creeping up the social strata. The tension between income and cost of living – strongly driven by the high cost of housing – has become so tight that some middle-class workers employed on good salaries struggle to pay the rent. Foreign financial investment is gargantuan, and it will likely be here for some years to come. But pat-terns of job losses, however intermittent, are causing many to wonder aloud how long the good times will last.

The Environmental Flashpoints

Enter James Price Point, an expanse of wilderness along the Kimberley coast 60km north of Broome. A multinational consortium and the WA state government are proposing a liquefied natural gas (LNG) station here – the biggest in the world.

James Price Point has become a leading symbol of tensions between the growing financial fortunes of the state and the less easily quantified value of a pristine, untouched landscape. Not only are mining interests, traditional land owners, politicians and environmentalists in fierce dis-agreement with each other but also divisions within these groups run deep. For locals in the relatively small community of nearby Broome, for instance, 'whose side you're on' is often common knowledge, and this lack of anonymity is a further source of strain.

For the state premier Colin Barnett, successful extraction of the gas at James Price Point would not just award him a badge of honour. It would mark the zenith of the state's contemporary achievements, and he would be leading the charge. In May 2012, in response to noisy but peaceful protestors, over 150 riot police were flown up from Perth to protect the site and quell the clamour.

The approval process for extraction of the gas is lengthy and com-plex. In July 2012 the state's Environmental Protection Authority (EPA), an independent statutory body that provides environmental advice to government, flashed up a green light of approval, subject to a series of restrictions and amendments that included which areas of land should remain untouched (there are dinosaur tracks in evidence) and when gas could be piped out (not at night during in the whales' migratory and breeding season, please).

Four members of the EPA board who helped develop the initial assessment were stood aside due to conflicts of interest. Two had su-perannuation shares in Woodside; one had worked for BP, one of the joint-venture partners of the project; and another had worked for a re-lated state government department. (In many respects, WA is – and al-ways has been – a 'small town'.) This left just one member standing: the

In *The Weather Makers*, Tim Flannery argues lucidly and passionately that there is an immediate need to address the implications of a global change in climate that is damaging all life on earth and endangering our very survival. An accessible read.

Keep your eyes peeled for the banded anteater, also known as the numbat. Tiny, light-footed and incredibly shy, the numbat is a solitary creature who will venture outside its neatly delineated terri-tory only to find a mate. Singular dietary require-ment: termites.

NINGALOO'S CLOSE SCRAPE

Some locals still sport 'Save Ningaloo' bumper stickers on their cars. No one seems to pay much attention to the faded stickers these days, but they're a reminder of one of the most high-profile and fiercely contested environmental campaigns the state has seen. 'Save Ningaloo', with its thousands of protestors, successfully blocked development of a massive marina resort (slated for 2003) on a loggerhead-turtle nesting ground. Comprising 280km of coral reef, and visited by species such as manta rays, whale sharks, dugongs, humpback whales and turtles, Ningaloo is one of the last healthy major reef systems in the world.

The area has nevertheless remained a site of interest for property developers and the resources sector. In late 2012 BHP Billiton submitted a proposal to the state government to explore for LNG some 5km from Ningaloo's perimeter. Regardless of whether exploration goes ahead, the condition of this World Heritage–listed reef will remain precarious and controversial.

WILDFLOWERS

chairman, Paul Vogel. That initial environmental approval for development of the world's largest LNG station was granted by one individual has been a source of consternation for many. Some claim that the environmental-assessment process was not rigorous enough, and that too much about the area remains unknown. Many others, though, see a seemingly endless expanse of coastline and red dirt and believe that, while the financial fruits of development would be expansive, environmental and cultural costs would be limited.

Aside from its dinosaur fossils, it is thought that the area is a playground for spinner and snubfin dolphins, dugongs and breeding bilbies. Humpback whales breed and calve along the coastline, and the rainforest backing the coast harbours a multitude of plant species. Not least, this is traditional Aboriginal land. Negotiating a native title deed this size would mark a historic achievement.

Elsewhere on the Land

But WA's environmental flashpoints are by no means limited to James Price Point. Aside from climate change and greenhouse-gas emissions – issues not unique to WA, of course – ground water has been utilised very freely for decades. Alternative water sources, using desalination plants, have been in place for some time. Old-growth forests, with their thousand-year-old karri trees, were logged until the 1990s. Today scientists cite lowered rainfall in the southwest as the result of deforestation. Other controversial sites slated for mining include the Burrup Peninsula on the Dampier Archipelago, also the location of a multitude of petroglyphs (rock art), archaeological wonders thought to date from the last ice age. Although disruption to the works began in the 1960s, in 2007 Woodside had several petroglyphs gingerly removed and fenced off in a separate area to better facilitate development. Some argue that the works are not discrete: disruption of one petroglyph compromises the entire site. Elsewhere in the state, four uranium mines are under consideration.

Much like other major cities in Australia, Perth is subject to suburban sprawl. Because the boom has driven much property development, the city now tails out across 100km, densely studded with so-called affordable housing. The environmental effects of the lifestyle out here are not immediately apparent but may nevertheless prove significant. Many housing estates are divorced from public-transport routes, so people must always drive for their litre of milk, and the roads are becoming increasingly congested. Many have long been calling for more high-density housing in and near the city of Perth.

For detailed directions on where and how to surround yourself with wildflowers, see the Wildflower Society of Western Australia's website (www.members.ozemail.com.au/~wildflowers).

But Still Booming

Stoushes over the environment are nothing new here. The argument over whether a resort should be developed at Ningaloo, up north, was particularly fierce in the early 2000s (so far development has not gone ahead). And the state is not naive about the environmental dangers of mining. In 2006 and 2007, dangerously high levels of lead were detected after Esperance locals sighted a number of dead birds around the township. Lead had been emitted by local industry, and the Esperance Port Authority has been convicted on lead-contamination charges.

But today the stakes seem higher. LNG exploration at James Price Point is a $30-billion project. The boom has spawned a handful of mega-rich mining magnates whose influence extends beyond resources and into politics and the media. Gina Rinehart, daughter of the late iron-ore magnate Lang Hancock, in 2012 became the largest shareholder in Fairfax Media. Much of the state's population has capitalised on opportunities afforded by the resources boom, and tougher times spent sweating over every utilities bill seem a distant memory. What's more, many of these same people have long said goodbye to steady nine-to-five jobs and embraced a more cosmopolitan lifestyle thanks to financial return from the mines; for them to maintain this lifestyle, such returns must continue to materialise. And yet behind all these competing interests, the fact remains that every new mine or gas plant much reach deep into pristine wilderness.

Locals are fond of wryly mentioning the increasing numbers of educated Irish now coming to toil as FIFO workers. At first glance it seems to be a modern echo of colonial days, but for many it's a reminder that the economic climate is altogether better in WA than overseas. Many Western Australians still feel lucky.

Boomtown 2050, by landscape architect Richard Weller, is a nicely packaged book about how a rapidly growing town like Perth could be developed – sustainably.

Indigenous Art in Western Australia

Experiencing the Indigenous art of Western Australia (WA) creates an indelible link for travellers to this land of red dirt and desert expanses. Ancient rock art echoes across the centuries, traditional designs and motifs inspire modern artists, and indigenous tour operators inform with stories of spirituality, bush tucker and country.

The Western Desert Mob (www.westerndesertmob.com.au) is a coalition of artists cooperatives of the Ngaanyatjarra lands of Western Australia. Mediums include *punu*, the traditional art of woodcarving.

Indigenous Art

Rock Art

Some Aboriginal rock paintings are believed to date back between 18,000 and 60,000 years and provide a record of changing environments and lifestyles over the millennia. For the local Indigenous people, rock-art sites are a major source of traditional knowledge – their historical archives in place of a written form.

The earliest hand or grass prints were followed by a naturalistic style, with large outlines of people or animals filled in with colour. Then came the dynamic style, in which motion was often depicted (a dotted line, for example, to show a spear's path through the air). In this era the first mythological beings appeared, with human bodies and animal heads. Following this were simple human silhouettes, and then the more recent x-ray style, displaying the internal organs and bones of animals.

Art of the Kimberley

The art of the Kimberley is perhaps best known for its images of the Wandjina, a group of ancestral beings who came from the sky and sea and were associated with fertility. They controlled the elements and were responsible for the formation of the country's natural features.

Wandjina images are found painted on rock as well as on more recent contemporary media; some of the rock images are more than 7m long. They generally appear in human form, with large black eyes, a nose but no mouth, a halo around the head (representative of both hair and clouds) and a black oval shape on the chest.

WHERE TO SEE ROCK ART

➡ Mulkas Cave, near Wave Rock and Hyden

➡ Around Esperance with Kepa Kurl (☑08-9072 1688; www.kepakurl.com.au; Museum Village)

➡ The Wandjina and Gwion Gwion images of the Kimberley

➡ Mitchell Falls in the Kimberley

➡ Mt Elizabeth Station on the Gibb River Road

BEST NORTHERN GALLERIES

- ➡ **Gecko Gallery** (☑08-9192 8909; www.geckogallery.com.au; 9 Short St, Broome; ◷10am-6pm Mon-Fri, to 2pm Sat & Sun dry season, shorter hours in wet season)
- ➡ **Short Street Gallery** (☑08-9192 2658; www.shortstgallery.com.au; 7 Short St, Broome; ◷10am-5pm Mon-Fri, to 2pm Sat)
- ➡ **Mowanjum Art & Culture Centre** (☑08-9191 1008; www.mowanjumarts.com; Gibb River Road, Derby; ◷9am-5pm daily dry season, closed Sat & Sun wet season)
- ➡ **Waringarri Aboriginal Arts Centre** (☑08-9168 2212; www.waringarriarts.com. au; 16 Speargrass Rd, Kununurra; ◷8.30am-4.30pm Mon-Fri, dry season 10am-2pm Sat)
- ➡ **Red Rock Art Gallery** (☑08-9169 3000; 50 Coolibah Dr, Kununurra; ◷10am-4pm Mon-Fri)

Each Wandjina traditionally has its own custodian family, and to ensure good relations between the Wandjina and the people, the images have to be retouched annually.

One of the other significant styles of painting found in the Kimberley is that of the Gwion Gwion figures (also named the Bradshaw images after the first non-Indigenous person who saw them). The Gwion Gwion figures are generally small and seem to be of ethereal beings depicted engaged in ceremony or dance. It is believed that they pre-date the Wandjina paintings, though little is known of their significance or meaning.

Western Desert Painting

Western Desert painting, also known as dot painting, is probably the most well known of indigenous painting styles. It partly evolved from 'ground paintings', which formed the centrepiece of dances and songs. These were made from pulped plant material, with designs made on the ground. While dot paintings may look random and abstract, they depict Dreaming stories and can be read in many ways, including as aerial landscape maps. Many paintings feature the tracks of birds, animals and humans, often identifying the land's ancestral beings. Subjects may be depicted by the imprint they leave in the sand – a simple arc depicts a person (as that is the print left by someone sitting cross-legged), a coolamon (wooden carrying dish) is shown by an oval shape, a digging stick by a single line, and a campfire by a circle. Men or women are identified by the objects associated with them: digging sticks and coolamons for women, spears and boomerangs for men. Concentric circles usually depict Dreaming sites, or places where ancestors paused in their journeys.

While these symbols are widely used, their meaning in each painting is known only by the artist and the people closely associated with them – either by clan or by the Dreaming – since different clans apply different interpretations to each painting. In this way sacred stories can be publicly portrayed, as the deeper meaning is not revealed to uninitiated viewers.

Buying Aboriginal Art Ethically

By buying authentic items you are supporting indigenous culture and helping to ensure that traditional and contemporary expertise and designs continue to be of economic and cultural benefit to indigenous individuals and communities. Unfortunately, some of the so-called indigenous art sold as souvenirs is ripped off, consisting of appropriated designs illegally taken from indigenous people or just plain fake, and sometimes made overseas by underpaid workers. Artworks should have

BEST SOUTHERN GALLERIES

→ **Art Gallery of Western Australia** (www.artgallery.wa.gov.au; Perth Cultural Centre; ⊙10am-5pm Wed-Mon) Perth.

→ **Indigenart** (www.mossensongalleries.com.au; 115 Hay St; ⊙10am-5pm Mon-Fri, 11am-4pm Sat) Perth.

→ **Japingka** (www.japingka.com.au; 47 High St; ⊙10am-5.30pm Mon-Fri, noon-5pm Sat & Sun) Fremantle.

→ **Tunbridge Gallery** (www.tunbridgegallery.com.au; 101 Bussell Hwy; ⊙10am-5pm Mon-Sat, to 3pm Sun) Margaret River.

→ **Kepa Kurl Art Gallery** (www.kepakurl.com.au; cnr Dempster & Kemp Sts; ⊙10am-4pm Mon-Fri & market Sun) Esperance.

a certificate of authenticity. Note that haggling is not part of Aboriginal culture.

The best place to buy art is either directly from the communities that have art collectives, or from galleries and outlets that are owned and operated, or supported by indigenous communities. You can then be sure that the items are genuine and that the money you spend goes to the right people. However, some indigenous artists continue to be paid small sums for their work, only to find it being sold for much higher prices in commercial galleries in cities that don't have the interest of the communities producing the art as their priority.

To negate this, it's vital to do some research. The Australian Commercial Galleries Association (www.acga.com.au) lists galleries considered to observe ethical practices. Another excellent organisation is Solid Arts, with its online portal (www.solidarts.com.au) offering support for indigenous artists and ethical considerations to keep in mind when purchasing indigenous art.

Survival Guide

Directory A–Z

Accommodation

Accommodation in Western Australia ranges from camping grounds to high-end hotels. Perth's accommodation is generally more expensive, although Margaret River, Broome, the Coral Coast and Pilbara mining towns come very close. For simplicity, reviews in this book use the same price categories throughout the state.

Over summer (December to February) and around school and public holidays, prices are at their highest. Outside these times discounts and lower walk-in rates can be found. One exception is the far north, where the wet season (November to March) is the low season and prices can drop by as much as 50%.

Accommodation in the Pilbara can be hard to find, due to the fly-in, fly-out (FIFO) mining phenomenon. Camping is often the best option.

B&Bs

Bed and breakfast (B&B) options range from rooms in heritage buildings to a bedroom in a family home. A full cooked breakfast is not the norm. Tariffs for couples are typically in the $150 to $250 range but can be much higher for exclusive properties. For online information, try www.australianbedand breakfast.com.au, www.babs. com.au or www.ozbedand breakfast.com.

Camping & Caravan Parks

For many travellers, touring with a tent or campervan is the consummate WA experience. In the outback and up north you often won't even need a tent. Check with visitor centres before heading out to confirm locations of free roadside stops. Many stops have been phased out immediately north of Perth but are more frequent further away from the city.

Designated camp sites in national parks cost $7/2 per adult/child with no or basic facilities. Sites with showers (including unpowered caravan sites) cost $9/2. You'll also need to pay entrance fees for many national parks, but only when you enter the park. If you're exploring several parks, pick up a four-week national-park holiday pass ($40). Some national-park camp sites can be booked online. See www.dec. wa.gov.au/campgrounds.

At WA's ubiquitous holiday parks, prices for two people range from $25 (unpowered tent sites) to $40 (powered caravan sites). Many caravan parks are phasing out unpowered sites because they are less profitable. Most holiday parks offer accommodation, from simple chalets to flasher motel units.

Pick up the free *Caravanning, Camping and Motorhoming in WA* at visitor centres or see www.cara vanwa.com.au.

Dongas

Commonly found in the outback, especially in mining towns, the donga is basically a prefab tin room (usually air-conditioned) with a single bed, TV and small fridge.

Farmstays & Station Stays

The Gascoyne and Pilbara areas are popular spots for station stays, and at some you may be asked to pitch in. Accommodation is either in the main homestead (B&B style, with dinner on request) or in adjacent self-contained cottages. Other farms provide budget options in outbuildings or former shearers' quarters. Search for 'Farmstay' online at www.tacawa. com.au.

BOOK YOUR STAY ONLINE

For more accommodation reviews by Lonely Planet authors, check out http://hotels.lonelyplanet.com. You'll find independent reviews, as well as recommendations on the best places to stay. Best of all, you can book online.

Hostels

Prices for dorm beds range from $23 to $35, private rooms from $65 to $90. Staff can often help in securing seasonal work.

Some hostels, especially in Perth, are popular as short-term accommodation for FIFO workers, changing the traditional travellers' vibe.

A **Youth Hostel Association** (YHA; www.yha.com.au) or **Hostelling International** (HI; www.hihostels.com) annual membership (in Australia $42) gives a 10% discount at participating hostels. Sign up at the first YHA you stay in.

VIP Backpackers (www.vipbackpackers.com) also offers discounts in participating WA hostels. A 12-month membership ($47) offers discounts on accommodation and some transport, tours and activities. Join online, or at VIP hostels.

Hotels & Motels

Full-service hotels are rare outside of Perth, and coastal properties tend to be resort-style, with standalone cottages or apartments. Rates vary widely, but there are benefits in booking early, directly with the properties, or at the last minute, on accommodation-booking websites.

In rural areas, book ahead, as motels are used by government workers and tour groups.

Pubs

You can sometimes rent a single room at a country pub for not much more than a hostel dorm. If you're a light sleeper, never book a room above the bar. Some pubs also have separate motel-style accommodation.

Rental Accommodation

The ubiquitous holiday flat resembles a motel unit but has cooking and often laundry facilities. They're often rented on a weekly basis, and nightly prices are higher

---

SLEEPING PRICE RANGES

The following price ranges refer to the cheapest double room per night.

$	less than $150
$$	$150 to $250
$$$	more than $250

---

for shorter stays. For listings of holiday homes, see www.stayz.com.au.

For self-contained accommodation, many of the places reviewed in this book will suit; with full kitchens, they're a good option to save money by not eating out. Check out the listings flagged as 'cottage', 'chalet', and 'apartment'.

In cities a good alternative is a serviced apartment. Number Six has apartments around Perth, Fremantle and Margaret River, and others are also listed in this book. See boxed text on p59 for tips to offset high accommodation prices, especially in Perth.

Customs Regulations

For comprehensive information on customs regulations, contact the **Australian Customs Service** (📱02-6275 6666; www.customs.gov.au).

On arrival, declare all goods of animal or plant origin, as it's vital to protect Australia's unique environment and agricultural industries. If you fail to declare quarantine items, you risk an on-the-spot fine of over $200 or even prosecution and imprisonment. For more information contact the **Australian Quarantine and Inspection Service** (AQIS; www.daff.gov.au/aqis).

Duty-free allowances:

➡ Alcohol – 2.25L

➡ Cigarettes – 50

➡ Other goods – up to $900 value; or items for personal use that you will be taking with you when you leave.

Discount Cards

The most common discount card for accommodation, transport and some attractions is the **International Student Identity Card**

GST REFUNDS

The goods and services tax (GST) is a flat 10% tax on all goods and services with the exception of basic food items (milk, bread, fruits and vegetables etc). By law the tax must be included in the quoted or shelf price, so all prices in this book are GST inclusive.

If you purchase goods with a minimum value of $300 from any one supplier (on the same invoice) no more than 30 days before you leave Australia, you are entitled under the Tourist Refund Scheme (TRS) to a refund of any GST paid. The scheme only applies to goods you take with you as hand luggage or wear onto the plane or ship. You can collect your refund at the airport up to 30 minutes before departure. At Perth airport, the refund counter is just after passport control. For more information, contact the Australian Customs Service.

(ISIC; www.isic.org), issued to full-time students aged 12 years and over. See the **International Student Travel Confederation** (ISTC; www.istc.org). ISTC also has an International Youth Travel Card (IYTC or Go25), for people between 12 and 26 years of age who are not full-time students. Benefits are equivalent to the ISIC.

Electricity

240V/50Hz

Embassies & Consulates

The principal diplomatic representations to Australia are in Canberra, but many countries are represented in Perth by consular staff.

Remember that while in Australia you are bound by Australian laws. Your embassy will not be sympathetic if you end up in jail after committing a crime locally, even if such actions are legal in your own country.

Canada (☎08-9322 7930; www.canadainternational.gc.ca; 267 St Georges Tce, 3rd fl)
France (☎0406 654 254; www.ambafrance-au.org; 4/105 Broadway, Nedlands)

Germany (☎08-9221 2941; www.canberra.diplo.de; 2 The Esplanade, Level 18, Exchange Plaza)
Irish Embassy (☎02-6214 0000; www.embassyofireland. au.com; 20 Arkana St, Yarralumla, Canberra, ACT)
Netherlands (☎08-9486 1579; http://australia.nlem bassy.org; 1139 Hay St)
New Zealand Embassy (☎02-6270 4211; www.nzem bassy.com; Commonwealth Ave, Yarralumla, ACT)
UK (☎08-9224 4700; www. fco.gov.uk; 77 St Georges Tce, Level 26, Allendale Sq)
USA (☎08-9202 1224; http://perth.usconsulate.gov; 16 St Georges Tce, 4th fl)

Gay & Lesbian Travellers

In general Australians are open-minded about homosexuality and, in WA, gays and lesbians are protected by anti-discrimination legislation and share an equal age of consent with heterosexuals (16 years).

Perth has the state's only gay and lesbian venues and its small scene is centred on Northbridge. It's very unlikely you'll experience any problems, although the further away from the main centres, the more likely you are to experience overt homophobia.

Useful resources:
Gay & Lesbian Community Service of WA (☎08-9420 7201; www.glcs.org.au; 2 Delhi St) Information and counselling line.

Gay & Lesbian Tourism Australia (GALTA; www.galta.

com.au) Has a handful of WA members offering accommodation and tours.
Q Pages (www.qpages.com. au) Gay and lesbian business directory and what's-on listings.

Health

Australia is a healthy country for travellers. Malaria and yellow fever are unknown, cholera and typhoid are unheard of, and animal diseases such as rabies and foot-and-mouth disease have yet to be recorded. The standard of hospitals and health care is high.

Few travellers should experience anything worse than an upset stomach or a bad hangover.

Before You Go

Bring medications in their original, clearly labelled, containers. A signed and dated letter from your physician describing your medical conditions and medications, including generic names, is also a good idea. If carrying syringes or needles, be sure to have a physician's letter documenting their medical necessity.

Insurance

If your health insurance doesn't cover you for medical expenses abroad, consider getting extra insurance – check www.lonelyplanet.com for more information. Find out in advance if your insurance plan will make payments directly to providers or reimburse you

---

REQUIRED VACCINATIONS

Proof of yellow-fever vaccination is required from travellers entering Australia within six days of having stayed overnight or longer in a yellow-fever-infected country. For a full list of these countries, see the **World Health Organization** (www.who.int/ith) or the **Centers for Disease Control & Prevention** (www.cdc.gov/travel).

later for overseas health expenditures.

Availability & Cost of Health Care

Health insurance is essential for all travellers. While health care in Australia is of a high standard and not overly expensive by international standards, considerable costs can build up and repatriation is extremely expensive.

Australia's health-care system is a mixture of privately run medical clinics and hospitals alongside a government-funded system of public hospitals. The Medicare system covers Australian residents for some health-care costs. Visitors from countries with which Australia has a reciprocal health-care agreement (New Zealand, the UK, the Netherlands, Sweden, Finland, Norway, Italy, Malta, Ireland, Slovenia and Belgium) are eligible for benefits to the extent specified under the Medicare program. If you are from one of these countries check the details before departure. In general the agreements provide for any episode of ill health that requires prompt medical attention. For further details see www.humanservices.gov. au and search for 'reciprocal'.

Over-the-counter medications are widely available at pharmacies. These include painkillers, antihistamines for allergies and skin-care products.

Some medications readily available over the counter in other countries are only available in Australia by prescription. These include the oral contraceptive pill, most medications for asthma and all antibiotics. If you take medication on a regular basis, bring an adequate supply and ensure you know the generic name, as brand names may differ.

Infectious Diseases

BAT LYSSAVIRUS

This disease is related to rabies and some deaths have occurred after bites. The risk is greatest for animal handlers and vets. Rabies vaccine is effective, but the risk to travellers is very low.

DENGUE FEVER

Also known as 'breakbone fever', because of the severe muscular pains that accompany the fever, this viral disease is spread by a species of mosquito that feeds primarily during the day. Most people recover in a few days, but more severe forms of the disease can occur, particularly in residents who are exposed to another strain of the virus (there are four types) in a subsequent season.

GIARDIASIS

Giardiasis is widespread in the waterways around Australia. Drinking untreated water from streams and lakes is not recommended. Water filters, and boiling or treating water with iodine, are effective in preventing the disease. Symptoms consist of intermittent bad-smelling diarrhoea, abdominal bloating and wind. Effective treatment is available (tinidazole or metronidazole).

MENINGOCOCCAL DISEASE

This disease occurs worldwide and is a risk with prolonged, dormitory-style accommodation. A vaccine exists for some types of this disease, namely meningococcal A, C, Y and W. No vaccine is presently available for the viral type of meningitis.

ROSS RIVER FEVER

The Ross River virus is widespread throughout Australia and is spread by mosquitoes living in marshy areas. In addition to fever the disease causes headache, joint and muscular pains and a rash,

before resolving after five to seven days.

SEXUALLY TRANSMITTED DISEASES

STDs occur at rates similar to those in most other Western countries. Always use a condom with any new sexual partner. Condoms are readily available in chemists and through vending machines in many public places including toilets.

VIRAL ENCEPHALITIS

Also known as the Murray Valley encephalitis virus, this is spread by mosquitoes and is most common in northern Australia, especially during the wet season (November to April). This potentially serious disease is normally accompanied by headache, muscle pains and light sensitivity. Residual neurological damage can occur and no specific treatment is available. However, the risk to most travellers is low.

Insurance

Sign up for a travel-insurance policy covering theft, loss and medical problems.

Some policies exclude designated 'dangerous activities' such as scuba diving, parasailing, or even bushwalking. Ensure your policy fully covers you for activities of your choice. Check you're covered for ambulances and emergency medical evacuations by air.

Worldwide travel insurance is available at www.lonelyplanet.com/travel_services.

Internet Access

Internet cafes are located across WA but are becoming less prevalent with the growth of smartphones and other internet-enabled mobile devices. Many backpacker hostels and public libraries offer connections. In smaller towns visit the

Community Resource Centre. The cost ranges from around $5 an hour in Perth to $10 an hour in locations that are more remote.

The best bets for free wi-fi connections are public libraries and cafes. Wi-fi is becoming more prevalent in accommodation; it's sometimes free in hostels but is often charged for in caravan parks and hotels.

Legal Matters

Police have the power to stop your car and see your licence (you're required to carry it), check your vehicle for roadworthiness, and compel you to take a breath test for alcohol.

First-time offenders in possession of small amounts of illegal drugs are likely to receive a fine rather than go to jail, but a conviction may affect your visa status. If you remain in Australia after your visa expires, you will officially be classified as an 'overstayer' and could face detention and expulsion, and be prevented from returning

to Australia for a period of up to three years.

Maps

Tourist-information offices usually have serviceable town maps. For more detailed information, the **Royal Automobile Club of WA** (RACWA; www.rac.com.au) has road maps available (including downloadable route maps). UBD publishes a handy *South West & Great Southern* book.

Hema Maps (www.he mamaps.com.au) Best for the north, especially the dirt roads.

Landgate (www.landgate. wa.gov.au) State-wide maps and topographical maps for bushwalking.

Money

All prices in this books are in Australian dollars, unless otherwise stated.

ATMs

Bank branches with 24-hour ATMs attached can be found

state-wide. In the smallest towns there's usually an ATM in the local pub. Most ATMs accept cards from other banks and are linked to international networks.

Cash

The Australian dollar is made up of 100 cents; there are 5c, 10c, 20c, 50c, $1 and $2 coins, and $5, $10, $20, $50 and $100 notes.

Cash amounts equal to or in excess of the equivalent of A$10,000 (in any currency) must be declared on arrival or departure.

Changing foreign currency or travellers cheques is usually no problem at banks throughout WA.

Credit & Debit Cards

Visa and MasterCard are widely accepted and a credit card is essential (in lieu of a large deposit) for car hire. Any debit cards connected to the international banking network (Cirrus, Maestro, Plus and Eurocard) will work. Diners Club and Amex are not as widely accepted.

Photography

Purchase memory cards, batteries and DV tape in larger cities and towns as they're cheaper than in the remote areas. Most photo labs have self-service machines to make your own prints and burn CDs and DVDs.

Public Holidays

New Year's Day 1 January
Australia Day 26 January
Labour Day First Monday in March
Easter (Good Friday and Easter Monday) March/April
Anzac Day 25 April
Foundation Day First Monday in June
Queen's Birthday Last Monday in September
Christmas Day 25 December
Boxing Day 26 December

PRACTICALITIES

→ Key newspapers are the *West Australian* or the *Australian*, a national broadsheet, from Monday to Saturday, and the *Sunday Times* on Sunday.

→ TV networks include the ad-free ABC, multicultural SBS, and commercial TV stations Seven, Nine and Ten.

→ Tune in to the ABC on the radio – pick a program and frequency from www.abc.net.au/radio.

→ DVDs sold in Australia can be watched on players accepting region 4 DVDs (the same as Mexico, South America, Central America, New Zealand, the Pacific and the Caribbean). The USA and Canada are region 1 countries, and Europe and Japan are region 2.

→ The metric system is used for weights and measures.

→ Smoking is banned on public transport and airplanes, in cars carrying children, between the flags at patrolled beaches, within 10m of a playground and in government buildings. It's also banned within bars and clubs but permitted in al-fresco or courtyard areas.

Safe Travel

Environmental Hazards

HEAT EXHAUSTION & HEATSTROKE

Heat exhaustion occurs when fluid intake does not keep up with fluid loss. Symptoms include dizziness, fainting, fatigue, nausea or vomiting. On observation the skin is usually pale, cool and clammy. Treatment consists of rest in a cool, shady place and fluid replacement with water or diluted sports drinks.

Heatstroke is a severe form of heat illness that occurs after fluid depletion or extreme heat challenge from heavy exercise. This is a true medical emergency: heating of the brain leads to disorientation, hallucinations and seizures. Heatstroke is prevented by maintaining an adequate fluid intake to ensure the continued passage of clear and copious urine, especially during physical exertion.

HYPOTHERMIA

Hypothermia is a significant risk, especially during the winter months in southern parts of Australia. Early signs include the inability to perform fine movements (such as doing up buttons), shivering and a bad case of the 'umbles' (fumbles, mumbles, grumbles, stumbles). The key elements of treatment include changing the environment to one where heat loss is minimised, changing out of any wet clothing, adding dry clothes with windproof and waterproof layers, adding insulation and providing fuel (water and carbohydrate) to allow shivering, which builds the internal temperature. In severe hypothermia, shivering actually stops – this is a medical emergency requiring rapid evacuation in addition to the above measures.

SCHOOL HOLIDAYS

The Christmas season is part of the summer school holidays (mid-December to late January), when transport and accommodation are often booked out, and there are long, restless queues at tourist attractions. There are three shorter school-holiday periods during the year that change slightly from year to year. Generally, they fall in mid-April, mid-July and late September to mid-October.

Animal Hazards

Australia is home to some seriously dangerous creatures. On land there are poisonous snakes and spiders, while the sea harbours deadly box jellyfish and white pointer sharks. The saltwater crocodile spans both environments.

In reality you're unlikely to see these creatures in the wild, much less be attacked by one. Far more likely is a hangover after a big night, or getting sunburnt after not wearing sunscreen.

BOX JELLYFISH & OTHER MARINE DANGERS

There have been fatal encounters between swimmers and box jellyfish on the northern coast. Also known as the sea wasp or 'stinger', they have venomous tentacles that can grow up to 3m long. You can be stung any time, but from November to March you should stay out of the water unless you're wearing a 'stinger suit' (available from sporting shops).

If you are stung, first aid consists of washing the skin with vinegar to prevent further discharge of remaining stinging cells, followed by rapid transfer to a hospital; antivenin is widely available.

Marine spikes from sea urchins, stonefish, scorpion fish, catfish and stingrays can cause severe local pain. If this occurs, immediately immerse the affected area in water as hot as is tolerable. Keep topping up with hot water until the pain subsides and medical care can be reached. The stonefish is found only in tropical Australia; antivenin is available.

CROCODILES

In northwest WA, saltwater crocodiles can be a real danger. They live around the coast, and are also found in estuaries, creeks and rivers, sometimes a long way inland. Observe safety signs or ask locals whether an inviting waterhole or river is croc-free before plunging in. The last fatality caused by a saltwater crocodile was in 1987, and attacks occurred in 2006 and 2012.

INSECTS

For four to six months of the year you'll have to cope with flies and mosquitoes. Flies are more prevalent in the outback, where a humble fly net is effective. Repellents may also deter them.

Mozzies are a problem in summer, especially near wetlands in tropical areas, and some species are carriers of viral infections. Keep your arms and legs covered after sunset and use repellent.

The biting midge (sandfly) can be found in WA's northern coastal areas. Locals often appear immune, but it's almost a rite of passage for those heading north to be covered in bites. Cover up at dusk.

Ticks and leeches are also common. For protection, wear loose-fitting clothing with long sleeves. Apply 30% DEET on exposed skin, repeated every three to four

TAP WATER & OTHER WATER SOURCES

Tap water is universally safe to drink in WA. Increasing numbers of streams, rivers and lakes, however, are being contaminated by bugs that cause diarrhoea, making water purification essential. The simplest way of purifying water is to boil it thoroughly. Consider purchasing a water filter; it's very important when buying a filter to read the specifications, so that you know exactly what it removes from the water and what it doesn't. Simple filtering will not remove all dangerous organisms, so if you cannot boil water it should be treated chemically. Chlorine tablets will kill many pathogens, but not some parasites like giardia and amoebic cysts. Iodine is more effective in purifying water and is available in tablet form. Follow the directions carefully and remember that too much iodine can be harmful.

hours, and impregnate clothing with permethrin.

SHARKS

In 2012 there were six major shark attacks in WA, five of them fatal, and most of them involved surfers at more remote beaches. Around popular coastal and city beaches, shark-spotting methods include spotter planes, jet skis and surf lifesavers, and at the time of writing, the WA government had also launched a $20-million program to track, identify and mitigate (ie kill) sharks that are considered to pose an imminent threat. A shark cull was also being discussed, a controversial proposal given that great white sharks are a protected species. See boxed text on p40 for guidelines on how best to avoid a shark attack.

SNAKES

There are many venomous snakes in the Australian bush, the most common being the brown and tiger snakes. Unless you're interfering with one, or accidentally stand on it, it's extremely unlikely you'll be bitten.

Australian snakes have a reputation that is justified in terms of the potency of their venom, but unjustified in terms of the actual risk to travellers and locals. They are endowed with only small fangs, making it easy to prevent bites to the lower limbs (where 80% of bites occur) by wearing protective clothing (such as gaiters) around the ankles when bushwalking.

The bite marks are small and preventing the spread of toxic venom can be achieved by applying pressure to the wound and immobilising the area with a splint or sling before seeking medical attention. Application of an elastic bandage (you can improvise with a T-shirt) wrapped firmly, but not so tightly circulation is cut off, around the entire limb – along with immobilisation – is a life-saving first-aid measure.

SPIDERS

The redback is the most common poisonous spider in WA. It's small and black with a distinctive red stripe on its body. Bites cause increasing pain at the site followed by profuse sweating and generalised symptoms. First aid includes application of ice or cold packs to the bite and transfer to hospital. White-tailed (brown recluse) spider bites may cause an ulcer that is very difficult to heal. Clean the wound thoroughly and seek medical assistance.

Hospitals have antivenin on hand for all common snake and spider bites, but it helps to know what it was that bit you.

Other Hazards

BUSHFIRES

Bushfires are a regular occurrence in WA and in hot, dry and windy weather, be extremely careful with any naked flame. Even cigarette butts thrown out of car windows can start fires. On a total fire ban day it's forbidden even to use a camping stove in the open.

Bushwalkers should seek local advice before setting out. When a total fire ban is in place, delay your trip until the weather improves. If you're out in the bush and you see smoke, even a long distance away, take heed – bushfires move fast and change direction with the wind. Go to the nearest open space, downhill if possible. A forested ridge is the most dangerous place to be during a bushfire.

CRIME

Western Australia is a relatively safe place to visit, but you should still take reasonable precautions. Don't leave hotel rooms or cars unlocked, and don't leave valuables unattended and visible in cars.

In recent years there has been a spate of glassings (stabbings with broken glass) at Perth venues. If you see trouble brewing, it's best to walk away. Take due caution on the streets after dark, especially around hot spots such as Northbridge. There have also been reports of drinks being spiked with drugs in Perth pubs and clubs. Authorities advise women to refuse drinks offered by strangers in bars and to drink bottled alcohol rather than that in a glass.

DRIVING

Australian drivers are generally a courteous bunch, but rural 'petrolheads', inner-city speedsters and drink drivers can pose risks. Open-road dangers can include include wildlife, such as kangaroos (mainly at dusk and dawn); fatigue, caused by travelling long distances without the necessary breaks; and excessive speed. Driving on dirt roads can also be tricky for the uninitiated.

OUTBACK TRAVEL

If you're keen to explore outback WA, it's important not to embark on your trip without careful planning and preparation. Travellers regularly encounter difficulties in the harsh outback conditions, and trips occasionally prove fatal.

SWIMMING

Popular beaches are patrolled by surf life-savers and flags mark out patrolled areas. Even so, WA's surf beaches can be dangerous places to swim in, if you aren't used to the often heavy surf. Undertows (or 'rips') are the main problem. If you find yourself being carried out by a rip, just keep afloat; don't panic or try to swim against the rip, which will exhaust you. In most cases the current will stop within a couple of hundred metres of the shore and you can then swim parallel to the shore for a short way to get out of the rip and swim back to land.

On the south coast, freak 'king waves' from the Southern Ocean can sometimes break on the shore with little or no warning, dragging people out to sea. In populated areas there are warning signs; in other areas, be extremely careful.

People have been paralysed by diving into waves in shallow water and hitting a sandbar; check the depth of the water before you leap.

Telephone

The two main telecommunications companies are **Telstra** (www.telstra.com.au) and **Optus** (www.optus.com.au).

Both are also major players in the mobile (cell) market, along with **Vodafone** (www.vodafone.com.au), **Virgin** (www.virginmobile.com.au) and **3** (www.three.com.au).

Local calls from private land lines cost 15c to 30c, while local calls from public phones cost 50c; both allow for unlimited talk time. Calls to mobile phones attract higher rates and are timed.

Although the whole of WA shares a single area code (☎08), once you call outside of the immediate area or town, it is likely that you are making a long-distance call. STD calls (Subscriber Trunk Dialling – a long-distance call within Australia) can be made from public phones and are cheaper during off-peak hours, generally between 7pm and 7am.

Phonecards can be purchased at newsagents and post offices for a fixed dollar value (usually $10, $20, $30 etc) and can be used with any public or private phone by dialling a toll-free access number and then the PIN number on the card. Call rates vary, so shop around. Some public phones also accept credit cards.

Mobile Phones

Australia's GSM and 3G mobile networks service more than 90% of the population but leave vast tracts of the country uncovered, including much of inland WA. Perth and

the larger centres get good reception, but outside these centres it's haphazard or nonexistent, especially in the north. Of the mobile telcos, Telstra has the best coverage for both voice and internet services.

Australia's digital network is compatible with GSM 900 and 1800 (used in Europe), but is generally not compatible with the US or Japanese systems. All the main service providers offer prepaid mobile services for short-term access.

Phone Codes

➡ ☎0011 International calling prefix (the equivalent of 00 in most other countries).

➡ ☎61 Australia's country code.

➡ ☎08 Area code for all of WA. If calling from overseas, drop the initial zero.

➡ ☎04 All numbers starting with ☎04 (such as ☎0410, ☎0412) are mobile phone numbers. If calling from overseas, drop the initial '0'.

➡ ☎190 Usually recorded information calls, costing from 35c to $5 or more per minute (more from mobiles and payphones).

➡ ☎1800 Toll-free numbers; can be called free of charge from anywhere in the country, though they may not be accessible from

---

A BIT OF PERSPECTIVE

Despite the recent increase in fatal shark attacks in WA, statistically it's still very unlikely that visitors will be attacked. Blue-ringed octopus deaths are even rarer – only two in the last century – and there's only ever been one confirmed death from a cone shell. Jellyfish kill about two people annually, but you're still 100 times more likely to drown.

On land, snakes kill one or two people per year (about the same as bee stings, or less than a thousandth of those killed on the roads). There hasn't been a recorded death from a tick bite for over 50 years, nor from spider bites in the last 20.

RESPONSIBLE INDIGENOUS TRAVEL

There are a range of protocols for visiting indigenous lands, but it's always courteous to make contact prior to your visit. In many cases you must acquire a permit to enter, so check with local Indigenous Land Councils and police stations before visiting.

Some indigenous sites are registered under heritage legislation and have conditions attached, or may be visited only with permission from their traditional custodians or in their company. Don't touch artworks, as the skin's natural oils can cause deterioration. Dust also causes problems – move thoughtfully at rock-art sites and leave your vehicle some distance away. Respect the wishes of indigenous custodians by reading signs carefully, keeping to dedicated camping areas and staying on marked tracks. Remember that rock art and engravings are manifestations of sacred beliefs and laws.

When interacting with Indigenous Australians, you'll generally find them polite and willing to share their culture with you – but it must be on their terms. Show respect for privacy and remember that your time constraints and priorities may not always be shared. In some areas, English is not a first language, but in others many people speak English fluently. Body language and etiquette often vary: the terms 'thank you', or 'hello' and 'goodbye', may not be used in some areas, or direct eye contact may be avoided. So take note of local practices: take them as they come and follow the cues. Some Aboriginal communities are 'dry'. There may be rules relating to the purchase and consumption of alcohol, or it may be forbidden altogether.

certain areas or from mobile phones.

➜ ☑1800-REVERSE (738 3773) or ☑12 550 For reverse-charge (collect) calls from any public or private phone.

➜ ☑13 or ☑1300 Cost of a local call. The numbers can usually be dialled Australia-wide, but may be applicable only to a specific state or STD district.

Note: ☑1800, ☑13 or ☑1300 numbers can't be dialled from outside Australia.

Tourist Information

For general statewide information, try the WA Visitor Centre in Perth.

Around WA, tourist offices with friendly staff (often volunteers) provide local knowledge including info on road conditions.

Travellers with Disabilities

Disability awareness in WA is excellent. Legislation requires that new accommodation meets accessibility standards, and discrimination by tourism operators is illegal. Many of the state's key attractions provide access for those who have limited mobility, and an increasing number of places are addressing the needs of visitors who have visual or aural impairments. It's advisable to contact attractions in advance to confirm the facilities that are available.

Useful contacts:

Association for the Blind of WA (☑1800 847 466, 08-9311 8202; www.abwa.asn.au)

Easy Access Australia (www.easyaccessaustralia.com.au) Available from bookshops and detailing accessible transport, accommodation and attraction options.

National Information Communication & Awareness Network (Nican; ☑02-6241 1220, TTY 1800 806 769; www.nican.com.au) National directory with information on access issues, accessible accommodation, sporting and recreational activities, transport and specialist tour operators.

National Public Toilet Map (www.toiletmap.gov.au) Over 2300 public and private toilets, including those with wheelchair access.

People with Disabilities WA (PWdWA; ☑08-9485 8900, 1800 193 331; www.pwdwa.org) Website detailing WA's major disability service providers.

Tourism WA (www.westernaustralia.com) Website highlighting all accessible listings (accommodation, restaurants, tours etc).

WA Deaf Society (☑08-9441 2677, TTY 08-9441 2655; www.wadeaf.org.au)

Visas

All visitors to Australia need a visa – only New Zealand nationals are exempt, and even they receive a 'special category' visa on arrival. Visa application forms are available from Australian diplomatic missions overseas, travel agents or the website of the **Department of Immigration and Citizenship** (☑13 18 81; www.immi.gov.au).

eVisitor

Many European passport holders are eligible for an eVisitor, which is free and allows visitors to stay in Australia for up to three months. eVisitors must be applied for online and they are electronically stored and linked to individual passport numbers, so no stamp in your passport is required. It's advisable to apply at least 14 days prior to the proposed date of travel to Australia. Applications are made on the Department of Immigration and Citizenship website.

Electronic Travel Authority (ETA)

Passport holders from eight countries that aren't part of the eVisitor scheme – Brunei, Canada, Hong Kong, Japan, Malaysia, Singapore, South Korea and the USA – can apply for either a visitor or business ETA. ETAs are valid for 12 months, and allow stays of up to three months on each visit. Apply online at www.eta.immi.gov.au.

Tourist Visas

Short-term tourist visas have largely been replaced by the eVisitor and ETA. However, if you are from a country not covered by either, or you want to stay longer than three months, you'll need to apply for a visa. Tourist visas cost $105 and allow single or multiple entry for stays of three, six or 12 months and are valid for use within 12 months of issue.

Visa Extensions

If you want to stay in Australia for longer than your visa allows, you'll need to apply for a new visa (usually a tourist visa 676) through the Department of Immigration and Citizenship at www.immi.gov.au/visitors/tourist. Apply at least two or three weeks before your visa expires.

Work & Holiday Visas (462)

Nationals from Bangladesh, Chile, Indonesia, Iran, Malaysia, Thailand, Turkey and the USA between the ages of 18 and 30 can apply for a work and holiday

visa prior to entry to Australia. It allows the holder to enter Australia within three months of issue, stay for up to 12 months, leave and re-enter Australia any number of times within that 12 months, undertake temporary employment to supplement a trip, and study for up to four months.

Working Holiday Maker (WHM) Visas (417)

Young visitors (those aged 18 to 30) from Belgium, Canada, Cyprus, Denmark, Estonia, Finland, France, Germany, Hong Kong, Ireland, Italy, Japan, Korea, Malta, the Netherlands, Norway, Sweden, Taiwan and the UK are eligible for a WHM visa, allowing visits of up to one year and casual employment.

The emphasis of this visa is on casual and not full-time employment, so you're only supposed to work for any one employer for a maximum of six months. A first WHM visa must be obtained prior to entry to Australia and can be applied for at Australian diplomatic missions abroad or online (www.immi.gov.au/visitors/working-holiday). You can't change to a WHM visa once you're in Australia, so apply up to 12 months before your departure to Australia.

Women Travellers

WA is generally a safe place for women travellers, although the usual sensible precautions apply. Avoid walking alone late at night in major cities and towns, and always keep enough money aside for a taxi home. The same applies to outback and rural towns with unlit, semi-deserted streets between you and your temporary home. Lone women should be wary of staying in basic pub accommodation unless it appears safe and well managed.

Lone hitching is risky for everyone, but women especially should consider taking a male companion.

Work

If you come to Australia on a tourist visa then you're not allowed to work for pay – working for approved volunteer organisations in exchange for board is OK. If you're caught breaching your visa conditions, you can be expelled from the country and banned for up to three years.

Seasonal Work

WA is experiencing a labour shortage and a wealth of opportunities exist for travellers (both Australian and foreign) for paid work year-round.

In Perth, plenty of temporary work is available in tourism and hospitality, administration, IT, nursing, childcare, factories and labouring. Outside Perth, travellers can easily get jobs in tourism and hospitality, plus a variety of seasonal work. Some places have specialised needs; in Broome, for example, there is lucrative work in pearling, on farms and boats.

INDUSTRY	TIME	REGION(S)
grapes	Feb-Mar	Denmark, Margaret River, Mt Barker, Manjimup
apples/ pears	Feb-Apr	Donnybrook, Manjimup
prawn trawlers	Mar-Jun	Carnarvon
bananas	Apr-Dec	Kununurra
bananas	year-round	Carnarvon
vegies	May-Nov	Kununurra, Carnarvon
tourism	May-Dec	Kununurra
flowers	Sep-Nov	Midlands
lobsters	Nov-May	Esperance

Information

Backpacker accommodation, magazines and newspapers are good resources for local work opportunities.

Useful websites:

Australian Jobsearch (www.jobsearch.gov.au) Government site offering a job database.

Career One (www.careerone. com.au) General employment site, good for metropolitan areas.

Centrelink (www.centrelink. gov.au) The Australian government employment service has information and advice on looking for work, training and assistance.

Gumtree (http://perth.gum tree.com.au) Great classified site with jobs, accommodation and items for sale.

Harvest Trail (http://job search.gov.au/HarvestTrail) Specialised recruitment search for the agricultural industry, including a 'crop list' detailing what you can pick and pack, when and where.

Job Shop (www.thejobshop. com.au) WA-based recruitment agency specialising in jobs for WA as well as the Northern Territory.

MyCareer (www.mycareer. com.au) General employment site, good for metropolitan areas.

Seek (www.seek.com.au) General employment site, good for metropolitan areas.

Travellers at Work (www. taw.com.au) Excellent site for working travellers in Australia.

West Australian (www. thewest.com.au) WA's main newspaper advertises jobs online.

Volunteering

Lonely Planet's *Volunteer: A Traveller's Guide to Making a Difference Around the World* provides useful information about volunteering. Organisations that take on volunteers include the following.

Conservation Volunteers Australia (CVA;☎03-5330 2600, 1800 032 501; www. conservationvolunteers.com. au) A nonprofit organisation focusing on practical conservation projects such as tree planting, walking-track construction, and flora and fauna surveys. Most projects are either for a weekend or a week and all food, transport and accommodation is supplied in return for a contribution to help cover costs ($40 per day, $208 for four nights).

Department of Environment and Conservation (DEC; www.dec.wa.gov.au) Current and future opportunities at national parks all over WA. Online, click on the Community & Education tab and then Volunteer Programs. Opportunities vary enormously, from turtle tagging at Ningaloo Marine Park to feral-animal control at

Shark Bay. Working with the dolphins at Monkey Mia is a popular program (contact: monkeymiavolunteers@ westnet.com.au).

Willing Workers on Organic Farms (WWOOF;☎03-5155 0218; www.wwoof.com. au) Work four to six hours each day on a farm in return for bed and board, often in a family home. Almost all places have a minimum stay of two nights. Not all places are farms – you might help out at a pottery or do the books at a seed wholesaler. Most placements have a connection to alternative lifestyles.

Earthwatch Institute (☎03-9682 6828; www.earth watch.org) Offers volunteer 'expeditions' focusing on conservation and wildlife.

Go Volunteer (www.govolun teer.com.au) National website that lists volunteer opportunities.

i-to-i (www.i-to-i.com) Volunteer holidays in Australia, focused on conservation.

Responsible Travel (www. responsibletravel.com) Volunteer travel opportunities.

STA (www.statravel.com.au) Click on 'Experiences' and go to the volunteer link.

Transitions Abroad (www. transitionsabroad.com) Listings of volunteer opportunities.

Volunteering Australia (www.volunteeringaustralia.org) Support, advice and volunteer training.

Transport

GETTING THERE & AWAY

Unless you're coming by land from other states in Australia, chances are you'll be touching down in Perth. Western Australia's (WA's) capital is considerably closer to Southeast Asia than it is to Australia's east coast – it's actually closer to Jakarta than to Sydney.

Flights, tours and rail tickets can be booked online at www.lonelyplanet.com/bookings.

Entering the Country

Global instability has resulted in increased security in Australian airports, in both domestic and international terminals. Customs procedures may be a little more time-consuming but are still straightforward.

Air

Airports & Airlines

If you're coming to Australia from Europe, Asia or Africa you'll find it quicker to fly directly to **Perth Airport** (PER; ☑08-9478 8888; www.perthairport.com). If you do fly to the east coast first, there are frequent connecting flights to Perth from major cities. Port Hedland has international flights to/from Bali, while Port Hedland and Broome both welcome interstate flights.

AIRLINES FLYING TO & FROM WA

All flights listed here are to Perth, unless otherwise specified, and all phone numbers are for dialling from within Australia.

Air Asia (D7;☑1300 760 330; www.airasia.com) Budget flights from Kuala Lumpur and Denpasar (Bali).

Air Mauritius (MK; ☑1300 332 077; www.airmauritius.com) Flies from Mauritius.

Air New Zealand (NZ;☑13 24 76; www.airnz.com.au) Flies from Auckland.

Airnorth (TL; ☑1800 627 474; www.airnorth.com.au) Destinations include Perth, Broome, Darwin, Kununurra, Karratha and Port Hedland.

Cathay Pacific (CX;☑13 17 47; www.cathaypacific.com) Flies from Hong Kong.

Emirates (EK;☑1300 303 777; www.emirates.com) Flies from Dubai.

Garuda Indonesia (GA; ☑08-9214 5101; www.garuda-indonesia.com) Flies from Denpasar and Jakarta.

Jetstar (JQ;☑13 15 38; www.jetstar.com) Runs cheapies from Sydney, Melbourne, Brisbane, Cairns, Adelaide and the Gold Coast. International routes include Jakarta and Denpasar.

Malaysia Airlines (MH; ☑08-9263 7043, 13 26 27;

CLIMATE CHANGE & TRAVEL

Every form of transport that relies on carbon-based fuel generates CO_2, the main cause of human-induced climate change. Modern travel is dependent on aeroplanes, which might use less fuel per kilometre per person than most cars but travel much greater distances. The altitude at which aircraft emit gases (including CO_2) and particles also contributes to their climate change impact. Many websites offer 'carbon calculators' that allow people to estimate the carbon emissions generated by their journey and, for those who wish to do so, to offset the impact of the greenhouse gases emitted with contributions to portfolios of climate-friendly initiatives throughout the world. Lonely Planet offsets the carbon footprint of all staff and author travel.

www.malaysiaairlines.com)
Flies from Kuala Lumpur.

Qantas (QF;☑13 13 13; www.qantas.com.au) Direct flights from Hong Kong and Singapore. Flies between Perth and all Australian state capitals (excluding Hobart), as well as Cairns, Alice Springs and Uluru (Ayers Rock). Also flies from Kalgoorlie to Adelaide and Perth, and from Melbourne to Broome year round, and from Sydney and Brisbane to Broome during school holidays.

Qatar Airways (QR;☑1300 340 600; www.qatarairways.com) Flies from Doha.

Singapore Airlines (SQ;☑13 10 11; www.singaporeair.com.au) Flies from Singapore.

Skywest (XR;☑1300 660 088; www.skywest.com.au) Regional and international destinations from Perth including Darwin, Melbourne and Denpasar. Bali to Port Hedland on weekends.

South African Airways (SA;☑1300 435 972; www.flysaa.com) Flies from Johannesburg.

Thai Airways International (TG;☑1300 651 960; www.thaiairways.com) Flies from Bangkok.

Tiger Airways (TR;☑03-9335 3033; www.tigerairways.com) From Melbourne and Singapore.

Virgin Australia (DJ;☑13 67 89; www.virginaustralia.com) Links Perth to other Australian state capitals, except Canberra and Hobart. International destinations include Denpasar and Phuket.

Land

The nearest state capital to Perth is Adelaide, 2560km away by the shortest road route. To Melbourne it's at least 3280km, Darwin is around 4040km and Sydney 3940km. Despite the vast distances, sealed roads cross the Nullarbor Plain from the eastern states to Perth, and

then up the Indian Ocean coast and through the Kimberley to Darwin.

Bus

The only interstate bus is the daily **Greyhound** (☑1300 473 946; www.greyhound.com.au) service between Darwin and Broome ($361, 27½ hours), via Kununurra, Fitzroy Crossing and Derby.

Car, Motorcycle & Bicycle

Driving to Perth from any other state is a *very* long journey, but it's a great way to see the country. Be aware that there are strict quarantine restrictions on fruit and vegetables when crossing the border into WA.

Hitching

Hitching is never entirely safe – we don't recommend it. Hitching to or from WA across the Nullarbor is definitely not advisable, as waits of several days are not uncommon.

People looking for travelling companions for driving to WA from Sydney, Melbourne, Adelaide or Darwin frequently leave notices in backpacker hostels. See also car-share websites (p267).

Train

The only interstate rail link is the famous Indian Pacific, run by **Great Southern Rail** (☑13 21 47; www.greatsouthernrail.com.au), which travels 4352km to Perth from Kalgoorlie (10 hours), Adelaide (two days), Broken Hill (2¼ days) and Sydney (three days). From Port Augusta to Kalgoorlie the seemingly endless crossing of the virtually uninhabited centre takes well over 24 hours, including the 'long straight' on the Nullarbor – at 478km this is the longest straight stretch of train line in the world. You can take 'whistle-stop' tours of some towns on the way.

Flexible one-way adult fares for the full journey are $783 (reclining seat), $1700 (sleeper cabin) and

$2178 ('gold service', including meals). Substantial discounts are available off the seat-only price for backpackers, students, children and pensioners, and non-cancellable 'Ready Rail' and 'Rail Saver' fares also offer significant discounts.

Cars can be transported between Perth and Sydney, Melbourne and Adelaide – a good alternative to driving across the Nullarbor Plain in both directions. Note that service is usually around 40% cheaper *from* Perth, than *to* Perth.

GETTING AROUND

The distances between key WA towns are vast, especially in the north.

Air

Unless you have unlimited time, consider internal flights.

Airlines Flying Within WA

Airnorth (TL;☑1800 627 474; www.airnorth.com.au) Routes include Perth–Kununurra, Karratha–Port Hedland, Karratha–Broome, Port Hedland–Broome and Broome–Kununurra.

Cobham (☑1800 105 503; www.cobham.com.au) Flies between Perth and Kambalda.

Qantas (☑13 13 13; www.qantas.com.au; 55 William St) WA destinations include Kalgoorlie, Paraburdoo, Newman, Exmouth, Karratha, Port Hedland and Broome.

Skippers Aviation (☑1300 729 924; www.skippers.com.au) Flies three routes in both directions: Perth–Leonora–Laverton, Perth–Wiluna–Leinster, Perth–Mt Magnet–Meekatharra, Perth–Carnarvon, Perth–Geraldton–Carnarvon and Perth–Kalbarri–Monkey Mia. Of most relevance to the mining industry. Also flies

Broome–Fitzroy Crossing–Halls Creek.

Skywest (XR;✈1300 660 088; www.skywest.com.au) Flies to Perth, Busselton, Albany, Esperance, Geraldton, Exmouth, Port Hedland and Kalgoorlie.

Alliance Airlines (✈1300 780 970; www.allianceairlines.com.au) Mine-industry services linking Broome and Karratha, but also can be booked by the public.

Virgin Australia (DJ;✈13 67 89; www.virginaustralia.com) Flies from Perth to Broome, Karratha, Port Hedland, Christmas Island and the Cocos Islands.

Bicycle

Bicycle helmets are compulsory in WA, as are white front lights and red rear lights for riding at night.

If you're coming specifically to cycle, bring your own bike. Check with your airline for costs. Within WA you can load your bike onto a bus to skip the boring bits of the country. Book well ahead so that you and your bike can travel on the same vehicle.

Suffering dehydration is a very real risk in WA and can be life-threatening. It can get very hot in summer, so take things slowly until you're used to the heat. A prudent plan is to start riding every day at sunrise, relax in the shade – bring your own shelter – during the heat of the day and then ride a few more hours in the afternoon. Always wear a hat and plenty of sunscreen, and drink *lots* of water.

Outback travel needs to be planned thoroughly, with the availability of drinking water the main concern. Those isolated water sources (bores, tanks, creeks) shown on your map may be dry or undrinkable, so you can't always depend on them. Also don't count on getting water from private mine sites as many are closed to the public.

Bring necessary spare parts and bike-repair knowledge. Check with locals (start at the visitor centres) if you're heading into remote areas, and always let someone know where you're headed before setting off.

Useful contacts for information on touring around WA, including suggested routes, road conditions and cycling maps:

Bicycle Transportation Alliance (✈08-9420 7210; www.btawa.org.au)
Cycle Touring Association of WA (www.ctawa.asn.au)

Bus

WA's bus network could hardly be called comprehensive, but it offers access to substantially more destinations than the railways. All long-distance buses are modern and well equipped with air-con, toilets and videos.

Main Companies

Greyhound (✈1300 473 946; www.greyhound.com.au) North of Geraldton, Greyhound is the main provider, with services from Perth to Broome via Geraldton, Carnarvon, Karratha and Port Hedland, and from Broome to Darwin, via the Great Northern Hwy. Multiday passes allow you to stop along the route.

Integrity Coach Lines (✈1800 226 339; www.integritycoachlines.com.au) Weekly buses between Perth and Port Hedland via the Great Northern Hwy, and also from Perth to Lancelin, Cervantes, Geraldton and Exmouth.

South West Coach Lines (✈08-9261 7600; www.veolia transportwa.com.au) From Perth to all the major towns in the southwest – your best choice for Margaret River.

Transwa (✈1300 662 205; www.transwa.wa.gov.au) The state government's transport service, operating mainly in the southern half of the state. Main routes include Perth–Augusta,

Perth–Pemberton, Perth–Albany (three different routes), Perth–Esperance (two routes), Albany–Esperance, Kalgoorlie–Esperance, Perth–Geraldton (three routes) and Geraldton–Meekatharra.

Car & Motorcycle

Providing the freedom to explore off the beaten track, travelling by vehicle is the best option in WA. With several people travelling together, costs can be contained and, if you don't have major mechanical problems, there are many benefits.

The climate is good for motorcycles for much of the year, and many small trails into the bush lead to perfect camping spots. Bringing your own motorcycle into Australia requires valid registration in the country of origin and a Carnet de Passages en Douanes, allowing the holder to import their vehicle without paying customs duty or taxes. Apply to the motoring organisation/association in your home country. You'll also need a rider's licence and a helmet. A fuel range of 350km will cover fuel stops up the centre and on Hwy 1 around the continent. The long, open roads are really made for large-capacity machines above 750cc.

The **Royal Automobile Club** (RAC; ✈13 17 03; www.rac.com.au) has useful advice on state-wide motoring, including road safety, local regulations and buying/selling a car. It also offers car insurance to members, and membership can secure discounts on car rentals and motel accommodation.

Also popular are car-share sites, especially for securing a lift to Broome, Perth, Denmark and Darwin. See the following websites: www.findalift.com.au, www.needaride.com, www.coseats.com, www.gumtree.com.au.

Driving Licence

You can use your own home country's driving licence in WA for up to three months, as long as it carries your photo for identification and is in English. Alternatively, arrange an International Driving Permit (IDP) from your home country's automobile association and carry it along with your licence.

Fuel

Fuel (predominantly unleaded and diesel) is available from service stations. Liquefied petroleum gas (LPG) is not always stocked at more remote roadhouses – if your car runs on gas it's safer to have dual fuel capacity.

Prices vary wildly in WA, even between stations in Perth. For up-to-date fuel prices, visit the government fuel-watch website (www. fuelwatch.wa.gov.au).

Distances between fill-ups can be long in the outback, but there are only a handful of tracks where you'll require a long-range fuel tank or need to use jerry cans. However, if you are doing some back-road explorations, always calculate your fuel consumption, plan accordingly and carry a spare jerry can or two. Keep in mind that most small-town service stations are only open from 6am to 7pm and roadhouses aren't always open 24 hours. On main roads there'll be a small town or roadhouse roughly every 150km to 200km.

Always carry two spare tyres and at least 20L of water.

Hire

Competition between car-rental companies in Australia is fierce, so rates vary and special deals come and go.

The main thing to remember when assessing your options is distance – if you want to travel widely, you need to weigh up the price difference between an unlimited kilometres deal and one that offers a set number of kilometres free with a fee per kilometre over that set number.

Local firms are always cheaper than the big operators – sometimes half the price – but cheap car hire often comes with restrictions on how far you can take the vehicle away from the rental centre.

Some, but not all, car-rental companies offer one-way hires, so research this option before you arrive. It's worth investigating and combining with an internal flight if you're travelling to somewhere like Exmouth, Broome or Esperance. A significant premium is usually charged. There are sometimes good deals for taking a car or campervan from, say, Broome back to Perth, but you'll need to contact local rental companies closer to the time of rental.

You must be at least 21 years old to hire from most firms – if you're under 25 you may only be able to hire a small car or have to pay a surcharge. A credit card will be essential.

Renting a 4WD enables you to safely tackle routes off the beaten track and get out to more remote natural wonders. Note that many 'normal' rental cars aren't allowed off main roads, so always check insurance conditions carefully, especially the excess, as they can be onerous. Even for a 4WD, the insurance offered by most companies does not cover damage caused when travelling 'off-road', which basically means anything that is not a maintained bitumen or dirt road.

Avis (☎13 63 33; www.avis. com.au)

4WD DRIVING TIPS

We don't need to see more 4WDs on tow trucks: the victims of a dirt-road rollover, a poorly judged river crossing, or coming to grief when meeting the native fauna on the road. Here are some tips to help keep you from riding upfront in a tow truck:

➡ Before heading off-road, check the road conditions at www.mainroads.wa.gov.au.

➡ Recheck road conditions at each visitor centre you come across – they can change quickly.

➡ Let people know where you're going, what route you're taking and how long you'll be gone.

➡ Don't drive at night: it's safer to stop in the mid-afternoon to avoid wildlife.

➡ Avoid sudden changes in direction – 4WDs have a much higher centre of gravity than cars.

➡ On sand tracks, reduce tyre pressure to 140kpa (20psi) and don't forget to reinflate your tyres once you're back on the tarmac.

➡ When driving on corrugated tracks, note that while there is a 'sweet spot' speed where you feel the corrugations less, it's often too fast to negotiate a corner – and rollovers often happen because of this.

➡ When crossing rivers and creeks, always walk across first to check the depth – unless you're in saltwater crocodile territory, of course!

Backpacker Car Rentals (📞08-9430 8869; www.backpackercarrentals.com.au) Good-value local agency.

Bayswater Car Rental (📞08-9325 1000; www.bayswatercarrental.com.au) Local company with four branches in Perth and Fremantle.

Britz Rentals (📞1800 331 454; www.britz.com) Hires out fully equipped 4WDs fitted out as campervans, popular on the roads of northern WA. Britz has offices in all the state capitals, as well as Perth and Broome, so one-way rentals are possible.

Budget (📞1300 362 848; www.budget.com.au)

Campabout Oz (📞08-9477 2121; www.campaboutoz.com.au) Campervans, 4WDs and motorbikes.

Hertz (📞13 30 39; www.hertz.com.au)

Mighty Cars & Campers (📞1800 670 232; www.mightycampers.com.au)

Thrifty (📞1300 367 227; www.thrifty.com.au)

Wicked Campers (📞1800 246 869; www.wickedcampers.com.au) Check the website for good last-minute discounts.

Insurance

In Australia, third-party personal-injury insurance is always included in the vehicle registration cost. This ensures that every registered vehicle carries at least minimum insurance. You'd be wise to extend that minimum to at least third-party property insurance as well – minor collisions with other vehicles can be surprisingly expensive.

If you're bringing your own car from within Australia, take out the most comprehensive roadside assistance plan you can. It's not a matter of if your car will break down, but when. Having the top cover will offset your recovery costs considerably.

For hire cars, establish exactly what your liability is in the event of an accident.

Rather than risk paying out thousands of dollars if you do have an accident, you can take out your own comprehensive insurance on the car, or (the usual option) pay an additional daily amount to the rental company for an 'insurance excess reduction' policy. This brings the amount of excess you must pay in the event of an accident down from between $2000 and $5000 to a few hundred dollars.

Be aware that if you're travelling on dirt roads you may not be covered by insurance. Also, most companies' insurance won't cover the cost of damage to glass (including the windscreen) or tyres. Always read the small print.

Purchase

If you're planning a stay of several months that involves lots of driving, buying a second-hand car will be much cheaper than renting. But remember that reliability is all-important. Breaking down in the outback is very inconvenient (and potentially dangerous) – the nearest mechanic can be a very expensive tow-truck ride away!

You'll probably get any car cheaper by buying privately through the newspaper (try Saturday's *West Australian*) rather than through a car dealer. Buying through a dealer can include a guarantee, but this is not much use if you're buying a car in Perth for a trip to Broome. Online, see www.carpoint.com.au and www.drive.com.au to buy a car.

There are local regulations to comply with when buying or selling a car. In WA a vehicle has to have a compulsory safety check and obtain a road-worthiness certificate (RWC) before it can be registered in the new owner's name – usually the seller will indicate whether the car already has a RWC. Stamp duty has to be paid when you buy a car; as this is based on

the purchase price, it's not unknown for the buyer and the seller to agree privately to understate the price.

To avoid buying a lemon, you might consider forking out some extra money for a vehicle appraisal before purchase. The **RAC** (📞13 17 03; www.rac.com.au) offers this kind of check in Perth and other large WA centres for around $198/220 for members/nonmembers; it also offers extensive advice on buying and selling cars on its website.

The beginning of winter (June) is a good time to start looking for a used motorbike. Local newspapers and the bike-related press have classified advertisement sections.

Fremantle has a number of secondhand-car yards, including a cluster in North Fremantle on the Stirling Hwy, while in Perth there's the **Traveller's Auto Barn** (📞1800 674 374; www.travellers-autobarn.com.au; 365 Newcastle St, Northbridge).

Road Conditions

WA is not criss-crossed by multilane highways; there's not enough traffic and the distances are too great to justify them. All the main routes are well surfaced and have two lanes, but not far off the beaten track you'll find yourself on unsealed roads. Anybody seeing the state in reasonable detail can expect some dirt-road travelling. A 2WD car can cope with the major ones, but for serious exploration, plan on a 4WD.

Driving on unsealed roads requires special care – a car will perform differently when braking and turning on dirt. Under no circumstances exceed 80km/h on dirt roads; if you go faster you won't have enough time to respond to a sharp turn, stock on the road, or an unmarked gate or cattle grid. Take it easy and take time to see the sights.

It's important to note that when it rains, some roads flood. Flooding is a real problem up north because of cyclonic storms. Exercise extreme caution at wet times, especially at the frequent yellow 'Floodway' signs. If you come to a stretch of water and you're not sure of the depth or what could lie beneath it, pull up at the side of the road and walk through it (excluding known saltwater-crocodile areas, such as the Pentecost River crossing on the Gibb River Road!). Even on major highways, if it has been raining you can sometimes be driving through 30cm or more of water for hundreds of metres at a time. **Mainroads** (☑13 81 38; www.mainroads.wa.gov.au) provides statewide road-condition reports, updated daily (and more frequently if necessary).

Road Hazards

Travelling by car within WA means sometimes having to pass road trains. These articulated trucks and their loads (consisting of two or more trailers) can be up to 53.5m long, 2.5m wide and travel at around 100km/h. Overtaking them is tricky – once you commit to passing there's no going back. Exercise caution and pick your time, but don't get timid mid-manoeuvre. Also, remember that it is much harder for the truck driver to control their giant-sized vehicle than it is for you to control your car.

WA's enormous distances can lead to dangerous levels of driver fatigue. Stop and rest every two hours or so – do some exercise, change drivers or have a coffee. The major routes have rest areas and many roadhouses offer free coffee for drivers; ask for maps from the RAC that indicate rest stops.

Cattle, emus and kangaroos are common hazards on country roads, and a collision is likely to kill the animal and cause serious damage to your vehicle. Kangaroos are most active around dawn and dusk, and they travel in groups. If possible plan your travel to avoid these times of the day. If you see a roo hopping across the road in front of you, slow right down – its friends are probably just behind it.

It's important to keep a safe distance behind the vehicle in front, in case it hits an animal or has to slow down suddenly. If an animal runs out in front of you, brake if you can, but don't swerve unless it is safe to do so. You're likely to survive a collision with an emu better than a collision with a tree or another vehicle.

Road Rules

Driving in WA holds few surprises, other than those that hop out in front of your vehicle. Cars are driven on the left-hand side of the road (as in the rest of Australia). An important road rule is 'give way to the right' – if an intersection is unmarked, you must give way to vehicles entering the intersection from your right.

The speed limit in urban areas is generally 60km/h, unless signposted otherwise. The state speed limit is 110km/h, applicable to all roads in non-built-up areas, unless otherwise indicated. The police have radar speed traps and speed cameras, often in carefully concealed locations.

Oncoming drivers who flash their lights at you may be giving you a warning of a speed camera ahead – or they may be telling you that your headlights are not on. It's polite to wave back if someone does this. Don't get caught flashing your lights yourself, as it's illegal.

Seat belts are compulsory, and not using them incurs a fine. Children must be strapped into an approved safety seat. Talking and texting on a mobile phone while driving is illegal.

Drink-driving is a serious problem in WA, especially in country areas, and random breath tests are used to reduce the road toll. If you're caught driving with a blood-alcohol level of more than 0.05%, expect a hefty fine, a court appearance and the loss of your licence.

Local Transport

Perth has an efficient, fully integrated public transport system called **Transperth** (☑13 62 13; www.transperth. wa.gov.au) covering public buses, trains and ferries in a large area that reaches south to include Fremantle, Rockingham and Mandurah. Larger regional centres, including Bunbury, Busselton and Albany, have limited local bus services.

Taxis are available in most of the larger towns.

Tours

The WA Visitor Centre in Perth has a wide selection of brochures and suggestions for tours all over the state. The tours listed here are only a selection of what's available. Prices given are rates per person in twin share; there's usually an extra supplement for single accommodation. Students and YHA members often get a discount.

The hop-on, hop-off bus options are a popular way for travellers to get around in a fun, relaxed atmosphere. Some adventure tours include serious 4WD safaris, taking travellers to places that they simply couldn't get to on their own without large amounts of expensive equipment.

AAT Kings Australian Tours (☑1300 228 546; www. aatkings.com.au) A long-established and professional outfit offering a wide range of fully escorted bus trips and 4WD adventures. At the time of writing it offered 17 tours in WA, ranging from a five-day Perth to Monkey Mia trip ($1825) to a 20-day

Perth to Darwin 'Western Discovery' ($8075).

Adventure Tours (☑1800 068 886; www.adventuretours. com.au) A wide range of WA tours, many with an off-the-beaten-track focus for active and adventurous travellers. Accommodation may include hostels and camping, and tour options include Perth to Broome ($2555, 14 days) and Monkey Mia, Kalbarri and the Pinnacles ($645, four days).

Outback Spirit (☑1800 688 222; www.outbackspirittours. com.au) Luxury all-terrain explorations including a Western Wildflowers Discovery tour ($5595, 15 days) and Pilbara, Karijini and Ningaloo Reef ($5995, 12 days).

Red Earth Safaris (☑1800 501 968; www.redearthsafaris. com.au) Operates a six-day Perth to Exmouth minibus tour ($745) with a two-day return trip ($200).

Train

The state's internal rail network, operated by **Transwa** (☑1300 662 205; www. transwa.wa.gov.au), is limited to the *Prospector* (Perth to Kalgoorlie), the *AvonLink* (Perth to Northham) and the *Australind* (Perth to Bunbury). Transperth's local train network reaches as far south as Mandurah.

Behind the Scenes

SEND US YOUR FEEDBACK

We love to hear from travellers – your comments keep us on our toes and help make our books better. Our well-travelled team reads every word on what you loved or loathed about this book. Although we cannot reply individually to postal submissions, we always guarantee that your feedback goes straight to the appropriate authors, in time for the next edition. Each person who sends us information is thanked in the next edition – the most useful submissions are rewarded with a selection of digital PDF chapters.

Visit **lonelyplanet.com/contact** to submit your updates and suggestions or to ask for help. Our award-winning website also features inspirational travel stories, news and discussions.

Note: We may edit, reproduce and incorporate your comments in Lonely Planet products such as guidebooks, websites and digital products, so let us know if you don't want your comments reproduced or your name acknowledged. For a copy of our privacy policy visit lonelyplanet.com/privacy.

OUR READERS

Many thanks to the travellers who used the last edition and wrote to us with helpful hints, useful advice and interesting anecdotes:
Roger Bailye, Christian Cantos, Jane Coffey, Lena Lise Ibsen, Paul Joyce, Karen Mein, John O'Connor, John O'Gorman

AUTHOR THANKS

Brett Atkinson
Huge thanks to the keen and professional staff at WA's visitor centres who smoothed the way for information gathering, allowing me to focus on the vital task of taste testing the craft breweries of Margaret River. In Perth, thanks to Amanda Keenan for the pre-trip hit list. Special thanks to my fellow scribe Steve Waters, and also to the LP in-house team, especially Maryanne Netto for her support. Final thanks to Carol for holding the fort back home in Auckland.

Steve Waters
Thanks to Karen from RACWA for not hanging up, Mick for the tow, Leonie and Nev for beer and watermelons, Dave and Thuman of Djarindjin for the sand rescue, Travis for the drive shaft, John in the Subie for the WD40, Colleen and Karen for dinner and great conversation, Trace and Heath, Brodie, Abbidene, Meika and Kaeghan for everything, Roz, Megan and Batty for caretaking, Friz and Ian for putting up with me, and the Bung-Bung crew for, well, Bung-Bung!

ACKNOWLEDGMENTS
Cover photograph: Camel caravan, Broome, George Steinmetz/Corbis

THIS BOOK

This is the 7th edition of Lonely Planet's *Perth & West Coast Australia* guidebook. Brett Atkinson was the coordinating author, joined by coauthor Steve Waters. Rebecca Chau contributed the Boomtown: Mining & the Environment essay. Michael Cathcart wrote the History chapter, with additions and updates by Brett Atkinson. The previous edition was written by Peter Dragicevich, Steve Waters and Rebecca Chau. This guidebook was commissioned in Lonely Planet's Melbourne office, and produced by the following:

Commissioning Editor Maryanne Netto

Coordinating Editors Victoria Harrison, Sarah Koel

Coordinating Cartographer Peter Shields

Coordinating Layout Designer Kerrianne Southway

Managing Editor Barbara Delissen

Senior Editors Andi Jones, Martine Power

Managing Cartographers Corey Hutchison, Diana Von Holdt

Managing Layout Designer Chris Girdler

Assisting Cartographers Valeska Cañas, Csanad Csutoros, Xavier Di Toro

Assisting Layout Designer Mazzy Prinsep

Assisting Editors Susie Ashworth, Trent Holden

Cover Research Naomi Parker

Internal Image Research Aude Vauconsant

Thanks to Ryan Evans, Larissa Frost, Mark Griffiths, Genesys India, Jouve India, Trent Paton, Kirsten Rawlings, Raphael Richards, Gerard Walker

BEHIND THE SCENES

Index

Map Pages **000**
Photo Pages **000**

Map Legend

Sights
- Beach
- Bird Sanctuary
- Buddhist
- Castle/Palace
- Christian
- Confucian
- Hindu
- Islamic
- Jain
- Jewish
- Monument
- Museum/Gallery/Historic Building
- Ruin
- Sento Hot Baths
- Shinto
- Sikh
- Taoist
- Winery/Vineyard
- Zoo/Wildlife Sanctuary
- Other Sight

Activities, Courses & Tours
- Bodysurfing
- Diving/Snorkelling
- Canoeing/Kayaking
- Course/Tour
- Skiing
- Snorkelling
- Surfing
- Swimming/Pool
- Walking
- Windsurfing
- Other Activity

Sleeping
- Sleeping
- Camping

Eating
- Eating

Drinking & Nightlife
- Drinking & Nightlife
- Cafe

Entertainment
- Entertainment

Shopping
- Shopping

Information
- Bank
- Embassy/Consulate
- Hospital/Medical
- Internet
- Police
- Post Office
- Telephone
- Toilet
- Tourist Information
- Other Information

Geographic
- Beach
- Hut/Shelter
- Lighthouse
- Lookout
- Mountain/Volcano
- Oasis
- Park
- Pass
- Picnic Area
- Waterfall

Population
- Capital (National)
- Capital (State/Province)
- City/Large Town
- Town/Village

Transport
- Airport
- Border crossing
- Bus
- Cable car/Funicular
- Cycling
- Ferry
- Metro station
- Monorail
- Parking
- Petrol station
- Subway station
- Taxi
- Train station/Railway
- Tram
- Underground station
- Other Transport

Note: Not all symbols displayed above appear on the maps in this book

Routes
- Tollway
- Freeway
- Primary
- Secondary
- Tertiary
- Lane
- Unsealed road
- Road under construction
- Plaza/Mall
- Steps
- Tunnel
- Pedestrian overpass
- Walking Tour
- Walking Tour detour
- Path/Walking Trail

Boundaries
- International
- State/Province
- Disputed
- Regional/Suburb
- Marine Park
- Cliff
- Wall

Hydrography
- River, Creek
- Intermittent River
- Canal
- Water
- Dry/Salt/Intermittent Lake
- Reef

Areas
- Airport/Runway
- Beach/Desert
- Cemetery (Christian)
- Cemetery (Other)
- Glacier
- Mudflat
- Park/Forest
- Sight (Building)
- Sportsground
- Swamp/Mangrove

OUR STORY

A beat-up old car, a few dollars in the pocket and a sense of adventure. In 1972 that's all Tony and Maureen Wheeler needed for the trip of a lifetime – across Europe and Asia overland to Australia. It took several months, and at the end – broke but inspired – they sat at their kitchen table writing and stapling together their first travel guide, *Across Asia on the Cheap*. Within a week they'd sold 1500 copies. Lonely Planet was born.

Today, Lonely Planet has offices in Melbourne, London and Oakland, with more than 600 staff and writers. We share Tony's belief that 'a great guidebook should do three things: inform, educate and amuse'.

OUR WRITERS

Brett Atkinson

Coordinating Author; Perth & Fremantle, Around Perth, Margaret River & the Southwest Coast, South Coast Brett's previous visits to Western Australia had involved museum- and bar-hopping in Fremantle, and taking on the mighty Nullarbor Plain. This time he expanded his WA horizons by immersing himself in Perth's restaurants and cafes, 'researching' craft breweries in the Swan Valley, and jumping from beach to forest and back to beach throughout Margaret River and the southwest. As a New Zealander, he's used to weird and wonderful wildlife but still thinks WA's quirky combo of woylies, numbats and whale sharks is something special. Brett's based in Auckland, and has covered more than 45 countries as a guidebook author and travel and food writer. See www.brett-atkinson.net for what he's been eating recently, and where he's travelling to next.

Steve Waters

Around Perth, Monkey Mia & the Central West, Coral Coast & the Pilbara, Broome & the Kimberley While researching the previous edition of this book, Steve descended into rental-car hell, so this trip he drove 15,000km in his own Subaru L-series, which took a hammering on the Tanami and almost drowned getting into Purnululu. Driving lights dropped off, shockers, tyres and drive shafts all broke. At least it only caught fire once. Slept in, eaten on, buried in Dampier Peninsula pindan, covered in Pilbara dust, pulled over by Cervantes cops, from Kununurra to Perth, the Subie kept going. Steve's also co-authored previous editions of *Australia*, *Indonesia* and *Great Adventures*; while not on the road, he frequents Lonely Planet's Melbourne office.

Read more about Steve at:
lonelyplanet.com/members/stevewaters

CONTRIBUTING AUTHORS

Rebecca Chau wrote the Boomtown: Mining & the Environment chapter. Rebecca first started learning about WA back in the '80s, when she started school in Albany, south of the state. After growing up on this land crinkled by beaches and coveted by whales, she moved to Perth, and later became a commissioning editor for Lonely Planet. Also an author on the previous editions of this guide, she heads back to WA a couple of times a year. She has long followed the mining boom with fascination.

Dr Michael Cathcart wrote the History chapter. Michael teaches history at the Australian Centre, the University of Melbourne. He is well known as a broadcaster on ABC Radio National and has presented history programs on ABC TV. His most recent book is *The Water Dreamers* (2009), a history of how water shaped the history of Australia.

Published by Lonely Planet Publications Pty Ltd
ABN 36 005 607 983
7th edition – July 2013
ISBN 978 1 74179 952 1
© Lonely Planet 2013   Photographs © as indicated 2013
10 9 8 7 6 5 4 3 2 1
Printed in China